PUCCINI

A Biography

PUCCINI

A Biography

Mary Jane Phillips-Matz

Northeastern University Press
BOSTON

Advisor in music to Northeastern University Press
GUNTHER SCHULLER

Library of Congress Cataloging-in-Publication Data
Phillips-Matz, Mary Jane.
Puccini : a biography / by Mary Jane Phillips-Matz.
p. cm.
Includes bibliographical references (p.   ) and index.
ISBN 1-55553-530-5 (cloth : alk. paper)
1. Puccini, Giacomo, 1858–1924.   2. Composers—Italy—Biography.   I. Title.
ML410.P89 P52 2002
782.1′092—dc21   2002009017

Designed by Dean Bornstein

Composed in Dante by Wellington Graphics, Hanover, Massachusetts. Printed and bound by Thomson-Shore, Inc., Dexter, Michigan. The paper is Supple Opaque Recycled, an acid-free stock.

MANUFACTURED IN THE UNITED STATES OF AMERICA
06   05   04   03   5   4   3   2

To my daughters and my son,
with grateful thanks

Mary Ann · Catherine

Margaret · Clare

Carlino

Contents

Illustrations

Foreword

GIACOMO PUCCINI came from a gifted, provincial family. His own gifts were quickly recognized, and, still in his youth, he began a brilliant career that brought him international fame and considerable fortune. He went everywhere, met everyone. But behind the apparent cosmopolite there was a man racked with indecision, with self-doubt, and also by private misfortunes. Biographers set about unraveling the knotted strands of this life and this personality while the composer was still alive, and in the decades since his death a number of biographies have appeared. Many of these are of interest and value, but no one book seems to grasp the full significance of the subject.

As anyone who has read her magisterial *Verdi* knows, Mary Jane Phillips-Matz has an uncanny gift for feeling the past. To begin with, she loves documents: there is hardly an archive in Italy that she does not know. She can happily spend days poring over parish registers, bank statements, scrawled letters, yellowing newspapers. But she is not one of your everything-including-the-laundry-list biographers. Still, when she does come upon a laundry list, she has the insight and sensitivity to extract the story, the human element from it.

And Phillips-Matz holds yet another trump. She knows Italy as few outsiders do. She has lived long and full years in that country; she has shopped for food, cooked it, raised a family, dealt with officials, gone to parent-teacher meetings. So when she learns that the young Puccini failed to be promoted one academic year, she can feel the terrible resonance in the Puccini household. She can gauge the dimensions of a scandal, the widening echoes of a success, the depth of an abysmal failure.

Early in her career as a writer, Phillips-Matz wrote frequently for *Opera News,* and her assignments brought her into contact with many retired singers, several of whom had played important roles in Puccini's operas (and even in his life). These recalled events lend a personal warmth to the story. And, for all its invaluable documentation, this new biography is a personal book. We feel the biographer's sympathy for her subject, her heart-deep understanding of his flaws, and we welcome her willingness to forgive (but never overlook) them. She is frank to admit her own favorite among his works: *La Fanciulla del West*. And, if I may also be personal—it is my own favorite, too.

Puccini's music is, I believe, almost impossible to dislike, though some listeners have tried. The man Puccini is more problematical, but there is no denying his great humanity, and this new biography conveys that to us, in a winning and definitive fashion.

WILLIAM WEAVER

Preface and Acknowledgments

THE PRESERVATION and publication of material about Giacomo Puccini is owed chiefly to five families: the Puccinis themselves, the Toscaninis, Ricordis, Marchettis, and Del Fiorentinos. All honored him in different ways, tending troves of documents and promoting and playing his music or writing about him. In short, they kept Puccini alive in the decades when most critics and scholars tended to dismiss him and his work.

Simonetta Puccini, the composer's granddaughter, has contributed her personal effort and the scrupulous scholarship of her publications, giving us a new understanding of her grandfather's character and life. Determined to preserve her family's traditions, she has also given us a full genealogical record that reaches back to the sixteenth century and traces the five generations of Puccinis who produced professional composers. She also edited Puccini's correspondence with Riccardo Schnabl and wrote "Puccini and the Painters," an important essay on the composer's friendships with several artists of his time. Acting to preserve and restore Giacomo Puccini's homes, she heads the *Associazione Amici delle Case di Puccini*. No granddaughter could have done more, and I am very grateful for her work.

Although I never interviewed Fosca Gemignani Leonardi Crespi, Puccini's beloved stepdaughter, I did have help from Fosca's daughter, Elvira Leonardi, who was for all intents and purposes Puccini's granddaughter. Known as Biki, the famous fashion designer, she let me interview her several times in Milan, beginning in May 1956; and I turned to her again later, when I began this book. I cherish Biki's last gift to me, a copy of her memoir, which she sent me in 1999. My thanks also to Hélène Blignaut, who gathered Biki's memories and wrote about them, and to Vera Bardelli Perinati, the daughter of the late baritone Cesare Bardelli. Vera helped me with research about Biki, her family, and her friends, in part because she and her mother knew Biki very well. Biki had attended the world premiere of *Turandot* at La Scala. Like everyone else in the audience, she left the theater after the death of Liù, at the point where Arturo Toscanini put

Preface and Acknowledgments

down his baton and turned to the audience, saying that was the last music Puccini had composed before his death. When Biki attended *Turandot* at La Scala more than sixty years later, she left at the same moment in the opera. She set off, walking home. Along the way, she met Maestro Riccardo Muti, and they began chatting about Puccini. Standing there in the dark, Muti mused about art, saying that it is a consolation, something that defeats loneliness. A divine hand touches anyone who writes music, or interprets it, or listens to it. After Biki thanked him for what he had done to make music "a window on the future," Muti returned her thanks, and they both walked on (Blignaut, p. 215).

Next, the Toscaninis. Although relations between Puccini and Arturo Toscanini were sometimes stormy, the conductor made a huge effort to help Puccini by conducting many productions of his operas, beginning with *Le Villi* and going on to the world premieres of *La Bohème* and *La Fanciulla del West*, and *Turandot*. Toscanini's wife and children also re-mained close to Puccini and his family. Walfredo, the conductor's grand-son, has stood by me for more years than I can count, spending hours on research for this book, answering questions, and giving me material I could never have found on my own. I also had a great deal of help from Walfredo's aunt, the late Wally Toscanini, Countess Castelbarco, who was Arturo Toscanini's daughter. Having met her in Spoleto, I became her tenant in her casetta at La Salute in Venice and was later her guest in Avio and Milan. She always spoke frankly about Puccini and shed a great deal of light on her father's association with him.

In the vaults of Casa Ricordi, Italy's most powerful music-publishing firm, four generations of Ricordis preserved the letters and musical scores of Puccini and many other composers. Their collection, dating back to the company's founding in Milan in the early nineteenth century, was tended by Giovanni Ricordi, then his son, grandson, and great-grandson, and finally by those who succeeded them; it remains available to scholars today. Without the Ricordis, much of this enormous archive might have been lost. Casa Ricordi asked Eugenio Gara to edit the *Carteggi pucciniani*, a hefty collection of Puccini's letters, related documents, and critics' ac-counts of his operas. At Casa Ricordi (now BMG–Ricordi) Ilaria Narici and Dr. Gabriele Dotto made it possible for me to use material from that archive.

In the Del Fiorentino family—vintage Tuscans all—almost everyone was a Puccini fan. Without their support I would perhaps never have begun Puccini studies, for my first mentor in this work was the late Monsignor Dante Del Fiorentino. Born in a village across Lake Massaciuccoli from Torre del Lago, where Puccini lived, Father Dante attended seminary in Lucca and was ordained there. After World War I he became the junior priest in Puccini's parish. In the early 1920s Puccini helped him find a post in the United States and entertained him when he returned to Torre del Lago in the summers. I first met Father Dante in autumn 1947, when he was the parish priest in Glen Cove, Long Island, and was presenting Saturday night concerts with Italian singers in the parish hall. Later he served at St. Lucy's in Brooklyn. He baptized four of my five children and was a generous, trusted personal friend. I first worked with Father Dante while he was writing *Immortal Bohemian,* his memoir of Puccini. Thanks to Mrs. August Belmont's efforts, Prentice-Hall published it. Although this book contains some serious errors, it remains a valuable firsthand account of Puccini's life and culture, written by someone who knew him as a Tuscan and a citizen of Lucca and the Lake Massaciuccoli community. Beyond that, Father Dante knew him as only a priest can know someone in his flock.

Thanks to him, I could examine Puccini's letters and other items in his large private collection; and it is very much to his credit that he kept this collection together when he could have made his life easier by selling it. In May 1956 Father Dante sent me to visit his sister and other relatives in Lucca, Quiesa, and Viareggio. They took me to all the "Puccini places," where I met people who had actually worked for the composer. In the decades that followed, I returned to this area for further study. Thanks to Father Dante's heir, 276 letters from his collection have been edited, annotated, and published by Dr. Giuseppe Pintorno. I also thank him for his help and his courtesy to me.

We owe special thanks to the Marchettis, especially to Arnaldo Marchetti, yet another Tuscan. Collaborating with one of Puccini's nieces, he published an important collection of their family letters, the remarkable *Puccini com'era.* Marchetti remained objective about the composer yet sympathetic to him; he understood him as few writers have. I also had help from Marchetti's heirs, particularly Francesca Marchetti Staderini, his granddaughter, and from Silvia Di Cataldo of Edizioni Curci in Milan.

My debt to these people is large, for they helped me as I pulled together the dozens of letters and documents that make up the body of this book. To these I added material from my interviews and a body of unpublished material from private and public collections.

I realize this book has neither the size nor the scope of my biography of Verdi, but Verdi wrote many more operas than Puccini did and lived twenty years longer, remaining active until he was almost ninety. Then there is the matter of Verdi's reputation as a national hero before and after the creation of Italy, for he was elected twice to public office, first in the Assembly of the Parma Provinces, then in the First Parliament of Italy. Puccini, on the other hand, avoided politics as much as possible and lived as privately as his international career would allow. Any biography of him will reflect that.

William Weaver, a much-loved friend, made a special effort in writing the foreword to this book. Among his many contributions, he published his translations of Puccini librettos, and he edited *The Puccini Companion*, which he co-authored with Simonetta Puccini. I called dear, dear William Ashbrook at all hours of the day and night, and at every stage in my research I used his articles on Puccini and his books—one by him alone, and one written in collaboration with Harold S. Powers, whom I also thank. Andrew Porter's *Music of Three Seasons: 1974–1977* clarified the background and substance of Puccini's popular operas and the unfamiliar ones such as *Edgar,* for which he has such respect.

John Freeman, long an editor of *Opera News,* often writes about Puccini, Toscanini, Mascagni, and their contemporaries. He brought his scrupulous editing to my manuscript, and suggested important changes and additions to this book. I also thank my publisher, William Frohlich, Editor in Chief at Northeastern University Press, and Ann Twombly, Sarah Rowley, and Jill Bahcall.

Robert Tollett, my friend for more than fifty years, recently deceased, and Richard Harr, his colleague, gave me photocopies of the Puccini letters in the collection of Tollett and Harman Autographs, so I could translate them for use in this book. Richard also let me copy and use photographs from his archive.

Jean Bowen and Susan T. Sommer, the former chiefs of the Music Division, The New York Public Library for the Performing Arts, Astor, Lenox and Tilden Foundations, stood by me through years of research for this book. They made available the Puccini materials in their division, and particularly those in the Toscanini Legacy and the Wanda Toscanini Horowitz Donation. Thanks, too, to Charles Eubanks, assistant chief; Frances Barulich, John Shepard, George Boziwick, Tema Hecht, Maxine Soares, and others in the Music Division. Linda B. Fairtile, now a librarian in the Music Division, is the former archivist of the American Institute for Verdi Studies at New York University and the author of *Giacomo Puccini: A Guide to Research,* an essential basic reference volume. Equally knowledgeable about Verdi and Puccini, she answers my questions about both. My list of Puccini's works, drawn up for this book, is based on the Work List in Linda's *Giacomo Puccini: A Guide to Research.* Dr. Dieter Schickling of the Centro Studi Giacomo Puccini also let me use the list of compositions that he compiled for the Web site of the center.

In the Map Division of the New York Public Library, the unfailingly helpful Alice C. Hudson, Chief, and Nancy Kandoian, her assistant, went well beyond the call of duty as they searched for Tuscan mountain hamlets so remote that they are not found on standard maps.

J. Rigbie Turner, the Mary Flagler Cary Curator of Music Manuscripts and Books at the Pierpont Morgan Library, New York, directed me to previously unpublished letters from Puccini and his wife. He also found and made available the extraordinary photograph of Puccini made in 1912, in mourning for one of his sisters and for Giulio Ricordi. It is the frontispiece for this book.

Much of my early "education" as a listener came from Licia Albanese, the beloved soprano who defined Puccini's most important female characters. Licia founded and remains the prime mover of the Licia Albanese–Puccini Foundation; but her commitment to the composer goes back to her student days. To pay homage, she even traveled the mountain roads of Tuscany to reach Celle dei Puccini, the family's ancestral hamlet, and track down Puccini's nieces.

At the Metropolitan Opera, I relied on Robert Tuggle, Director of the Archives, and John Pennino, Assistant Archivist, to steer me toward essential documents and photographs. In the Archives, Jeff McMillan and Charles Mintzer also gathered material for this book, with Charles shedding new light on the humiliating moment during a rehearsal for *Nerone* at La Scala, when Toscanini told Puccini to leave the theater. Tom Lehmkuhl searched the files of the Metropolitan Opera Press Office for data on the company and its singers.

As always I am grateful for support from the Metropolitan Opera Guild, and particularly to Rudolph S. Rauch, Managing Director of the Guild and Editor and Publisher of *Opera News;* Paul Gruber, the Guild's Executive Director, Program Development; Jane L. Poole, Director of External Relations; F. Paul Driscoll, Executive Editor of *Opera News,* and Brian Kellow, Features Editor. John Freeman's help is mentioned above. The Guild, through the late Lauder Greenway and Mary Ellis Peltz, made possible my first trip to Italy.

Edward Young of Nashville, Robert Baxter of Philadelphia, and Edward F. Durbeck III of California sent me tapes of hard-to-find recordings, while Dr. Jesse Rosenberg of Northwestern University, Dr. Helen Hatton, and Dr. Harry Dunstan and Henry Grossi of Catholic University of America gave me hard-to-find printed material. Dr. Dunstan, a passionate advocate for Puccini, was always ready to discuss issues about his merit and air his own personal view of *La Fanciulla del West.* Steven Mercurio added insight on Franco Alfano's original and revised endings for *Turandot.* Cavaliere Ufficiale Aldo H. Mancusi, founder of the Enrico Caruso Museum of America, Inc., let me publish Puccini's doggerel poem about Caruso and *La Fanciulla del West.* I am also grateful to him for finding Giuseppe Giacosa's commemorative oration on Verdi's death. The "Puccini Seminar" conducted by Dr. Frank Celenza and Andrea Celenza also opened new avenues of research on *La Fanciulla del West* for me, and I am grateful to Raquel Celenza, who oversaw the event.

In a telephone interview in New York, Cody Franchetti shared information about Alberto Franchetti's relationship to Puccini and the controversy over *Tosca;* in several personal interviews, Dr. Deborah Burton discussed her studies with me; and Michele Girardi and Virgilio Bernardoni, both associated with the Centro Studi Giacomo Puccini in Lucca, have added important books to the Puccini literature. Gaspare Nello Vetro contributed material that is essential to our understanding of the early years of Puccini's career and the negotiations for *Tosca.* Grateful thanks to Professor Corrado Mingardi, Librarian, and the Biblioteca della Cassa di Risparmio di Parma e Monte di Credito su Pegno di Busseto for permission to use Emanuele Muzio's letters. My thanks go also to Patricia Blankenship, president of the Dallas Chapter of the Puccini Society, and to Marilyn and Ward Halla and Puccini's other loyal fans. And special thanks to Howard Greenfeld, who knows Tuscany so well.

Dr. Bernard Foccroule and his staff at the Théâtre Royal de la Monnaie in Brussels helped me with research on Puccini's last illness and death while I was in Belgium. Jan Van Goethem, the Monnaie's archivist, provided a chronology and some 1924 newspaper coverage. Other clippings about Puccini's last weeks came from Dr. Anne Vandenbulcke, Archivist-Conservator of the Archives, City of Brussels, Department of Culture. I add a special word of thanks to Christina Kolb, my assistant in Brussels.

My thanks to the New York City Opera for its riveting production of Puccini's 1904 version of *Butterfly,* and to Gian Carlo Menotti for directing Puccini's work in many theaters, with a special mention of his *Manon Lescaut* at the Metropolitan Opera. My gratitude also goes to Enrico Aloi; Carlo Bergonzi; Patricia G. Brown; Vittoria Casarotti, R.C.S. Libri SpA; Maria Casati, Istituto Nazionale di Studi Verdiani, Parma; Wally Cleva Riecker; William Crawford; Donna De Laurentis; Stephen De Maio; Plácido Domingo; Richard Fischer, M.D.; Gene Galasso; Norina Greco Nobile; Joshua Gurin, M.D.; Dr. Floyd Herzog, Director, Anderson Center for the Arts, Binghamton University, State University of New York; Jerome Hines; Jean Kashmer, C.S.W.; James Keolker; Bruce Kubert; Evelyn Kupin; Jeffrey Langford, Manhattan School of Music; Dr. Liana Lara, former president of the Casa di Riposo per Musicisti (Casa Verdi) in Milan; Lisa Mancusi; Alba Mazza; Sherrill Milnes; Anna Moffo; Nicholas Muni, artistic director, and the staff of the Cincinnati Opera; Nino Pantano, Mrs. Verna Parino; Maribeth Payne, W. W. Norton, Inc., New York; Florence and Ralph Postiglione; Joseph Pugliese; Charles Riecker; Tony Russo; Leon and Dorothy Schmidt; Renata Scotto; Sherwin Sloan; William R. T. Smith and Ruth Smith; Renata Tebaldi; Mrs. Elaine Toscanini; Betty Toy; Ellen Wolf; and Joanna Wright, Macmillan, Ltd., London. I also thank the National Opera in Prague for its 1995 production of *Bohème,* the finest I ever saw.

Among many colleagues who are no longer living are Monsignor Del Fiorentino, Biki Leonardi, Robert Tollett, Cesare Bardelli, and Arnaldo Marchetti, all mentioned above. To the late Anthony L. Stivanello, his father, and his brother I offer my eternal gratitude, because they truly opened the doors of opera to me. Further thanks: Salvatore Baccaloni, Jussi Björling, John Brownlee, Fausto Cleva, Eugene Conley, Mina Cravi, Gilda Dalla Rizza, Giuseppe De Luca, Max De Schauensee, Mario Del Monaco, Vivian Della Chiesa, Lucia Evangelista, Geraldine Farrar,

Claudio Frigerio, Fortune Gallo, Dorothy Kirsten, Hizi Koyke, Charles Kullman, Bruno Landi, Virgilio Lazzari, Giovanni Martinelli, Nino Martini, Edith Mason, Dimitri Mitropoulos, Carlo Moresco, Aureliano Pertile, Angelo Pilotto, Ezio Pinza, Hilde Reggiani, Rosa Ponselle, Rosa Raisa, Francis Robinson, Stella Roman (for her unforgettable Mimì and for Manon, Tosca, and Butterfly as well), Alfredo Salmaggi, Bidú Sayao, William Seward, Margherita Sheridan, Martial Singher, Michael Sisca, Eleanor Steber, Ferruccio Tagliavini, Lawrence Tibbett, Armand Tokatyan, Peter Treves, Vittorio Trevisan, Richard Tucker, and Giuseppe Valdengo.

As always, I thank my daughters and my son, to whom I dedicate this book. Clare lived and worked for several years in Castelvecchio Pascoli, near the Puccinis' ancestral village; it is also the town where the poet Giovanni Pascoli lived. She also hunted material for me in Tuscany and went with me to Viareggio and Torre del Lago. Carlino saw me through computer-generated emergencies. Although the translations in this book are mine, Carlino, Clare, and Margaret set me straight on many Italian and dialect phrases. I also used the *Cambridge-Signorelli Dizionario Italiano-Inglese, Inglese-Italiano,* on which my daughter Catherine worked as an editor and translator.

Abbreviations Used in Source Citations

AB	Antonio Bettolacci	GG	Giuseppe Giacosa
AB-P	Arturo Buzzi-Peccia	GR	Giulio Ricordi
AE	Angelo Eisner-Eisenhof	GV	Guido Vandini
AMP	Albina Magi Puccini	LI	Luigi Illica
AP	Antonio (Tonio) Puccini	LP	Luigi Pieri
AT	Arturo Toscanini	MP	Michele Puccini
CC	Carlo Clausetti	MV	Margit Vészi
CN	Carlo Nasi	NP	Nitteti Puccini
CP	Carlo Paladini	PM	Pietrino Malfatti
CR	Cesare Riccioni	RA	Rose Ader
CT	Carla Toscanini	RP	Ramelde Puccini
EBG	Elvira Bonturi Gemignani	RPF	Ramelde Puccini Franceschini
EBP	Elvira Bonturi Puccini	RS	Renato Simoni
EL	Ervin Lendvai	RSR	Riccardo Schnabl Rossi
EP	Ettore Panizza	SL	Salvatore Leonardi
FF	Ferdinando Fontana	SS	Sybil Seligman
FL	Fosca Leonardi	TPG	Tomaide Puccini Gherardi
GA	Giuseppe Adami	TR	Tito Ricordi
GD	Gabriele D'Annunzio		
GDR	Gilda Dalla Rizza		

PUCCINI

A Biography

CHAPTER ONE

~❧~

A Musical Dynasty: 1600–1880

G IACOMO PUCCINI was born in 1858. As his family's oldest son and the descendant of four generations of respected professional musicians, he was expected to follow his ancestors' path, his father's path, if he could. To do that, he had to master his self-doubt and his annihilating inability to make firm decisions. Driven by tradition and by his ambitious mother, he moved beyond a secure career as a church organist and went on to conquer the larger world, becoming the fifth-generation composer in his line. He revealed his gifts gradually, first in conservatory efforts and then in a short opera that attracted attention in music-mad Milan. Giulio Ricordi, the head of Italy's most powerful music publishing house, became Puccini's mentor in 1883, managed to establish his protégé in the opera business, and fought off his rivals for almost thirty years, in defense of the man who came to be called Italy's long-awaited successor to Giuseppe Verdi.

Puccini's earliest operas were *Le Villi* and *Edgar. Manon Lescaut* was the first to win him a niche in his field. He then wrote three of the most popular works of his time, *La Bohème, Tosca,* and *Madama Butterfly.* After 1896, these made him a rich international celebrity. That success, however, left him dissatisfied with his own work. Believing that audiences had begun to tire of what he called his "sugary music," he changed direction and embarked on years of anguish as he sought to create works of greater resonance. *La Fanciulla del West* was the first of these, but it had only a limited commercial success. After Giulio Ricordi's death in 1912, Puccini faced a hostile professional environment and a struggle with Ricordi's son, Tito (he was the second Tito in the firm), the new head of the firm. *La Ron-*

dine and *Il Trittico* followed. In 1924, Puccini died, leaving *Turandot* un-finished.

In spite of the enormous popularity of his operas, Puccini was often at-tacked as a commercial hack, a cynical, shallow man of limited imagina-tion who aimed at the lowest possible level of common taste. He certainly chose modest subjects, his "little things," his *"cosettine,"* as he called them. Where was his *Tristan und Isolde?* Where were his *Don Carlos* and his *Aida?* To those closest to him he seemed incapable of writing a big opera. Some Italian critics also felt that he lacked a patriotic impulse, focused as he was on the music of other countries. He was too international, they said. Among many other aspects of his art that offended his critics were the sa-dism and gratuitous cruelty he injected into some works; critics found him lacking in moral substance. After his death, most of his operas were considered unworthy of serious critical attention. Only in the last half-century have scholars begun to see him as an important composer, but even now some find him insignificant. Nevertheless, his critics cannot deny that he left a legacy of music. Only time will tell whether it will last.

This much is fact: the early Puccinis enriched the culture of Lucca for more than a hundred years; Giacomo Puccini extended their reign over another century and broadened their geographical reach. His influence extends even to popular music and the Broadway theater, with *Miss Sai-gon* and *Rent* offering further proof of his influence outside the opera house today. His greatest achievement, however, is his popularity, for his staples hold the stage year after year. Nor are his lesser works completely neglected. In spite of the expense of staging it, even *La Fanciulla del West* is sometimes performed and is sold as a popular video. *La Rondine* and *Il Trittico* (integral or fractured) are given by professional companies, schools, and conservatories. On another cultural front, three Puccini homes have become museums, one in Celle, one in Lucca, and another in Torre del Lago. Puccini scholarship thrives; and he is at last getting the at-tention he deserves, as a musician and as a man. Even though many con-sider him an international composer, he is now recognized for his Tuscan virtues. Italians today describe the rugged folk who live in the mountains near his ancestral village as having "big shoes and sharp minds." Puccini had both.

"What are Tuscans like?" I asked Dario, my granddaughter's friend, who is twenty and was born near Lucca.

"As good as bread," he shot back, without a second's hesitation. Like young Puccini, Dario aspires to a career in music, and he is very much at home in the composer's home territory.

Puccini was that: as good as bread, simple, modest, rather shy, unpretentious, good-natured and playful, especially among his male friends. Flirtatious with women, he had several serious affairs and a few long, platonic relationships, among them one with Sybil Seligman and another with Margit Vészi. Elvira Bonturi Gemignani became his mistress in the mid-1880s and married him in 1904. Careful about money, he was generous to a fault in writing letters of recommendation and helping people find work and get significant honors. Although he loved nature, he hunted all his life. He loved his boats and cars. He loved his homes, and they were several. Among the many members of his extended family, he helped nieces, nephews, a stepdaughter and her children, a stepson, and several in-laws who entered his circle.

Industrious Lucca and the Very Serene Republic

Puccini's native city lies in the marshy valley of the Serchio River, about forty miles from Florence and fourteen miles from the Mediterranean Sea. Lucca boasts very ancient origins. It was an Etruscan city that became Roman, only to fall under the dominion of the Lombards and the Franks. Later ruled by Florence and then by Pisa, it became a republic in 1369. Known as *Lucca Industriosa*, it grew as a center of commerce. When Napoleon invaded Italy in 1799, it fell. He gave it to his sister, Duchess Elisa Bonaparte Baciocchi, as the Duchy of Lucca. Ceded to Tuscany in 1847, it became part of unified Italy in 1861, three years after Puccini was born. In his youth, Lucca had a population of about twenty thousand. The city's lifeblood has always been trade, which made it a busy place with people tightly packed within its imposing ramparts. "A miniature Florence, without the art," critics unfairly said. Lucca is a medieval city, with its art, paintings, sculpture, and above all, architecture. Many churches date from the early Middle Ages. The Church of San Frediano was founded in the seventh century; its present facade was raised in the thirteenth. San Michele, founded in the eighth century, was rebuilt in the twelfth. The religious heart of Lucca is the Cathedral of San Martino, built in the eleventh century. Its magnificent facade dates from 1210. Here the Puccinis held the posts of organist and Maestro di Cappella, composing original works for the cathedral, performing the music of others, and directing the choirs. While these are the greatest churches, others also kept high musical standards.

Testimony to the importance of spectacle and the theater in Lucca's rich urban life is found in its history and architecture. When Puccini was a boy, parts of the Roman amphitheater survived, with some of its arcades clearly identifiable and many buildings that had been constructed on its ancient foundations. Outdoor spectacles were given in medieval times in open squares in front of churches; after 1650 performances were given in large halls. Because those often were too small, the Council of the Republic named a commission of citizens in 1672 to authorize the building of a new theater. The whole complex was intended to house *rappresentazioni profane, balli e commedie,* secular dramas, dance, and comedies. Thus the Teatro Pubblico was built as a full-program theater. Destroyed by fire in 1687, it was quickly rebuilt. Today the Teatro del Giglio, built in 1817, is the city's busiest stage.

In Lucca one annual celebration was the *Festa delle Tasche,* the Feast of the Pockets, a holiday that originally marked the election of magistrates, when the ballots were dropped into "pockets." Important pieces of music were specifically composed for it. Even more popular was the two-day September holiday called the *Festa del Volto Santo,* the Feast of the Holy Face, which honored the image of Christ on a cedarwood crucifix. The Lucchesi believe that Saint Nicodemus carved this relic, which was brought to their city in the eighth century. It was normally kept in a small chapel in the cathedral, but in late summer, the priests and members of the congregation organized a religious procession and carried it through the city. After the Volto Santo was returned to the cathedral, a Mass was celebrated and the organist-choirmaster directed the choir and instrumentalists in a cantata that he had composed for the occasion. Puccini's ancestors wrote many of these works. Like some cities and towns, Lucca also celebrated Saint Cecilia's Day, November 22, with musical events planned by the Santa Cecilia *confraternità,* a kind of club made up of laymen who assumed responsibility for certain functions connected with the churches. As its name indicates, the group oversaw musical events connected to that saint's day.

The several local music schools, functioning as early as 1800, were brought together under one roof in 1842. In 1867 the director was the composer Giovanni Pacini. Pacini, a native of Catania, had left Sicily and emigrated north, settling finally in Viareggio, a seashore town near Lucca, where he opened a school of music. Later he moved to Lucca, where he worked with Giacomo Puccini's father. The old Istituto Musicale was renamed the Istituto Musicale Pacini after his death in December 1867. (It is now called the Istituto Musicale Pareggiato "Luigi Boccherini"; it is of interest today because of its ties with the Puccinis and its archive, which holds a collection of their scores.)

The Puccini Dynasty

The Puccini family figured prominently in this rich culture. Exactly at the moment when the government of the Republic began to focus on artistic matters, Domenico Puccini (1679–1781), a villager from the hamlet of Celle, moved from the hills down to the capital. Today Celle, in the modern municipality or commune of Pescaglia and the province of Lucca, is called Celle dei Puccini, in honor of its famous historic family. Lying on a hillside above a stream flowing toward the Pedogna River, it has a museum, which was opened in the early 1970s in their ancestral home. Primitive and remote even now, Celle is above the dark valleys of the Apennines, tucked away on a dangerous road that snakes along rough terrain west of the Serchio River. Even in the late years of Giacomo Puccini's life, Celle remained a small cluster of houses surrounded by chestnut, oak, and walnut trees and reachable only by a road scarcely better than a mule track. His family's house, however, was the largest in the village. Peasants tended their pigs, sheep, and goats, gathered nuts and berries in the woods, spun and wove, and made rough wine or spirits. Because early travel was limited to the immediate neighborhood in the mountains, people rarely left home, save when they took goods to market. In general, they lived in a largely self-sufficient economy.

Even today Celle is difficult to reach without a car; the trip on the old-fashioned local train from Aulla down to Lucca shows how hard travel was when Puccini was a boy and later, when he was a young organist. The little carriages jolt their way along a single-track rail line and creep through tunnels, some as long as six miles. The train finally reaches the Serchio and runs through the deep gorges of the region called the Gar-

fagnana. On one ridge stands tiny Castelvecchio, the home of the poet
Giovanni Pascoli, Puccini's friend. It has been renamed Castelvecchio
Pascoli in his honor. Farther south is Bagni di Lucca, where young
Giacomo Puccini played the piano for small fees in the late 1800s. Near
Bagni, the provincial road turns off westward, toward Pescaglia and Celle.

The Puccini Museum in Celle was founded by the *Associazione Lucchesi
nel Mondo,* the worldwide association of emigrants from Lucca who
bought the old Puccini homestead; its formal inauguration in 1970 was
widely covered in the Italian and Italian-American press. Among the
guests were two cabinet ministers from Rome, corporation heads, local
and provincial dignitaries, and members of the Puccini family, including
the composer's niece, Albina Franceschini Del Panta. In the evening, the
RAI Symphony Orchestra gave a concert honoring Puccini in the Teatro
del Giglio in Lucca. Among many later visitors to Celle was the soprano
Licia Albanese, who made her own emotional pilgrimage to the place.
William Weaver, writing in *Opera News* in July 1974, described the museum as "lovingly and intelligently restored," with rooms full of furniture
from the family. The collection of memorabilia includes the bed in which
Puccini was born, his baptismal gown, portraits, the piano on which he
composed part of *Madama Butterfly,* letters, some musical exercise note-
books from his youth, and the phonograph that Thomas A. Edison gave
to Puccini. He, in turn, gave it to his niece.

According to Simonetta Puccini, who published her genealogical research in *The Puccini Companion,* the three earliest traceable Puccinis lived
in Celle in the sixteenth and seventeenth centuries. (The following information about the family is taken from her essay, "The Puccini Family," in
that book.) Michele had a son named Giuliano; he, in turn, had a son
named Jacopo. Those three generations preceded the birth of Domenico
Puccini, the first of the family to move to Lucca, where he died. Domenico's son, Giacomo (1712–1781), was born in Lucca and became the first
composer in the family. This early Giacomo studied music in Lucca and
Bologna.

The most venerable lay musical institution in Bologna was the
Accademia Filarmonica, a select society whose members were chosen by
recommendation and nomination. To be a member was perhaps the
greatest professional honor that could be conferred on a musician in Italy
at that time; and the fact that an early Puccini was a member proves how

able and respected he was. At one time Francesco Antonio Uttini, Verdi's distant cousin on his mother's side, was the *prence* or *principe,* the Accademia's elected head. Returning to Lucca in 1739, this early Giacomo Puccini won the city's highest musical post when he became the organist of the Cathedral of San Martino. In 1740 he was also named Maestro di Cappella of the Republic of Lucca. A distinguished composer, he wrote for both the church and the stage and composed for the celebrations of the *Tasche* and the feast of Santa Cecilia. In 1742 he married Angela Maria Piccinini, whose surviving portrait shows a woman of striking beauty, very much a grand lady in a richly ornamented, lace-trimmed gown, wearing jewels and a fine white wig.

Antonio Benedetto Maria Puccini (1747–1832) left Lucca, studied in Bologna as his father had done, and returned in 1772 to take over his father's duties. He too was attached to the cathedral and the Cappella Palatina and wrote for the *Tasche.* In 1771 Antonio married Caterina Tesei, a Bolognese who was a gifted organist in her own right. After her husband died, she often took over his duties at the cathedral; she did the same for their son while he studied. He then took up his father's profession.

Domenico Vincenzo Maria Puccini (1772–1815), the son of Antonio and Caterina, is the grandfather of Giacomo Puccini. Domenico also studied in Bologna, with the illustrious Padre Stanislao Mattei, then in Naples with Giovanni Paisiello, a revered composer. Back in Lucca, Domenico served as organist of the cathedral and Maestro of the Cappella Palatina. Later, Duchess Elisa Bonaparte Baciocchi, the ruler of the little state, named him director of the Cappella Municipale. In 1805 Domenico married Angela Cerù.

In the summer of 2000, fresh attention was drawn to Domenico Puccini's compositions. One is a Te Deum that he conducted in June 1800 in the Cathedral of San Martino to celebrate the reported defeat of Napoleon in the Battle of Marengo. According to a contemporary account, the work was received with "universal applause." Soon, of course, people learned that Napoleon in fact had won, not lost. These same historical moments are represented in the first and second acts of Giacomo Puccini's *Tosca,* when the Te Deum is sung to mark the supposed victory. In the next act the truth comes out. Two American scholars brought Domenico's Te Deum to its first modern hearing in July 2000, during a program of a conference on *Tosca* in Rome. Herbert Handt, who conducted it, found this piece in 1969 in Giacomo Puccini's villa at Torre del Lago. Dr. Deborah Burton successfully connected it to *Tosca,* which had its premiere in 1900. William Weaver, writing in the *New York Times* about the celebrations of Puccini during the Rome conference, described the nobility and lyricism of Domenico's composition. He also pointed out the similar circumstances in its first performance and those in *Tosca.* Another of Domenico's works, the opera *Il Ciarlatano,* was revived in the Teatro del Giglio in Lucca the same summer (Weaver, "In *Tosca,* a Touch of Family History").

After Waterloo, Domenico became director of the duchy's orchestra. When his director's stipend was cut off, he appealed to the duke, who decided he should be the Maestro and director of a new municipal music school. Under these more favorable working conditions, Domenico wrote two operas and additional religious music. He died young; it was rumored that he was poisoned for his too liberal political views, for he remained an ardent democrat at the very moment when Austria was struggling to suppress revolt in northern Italy, most of which it ruled after the Napoleonic Wars. Domenico's formidable widow was left to keep the family going.

Michele Puccini (1813–1864), the son of Domenico and Angela Cerù, was born in the year that also marks the births of Giuseppe Verdi and Richard Wagner. As the fourth-generation musician among the Puccinis, he followed custom by studying first at home and then in Bologna, where he became a pupil of Giuseppe Pilotti and was eventually named to the Accademia Filarmonica. As his father had done, he left for Naples, in his case to study with Saverio Mercadante, another of Italy's respected opera composers. Michele's second teacher in Naples was Gaetano Donizetti, who dominated Italian opera before Verdi emerged with *Nabucco.* In Lucca, Michele became the organist at San Martino. In 1848 or 1849, according to Simonetta Puccini, Michele married Albina Magi, the daughter of a prominent local clan. At the time of their marriage, he was thirty-seven, while she was only nineteen. A woman of great presence, she was called Donna Albina. Even her sons addressed her in their letters with the formal *"Lei"* instead of the familiar *"Tu."*

When Michele Puccini married Albina Magi, a senior spokesman for the family was Nicolao Cerù, a nephew of Angela Cerù. Nicolao, born in

1817, was about Michele's age; he became a respected, prosperous citizen and amassed a fair fortune. Angela herself, the widow of Domenico Puccini, remained the revered family matron, mistress of her home in Via di Poggio. Now open to the public, it is called the Museo Casa Natale Giacomo Puccini. With the recovery of his birthplace, the directors have created a museum to illustrate his early life and much of his career. Among the several rooms is the "Room of the Puccini Family," which contains a family tree; in the great hall are portraits of the early Puccinis, beginning with Giacomo Puccini the Elder, born in 1712. In a cabinet is the autograph score of a Mass written by Michele Puccini. Another room, a center for the *Fondazione Puccini*, may be the place where Puccini was born; in 1858 it was his parents' bedroom. Here also autograph scores are displayed. The kitchen, which is the heart of every Italian home, is next to a recently recreated studio similar to one where Puccini first composed. Letters and photographs fill the room. In the "Room of Triumphs," important documents recall the great moments of his career, among them the scenic designs for the historic 1923 *Manon Lescaut* that Toscanini conducted at La Scala. The "*Turandot* Room" marks the success of Puccini's last opera. Galileo Chini's designs for the settings for the 1926 La Scala production are here, as is Puccini's piano from his villa in Viareggio, the instrument he used when he composed the opera. Among other memorabilia are the notes he scribbled on a pad before his death in Brussels.

Soon after their marriage, Michele and Albina moved into this house, to live with his mother. Michele was rising steadily in his profession as organist, teacher, and composer. He continued to direct music for the Cathedral of San Martino, as his antecedents had done. In 1857 he was also named Inspector at the Istituto Musicale, where he taught organ. He wrote music for the *Tasche* and was recognized as the official composer for the religious festivals of Santa Cecilia and the *Volto Santo*. Beyond those events, he composed for the regular cycle of civic festivals, those public duties falling to him because he headed the Cappella Municipale. His two operas, *Antonio Foscarini* and *Giambattista Cattani*, never entered the repertory; but as a composer of ecclesiastical music and a teacher he was wholly successful. The author of texts on harmony and counterpoint, he taught Albina's younger brother, Fortunato Magi (1839–1882).

Another of his pupils, at least for a short time, was a young Lucchese, Alfredo Catalani (1854–1893). Catalani, who was also Magi's pupil, went on to advanced study in Milan and became an opera composer.

Michele and Albina had a large family, whose birthdates Simonetta Puccini has recorded. Their daughter Otilia, born in 1851, was followed by Tomaide in 1852. Another daughter, called Temi or Zemi, was born in 1853 and died one year later. Then came Nitteti, in 1854, and Iginia, in 1856. After Giacomo's birth in 1858, his mother had two other daughters, Ramelde in 1859, and Macrina in 1862. As we shall see, a second son, Michele, was born after Michele's death. Remarkably, given the high rate of child mortality in the nineteenth century, only Temi died in infancy; Macrina died in 1870, when she was eight and Giacomo eleven. Of these children, Otilia, Giacomo, and Michele showed a talent for music.

Giacomo Puccini's Birth, Childhood, and Youth

Giacomo, the son of Albina Magi and Michele Puccini, was born in Lucca on the night of December 22–23, 1858, in his parents' apartment in the old Cerù-Puccini house on Via di Poggio. His parents baptized their first son with five names, Giacomo Antonio Domenico Michele Secondo Maria, honoring past generations of Puccini composers. Their house was a storehouse of family lore, where they had lived for almost a century. Portraits of distinguished ancestors hung on the walls, while music scores by famous composers and by Michele and his forebears filled the cabinets and shelves. Because of Michele's many responsibilities, music truly defined the family's daily routine. He kept to his schedule, covering several posts, composing and directing the music at the cathedral, and teaching at the Istituto Musicale. In church, at home, and outside, during public events, the children heard their father's direction of his own compositions as well as the works of others. Nor was Michele the only musician in the clan, for soon Fortunato Magi was poised to launch his own career in music. After studying with Michele at the Istituto, he joined its faculty in 1857. There, as we shall see, he later tried to teach his obstreperous nephew. Magi went on to direct several of Italy's best conservatories, including the Benedetto Marcello Conservatory in Venice. Thus, it seemed that the traditions of the Puccini and Magi clans made little

Giacomo's future almost inevitable: he would follow the paths of his ancestors, his father, and his uncle.

Life for the whole family changed abruptly on January 23, 1864, when Michele Puccini died suddenly, just a month after Giacomo's fifth birthday. He was fifty-one. Albina, his widow, was then about thirty-four, with seven children, the oldest twelve and the youngest sixteen months old. With that, her situation was dire enough; but she was also six months pregnant. At the public funeral, which the city of Lucca offered to honor its composer, Pacini delivered the oration and spoke of little Giacomo and the expectation that he would carry on the family tradition. The post of choir director and organist at the cathedral was secured for the little boy; and it was stipulated that Michele Puccini's successor "should and must turn the post of organist and Maestro di Cappella to Signor Giacomo, son of the late Maestro, as soon as the said Signor Giacomo is able to discharge his duties." Fortunato Magi, Giacomo's uncle, held the director's post temporarily. Giacomo Puccini's life was thus prescribed and planned for him, even before he began elementary school.

In spite of the family's position in Lucca, Albina found herself in financial straits, for none of her daughters was old enough to work. The family had two housemaids, and much has been made of them, as if they proved that the Puccinis were well off; but Albina may not have been paying them. That task may have fallen to Angela Cerù. Or those two maids, like thousands of other people who found themselves jobless in the economic collapse after the unification of Italy, may have been members of the underclass known as *famigli a spesa,* room-and-board laborers, who were given token wages, or none. Many, many servants were designated that way in the national and parish censuses. Years would pass before Albina could get financial help from her daughters. Living with a strong-willed mother-in-law and bearing the burden of a very large family, she awaited the birth of her ninth child; he would be named Domenico, for his grandfather, and Michele, for his late father. Always called Michele and nicknamed Mi'ele and Belatti, this boy was born in April 1864, three months after his father's death. With his arrival, Albina had eight children to care for, two of them under two years of age. Her oldest daughter was only thirteen, and the next girl was not yet twelve.

An account of their family life written by Ramelde Puccini in 1906 read: "[Our mother's] first concern was the education and training of her older daughters; and, obedient to their mother's wishes, they were soon able to support the family" (S. Puccini, "The Puccini Family," p. 10). After his death, Albina petitioned the city for a pension, which was paid at the rate of sixty-seven lire a month, a modest sum, with no increase over the years. After her mother-in-law's death in 1865, she was left alone to provide for the children. She raised them in dignity and educated them, certainly with the help of Dr. Cerù. When they were little, the family lived in respectable poverty in Lucca and spent delicious moments in the summer in Celle, the family's ancient village, and in Mutigliano, near Lucca. Albina eventually saw her daughters honorably settled.

From the beginning, Albina fixed her hopes on Giacomo. Her daughters, she supposed, could marry. But finding a way for Giacomo to continue the family tradition became this ambitious mother's mission as she guided him toward music, expecting that he would fill his late father's posts. According to Ramelde's account, "All [the Puccini family] did their best, following a path illuminated by great hope. This hope, for our good Mamma, was Giacomo, who was endowed with a very lively mind and a sensitive heart. But the darling boy, perhaps because of the extraordinary vitality and restlessness of his character, refused to take an interest in any kind of study. Mamma wanted her Giacomo to study the classics before devoting himself to music, because she sensibly used to say: '*Puro musico, puro asino* [Pure musician, pure jackass].' But the ebullient Giacomo, although he loved his mother deeply, was no good at sitting long at a school desk and was frequently expelled, to be readmitted only through his mother's petitions" (S. Puccini, "The Puccini Family," p. 10).

Year after year, as each of his older sisters entered school or was tutored at home, this older son laid a larger claim to his mother's time. Albina could devote herself more fully to him after 1865, when, with her husband dead just a year, she put Nitteti, age ten, and Iginia, age nine, in the Augustinian convent in Via San Nicolao in Lucca. Nitteti remained there until she was nineteen, leaving the convent in 1873. Iginia became a nun. Giacomo, from infancy through his childhood and teen years and well into his twenties, had a special and privileged attachment to his mother. Fiercely protective of him, resolved to direct his education and fight his battles, she followed her instincts and, to a remarkable extent, determined much of the course of his life. Albina's ambition drove him forward through elementary and secondary schools and his later music courses at the Istituto. Then, in 1880, she even managed to pay for his advanced education at the Milan Conservatory.

Given the rules of custom and culture, an Italian boy reared by a widowed mother in a sea of sisters is likely to be an authentic *cocco di mamma,* a spoiled child who is looked upon as the future savior of the family. So it was with "the darling boy," Giacomo, whose status as firstborn son defined his position. Admittedly, he was his mother's favorite, although all her children agreed that Albina was a very good mother. And these siblings, so close to each other in age, developed strong bonds of love and trust that endured until their deaths, with Giacomo's affection for Tomaide and Ramelde particularly strong. The most respected older men in Giacomo's early life were Dr. Nicolao Cerù, the man from his grandmother's generation whom the orphaned children often visited on holidays, and a priest, his father's first cousin, Don Roderigo Biagini. Both lived in Lucca. Don Roderigo, a respected canon of the church, arranged for Giacomo to stay with him in Chiatri, a village in the nearby mountains, where he owned an old house used for brief vacations in summer or fall. He also had a connection to opera and the theater, for he knew the spirited poet-playwright-librettist-journalist Luigi Illica. As adults, both Iginia and Giacomo corresponded with this priest. The boy felt more comfortable with him than with Fortunato Magi, his uncle, who was a severe taskmaster.

Giacomo attended the Seminario di San Michele and, later, the Seminario di San Martino, which was affiliated with the cathedral. He apparently began to sing in the boys' choir at the cathedral when he was about ten. As one of his sisters admitted, he was a poor student. A surviving record from his school days shows that he was promoted every year from 1867–1868 through 1870–1871. However, he failed one subject in the year of 1871–1872 and was sent back as a repeating scholar. Anyone who has ever raised school-age children in Italy knows the shame of having a son or daughter *rimandato* in a culture where parents love to brag about their children's grades. Being *rimandato* in the crucial final year brought dishonor on the student and his family. This meant that the wayward teenager had to face his mother, tell her he had failed (if someone else had not already done that), explain himself to relatives and neighbors, and stand aside while his classmates graduated.

Puccini's record reads:

PUCCINI, Giacomo
Son of Michele

1867–68	First [year of] *Ginnasio,* Elementary Grammar
1868–69	Second *Ginnasio,* Advanced Grammar
1869–70	Third *Ginnasio,* Advanced Grammar
1870–71	Fourth *Ginnasio,* Advanced Grammar
1871–72	Fifth *Ginnasio,* Advanced Grammar
1872–73	Repeat

Examinations:

August 25, 1871: Oral Examination in Humanities. Approved with minimum marks.

August 26, 1872: Oral Examination in Rhetoric. Not approved. [Del Fiorentino, p. 9]

Puccini finally passed his final exam in Rhetoric a year later, on August 25, 1873. The record reads, "Oral Examination. Approved." His professors' remarks, written in the margins of the report, characterized him as inattentive, lazy, and disruptive. One teacher wrote, "He comes to school only to wear out the seat of his pants. He pays no attention to anything"; another noted, "He never reads a book" (Del Fiorentino, pp. 9–10).

The situation of Albina's family changed in 1872, when Otilia, her oldest child, married. Earlier, according to Simonetta Puccini, Otilia had studied music and had even performed in public, perhaps influenced by her father, to whom she, as the firstborn, was close. Her husband, Massimo del Carlo, was a physician; later he had a political career, becoming mayor of Lucca. Although Otilia and her husband remained in the city, she, as a married woman, had a household of her own to run; and soon she had a son to care for. Albina was then alone with her large family, and Tomaide, her next daughter, helped in the household. Later Nitteti also helped. Nothing, however, changed Giacomo's position at home. Had Albina not been so determined to see him succeed, his disappointing performance in the *ginnasio* might have meant the end of his formal education, given the family's difficult financial situation. Another mother in similar straitened circumstances would have apprenticed her son to some local shopkeeper. But Albina, whose brother had taken over the direction of the Istituto Musicale in 1872, had another option, and that was to enroll Giacomo there. Magi began overseeing his nephew's musical training.

The Learning Process

At the Istituto, Giacomo first studied under Magi, his hot-tempered uncle, who found the boy restless and disrespectful, an impossible scholar. After many failed attempts to bring him to heel, Magi decided Giacomo did not belong in a serious institution and was not worthy of the education Albina was fighting to give him. Magi reported this to his sister, but she would not accept his fiat. As always, she stood behind her son. He must stay in the Istituto, she said. Against his best judgment, Magi agreed, but another professor was then charged with Giacomo's education. This was Carlo Angeloni, another of Michele Puccini's former students. Angeloni taught harmony at the Istituto until 1872, when he replaced Magi as a professor of composition and counterpoint. A composer in his own right, he also loved opera. Angeloni was a significant influence on him from 1874 until the day Puccini left for Milan, although an undoubtedly prejudiced Ramelde Puccini thought him far inferior to her father as a teacher and musician. One early composition from Giacomo's hand that has survived is *"A te,"* published in Michael Kaye's *The Unknown Puccini*. Kaye believes that this song for voice and piano dates from 1875 and that it was composed while Giacomo was still at the Istituto and may have been a "required student work" (Kaye, pp. 3–11). Giacomo may also have begun playing the organ in small village churches around Lucca, for he wrote pieces for the organ that year.

In his teen years, he was caught in a number of pranks, two of which got him in trouble with local authorities. Anecdotes about these appeared in books by Father Pietro Panichelli, Monsignor Dante Del Fiorentino, and others. Once Giacomo and Michele stole organ pipes from a church and sold them for scrap metal so they could buy tobacco. Another time Giacomo and Zizzania, a boyhood pal, were caught by the police after they faked Zizzania's suicide. In that case, they made a dummy of the body, added a painted death mask, and hung it in an elderly woman's cellar while she was in the country. When she found it, she nearly fainted from shock and called in the Carabinieri. The search for the pranksters quickly led to the still-missing Zizzania and Giacomo, who confessed.

After Zizzania surrendered, both youths had to answer for their conduct in court. Eventually they were acquitted with a reprimand. Del Fiorentino heard this story from Father Antonio Del Fiorentino, his great-uncle, who was a member of the bishop's council in Lucca (Panichelli, "*Il 'Pretino' di Giacomo Puccini racconta,* cited in Carner, p. 19n.7; Del Fiorentino, pp. 15–19).

Perhaps at Angeloni's urging, Giacomo and a group of friends went to Pisa on March 11, 1876, to see *Aida.* Although this event is often said to have marked the beginning of his interest in opera, it is certain that he had seen at least one staged performance earlier in Lucca; he also said he had studied the scores of other operas, *Il Trovatore, Rigoletto,* and *La Traviata* among them. Many years later, the composer remembered that *Aida,* saying, "When I heard *Aida* in Pisa, I felt that a musical window had opened for me." In his essay in *The Puccini Companion,* Michael Elphinstone stresses the fact that Puccini said "heard" and "musical," but did not mention "seeing" the opera or being impressed by its spectacle. He also notes that the next piece Giacomo composed after the trip to Pisa was his *Preludio sinfonico* for orchestra, some of which might suggest the score of *Aida.* In the 1950s the Milanese collector and music shop owner Natale Gallini described this composition's "striking" orchestration, "the clarity of the timbral combinations, [and] the correctness of the instrumental writing." From his description, Elphinstone believes, one might conclude that the prelude to *Aida* served as a model for the work (Elphinstone, p. 63).

One year later, still a student, Giacomo wrote a patriotic cantata called *I Figli d'Italia Bella.* In 1878 something far more tempting engaged him. He was hired to play the piano in the gambling casino of the fashionable spa at Bagni di Lucca. He also played the organ in a church there. Located in the hills about sixteen miles northeast of the city, Bagni had been favored even in the Middle Ages for its hot mineral waters and its beautiful site. After the unification of Italy, this watering place was chiefly known for attracting noble families, gamblers, and rich tourists from abroad. It boasted an especially impressive clientele in the fall; its elegant hotels housed Italian, French, English, and American vacationers, who could even count on having an English pharmacy.

When Giacomo was playing there, just getting to Bagni took time and energy. As late as the 1890s, the trip from Lucca lasted for two and a half hours, as Baedeker warned travelers. Even after the development of the national railroad network, the line to Bagni was still under construction, with only five miles of track, so the last lap had to be made by carriage or omnibus. When Giacomo was working there in the 1870s, the trip was even longer and more tiring, but it was worth the trouble, because of the contacts he could make. Among the people he met was Dr. Adelson Betti, the owner of the English pharmacy. Giacomo went to Bagni not as a boy but as a professional, hired to play in the Royal Casinò Ridotti, which had a ballroom, billiard hall, and reading room. His work earned him his first out-of-town commission when Dr. Betti, a passionate music lover, asked him to write something for the local parish church. He responded with a *Vexilla regis*.

Fifty years later, Adolfo Betti, the doctor's son, told how the commission came about. A violinist, Adolfo went to New York and, under the patronage of Carolyn Perera (the wife of Lionel Perera) and others, played for many years in the Flonzaley Quartet. He wrote, "[Giacomo] usually arrived before the time of the show and took supper with us, occasionally showing to my father his latest compositions or playing excerpts from the operas he admired most. On one of these visits, my father, who was the acting organist and choirmaster of our little church, asked if he would write a ['little' crossed out] composition for one of the forthcoming festivities. Giacomo agreed. The price (!) was stipulated as follows: ten lire cash (about 80 cents!) and . . . one of the special cakes for which Bagni di Lucca was famous! And so the *Vexilla* came into existence!" (from *Report of the Librarian of Congress, 1935–1936*, reproduced in Kaye, p. 13). The text was by Venantius Honorius Clementianus Fortunatus and may have been written in 569, when the Emperor Giustiniano II gave Queen Radegonda a gift of wood fragments that were believed to have come from the cross of Christ.

By writing for the Passion Week rites in a parish that welcomed rich Italians and foreigners, Giacomo had the opportunity to have his music performed before a knowledgeable audience. His *Vexilla regis,* which dates from about 1878, was composed for tenor and bass solo or for two-part men's chorus and organ or harmonium. In that same year he presented two other works during the celebrations for the feast of San Paolino in Lucca, a Credo for solo voices, chorus, and orchestra, and a motet for four voices. He was also beginning to earn small fees as the organist in the parish churches of Mutigliano, San Pietro Somaldi, and perhaps Celle, as well as in the Church and the Oratorio of the Benedictine Sisters of Saints Giuseppe and Girolamo. His Mass for four voices and orchestra was given in the church of San Paolino in Lucca in 1880.

As Giacomo's mother and his teachers judged, he needed training in a large conservatory. Albina called up all her reserves so she could send her son away. Among those she approached was Queen Margherita, through one of the ruler's ladies-in-waiting. Her pleas were answered when Giacomo received a study grant from the queen; then Dr. Cerù agreed to supplement it. With this financial aid, Giacomo could leave Tuscany and move to Milan, the commercial and artistic capital of the new Italy.*

* I am indebted for the material in this chapter to *The Puccini Companion: Essays on Puccini's Life and Music,* edited by William Weaver and Simonetta Puccini. Copyright 1994 by William Weaver and Simonetta Puccini. Used by permission of W. W. Norton and Company.

CHAPTER TWO

~e9~

Milan and the Old Guard: 1880–1883

W HEN PUCCINI left home in October 1880, he had to travel almost two hundred miles to reach Milan, a full day's trip and more. The most convenient route would have taken him from Lucca to Pisa and from there to the north. Express trains, which could reach thirty miles an hour, were very expensive. Local trains, more popular by far, had an average speed of about twelve miles an hour. However slow, any train was preferable to the lumbering, accident-prone coaches that had carried travelers over the Apennines for centuries.

A Student in Milan

At the end of the journey was Milan's handsome railway station, the Stazione Centrale, built in 1864 and decorated by famous artists and sculptors. Omnibuses from the great hotels waited at the station door, but Puccini may have taken public transportation. If he carried anything larger than hand baggage, he had to hire a hansom cab and pay extra for large items. Most people used the horse-drawn tramways to get to the center of Milan. As the tram left the station, it made its way through swarming, noisy streets amid a hubbub that the young, aspiring music student had never experienced in tight, ancient, conservative Lucca.

In the autumn of 1880 Great Milan, *Milano la Grande,* as it was called, had a population of about three hundred thousand people. The financial capital of the new nation of Italy, it stood as a busy working witness to its citizens' well-being. As a Baedeker guide put it in 1886, Milan had "a high degree of prosperity." Under the Romans it had been one of Italy's largest cities, and it had remained strong over the centuries, although after 1815 it had functioned chiefly as a center of Austrian provincial rule. After the founding of the Kingdom of Italy and the complete unification of the peninsula, Milan gradually saw radical change in every phase of daily life. Urban growth affected the whole city as a new planning commission finished writing its orders for the grand revitalization project. By 1880, construction had begun on new streets; whole new quarters were going up; soon some people had running water in homes, modern sewers functioned, and electric streetlights went up in the center city. Certain trams would begin to run on overhead electric wires, although horses were still everywhere, and many interurban tramways ran on steam. When Puccini got to Milan, people were still using oil lamps or gas in their homes. The director Luchino Visconti remembered that in the neighborhood around the Teatro alla Scala, gaslights in private houses dimmed every evening when the theater turned up the lights in its huge auditorium. Later, even La Scala converted to electricity.

With its important archdiocese and its huge cathedral, Milan was the heart of the Catholic faith in northern Italy, being one of the country's most important sees. Liberals and even some Catholics called the province "Black Lombardy" because of the zeal of the priests, who were seen everywhere in their floor-length, black cassocks. Quite naturally, the archbishop of Milan had a planning commission of his own. After five hundred years, the final touches were being added to the Duomo, the great Gothic cathedral founded in 1386 by Duke Gian Galeazzo Sforza. Every ruler and prelate had added something to the structure, and the facade was still unfinished when Napoleon ordered work resumed on it.

The Duomo covered fourteen thousand square yards of land. According to the 1895 Baedeker, it could hold about forty thousand people and was the third largest church on earth. With nearly one hundred turrets and about two thousand marble statues on its outside surfaces, it stood at the head of a large public square. The young architect Giuseppe Brentano was about to win the competition for restoration of its gorgeous facade, a project young Puccini followed with some interest.

Around the Duomo were several churches and towers dating from the fourteenth, fifteenth, and sixteenth centuries; crowded streets were edged with houses that were centuries old. To the north of the Duomo was the

Galleria Vittorio Emanuele, that glass-roofed marvel crossroad that linked Piazza Duomo to Piazza della Scala and nearby streets. Built in the 1860s, the Galleria had become one of Europe's busiest meeting places, with dozens of shops, cafés, and restaurants. In one of the apartments on the third floor, just under the glass roof, lived the head of the claque from the Teatro alla Scala, who could make or break a performance by directing the paid members of the claque to applaud on cue or create noisy disturbances, depending on what singers, composers, ballerinas, or impresarios had paid for. The Galleria soon became Puccini's second home.

Puccini roomed successively in several apartments in the city. He lived first in the house at Via Monforte 26, near the conservatory, but soon moved, complaining that his room was cold; worse, no one would wash his clothes and polish his shoes. In February 1881, he moved to Via Zecca Vecchia 10, near Piazza San Sepolcro, a twenty-minute walk from his school. Later, he found a place with a small stove. He also lived at 2 Vicolo San Carlo, a few hundred feet from the Galleria and the Duomo and a few blocks from the Milan Conservatory. This little street survives today as an ell at the end of Via San Carlo, across the street from the church of the same name.

As he settled in, several former Lucchesi offered him hospitality. Among them was Carlo Biagini, a cousin who was perhaps his closest friend at that time. He may have been the unidentified "Carlo" of early letters found in Arnaldo Marchetti's invaluable book, *Puccini com'era*. This Carlo helped Puccini with small gifts of money, enough to pay for about half of a dinner. In his letters home, Puccini also mentioned having dinner at Marchi's restaurant with a young soldier named Santori, who was doing military service in Milan. Other Lucchesi included a former theatrical impresario and several men in commerce. Puccini's best-known musical compatriot was Alfredo Catalani, Fortunato Magi's former student, who helped and encouraged him. Born in Lucca on June 19, 1854, only two blocks from the Puccinis, Catalani had begun his studies at the Istituto when he was nine and had remained there until he was eighteen. Instead of going straight to Milan or Naples after graduation, he set out for Paris, where he studied briefly at the conservatory. Dissatisfied there, he finally settled in Milan. Catalani graduated from the Milan Conservatory in 1875, and within a year he had begun to build a reputation with his well-received chamber compositions. His opera *Elda* had its premiere at the Teatro Regio in Turin in January 1880, before Puccini reached Milan. Graceful and serious, Catalani was popular in Milanese musical circles.

The Royal Conservatory

The Milan Conservatory was then respected as one of Italy's finest training grounds for composers, singers, and instrumentalists. Established by Napoleon and by an edict of Eugène Beauharnais in 1807–1808, it stands next to the Church of Santa Maria della Passione and occupies the former home of a religious order. Its baroque facade hides a handsome sixteenth-century structure with a spacious square courtyard surrounded by an arcade and rows of finely carved columns. In the early days of the conservatory, its dormitories had housed music students, for it, like all Italian schools of its kind, had been a boarding facility, where they slept, studied, and ate. By Puccini's day, students had to live outside the school, although Verdi had long urged a return to the old boarding-school system. His proposed reforms, however, were never carried out. Students of composition had to pass an entrance exam, then begin a three-year course of study. Those who remained for an extra year received an advanced diploma.

Among Puccini's professors were Antonio Bazzini, a modernist, who taught composition, and Amilcare Ponchielli, whose most popular opera, *La Gioconda,* had had its premiere in 1876. This, then, was the institution where Puccini hoped to complete his formal musical education, although there was so much competition for the few available places that he was not even sure he could get in. The well-known story of the Milan Conservatory's rejection of the nineteen-year-old Verdi was still common currency in musical circles and in biographies, for many knew the ridiculous story. In 1832, when Verdi applied for admission, he was turned down. *"Fu bocciato,"* he wrote across his letter of application after it was returned to him: "It was rejected."

In fact, Verdi was denied admission for some reasons that might also have made Puccini ineligible: only a few new students were being admitted in 1880, the school was short of space, and Puccini, like Verdi, was older than most students. He was later told that age would not matter, provided his exam showed him to be "one of the best" (GP to AMP, in Marchetti, p. 15).* Even at twenty-one, he still felt he had a chance, although he certainly looked like a poor young man at the time, badly needing new clothes and shoes. His shoes were so worn that he was ashamed to wear them to an appointment with Giovannina Lucca, the formidable head of one of Italy's three major music publishing houses.

In any case, he took the entrance exam and then wrote to his mother.

Dearest Mamma, So far I haven't heard anything about my admission to the conservatory, because on Saturday the council met to decide about the students who took the examination, that is, to see which students they can admit, because there are very few available openings. I have very fair expectations about getting in, because I got the highest marks, and I hope they will overlook my age. Tell [Maestro Carlo] Carignani that the examination was very, very easy for me, because they made me harmonize an unfigured bass, very easy, and then they made me develop a melody in D major, which came out very well.—No more about that; it went perhaps even better than it should have gone. The melody was this:

[Here Puccini drew a stave and wrote out the musical line for his mother, who could read music, although one of Albina's daughters later said her mother was not a trained musician.]

I forgot to tell you that the schools, which should have opened on the sixteenth, will open later here because the council has not yet decided about the students' admission. I often visit Catalani, who is extremely kind. In the evening when I have money, I go to a café, but on many, many evenings I don't go, because a glass of punch costs forty *centesimi!* But I go to bed early; I get bored with walking back and forth in the Galleria. I have a pretty little room, clean, with a beautiful, polished walnut writing table that is magnificent. All in all, I'm happy to stay here. I'm not suffering from hunger. The food is quite bad, but I fill up on minestrone made with 'thin broth . . . and . . . other things.' My belly is full. [GP to AMP, (November 1880), in Gara, p. 1]†

* Arnaldo Marchetti, *Puccini com'era*. With kind permission from EDIZIONI CURCI, S.r.l., Galleria del Corso 4, 20122 Milan, Italy. Copyright 1973 by EDIZIONI CURCI, S.r.l., Milan. All rights reserved.
† Eugenio Gara, *Carteggi Pucciniani,* copyright 1958 by CASA RICORDI-BMG RICORDI S.p.A.

On November 10, Puccini wrote again to tell his mother the good news: he had gone that morning to the conservatory, where the examination marks were posted, and had seen that he was "the best of all, all modesty aside" (GP to AMP, November 10, 1880, in A. Marchetti, p. 15). Soon he was told that he had been admitted despite his age. By December 18, he had had at least two lessons from Bazzini. Popular among his colleagues, Bazzini had enjoyed a respectable career as a concert violinist and composer before he joined the conservatory faculty. In 1867 he gave the world premiere of his opera *Turanda,* based on Carlo Gozzi's fable about a Chinese princess. It was given at La Scala, where it survived for twelve performances. After Rossini's death in 1868, Verdi asked Bazzini to compose one section of the requiem Mass, the *Messa per Rossini,* that he planned as part of a national event to honor the great composer. As Verdi conceived it, this would be a shared effort by several Italian composers, each to compose one part of the Mass. The *Messa per Rossini* project was later abandoned. In 1873 Bazzini, an advocate of modern music, became a professor of composition at the conservatory, just in time to have Catalani in his classes; in 1882 he became the school's director.

Among the professors, Amilcare Ponchielli became closest to Puccini, acting as his mentor. After working as a bandmaster in Cremona and Piacenza, Ponchielli had begun composing ballets and incidental music and had also written three operas besides his popular *La Gioconda.* He premiered yet another, *Il Figliuol Prodigo,* in 1880. Ponchielli's wife, the soprano Teresina Brambilla, had a distinguished career in her own right, and she was still singing when Puccini was introduced to her. Born into a family of professional musicians, she was the niece and namesake of the famous soprano Teresa Brambilla, who had been Verdi's first Gilda in *Rigoletto* in 1851. Another aunt, Marietta, had created roles in Donizetti operas and was a respected voice teacher. Teresina had created Lucia in Ponchielli's *I Promessi Sposi* in Milan in 1872 and gone on to become a famous Gioconda and Aida. Although she was married and had children, she continued to sing until her retirement in 1889. As a couple, Ponchielli and his wife helped Puccini in the last year of his studies and after graduation, directing him toward opera.

As Puccini reported to his mother in one letter, his lessons with Bazzini were going splendidly. He had had no other classes, but he was to begin aesthetics almost at once.

I made a schedule for myself, and this is how it goes. In the morning I get up at eight-thirty; when I have a lesson, I go to it; otherwise I study piano for a while. I don't need much, but I do have to study it. Now I am about to buy a very good [study] method by [Antonio] Angeleri; it is one of those methods where you can learn by yourself, and it is very, very good. Next: at ten-thirty I have a meal and then I go out. At one I go home and study a couple of hours for Bazzini; then between three and five I go back to the piano and do a little reading in classical music. Actually, I'd like to sub- scribe [to one of the circulating libraries for music scores], but I don't have enough money. Right now I am looking over Boito's *Mefistofele,* which I borrowed from a friend, [Alberto] Favara [Mistretta], who is from Palermo.

At five I go out for a frugal dinner (but really frugal!) and I eat mine- strone Milanese style, which, to tell the truth, is very good. I eat three dishes of it, then something else to fill up, a small piece of *cacio* [fresh pec- orino] cheese with young fava beans and a half-liter of wine. After that, I light a cigar and go to the Galleria to walk back and forth, as usual. I stay there until nine, and I go home, dead tired from walking. When I get home, I do a little counterpoint, [but] I don't play, because at night no one is allowed to play. After that, I slip into bed and read seven or eight pages of some novel. That's my life! [GP to AMP, (December 18?), 1880, in Gara, pp. 2–3]

In this letter, which was probably written on December 18, Puccini went on to ask his mother to send him some Tuscan olive oil. He needed it, he said, because in Milan he could get only sesame or linseed oil for his beans. He even asked her to get very good oil from a specific provider, Eugenio Ottolini, who had already sent some to the tenor Vincenzo Papeschi, another Lucchese living in Milan. At the end of the letter, Puc- cini added an emotional note. "You can't imagine how much I want to see you again," he wrote, "and if I have made you angry so often, it is not be- cause I don't love you; it's because I am an animal and a rascal; I know that about myself" (ibid., p. 3). Puccini also wrote frequently to his sister Ramelde. As Simonetta Puccini said in her essay in *The Puccini Companion,* Puccini was fonder of Ramelde than of his other siblings. She was close to him in age and similar in character, lively and funny. On December 9 he sent Ramelde the news of the latest Milanese women's fashions: long capes, tight at the waist, dark and tobacco-colored, with the hood lined with lighter satin. A large department store was selling them for thirty-five, forty, and fifty lire. He went on to describe simple wool dresses, pleated skirts, big scarves, and fur hats garishly ornamented with gilded animal claws (GP to RP, in A. Marchetti, pp. 16–19). This and many other chatty letters to Ramelde show the loving affection that existed between her and her brother. This bond was never broken.

Student life in a very expensive city proved challenging to a young man with little money to spend, but Puccini rarely knew real hardship, because his mother responded to virtually every request. He also had help from Ramelde. In April 1881 she sent him a suit, for which he thanked her: "You cannot imagine the effect this sweet act of yours had on me. Tears came to my eyes." To repay the favor, he promised to send her a hat as soon as he got some money; for the moment, he said, he was completely broke. In the same letter Puccini mentioned the engagement of his sister Tomaide, who taught French, to Enrico Gherardi, another teacher. Her fiancé was a widower with two small children. Puccini, expressing mixed feelings about the event, said he regretted the marriage because Tomaide was such a consolation for the family and had done so much for all of them. On the other hand, he conceded, she deserved happiness. (GP to RP, April 4, 1881, in A. Marchetti, pp. 29–30). Many of these letters sound as if he were homesick, even with many friends nearby. In addition to Catalani and the other Lucchesi, he had met young people like himself at school and had also found companions among the tenants in his rooming house.

Given the sacrifices Albina had made to get her son into the Milan Conservatory, one might expect Puccini to have been a model student, but he was not, although he was clearly as gifted as anyone in his class. In fact, he got in some trouble with his professors there, just as he had at the Seminario di San Martino and as he had with Magi at the Istituto in Lucca. Inattentive and restless in his Poetic and Dramatic Literature lessons, he used class time to write letters. On March 9, 1881, he wrote to his mother, "I'm here in my Dramatic Literature class, which bores me to tears" (GP to AMP, in A. Marchetti, pp. 27–28). And in a notebook he wrote, "Alas!!!! O! O God!!! Help, for pity's sake!!! Enough!!! It's too much!!! I'm dying!!!" Then later he added, "It's a bit better!" (L. Marchetti, ill. 20). In another note like this, he admitted to dozing off in class.

He missed so many classes that he was called before the Conservatory

Council. "Because of his continued unjustified absences, the Academic Council, at its meeting of June 26, 1881, inflicts a fine of 10 lire" (Weaver and S. Puccini, pp. 66–67). The note about the absences and the fine went on his record at a time when he, like all the other first-year students, was on a kind of probation. In fact, the council's reprimand sounds like something handed out in a *ginnasio* or high school; but Puccini was no teenager. He was then twenty-two, jobless, living on the grant from Queen Margherita and money from his mother and Dr. Cerù, asking others for further help, wearing the clothes Ramelde had sent him, and borrowing money that he could not repay.

He was, however, writing music. In his essay in *The Puccini Companion*, Michael Elphinstone described the importance of the compositions of the conservatory years and analyzed their place in the culture of the times in Milan. These included *Salve Regina*, for soprano and harmonium (1882 or 1883); *Melanconia*, for baritone and piano (1881, now lost); and *Ad una morta!*, also for baritone and piano (1882 or 1883). All three had texts by Antonio Ghislanzoni, the eccentric former baritone, journalist, and poet who had written the libretto for Verdi's *Aida*. In 1883 Puccini composed *Storiella d'amore*, to a Ghislanzoni text. During the early 1880s he also wrote a Suite for piano, a *Scherzo* in A minor for a string quartet, a *Largo adagietto* in F major for orchestra, a *Preludio sinfonico* in A major for orchestra (composed for the school's end-of-year concert in 1882), a Trio for two violins and piano, three fugues, and the String Quartet in D major. In 1883 he wrote *La Sconsolata*, for violin and piano, and the *Capriccio sinfonico*, which was performed for the end-of-year concert as he left the conservatory. An *Adagio* in A may date from 1881. These compositions are listed by Linda B. Fairtile in *Giacomo Puccini: A Guide to Research*.

Puccini wrote to his mother about Verdi's revised *Simon Boccanegra*, which was on the program at La Scala. In 1881 Franco Faccio, the leading conductor at La Scala, conducted it with Victor Maurel in the title role, the Austrian soprano Anna d'Angeri as Amelia/Maria, and Francesco Tamagno as Gabriele. This was d'Angeri's last year at La Scala, for she married and retired, so that when Verdi asked her to come back to sing the first Desdemona in his *Otello*, she refused. The reprise of *Simon Boccanegra* in 1882 had Maurel backed by less famous singers. Tickets were in great demand, and Puccini was, as usual, short of money. Good seats cost five lire and, as he wrote to his mother, were all sold out. He wrote,

"How rich Milan is!" And how expensive! It is not known whether he ever saw *Simon Boccanegra,* although his letter to his mother probably refers to the event of 1881. He did see *Carmen, Fra Diavolo, La Stella del Nord,* and Catalani's *Dejanice.*

Sometime at the end of 1882, Albina Puccini wrote to ask Ponchielli how her son was faring and urged, even begged, him to help her Giacomo. On January 8, 1883, Ponchielli replied. In a surprisingly long answer, he reassured her, saying that although Puccini was among his best pupils, his work was not fully satisfactory. His attention flagged, Ponchielli said; he was not working steadily enough. But, he said, "If he wants to, he can do very good work." He then warned Albina about other things her son should be doing, such as studying the works of great composers of the past and spending more time composing. Ponchielli evidently believed he had not learned enough, for he had advised the young man not to leave the conservatory in July, but to return in the fall for an additional year. With further study, Ponchielli said, he would be better prepared for his profession. Ponchielli appealed directly to Albina, asking her to tell her son "not to miss the other courses, so he can get a full Certificate." He closed by saying that he would do everything possible to help him and would try to get him a teaching position after graduation (Ponchielli to AMP, in L. Marchetti, ills. 29, 30).

True to his word, Ponchielli continued to mentor Puccini, even after he decided not to enroll for the extra year. Albina evidently solicited and got another report on her son's progress from Bazzini, his composition teacher (Bazzini to AMP, cited in Fairtile, p. 69). This letter came at a busy time in Albina's life, when Ramelde was planning to marry Raffaello Franceschini, a Lucchese. The couple remained in the city for some time, so Ramelde could help her mother, who was ill; then they moved to Pescia, where Franceschini was a tax collector.

Puccini left the Conservatory of Music on July 16, 1883; as it turned out, he was remarkably successful there. Earlier that week, his *Capriccio sinfonico,* written for the end-of-year concert, had been conducted by Franco Faccio, the foremost Italian conductor of his time. Puccini said that he had composed the piece on the run, scribbling on scraps of paper at home, in the Osteria Aida or the Excelsior Restaurant, and even as he walked in the street. No matter what the circumstances of its composition, the work was well received and even got reviewed by Filippo Filippi,

Italy's leading music critic. Faccio promised to put it on a concert program at La Scala. A triumphant Puccini wrote to his mother to say that its success would have satisfied the most demanding person on earth. But his work had just begun. He had to get a fresh copy of his *Capriccio* and get it to Giovannina Lucca, so he could strike before she lost interest in him.

The Sonzogno Competition

A theatrical magazine reported in the spring of 1883 that the publisher Edoardo Sonzogno would offer a prize for a new one-act opera. At the time of the announcement, Puccini was finishing his final year at the conservatory. Then came his final examinations. However, he evidently discussed the competition with Ponchielli, either just before or shortly after graduation. They both knew that deadline for delivery of the score to Sonzogno was December 31, 1883.

True to his promise to Albina, Ponchielli followed his promising student's fortunes after graduation, when Puccini urgently needed his support. His circumstances were so desperate that summer that even after he pawned his watch and gold pin, he could not cover his room and board. Under such pressure, he might well have given up hope and gone back to Lucca to take over as the organist at San Martino. But he did not look to the church for a position, nor did he accept the teaching post offered later by the Istituto Musicale. Both he and his mother believed that his future lay in Milan, where he had already impressed Ponchielli and Faccio, where Catalani had introduced him to other influential men.

Many doors opened for Puccini when Ponchielli invited him for a four-day visit in summer 1883 to Maggianico, a village near Lake Como. Given the importance of personal recommendations in the music business, it is surely no exaggeration to say that his fortunes changed when he was introduced to the circle of artists, writers, and musicians who summered there. Como is perhaps the most beautiful lake in Italy. Its shores are dotted with picturesque villages and vineyards. Magnificent villas perch on the hills above the water; the gardens are lush with tropical plants and trees. The Alps loom above at a height of about seven thousand feet, providing a backdrop for the lake itself and for forests of chestnut and walnut trees. The community has two "capitals," the city of Como to the west and Lecco to the east. When Puccini first went there, most of Lecco's year-round residents earned their living from fishing or from manufacturing silk, cotton, and iron. The region is marvelously described in Alessandro Manzoni's *I Promessi Sposi,* part of which is set on "that branch of Lake Como,"—the Lecco branch—as the famous first line of his novel reads. Ponchielli had a particular love for the book and the place, because he had composed an opera based on Manzoni's novel.

The colony of musicians gathered in the summer in a region south of Lecco, where certain villages had gradually become little private Edens for the intellectuals of the aesthetic movement called the *Scapigliatura Milanese.* The movement's name means "the Disheveled Ones from Milan." It had first flourished in the 1860s and 1870s, when many novelists, artists, journalists, librettists, poets, and composers had begun identifying themselves with it. The *Scapigliati,* who often looked to Germany and France for inspiration, wanted to modernize Italian art, music, and theater; in doing so, they turned their backs on the "Old Guard," which was represented chiefly by two venerable celebrities: Verdi and Manzoni.

Among the original *Scapigliati* were the composer-librettist Arrigo Boito; his close friends Emilio Praga and Franco Faccio; the music critic Filippo Filippi, who had given Puccini his first favorable review; the novelist Giuseppe Rovani; the journalist-poet-composer Marco Sala and one of his brothers; the poet-librettist Ferdinando Fontana, who would be the author of the librettos for Puccini's first two operas; the music publisher and composer Giulio Ricordi, who was then poised to take over his family firm; and the editor-historian Leon Fortis. An early member who had defected from the movement was the librettist Ghislanzoni. Ponchielli's own Verdian style of composition and his respect for Manzoni had kept him from being an authentic *Scapigliato,* but he knew and loved many members of the movement, and they loved him.

In the 1860s Verdi's trusted friend Countess Clara Maffei had been a ready supporter and patron of the *Scapigliati,* particularly attached to Faccio and Boito. In 1863, though, Boito ripped a large hole in the fabric of Italian culture by insulting Manzoni and Verdi, Italy's revered "Old Men." He delivered his outrageous slap at them during a banquet organized to honor Faccio and his new opera, *I Profughi Fiamminghi,* for which Ghislanzoni was the librettist. Near the end of the evening Boito read a long ode to the health of Italian art. In it he railed against the older generation and added an offensive line that Verdi never forgot. The old men were, Boito said, "scrofulous" and "idiotic," and they had left "the altar of Italian art soiled like a whorehouse wall." Not surprisingly, after this event Verdi cut Boito out of his life for about twenty years.

Faccio's next work was *Amleto,* an opera based on *Hamlet.* Its heavily publicized 1865 premiere at the Teatro Carlo Felice in Genoa stood as a milestone in the history of the *Scapigliatura,* whose adherents traveled from Milan in droves to attend. "Every artist in Milan" turned out for the event, one journalist said. Critics wrote extensively about it, hailing Faccio as the new messiah of Italian music, but high hopes for him faded as audiences for his opera grew smaller and smaller. The *Scapigliati* invested a similar amount of energy in Boito's career as he was composing his *Mefistofele.* Unfortunately, its premiere at La Scala in 1868 was a clamorous fiasco. He then revised the opera and gave the new version in 1875 in Bologna, a city where German music was welcome. But after *Mefistofele,* Boito spent much of his time composing *Nerone,* which was not premiered until six years after his death in 1918. He also wrote the libretto for Ponchielli's *La Gioconda* and those for Verdi's *Otello* and *Falstaff.*

By the time Puccini visited the summer colony on Lake Como, both Boito and Faccio were back in Verdi's favor and had even come to revere him. Nevertheless, many of the unreconstructed *Scapigliati* still had "Wagner" and "Germany" written in their hearts. Well into the 1890s, they continued to promote German music and denigrate many creative figures in Italy, wielding particular power through the newspapers and publishing houses and on the opera stage. Thus, Puccini's first two operas were conceived in the dying embers of the *Scapigliatura Milanese.* On Lake Como in 1883 Ponchielli was respected as the loyal old friend of the *Scapigliatura,* just as Verdi was enshrined as the "Grand Old Man" of Italian opera, the *"Gran Vegliardo."*

Ponchielli held forth in Maggianico, a small village beautifully situated in the shelter of looming Mount Resegone where the houses overlooked the lake and the panorama of the Alps. For more than ten years this village and nearby Malgrate and Caprino Bergamasco had been a mecca for the creative community from Milan. About six miles apart from each other, these three little communities were full of people who visited back and forth from house to house, shopped in the same stores in Lecco, and used the same railroad station. Coming and going, everyone took the train together. Apart from the physical beauty of the area, Maggianico and Caprino offered a forum for business. The summer homes of the various *Scapigliati* housed those who could not be accommodated in Caprino, where Ghislanzoni owned and ran a famous little hotel, Il Barco.

Earlier in 1883 Ponchielli and his wife had entertained Puccini in their home in Milan, and they were obviously comfortable having him visit them in Maggianico that summer. After ten years there, they had attracted other colleagues and thus had friends all around Lake Como. The Ricordi family's villa was on the western shore at Bellano, near Cernobbio. The extravagant Brazilian composer Antonio Carlos Gomes, Giulio Ricordi's protégé of the moment, had settled first in Malgrate and then moved to Maggianico, where he was Ponchielli's next-door neighbor. Ghislanzoni, whose poems Puccini had set to music, was the resident eccentric in Caprino, where the poet, dramatist, and librettist Ferdinando Fontana also vacationed. Around the table of the best restaurant in Maggianico the Ponchiellis and Ghislanzoni would sit with Boito and his friend Marco Praga. Nearby were the critic Domenico Oliva, who several years later would become one of Puccini's librettists for *Manon Lescaut,* Gomes and his wife, and the powerful critics Filippi and Eugenio Bermani.

In Maggianico Gomes and Ghislanzoni had worked together on the librettos of *Fosca,* which had had its premiere at La Scala in 1873, and *Salvator Rosa,* which followed a year later at the Teatro Carlo Felice in Genoa. As late as 1884, one year after Puccini's first visit, Gomes was composing to one of Ghislanzoni's librettos. Ponchielli and his wife were Ghislanzoni's closest friends; they were also very fond of Gomes, who flew the Brazilian flag at the door of his villa every day and filled his home with parrots and other exotic birds that he had brought back from Brazil in 1880. Other regulars who summered in this area include the composers Errico Petrella and Catalani; Amintore Galli, Puccini's professor at the Milan Conservatory; Costantino dall'Argine and Pietro Mascagni; Antonietta Anastasi-Pozzoni, the first Aida in the world premiere in Cairo, and Salvatore Anastasi, her husband; and Ponchielli's sisters-in-law, the ubiquitous Brambillas. Francesco Tamagno, the heroic tenor, headed a colony of singers and conductors that included Faccio and the soprano Romilda Pantaleoni, who would be Verdi's first Desdemona and would sing the leading soprano role in at the premiere of Puccini's second opera.

In his four days in Maggianico, Puccini made such an impression on

Ponchielli that the older man decided to help him further. He also managed to get the young composer his first opera libretto. One day when the two men were in Lecco, they ran into Fontana, whom Puccini had met earlier in Milan. Here is Fontana's account of that meeting:

> To graduate from the conservatory with the moral and material diploma as Maestro did not mean an end, but the beginning of a terrible struggle in that huge conservatory called The World. Giacomo Puccini was poor, but he had a strong calling to be a composer; however, he would likely have to give up composing in favor of teaching, so as not to starve. Nonetheless, he did not lose courage. Casa Sonzogno had announced a competition for an opera, and he wanted to go for it. It was August 1883.
>
> One beautiful morning, I had left Ghislanzoni's retreat in Caprino Bergamasco for Lecco. As I was headed back to the station, I met several members of the summer artists' colony from Maggianico: Ponchielli, [the composer and teacher Cesare] Dominiceti; [Michele] Saladino [another professor at the Milan Conservatory], and other important people. Puccini was with them. We knew each other very slightly, but on those few occasions when we had spent time together, a strong current of mutual understanding had flowed between us. After we all got in the railroad carriage with Ponchielli, he told me his pupil intended to enter the Sonzogno competition; and he suggested I should write the libretto for him. Right then, with the vivid memory of his *Capriccio sinfonico* in my head, I thought the young maestro would want a subject full of imagination, and I summarized the plot of *Le Villi* for him. He accepted it. The libretto was finished at the beginning of September. [Adami, p. 32]

In the event, it was not quite so easy, for Fontana had indeed written a scenario of the opera, but he had given it to another composer, Francesco Quaranta, who then had to agree to release it to Puccini. Fontana took care of that, as he informed Puccini in a letter of August 2. Fontana's scenario and libretto were based on traditional German and Eastern European folktales and on Alphonse Karr's French story *Les Wilis,* written in 1852. At first, the opera was also called *Le Willis,* named for the dancing witch-maidens familiar to ballet audiences from *Giselle.* Like *Giselle,* the 1841 ballet, it is a tale of love, betrayal, and high Romantic horror. Among its characters are an innocent village girl, her father, her inconstant fiancé, and the ghosts called the Willis, the spectral creatures who force Giselle's lover to dance until he dies. The choice of author and plot reflects Fontana's interest in the northern subjects loved by the *Scapigliatura Milanese.*

In Puccini's August letter to his mother, he told her about his meeting with Fontana.

> Dear Mamma, I went to visit Ponchielli and stayed four days. I spoke with Fontana, the poet, who was on vacation up there near Ponchielli; and we almost reached an agreement about a libretto. [And] he told me he liked my music. Then Ponchielli also got into the discussion, and gave me a warm recommendation. A good subject would be available, one that someone else has had but which Fontana would rather give to me, especially because I really like it a lot, for it means working a great deal in the symphonic and descriptive genre, [and that] pleases me very, very much, because it seems to me I ought to be successful with it. Thus I could take part in the Sonzogno competition. But this matter, dear Mamma, is very uncertain. Think that the competition is national in scope, and not restricted to local people, as I had thought. And then, time is short. [GP to AMP, August 1883, in Adami, p. 37]

At the end of the letter, he gave her the bad news: he was broke, he owed for fifteen days' room and board, had pawned his watch and a gold pin, and needed twenty lire to get them out of the pawnshop.

Given his situation, he had no money to pay his librettist, as composers customarily do; so Ponchielli persuaded Fontana to reduce his terms for a poor young man barely out of conservatory. Puccini was indeed very lucky to have established a friendship with Fontana, who soon had the libretto ready for him. The composer, however, did not begin the opera at once. That summer and autumn, Puccini and his collaborator became close friends, making a handsome pair, the gentle, blond Fontana and the tall, dark-haired Tuscan. At one point, Ponchielli arranged another important meeting for Puccini, making it possible for him to play a kind of one-on-one audition for Giulio Ricordi. The all-powerful publisher, who might otherwise never have received him, let Puccini play through the soprano's "Flower Aria" from *Le Willis.* "He was very happy with it," Puccini wrote to Fontana (GP to FF, in Gara, p. 9).

Whether Fontana was a competent librettist is open to question, but at least the arrangement with him catapulted Puccini into the opera business soon after graduation. However, some reservations about the librettist's character seem to have troubled others in the trade. In 1885 an acquaintance of Verdi's, the Cremonese journalist and playwright Alfonso Mandelli, wrote to tell Gomes that he was about to collaborate with Fontana on a play. Mandelli may not have asked Gomes's opinion, but the Brazilian composer offered one: "In your first letter you spoke of proposing a collaboration between you and Fontana. From that I see you do not know him very well. It is great to have talent, of course, but it is also great to be a gentleman, and I don't know whether Fontana is one" (Gomes to Mandelli, March 22, 1885, in Vetro, letter 129).

In the same letter Gomes referred to Puccini's new opera and Fontana's libretto for it. Gomes's reservations notwithstanding, Fontana behaved like a gentleman toward Puccini. The two men became good friends as they worked on *Le Willis,* sharing their private concerns and pursuing their careers. Still later they collaborated on *Edgar.* During most of their association, Fontana lived in Milan in the winter and near Lecco in the summer. Then and later, he offered Puccini good advice about professional and personal matters and helped him materially, as Ponchielli and Catalani had also done, by having him as a guest in his house and introducing him to influential people.

After Puccini left the little colony, he went to Milan and on to Lucca. Although he might have plunged straight into the composition of *Le Willis,* he apparently did little work on it. Michael Elphinstone has found a letter to Ponchielli, written on October 29, when Puccini had been home in Lucca for about three months. In it, he admitted that he was bored and lazy; he had also been "slightly ill" and sounded as if he did not know where to turn. "There is nothing to do here, and I, instead, need to find something to do." As he was revising the *Capriccio sinfonico,* he asked Ponchielli to try to get it performed in concerts, as the older man had promised he would do; and he also discussed its possible publication. Surprisingly, he asked Ponchielli for Fontana's address, so he could ask him for "the corrections of some spots in the little work I'm composing," as if he had not been in touch with his librettist since their first meeting (GP to Ponchielli, October 29, 1883, in Elphinstone, p. 72). Elphinstone believes that Puccini actually wrote most of *Le Willis* in a matter of weeks, just before the deadline for the competition.

Puccini's sister Ramelde painted a different picture, when she later provided a glimpse of her brother at work on his first opera, although she did mention his doubts about whether he would win the Sonzogno competition.

> Having returned to Lucca, Giacomo set to work with such ardor that it seemed the opera would soon be finished. But after a little while, he was assailed by discouragement and doubt and, at the same time, inertia. However, a guardian angel was watching over his destiny, and that was his Mamma, who, thinking of her son's future, devoted all her strength to exhorting him, encouraging him, and acting as critic of what he was writing. Every piece of the work was passed to her to judge, and Giacomo accepted her judgment and revised and rewrote. His loving Mamma did not know music, but her opinion was valuable because, having lived among artists, intelligent as she was, and of sincere spirit, she had acquired taste and knowledge. What anxiety, what effort, what trepidation, how many nights she spent with her Giacomo! (Because Giacomo wanted to compose amid silence, as he does now.) Finally the work was finished at midnight of the day set as the deadline for the competition. [S. Puccini, "The Puccini Family," p. 16]

Fontana knew that Puccini's score was presented at the last moment, and that he had to turn it in without making a fair copy of it. Sitting on the panel for the competition were some who were already familiar with his music: Ponchielli, Faccio, who had already conducted the *Capriccio sinfonico,* and Cesare Dominiceti and Amintore Galli, both from the summer colony at Como, who also taught at the Milan Conservatory. They might have weighed in for him, but they apparently did not. About two months passed before Puccini, his mother, and his sisters learned from a newspaper article that he had not won, or even received an honorable mention. The prize was divided between two composers. Guglielmo Zuelli was a student at the conservatory who later became the head of the Parma Conservatory. His *La Fata del Nord* and Luigi Mapelli's *Anna e Gualberto,* the other winner, were produced at the Teatro Manzoni in Milan. Ramelde remembered Puccini's dejection, for he was quite overwhelmed by such a disgraceful loss in a competition that was widely publicized and gossiped about in the music business. But, she said, their mother was undaunted. In letter after letter, Albina kept pushing her son to seek new support for their family's cause.

CHAPTER THREE

❧

Le Willis, *Later Called* Le Villi: 1884–1886

AFTER the Sonzogno competition, Puccini seemed utterly defeated, for even before the winners were announced, he had told his mother he had very little hope. At the least, he might have expected an honorable mention for *Le Willis;* but as a losing opera, it was effectively dead. With no money to pay for a new libretto, he could not begin a second work, nor could he easily turn again to Ponchielli, who had already risked a lot for him. Shorter of funds than before, he often wrote home for money. Luckily for him, Fontana had determined not to see their opera sink without a trace. Albina also continued to plead with Ponchielli and other influential people in Milan, begging them for recommendations for her son and adding gifts such as the book she gave to Amintore Galli.

"I am very sad because you aren't finding anything," Albina wrote to Puccini in February 1884, again urging him to deliver the letters she had written to those who might help him. Catalani, who was then in Lucca, was ruled out as a possible source of support, for she had been told that he thought only of himself (AMP to GP, February 12, 1884, in A. Marchetti, p. 43). A few weeks later, she told Puccini he should be "beating the streets" to find people who could help him. As she said, she could not rest because she thought of him all the time. Had he gone to the right theatrical agencies? Had he tried to find pupils and give lessons? He should have Ponchielli tell Ricordi to hire her son as the *maestro concertatore;* "and that would be the way to help you" (AMP to GP, March 3, 1884, in A. Marchetti, pp. 47–48). One hopeful sign came when Ponchielli took him to a meeting with Ricordi and gave him a strong personal recommendation.

Although Puccini told his mother that nothing would come of it, his association with Ricordi proved to be the most important of his career.

By March the young Michele Puccini was in Milan, where he was enrolled in the conservatory. He was also working as his brother's music copyist. In April Puccini found him a job in Alessandro Pigna's music shop in the Galleria and kept him on a short rein, in best big-brother style. Later Michele helped Puccini stage *Le Willis*. At first Puccini had no room for him, but he oversaw his schooling. Later the two lived together; a cousin also shared their quarters briefly, as did Pietro Mascagni, the future composer of *Cavalleria Rusticana*. One of Puccini's friends from the conservatory was Arturo Buzzi-Peccia, who remembered Puccini and Michele living on the third floor in an old house on Piazza Beccaria, which was just behind the cathedral.

> Michele had the habit of cooking lunch (usually a couple of eggs) on a little alcohol stove placed on top of the piano, an old upright, but a hero that could stand four or five hours of playing a day of any kind of music that happened to come to hand. One day, we were playing the Prelude to *Meistersinger* with great gusto, when, just at the climax, at the very moment when all the themes come together—Krak!—the stove, frying pan, the eggs, butter, all fell into a heap into the piano, burning the felts, greasing the strings and stopping the action of the keyboard, which was covered with butter. The only liquid on hand was a bottle of Chianti, and we had to sacrifice Bacchus to save Euterpe. Puccini that day had to go to the [Trattoria] Aida for his lunch. This was a Tuscan restaurant very popular among the students. [Buzzi-Peccia]

The daily menu included tough steak, a serving of Tuscan-style beans, and a half-glass of Tuscan Pomino, a light Chianti.

Buzzi-Peccia also recalled his evening strolls with Puccini in the Galleria Vittorio Emanuele and their card games in the Caffè Savini. He and Puccini cheated the other players by humming a melody that was in fact a code that corresponded to the values of the cards they held. The first note of the phrase told the partner what key the phrase of melody was in; the following notes tipped him off to the actual hand. "The theme of *Lohengrin* was "mi-la-ti-do-mi-mi," which meant "I hold one ace, one 2, one 3 and two 5s." A phrase from a duet from *Aida* meant "I have a 7, and an 8, and a 5." One night when they were playing with the librettist Luigi

Illica and another friend, Illica finally had had enough. "We are not great musicians," he said. "Would you mind announcing your cards by speaking instead of by singing the intervals? It would be fairer to us and more honest." Puccini said, "All right. Just as you say," but he played one more trick, cuing Buzzi-Peccia with another hint: "Clarinets in B flat," he said. Illica and their friend, bewildered, continued to lose money. Finally, Puccini and Buzzi-Peccia agreed to give away their secret if the other two would pay for their dinner.—Done! When summer came, the merry crew spent a week together at Cadenabbia on Lake Como (Buzzi-Peccia). When they were older, the two men exchanged letters; Puccini wrote doggerel verse to his old friend and always addressed him as *"tu,"* the intimate form of "you."

Later, Puccini asked Michele to move from his apartment, but he still kept close watch on him. Both continued to follow the vicissitudes of the opera business, although they rarely went to the theater. April found Puccini saying that his future looked brighter, so Dr. Cerù sent him money and a good-luck note. Albina too could see progress, although a note of desperation persisted in her letters, perhaps because she was so ill. In February 1884 she had begun to feel the first symptoms of the stomach cancer that killed her five months later.

Saving *Le Willis*

Puccini's own initiatives were directed for months toward Giovannina Strazza Lucca, the feared, respected music publisher whom he often mentioned in his letters to his family. She and her husband, Francesco, veterans in their profession, began operations as a couple in the 1840s, but in many ways Giovannina had always been the creative force in the company, the militant rival of Casa Ricordi and the standard-bearer in Italy for Wagner, many French composers, and Meyerbeer. In 1842 the Luccas had courted Verdi, who had just become famous with *Nabucco;* although he was associated for decades with the Ricordis, he also dealt with the Luccas, under a contract for some early operas. He soon ended his association with them, chiefly because he heartily disliked Francesco Lucca, but he certainly respected Giovannina, who aggressively pursued him. The Luccas, passionate advocates of Wagner, succeeded in getting *Lohengrin* produced in Bologna in 1871; this was the first Wagner opera given in Italy.

After Francesco's death in 1872, Giovannina ran the firm alone. Like the Ricordis, she was always looking for young composers and had noticed Puccini in 1883, when he won the annual scholarship she awarded to the most promising graduate from the Milan Conservatory. She also published his *Capriccio sinfonico* as part of her award and later offered to commission a symphony from him, an offer he refused, perhaps because he hoped for a more profitable relationship with Ricordi. His limited contacts with Madame Lucca, however, were helpful in these first years of his career.

In the end, however, it was Fontana who finally got *Le Willis* onstage in Milan. As he told Puccini, he was sure he could raise the money for the production, but first he had to interest influential people in it. Among these were two journalists, Aldo Noseda and G. Borghi, who wrote for the newspaper *Italia*. Fontana also enlisted Ponchielli's help in arranging for Puccini to play the score of *Le Willis* for a small, select audience. This private concert took place in the home of Marco Sala, a *Scapigliato* and a wealthy patron of young musicians. Sala was one of three music-mad brothers in a family of amateur musicians. A critic, poet, and composer, he played the violin in the orchestras of amateur philharmonic societies and hosted private evening concerts in the salon of his family's palazzo. His brother Giovanni, also a composer, wrote popular waltzes that were played at society balls in the city's great palazzi.

In the early 1860s Sala had emerged in Italy as a passionate advocate of the "new music," a term that referred mostly to the works of composers who might "cleanse" Italy of the "filth" left by old men such as Verdi. Like many of the *Scapigliati* and other forward-looking artists of his time, Sala had belonged to the Società del Quartetto and had written articles for its avant-garde periodical, the *Giornale della Società del Quartetto*. As early as 1865 Sala, the *Scapigliati,* and the Società del Quartetto had begun to search for new poets, novelists, and especially a young Italian composer who would embrace their modernist ideas. As the *Scapigliato* painter Carlo Mancini crudely put it, he and his friends wanted to drive the Italian "monsters and mastodons" into museums. Soon their hopes for "killing Verdi off" were crushed, for with the huge success of *Aida* after 1871, the *Scapigliati* had little hope of keeping its composer in a museum. But because they believed that *Aida* would be his last opera, they went on searching for new talent, for a young composer who would look beyond the Alps for inspiration. In a way, Puccini seemed made to order for them.

With his private event in Marco Sala's salon, Puccini was finally introduced to Boito and other influential members of society. In this he followed in the footsteps of Donizetti and Verdi, who had also used salon recitals to ask Milanese noblemen and noblewomen to judge their work, something they were fully qualified to do, for in the closed world of the Lombard elite, music ruled. Raffaello Barbiera described the culture of these families as a kind of musician's paradise, where everyone sang and played, creating "a perfect philharmonic society" at home. Many were even respected composers in their own right, cultivating music so avidly that they made professional musicians jealous, he added. Their wives and daughters played instruments and sang. And, one and all, they helped promising young musicians.

Fontana, comfortable in this world as Puccini was not, felt free to ask the guests for money for the planned production of *Le Willis*. Full of confidence, he stayed on in Milan to promote the project, while Puccini went home. First came the news that Marco Sala and Boito had each offered fifty lire; Marco's "unknown lady friend" also gave fifty lire, while two of Sala's brothers contributed twenty. One of the industrialist Vimercati family topped them all at sixty lire. At that point, Fontana was sure of getting more from other acquaintances, among them Duke Giulio Litta, who had been a dedicated patron of music and the arts for more than twenty years. In all, he thought he could raise 330 of the 450 lire they needed for copying the score and renting costumes. He had also arranged for a scenic designer to make sketches for the sets, and he sent them on to Puccini. Fontana also said he was making necessary changes in the libretto and was about to send it to Ricordi, who agreed to contribute the cost of printing it.

Le Willis at the Teatro Dal Verme

At that point Puccini returned to Milan. He sent his mother the good news on May 13:

> Dear Mamma, As you already know, I am giving my little opera at the Dal Verme. I had never written to you about it because I wasn't sure. Many

people from here are helping to produce it, and among them are important men such as A. Boito, Marco Sala, etc., each of whom has pledged money for it. I've written to my relatives and to Cerù for help with making copies of the score, which will cost more than 200 lire; right now I don't know; it could even be more. How are you? I know your health is always the same, poor Mamma! Michele is all right and sends you many good wishes, then he will write more; I have so much to do that I don't even have time to write to my good and dear Mamma. Be happy. A kiss. [GP to AMP, May 13, 1884, in Gara, p. 11; original reproduced in L. Marchetti, ill. 49]

Le Willis was described as an *"opera-ballo,"* an opera-ballet. It had its world premiere on May 31, 1884, on a triple bill with Filippo Marchetti's *Ruy Blas* and a ballet, *La Contessa d'Egmont,* whose composer and choreographer were neither named on the posters nor mentioned in the reviews. The conductor was Achille Panizza, a member of another musical dynasty; the singers for Puccini's opera were the soprano Regina Caponetti as Anna, the tenor Antonio d'Andrade as Roberto, and the baritone Erminio Peltz as Guglielmo Wulf. On that evening, Marchetti's hefty score might easily have overwhelmed Puccini's one-act work, because *Ruy Blas* was a long, violent tragedy. The theatrical agent–impresario Carlo D'Ormeville, the librettist for Catalani's *Elda,* had also written the studied libretto of *Ruy Blas.* As Thomas G. Kaufman showed in *Verdi and His Major Contemporaries, Ruy Blas* quickly entered the general repertory after its world premiere at La Scala in 1869 and played in many European theaters and in South America. It later reached the New York Academy of Music, Her Majesty's Theatre in London, and cities as remote as Constantinople, Hong Kong, and Calcutta.

To the immense satisfaction of Puccini and his sponsors, *Le Willis* held its own against Marchetti's work and had a huge success. Many years later, Puccini recalled that event in a conversation with Giuseppe Adami. On the night of the premiere, he said, he was broke, had only forty *centesimi* to his name, and was wearing a simple brown suit, the only one he owned. From beginning to end of the opera, applause rocked the walls of the Dal Verme, a major theater. The audience demanded two encores of the intermezzo called *"La Tregenda,"* the "Witches' Sabbath." One witness to this triumph was Pietro Mascagni, Puccini's friend and former roommate, who played in the orchestra. At the end of the evening, an embarrassed and awkward Puccini stepped to the footlights, thanked the cheering audience, and accepted flowery praise and a laurel wreath offered by his patrons as a tribute to their protégé.

Although *Le Willis* was scheduled so late in the season that it ran for only four performances, its success established Puccini as the most promising young composer of the time. Filippo Filippi's article carried the headline "PUCCINI ALLE STELLE," "PUCCINI REACHES THE STARS." Marco Sala wrote his own glowing review, saying, "Puccini's opera is, in our opinion, a small, precious masterpiece from beginning to end." Given his financial interest in this production, Sala's article might justly be dismissed as self-serving, had he not been so dependable a critic. The review in the periodical of the publishing house of Sonzogno read, "At the Dal Verme, we do not remember ever having seen a young maestro receive such acclaim as Puccini did." In the *Corriere della Sera,* the critic Antonio Gramola wrote: "The values found in this opera *Le Willis* reveal Puccini's musical imagination, which leans markedly toward melody. In the music of the young Maestro from Lucca there is freshness of imagination, phrases that touch the heart because they came from his heart. And there is a most elegant technique, so that from time to time it seems that we don't have a young composer standing before us, but rather a Bizet, a Massenet." To this forceful declaration he added his prediction: "We honestly believe that Puccini may be the composer for whom Italy has been waiting for a long time" (reviews in Gara, p. 11).

On the day after the premiere, Puccini sent his mother a telegram describing his triumph. As he later learned from one of his sisters, Dr. Cerù wept with joy when he heard about it. Michele also sent his mother a report on the last performance. Soon the family in Lucca had even greater reason to rejoice, for Giulio Ricordi acquired *Le Willis* for Casa Ricordi, assuring Puccini of that prestigious firm's support. The announcement came out on June 8, 1884, in the firm's popular *Gazzetta Musicale di Milano:*

TITO [SON] OF GIO[VANNI] RICORDI
Music Publishing House in
Milan, Rome, Naples, Florence, London, Paris,
announces that it has acquired absolute rights,

including the right to publish, produce, and
translate in all countries, the opera
LE WILLIS
Poetry by FERDINANDO FONTANA
Music by
GIACOMO PUCCINI
presented with immense success
in the Teatro Dal Verme in Milan.
It has also commissioned Maestro Puccini to compose a
new opera with libretto by FERDINANDO FONTANA.

Verdi, who had heard about the success of *Le Willis,* wrote that autumn to Count Opprandino Arrivabene, his friend of a half-century:

I've heard a lot of good things about the composer Puccini. I've seen a letter that speaks very well of him. He follows modern techniques, and that is natural, but he remains committed to melody, which is neither ancient nor modern. It seems, though, that in his music the symphonic element is dominant! There's nothing wrong with that. But one has to be careful with it. Opera is opera, symphony is symphony, and I don't believe that in an opera it is good to write a section of symphonic music just to make the orchestra dance. I say this just to be saying it, without attaching any importance to it, without being sure that I've said the right thing, or rather, being certain that I have said something that goes against modern tendencies. All epochs have their hallmarks. History tells us later which era is good and which is bad. [Verdi to Arrivabene, October 6, 1884, in Alberti, pp. 311–315]

Albina Magi Puccini's Death

At the very moment when Puccini had finally caught the attention of Verdi, Ricordi, and others who dominated the music business, he could have profited from staying in Milan, but he did not. Instead, he went home on the very day Ricordi's announcement was published; and at ten in the evening, Ramelde and Nitteti, their husbands, and Dr. Cerù cheered for him on the station platform in Lucca. It was a grand moment, with his success the talk of the city. Albina's deteriorating condition, however, worried everyone, and it left Puccini and one of his brothers-in-law as the heads of the family, with duties to discharge. Quite apart from any moral obligations, Puccini profoundly loved his mother. Without her, he would perhaps never have finished school or become a composer. Now, in these last weeks of Albina's life, the son came home, armed with a contract from Ricordi and the ceremonial laurel wreath he had been given at the Dal Verme. But he was so distracted that he even failed to take care of important professional matters. After Ricordi wrote to congratulate him on the success of *Le Willis,* the letter went unanswered until June 12. Then Puccini apologized to Ricordi, saying he was "so troubled" that he "could never manage to do anything."

However, he did make two brief business trips, one to Turin for a concert featuring his *Capriccio sinfonico.* Conducted by Faccio, this gala with the La Scala orchestra was part of the festivities for the International Exposition. To the composer's joy, his piece was encored; and the critics saw a glorious future for him. Leaving Turin, he traveled to Lake Como to see Giulio Ricordi, but he put off a planned visit to Caprino Bergamasco to discuss the revision of *Le Willis* with Fontana. Instead, he went home and stayed with his mother until the end. In one emotional moment, she took off her wedding ring and put it on her son's finger. He wore it all his life.

Albina died on July 17, 1884. As a last gesture of love, Puccini laid his laurel wreath on her coffin. Then, distraught with grief, he went back to Milan, where Fontana was waiting. In August Puccini wrote to Ramelde, "I think about *Her* all the time, and last night I even dreamed of her. And today I am even sadder than usual. No matter what triumph art can bring me, I will never be happy without my dear mamma. Keep your spirits up as best you can, and find that courage I have not been able to find" (GP to RPF, [August 1884], in Gara, p. 14). By October he was back in Lucca.

One day he found consolation on the lonely shores of nearby Lake Massaciuccoli. There he visited the tiny lakeside hamlet called Torre del Lago, where people lived by fishing, hunting, and harvesting the coarse marsh hay called *falasco.* In this desolate place Puccini found some small comfort after his mother's death. Several years later it became his home. Dante Del Fiorentino, the priest who would become the composer's friend, parish priest, and biographer, later tracked down people whom Puccini had met in Torre that year. Among them was a fisherman, Old Nofori, who ferried people across the lake to supplement his income. Nofori told Del Fiorentino about his first impression of the grief-stricken man. He looked "like a ghost," the fisherman said. Nofori "remembered the time when Giacomo first came to stay in the fishing village." Nofori asked him his trade. "'I'm a composer,' Giacomo replied, 'but after my mother's death, I became a corpse'" (Del Fiorentino, p. 57).

Narciso and Elvira Bonturi Gemignani

Not surprisingly, Puccini admitted to Ricordi that Albina's death had left him shattered. He idled away his days in Lucca, strolling in the piazzas, sitting in cafés, and taking long walks on the medieval ramparts of the city. These long visits covered parts of the summer and fall in 1884, then March, April, June, November, and December 1885, during which Puccini stayed with Pericle Pieri, a friend. In fact, he ordered Michele to tell their landlady that he was giving up his room in Milan. After Albina's death one of the family's main concerns was the sale of her furniture and the disposition of the house. Fiercely protective of it, Puccini arranged a contract of sale that guaranteed him the right to buy it back before the final conveyance of the deed. This he was able to do. During some absences, he also oversaw productions of his opera, which he and Fontana had finished revising. As Fontana wished, it was now called *Le Villi*.

At that time, however, Puccini had to deal with something far more serious than family property or the future of his opera. As Michele Puccini and others well knew, Giacomo had fallen in love with a married woman, Elvira Bonturi Gemignani, in the summer or early autumn in 1884. Writing to Puccini in June 1885, Michele masked her name by calling her La Buchignani and reported that a man named Rantacchio, probably a Lucchese living in Milan, had discussed the matter with him. "What are you doing?" Michele asked his brother. "[Rantacchio] says you are not leaving [Lucca] because you are too interested in La Buchignani, and that you are doing just as you did in November [1884], when you wanted to leave and did not" (MP to GP, June 5, 1885, in A. Marchetti, pp. 107–108). So the secret was out, at least in some circles, although for a long time Elvira's husband suspected nothing.

Puccini and Elvira had certainly seen each other earlier in Lucca, for she was the wife of Puccini's former schoolmate Narciso Gemignani, whom Michele and Puccini's sisters also knew. According to Arnaldo Marchetti, she was born on June 13, 1860. The Gemignanis had two small children, Fosca, their daughter, about five, and Renato, their son, about two. Narciso was in trade, a grocer and traveling salesman for a wine wholesaler. Elvira, tall and fashionably dressed, had dark blonde hair that she pulled loosely into a twist at the back of her head. The Gemignanis lived in an apartment on the third floor of a house in Piazza Bernardini and had a local girl working as their housemaid and nurse for the children.

Many details of Puccini's close association with the Gemignanis were gathered later by biographers, especially by Del Fiorentino, who heard local gossip about this period during and after his seminary years in Lucca. In *Immortal Bohemian*, Del Fiorentino described Puccini's situation in the year after his mother died. Stricken with grief, he faced ongoing expenses, with his debt to Cerù unpaid. Often pawning his personal property, he lived from day to day on Ricordi's stipend, which was enough for no more than his basic needs. He also bore a certain responsibility for Michele, who wanted to go on studying at the Milan Conservatory. Giving piano or organ lessons could bring in extra income; and it was in his role as a music teacher that Puccini first became closely associated with the Gemignanis.

Narciso Gemignani, like many Italian men, belonged to a Società Filarmonica, a group of amateur musicians who regularly put on private concerts of vocal and instrumental works. These events, called *accademie,* featured the members themselves and their friends and relatives. The directors of the philharmonic societies often commissioned works from young composers; the Società Filarmonica in Busseto had given Verdi his first chance by letting him work as its music copyist, composer, and conductor. Given the reputation the Puccinis had in Lucca, and given the success of *Le Villi*, it is not surprising that music brought Puccini together with Gemignani, a Società Filarmonica member who was also an amateur baritone. Puccini even seems to have written a song for him. Elvira too had sung in public at least once.

After Gemignani learned of the success of *Le Villi* and Ricordi's contract with Puccini, his interest in the local composer grew. In casual meetings the two men exchanged remarks about the weather and about music; then Gemignani asked Puccini to give Elvira piano lessons. In the early 1830s the same set of circumstances had brought young Verdi together with his patron, Antonio Barezzi, the head of the philharmonic society in

Busseto. Barezzi asked Verdi to give piano lessons to Margherita, his daughter, who was also an aspiring soprano. Verdi courted Margherita, and they fell in love. A similar scenario played out in Puccini's life, but in his case Elvira was already married and the mother of two small children. Gemignani asked Puccini to give Elvira two or three lessons a week. Although we have no idea how many lessons she actually took in 1884 or 1885, she saw Puccini fairly regularly. Soon they began a sexual relationship, which they managed to hide for about a year.

Le Villi in Turin and Milan

In October 1884 Puccini was staying in San Martino in Colle, a hamlet in the mountains between Lucca and Montecatini. Raffaello Franceschini, Ramelde's husband, owned property there, including several houses and the vineyards that produced Puccini's favorite red wine. Albina had also visited San Martino in the spring that year, so it was natural that Puccini should have fled to this remote place. His main job was the revision of his first opera. Puccini finished the orchestration of the two-act version at the end of the month and sent his score to Ricordi. In the coming winter the opera was on the program of the Teatro Regio in Turin, where it was to open the season on December 26. The very fact that it was being produced in an important city on opening night is a measure of Giulio Ricordi's power, for Puccini was, after all, an untested composer.

This engagement broadened his professional and aesthetic horizons, for Turin was no ordinary provincial town. An ancient city on the Po Plain, it had been a Roman center and, later, the medieval capital of the Piedmont. After the fifteenth century, Turin became the main residence of the Savoy dukes and their royal descendants, who ruled the Piedmont region on the mainland and the island of Sardinia. In the early 1800s Turin had also served as a base for patriots fighting for the unification of Italy; and in 1861 it quite naturally became the new country's capital. Parliament sat there, as did Turin's Savoy monarch, Vittorio Emanuele II, Italy's first king. With his centuries-old pedigree, he was held in some awe as a descendant of one of Europe's oldest ruling families and therefore gave Italy an authenticity that many new nations did not have.

In Puccini's lifetime Turin remained a major center of Italian commerce and learning, even though the capital of Italy was then Rome.

With its population of 272,000, Turin was only slightly smaller than Milan. A beautiful, orderly place, it had one of Italy's finest universities and the famous Accademia delle Scienze and Museo Egizio, an already renowned museum of Egyptian antiquities. Commerce and industry sustained the city's economy. Turin also had a long history in the performing arts. Opera was first heard there in 1622 in the Royal Court Theater. The Teatro Regio, built in 1741, was followed in 1753 by the Teatro Carignano. In 1884 the Regio, with its twenty-five hundred seats, seemed small compared to La Scala, but its programs included important opera productions and ballets. As Puccini knew, Catalani's *Elda* had had its world premiere in Turin in 1880, so, in a sense, he was following his older compatriot when he went there to present his first opera.

Puccini and Fontana went to oversee rehearsals for *Le Villi*, first staying in an expensive hotel, then moving to a private home. Many of their expectations for their opera were shattered when they began to work with the orchestra and cast, for nothing went smoothly. As the weeks wore on, Puccini despaired over almost every aspect of the production. His first problem was the singers, who were *"brocchi di ripiego,"* second-rate crocks, as Fontana described them to Ricordi in a letter that he and Puccini cosigned. The cast included the soprano Elena Boronat, the sister of a famous prima donna, Olimpia; the tenor Enrico Filippi-Bresciani; and the baritone Agostino Gnaccarini. Giovanni Bolzoni, the respected conductor, had trouble holding the production together and let his lethargic orchestra override the "weak" chorus, which at times could scarcely be heard. When Puccini finally protested, someone in the company answered him sharply. The situation was chaotic, for even as late as the day of the dress rehearsal, neither the cast nor the orchestra had rehearsed with the scenery onstage. Fontana, who had seen the sets, described them as "unspeakable" and complained about the amateurish ballet corps and the "positively second-rate lead dancer," who was also the choreographer. In spite of the bad omens, though, Fontana believed in their opera. Puccini, on the other hand, had "little hope." (Gara, p. 15). The two men need not have worried. *Le Villi* got onstage at the Regio on the day after Christmas, as scheduled. Puccini's first venture in a theater outside Milan might easily have been a fiasco that would end his career. Instead, the performance went so well that the composer could take bows. It also won praise from the city's influential critics.

With the Turin production behind them, Puccini and Fontana had to return to Milan for yet another production of *Le Villi,* which was to be given at La Scala on January 24, 1885. Faccio would conduct, and Puccini had an experienced leading soprano in Romilda Pantaleoni, Faccio's mistress. Born in 1847, Pantaleoni had begun her career in the early 1870s and had sung many of Verdi's works, from *Un Ballo in Maschera* to *Il Trovatore* to *La Forza del Destino* to *Aida.* In 1887 she would be cast as Desdemona in the world premiere of Verdi's *Otello.* The tenor in Puccini's opera was Andrea Anton, and the baritone was Delfino Menotti, who later sang Iago and other leading roles. Unfortunately, the same critics who had praised Puccini to the skies when he introduced *Le Villi* at the Dal Verme now attacked him in force, leaving him very much at risk in this tight community. One critic said Pantaleoni had saved the evening and that her colleagues belonged in a third-rate opera house. The heavy orchestration was also mentioned. Things went better after the baritone fell ill and a replacement was called in.

Among the early critics of *Le Villi* one of the most important was Emanuele Muzio, Verdi's former protégé and trusted friend, who was then living in Paris. A composer, conductor, and respected voice teacher, Muzio showed some early interest in Puccini, but in 1885 he studied *Le Villi* from a score and found it disappointing. He wrote to Verdi: "It seems to me that because he is young, Puccini should have ideas and fire; and when a young man has them, they are exciting. In this opera I expected to find something; and it seems cold to me and unpleasantly heavy [*pesantuccia*]. It may be different on the stage, but when the audience gets smaller and smaller at the second and third performances [as it apparently did in its first week at La Scala], it is an ugly sign. [The celebrated voice teacher Francesco] Lamperti wrote to me, saying the music is made from beer, not wine" (Muzio to Verdi, [January ?], 1885, in Vetro, p. 220).* Given Lamperti's well-known pro-German stance, he might have been expected to respect Puccini more because of his supposed debt to German music, but in fact his laconic observation was meant quite negatively. Lamperti's opinion cannot be easily dismissed. An influential professor at the Milan

---

* Muzio's letters reprinted with kind permission of the Biblioteca della Cassa di Risparmio di Parma e Monte di Credito su Pegno di Busseto; and of Professor Corrado Mingardi, Librarian.

Conservatory, he had taught dozens of leading singers, including Sofia Loewe, Sofia Cruvelli, Maria Waldmann, and Teresa Stolz, four of the century's grand divas. He also wielded influence in casting operas in Italy and abroad. With his solid knowledge of opera, he might have recognized in Puccini someone who could write for the voice, but he apparently did not. Nor could Lamperti have been accused of a preference for Verdi, whom he had attacked in print for wrecking singers' voices. Thus, when Lamperti dismissed Puccini's music with the clever, tossed-away phrase about beer and wine, he expressed a view that echoed the critics in part and ran contrary to the barrage of praise that Ricordi was putting out to promote his new composer.

Another influential voice raised against Puccini was that of Stolz, who was then retired and living as a grande dame in Milan. She often attended La Scala and entertained people from the opera business in her salon, which was famous for its Egyptian and oriental décor. And she sent Verdi frequent bulletins that kept him informed about theatrical matters. After seeing the first *Le Villi* at La Scala, Stolz offered him a singer's view: the score was heavy with descriptive orchestral music, and at times the orchestration was so thick that it completely covered the tenor's voice and left him looking like a mime. The ballet music reminded her of Bizet, she said, adding that the audience did not particularly like the opera, which contained nothing new or important. No one applauded the Prelude; Pantaleoni was "very good," and her first aria was "pretty"; the tenor was bad, and the baritone very bad and sometimes "scandalously" flat. Once during the opera and then at the last curtain, Puccini and the singers took several bows, but otherwise the audience was cool. And, Stolz said, the management had packed the house by giving away many orchestra seats; otherwise, few people would have come. In her opinion, the opera would never be popular (Stolz to Verdi, January 25, 1885; copy in Istituto Nazionale di Studi Verdiani, Parma; brief excerpt reproduced in Carner, p. 45). In spite of such reports and some bad reviews, *Le Villi* stayed on the boards in Milan for a respectable run of thirteen performances, although it was so short that it was sometimes paired with a ballet to fill out the evening.

In the spring Ponchielli had a chance to discuss *Le Villi* with Verdi during a visit in the old composer's suite in the Grand Hotel. Reporting to his wife, Ponchielli said both he and Verdi disliked the opera and thought

Puccini was on the wrong track: "Then we talked about the opera of Puccini, whose type of music we do not like, because it follows in the footsteps of Massenet, Wagner, etc." (Ponchielli to Teresa Brambilla Ponchielli, [April 1885], in Abbiati, p. 261).*

Seizing upon this modest success, Ricordi kept *Le Villi* in the repertory in other cities after its run ended at La Scala. Puccini oversaw one important production in Bologna, where "modern music" was always welcome. He also helped to prepare the unfortunate 1888 premiere in Naples, where his opera was almost whistled off the stage at the Teatro San Carlo. This was perhaps the first big fiasco of Puccini's career, matched later by the catastrophe of *Madama Butterfly* at La Scala in 1904. In 1886 *Le Villi* reached Venice and Buenos Aires; and in 1887, Trieste; Gustav Mahler conducted it in Hamburg in 1892; and it was produced at the Metropolitan Opera in New York in 1908, under Arturo Toscanini. According to Linda B. Fairtile, it was the 1890 production in Brescia that brought Puccini and Toscanini together for the first time and marked the beginning of their sometimes stormy association. This production also launched Puccini's long, successful relationship with the impresarios and audience of the Teatro Grande, an architectural showcase in that harsh industrial city. In *Musical Italy Revisited,* Siegmund Levarie described the Grande, built in the early 1700s and rebuilt in 1782 and again in 1811, as a splendid building with a grand staircase and "excellent proportions and acoustics" in its wooden hall. Luckily for Puccini, the public of Brescia remained loyal from the very start of his career until its end. Even many years later, when he complained about the Grande's incompetent singers and poorly prepared orchestra and raged about the heat during a summer opera season, he could still mount acceptable productions there and count on the support of its audience.

---

* Franco Abbiati, *Giuseppe Verdi.* Copyright 1959 by CASA RICORDI—BMG RICORDI S.p.A.

CHAPTER FOUR

❦

Edgar, *Elvira, and Antonio: 1886–1889*

Under his agreement with Casa Ricordi, Puccini was to write another opera, again with Fontana as his librettist. As for the subject, Fontana may have suggested the Abbé Prévost's *L'Histoire du Chevalier Des Grieux et de Manon Lescaut,* which he had first proposed to Puccini in 1884. Instead, they turned to *Edgar,* which was taken from Alfred de Musset's *La Coupe et les lèvres.* Then and later confusion arose over the author's rights, which Musset's heirs and their representatives had held since 1857. Apparently neither Ricordi nor Fontana had received permission to use the text, nor had they paid for it. Because the libretto was taken from the French original, Puccini was threatened with a lawsuit in a matter about which he may have known little or nothing.

Work Begins on *Edgar*

Puccini received the finished libretto in May 1885. Soon after he began composing, he asked for revisions, which Fontana provided, but work went slowly. In June Puccini had also begun corresponding with the distinguished conductor Luigi Mancinelli, who had taken over the Liceo Musicale and the Teatro Comunale in Bologna, where *Le Villi* was under consideration for the autumn program. It was Michele Puccini who urged his brother to contact Mancinelli. Like the *Scapigliati,* the conductor was interested in symphonic music, the aspect of Puccini's work that may have led him to lean toward *Le Villi.* The composer thanked Mancinelli for his support and continued work on *Edgar.* Michele, who by then was deeply involved in his brother's affairs, stopped at the Comunale en route from Lucca to Milan and sent back the news that Mancinelli would indeed produce what Puccini called "my poor *Villi*." The composer went to Bologna to help with the production. To everyone's relief, it was well received.

In November he wanted Fontana to join him in San Salvatore di Montecarlo, a town some twenty-six miles from Lucca on the rail line to Montecatini. There, he felt, they could work together in peace. Puccini wrote to Fontana: "I have received your very dear [letter]; it's clear you really were [feeling] fairly moody [*proprio che avevi la luna per benino*]! We are waiting for you. If you do come, get a ticket for S[an] Salvatore Montecarlo. It is raining now. I am working very little, but I have already done all the beginning, and I'm up to Tigrana's entrance. The little offstage chorus came out very well, as did the entrance of Zaroè [later called Fidelia] and the tale of the almond tree. We hope this blessed part of the second act will come to you soon, because I really need to have everything. That's enough! Have courage!" Puccini also sent good wishes for Fontana's little son, who was ill, and complained about his own financial situation. Ricordi had sent him a money order for only one hundred lire, one-half of his monthly stipend. "What is this all about?" he asked Fontana. "Didn't you tell me they would not withhold anything? For heaven's sake, please go over there yourself, I beg you, because you know what my situation is. Go over there right away, and *let me hear from you,* I beg you" (GP to FF, [November 1885], in Gara, p. 18).

As before, Fontana acted as the composer's sole contact with Eugenio Tornaghi, the comptroller of Casa Ricordi. Although both men were desperately poor, Puccini borrowed so much money from his friend that sometimes Fontana could not make ends meet without deducting some part of the debt before sending Puccini what remained. Fontana also helped Michele, who was studying at the conservatory and was obviously under the librettist's wing. He carried out his duties, went to San Salvatore di Montecarlo to work with Puccini, and then went on to Lucca.

Scandal

Elvira was still living in her husband's house at the beginning of 1886. In the first years of her relationship with Puccini, they were rarely able to be together, chiefly because her family and his ordered them to stay apart. Another factor was his fear of scandal. Unwilling to break with his respectably married sisters or their husbands, or with his sister Iginia, who was a nun, he also could not afford to alienate powerful people in Lucca or Milan. Nor could he risk a public or physical confrontation with Gemignani, who could easily have sued for the alienation of his wife's affections, challenged Puccini to a duel, or had him and Elvira arrested. Puccini spent part of the year in Lucca, fitting the score of *Edgar* to Fontana's revisions as they came. In January 1886 he wrote to say that he was working like a dog, *"con assai accanimento,"* and for the first time mentioned his relationship with Elvira to his librettist. "For several days I have been applying the sensible advice you gave me about lovvve [*l'amorrre*]. Elvira sends you greetings" (GP to FF, [January 1886], in Gara, pp. 21–22). Even Michele accused Giacomo of refusing to leave Lucca because of Elvira.

The chronology of their relationship is not clear, but Puccini was certainly in love with Elvira by November 1884. Given the role of gossip in a small city such as Lucca, it was astonishing that they were able to hide their affair. As it happened, Gemignani's long business trips helped them. He also was a womanizer who had relationships with women in other cities. By summer 1885, however, Elvira's friendship with Puccini led to gossip. The Del Fiorentinos, like other Lucchesi, were scandalized when they noticed the composer taking long walks with her; and they began to suspect this was no longer the innocent relationship of teacher and pupil.

Puccini moved in and out of Lucca over a period of several years, but was there in February and March 1886. He returned in April after a short business trip to Milan and was still in the city in the beginning of May. In that late winter Elvira became pregnant with Puccini's child. Writing from Milan on June 7, 1885, he sent news to Carlo Clausetti, Ricordi's representative in Naples, on a government postal service postcard, the cheapest way to write. "Greetings with hugs and handshakes. *She* is pregnant. *He* is ever on the lookout for subjects [for his operas]. We [are] all right. I am working slowly but I hope well. Your aff[ectionate] Omocaig [Giacomo in reverse]" (Tollett and Harman Collection, catalogue 20). Gemignani apparently suspected nothing, although he might have seen signs of a failing marriage in the untoward amount of time Elvira spent with Puccini.

By autumn she could not hide her pregnancy, although at that point most people probably believed Gemignani was the father of the child. All evidence indicates that he remained ignorant of the rumors flying around the city. Then came the night when he returned from a trip to be greeted by the sobbing maid, who told him Elvira had abandoned him and their children and run away to live with Puccini. Only later could she have Fosca with her; Renato would remain with his father.

In an 1891 letter to Ramelde, Puccini offered his account of what had happened, saying that he and Elvira had not intended to leave Lucca permanently in 1886. Their flight was a temporary solution, *provvisoria,* because, as he indelicately wrote, "The tripe [*la trippa*] was at such a point that it could no longer be hidden." "The tripe" was his term for the pregnant woman's belly. When Elvira left her husband, she told everyone that she was going to Palermo, a lie that some believed, at least for a while (GP to RPF, [end of April 1891], in A. Marchetti, pp. 160–161). But when the Lucchesi finally learned what had happened, they were outraged. Del Fiorentino said that when the story got around, the little city positively exploded with gossip. "Giacomo has disgraced our town," said one of his proper relatives, while an aunt even refused to speak Puccini's name.

As a shamed mother and adulterous wife, as a woman who abandoned the *tetto coniugale,* the "conjugal roof," Elvira had no leverage whatever, and Gemignani had Italian law wholly on his side. Under the codes that governed *patria potestà* and *potestà maritale,* he alone had legal authority, both the paternal power and the husband's power. According to Puccini's account, Gemignani took no action at first because no one knew where he and Elvira were. Frightened, Puccini would not even let his family mail letters from the Lucca post office, out of fear that Gemignani would discover his address and commit violence against him. Instead, the Puccinis had to take their mail to the box in the train station, where only railroad employees handled it. When Gemignani found out where his wife had gone, he was justifiably furious, refusing her even short visits with Fosca at first. Later Fosca joined Puccini's household as his stepdaughter, but Elvira's arguments with Gemignani went on for years, always aggravated by his legitimate claims.

Sometime before December, Puccini and Elvira moved to a furnished apartment in the building at Borgo Milano 8 in Monza, the city he had visited during the day trips of his student days. Some sources say Fontana found the place for them. Arturo Buzzi-Peccia, Puccini's fellow student from the Milan Conservatory and lifelong friend, left a marvelous description of the couple's life at that time. He said that "Giacomone," or "Big

Giacomo," as his friends called him, rented a half-ruined house called the Castello di Monza for fifteen lire a month; he then brought Elvira and Michele to live with him in its three habitable rooms. Friends from Milan came to Monza occasionally, and, as Buzzi-Peccia described:

Elvira used to fix an excellent minestrone and lovely *fagiolini alla Toscana* [green beans Tuscan style] for us. One day, with Catalani, Illica, Mascagni, Fontana, and some other friends, we called at the Castello as a surprise party. It was a surprise, all right, because to improvise a dinner for all of us was really a very hard problem to solve. But Michelino [Giacomo's brother] had a splendid idea. He took the blackbird (a cohabitant in the Castello), went to the market, and sold bird and cage, which unfortunately didn't provide quite enough money for the meat to make the *stufato* [stew]. Cupid came to help. Michelino had a sweetheart, the young daughter of the tobacco seller. He told the girl that his brother had to send much music to London and needed a lot of postage stamps. A lovely smile and a few sweet words won the stamps from the delicate hands of the sweet girl, and Michelino hurried to the butcher, where the stamps were converted into a big piece of good beef that Madame [Elvira] fixed up in a fine dish of beef à la mode. [Buzzi-Peccia]

Buzzi-Peccia also remembered that while Puccini was composing *Edgar,* he could be seen "promenading in the Galleria in Milan, wearing a big cloak of glaring red, like those the cowherds wear in Tuscany; but he walked like the Prince of Wales—as if he had on [an overcoat] of the latest style" (ibid.).

On December 22, 1886, Antonio Puccini, Elvira's third child and her second son, was born. Always called Tonio, the boy had a childhood as chaotic as Fosca's, rarely living in a settled household, and surviving several major family crises between 1886 and 1891. Because Puccini was too poor to provide for a family, they moved from place to place and were often separated when the Puccinis and the Bonturis harassed them. When Tonio was several months old, Puccini was staying in Lucca with Pericle Pieri, pretending that his affair with Elvira was over, while she and the baby lived with her sister in Florence. Whenever they were together he had to cover the extra expenses, and on the few occasions when Fosca stayed with them, she was another mouth to feed. Puccini also tried to help Michele, who remained in Milan until 1889, when he decided to emigrate with a friend to South America. Because Gemignani never granted his wife a legal separation, under the law she remained Elvira Bonturi Gemignani.

Composing Edgar

In spite of the confusion and scandal, Puccini went on composing, writing some of the opera in Monza, as Buzzi-Peccia remembered, and some in Sant'Antonio d'Adda, a hamlet in the mountains near Caprino Bergamasco. Even at this stage, Elvira could not always be with him. Everything looked promising, for the soprano Medea Mei and the tenor Nicolai Figner, two important singers, were scheduled to sing in the premiere of Edgar. They visited Puccini and Fontana in Caprino and ran through the score with them. (As it happened, neither sang in the opera.) At that point, Ricordi was ready to sign a contract with a theater, but he needed the completed score. Puccini, still in Caprino, advised Mancinelli that the end was in sight, but he had to do the orchestration.

With his Ricordi contract almost at an end, Puccini risked complete ruin because he had not finished Edgar. No one had offered him a renewal or extension, so he was reduced to begging the publisher to keep him on stipend until he could finish. The situation was this: he had had Fontana's libretto for more than a year and was still working, although Fontana was constantly being asked for revisions. As Puccini said, the project was important and difficult; but his money problems seemed beyond solution. He wrote frankly to Fontana about them, saying he would be left flat on the bare ground, "sulla nuda terra," if Ricordi cut him off. In the end, Ricordi agreed to continue the payments, but only after reviewing the situation with Casa Ricordi's board of directors. Others in the firm wanted to stop the flow of money to this apparently unproductive composer, a man nearly thirty years old whose only opera had had no more than a modest success. But Ricordi prevailed, so that for a while at least Puccini could count on getting his stipend.

In 1886 and 1887 he traveled back and forth between Milan and Lucca, where family matters called and confrontations with his sisters and their husbands continued. Sometimes he also worked in Caprino Bergamasco, to be close to Fontana; in the summer of 1888 he stayed in Pizzameglio, near Chiasso in the Ticino canton in Switzerland. December of that year found him in Milan, where he remained for the first four months of 1889, preparing for the premiere of *Edgar*. He also continued to follow the fortunes of *Le Villi*.

On April 21, 1889, *Edgar* had its world premiere at La Scala. Quite properly, it was dedicated to Ricordi. With Pantaleoni in the mezzo-soprano role of Tigrana, the tenor Gregorio Gabrielesco as Edgar, the solid soprano Aurelia Cataneo-Caruson as Fidelia, and the baritone Antonio Magini Coletti as Frank, Puccini had a very good cast. He also had Faccio, Italy's most respected conductor. Nevertheless, the opera fared badly with some critics, who saw improvement in his work, but dismissed it all the same. One important reviewer said that in some ways it was better than *Le Villi* and in some ways worse. He did, though, want to hear more from Puccini. Pantaleoni disliked the opera, something that was surely bruited about in Milan. *Edgar* was removed from the La Scala program after only two performances, and a proposed return to that stage was canceled, although the opera later appeared in other theaters. Puccini oversaw preparations for an important production of it in 1892 in Madrid, where the celebrated tenor Francesco Tamagno sang Edgar. Chosen by Verdi for the title role in the world premiere of *Otello,* he was one of the world's most famous singers. Luigi Mancinelli conducted.

But not even these occasional successes could save the opera; and after several revisions, even Puccini finally gave up, calling it a *cantonata,* a blunder. In the score of *Edgar* that belonged to Sybil Seligman, his friend in England, he later scrawled through the title so it read, *"E Dio ti GuARdi da quest' opera,"* "May God protect you from this opera" (Seligman, p. 19).* After the line "Yes, for Edgar lives" he wrote, "A lie!" and after the word *"orrore"* (horror), he wrote, "How right they were." Still, it was not completely dead after its premiere, for people in Milan heard a rumor about Verdi's putting pressure on the Corti brothers, the impresarios of La Scala, to bring it back, again with Pantaleoni (Catalani to Giuseppe Depanis, August 20, 1889, in Carner, p. 30). Given the gossip in circulation, Catalani's letter might be dismissed completely, but it seems to confirm what Puccini's friend Pericle Pieri wrote to Ramelde's husband about Verdi's plan to attend the premiere (Pieri to Franceschini, April 18, 1889, in

* Vincent Seligman, *Puccini among Friends,* Macmillan, 1938. Reproduced with permission of Palgrave Macmillan.

A. Marchetti, pp. 134–136). As Marchetti remarked in his note to that let-ter, Verdi later mentioned Puccini's "theatrical intuition," something that may have impressed him in *Edgar,* if indeed he ever saw it. He may only have seen the score.

After hearing *Edgar* in 1977 in a concert performance conducted by Eve Queler for the Opera Orchestra of New York, Andrew Porter, who had heard two earlier productions of it, wrote a spirited defense of the opera. As he noted, two important singers, Renata Scotto and Carlo Bergonzi, contributed to the success of the evening; but Puccini had made his own strong statement with this opera. Because Queler used the third version, prepared in 1905, this *Edgar* was more polished and more sophisticated than the earlier vocal scores. Porter found it "an arresting piece" with "en-joyable" music, an opera composed to a "peculiar" libretto. Although the characters are stereotypes, the work has "high poetic power." He went on: "By intention, at least, it represents opera of a different kind from that of [Puccini's] popular successes—more ambitious, more elevated. The music is enjoyable. There are influences from Verdi, Wagner, Ponchielli, Berlioz and Meyerbeer; shadows are thrown forward to *Turandot,* to which *Edgar* is closer in tone than to the other Puccini operas." Porter also praised the orchestration and vocal writing (Porter, pp. 578–580).

In the 1890s, though, nothing could save it. An apparent failure such as this might have caused Ricordi to reconsider his support for Puccini, but instead he encouraged him to write a third opera. In May 1889 Puccini mentioned *Tosca,* which Fontana had suggested to him. At that time, the composer was hoping to secure the rights to the Sardou play, but he soon abandoned the idea. In the summer of 1889 Ricordi had also sent Puccini abroad as his ambassador, letting him go to Paris with the Cortis of La Scala and the scenic designer Adolfo Hohenstein. There they attended the International Exposition and saw the Eiffel Tower, which had just been formally inaugurated. Ricordi corresponded with Faccio, who was in London to conduct *Otello* at the Lyceum and see how Mancinelli handled *Die Meistersinger.* Emanuele Muzio was there on Verdi's behalf. Because the Cortis intended to give the Wagner opera at La Scala, Ricordi also sent Puccini and Hohenstein to Bayreuth to plan the Milan production, which was scheduled for December 26, the season's opening. Puccini's job was to make the "merciless cuts" in the Wagner score that Ricordi de-manded. Among other things, he wanted Puccini to take out anything that was repetitious or "uselessly long." Having seen the cuts made in the score used by the Vienna Opera, he had decided that Puccini should shorten the opera even further. In another letter to Faccio, he went on: "The greatest problem lies with the cuts, for the opera is impossibly long. But between you, Puccini, and me, we aren't three idiots [*tre zucche*] and won't fail" (GR to Faccio, undated, in Abbiati, pp. 378–379).

In Bayreuth, Puccini saw not one Wagner opera but two: *Die Meistersinger* and *Parsifal*. Fully prepared, he had taken Giovannina Lucca's piano-vocal score of the latter opera with him. In it he wrote the singer's names and made short comments about the productions. "Bayreuth . . . 25 July 1889, splendid performance, very impressive" (Abbiati, p. 379; the Tuscan conductor-composer Pietro Vallini gave Abbiati this score). By the time Puccini got back to Milan, he was less enthusiastic. As Ricordi wrote to Faccio, Puccini came in to report on the production. That summer Puccini moved to Vacallo, another village in the Ticino canton. In July he had decided that Manon Lescaut and the Abbé Prévost's novel would be his next project. Leoncavallo, who was also spending the summer in Vacallo working on his own music, became the first librettist of the opera, which Ricordi began to see as a serious addition to his catalogue. Even Verdi and his wife took an interest in it, asking Ricordi to keep them informed on how Puccini's work was going.

Left out of the plans was Catalani. He was furiously jealous of Puccini and angry about the desecration of Wagner's score. When he wrote in August 1889 to the critic Giuseppe Depanis, he described a Puccini "armed with a pair of scissors and told by the publisher himself to make the necessary cuts in *Meistersinger* and alter it, like a suit of clothes, to fit the good people of Milan. But the Milanese are beginning to rebel and say they want the exact same suit that the Germans have worn until now; and the press, too, has begun to complain. So we should not be surprised if those same scissors that were to be used to cut Wagner would instead be used to cut all the lines of publicity that [Ricordi] has sent out for [Puccini], his favorite composer; and in that case the tailor [Puccini] will look ridiculous." Complaining further, Catalani, bitter and ill, said he feared "what is going on, now that there is only one publisher [because Ricordi had bought out Giovannina Lucca], and this publisher won't hear of anyone except Puccini." Desperate, he went on, "But this is only right, because now these 'dynasties' reign in the realm of art, and Puccini must be the successor to Verdi, who, like a good king, often invites the crown prince to dinner" (Catalani to Depanis, [1889], in Abbiati, pp. 377–378).

In fact, the living members of the Puccini dynasty taught Catalani a nasty lesson, for when one of his operas was performed in Lucca, they mounted such a campaign against it that he feared his evening would end in a fiasco. And Catalani was absolutely right about that other dynasty, the Ricordis. True, Giulio Ricordi had decided to promote Puccini; but in any case, he could not support several budding geniuses at once, as Casa Sonzogno was doing. He even had trouble persuading his board of directors to continue Puccini's stipend. Casa Ricordi was not so prosperous as it looked, for in December 1887 Giulio had to ask Verdi to lend the firm a very large sum, two hundred thousand lire. This may have helped to finance the purchase of Casa Lucca, but whatever advantages it brought, Ricordi was never able to pay Verdi back. The debt remained in 1901, when Verdi died.

As it happened, Verdi, who might have favored Catalani, was furious at Italian composers who, he felt, were betraying their country by looking to Germany for inspiration. When Faccio, writing to Verdi with news of the London season, mentioned "a triumph for Italian art," Verdi shot back: "You talk about *a triumph for Italian art!!* You are deceiving yourself. Our young Italian maestros are not good patriots. The Germans got to Wagner by starting with Bach, [so] they are operating like good Germans. But we, Palestrina's descendants, commit a musical crime by imitating Bach, and we are doing something useless and even ruinous" (GV to Faccio, [summer 1889], in Abbiati, p. 379). As Puccini's career developed, this was exactly the accusation others raised against him: that he was not a patriotic Italian, because he looked across the Alps for inspiration.

In spite of Catalani's jealousy, the fact that Ricordi favored Puccini did not leave him free of competition. In 1888 and 1889 Catalani was certainly a threat, with his operas passionately promoted by Arturo Toscanini. The stunning success of *Cavalleria Rusticana* in 1890 catapulted Mascagni to the top of his profession and temporarily, at least, gave the Sonzogno firm an advantage over Ricordi. Another competitor was Alberto Franchetti, a close friend of Fontana's and a man with whom Puccini had a long, turbulent association. Soon after the production of *Le Villi* at the Dal Verme, Franchetti had invited Fontana and Puccini to spend several weeks in his family's villa; but Puccini did not go. Franchetti held the title of baron in a noble family. Unlike Puccini and, later, Mascagni and Leoncavallo, he had wealth and position that gave him a substantial material advantage over them. He was also a very good musician, whose works got solid reviews. Alvise Zorzi described Franchetti in *Canal Grande* as "an extremely cultured and productive composer." According to the lore of the time, the Franchettis gave banquets where the women's "party favors" were unset diamonds, which the host hid in their napkins. Puccini, of course, could never compete at that level and certainly had every reason to be jealous of Franchetti. In 1887, as Franchetti was preparing for the world premiere of his *Asrael,* Puccini, burdened with Elvira and Tonio, was so poor that he did not even have enough money to get through the month.

Franchetti had no such worries. His family owned several residences, including a castle and two gothic Venetian palaces on the Grand Canal. One of those was the most famous private house in Venice: the Ca' d'Oro, the House of Gold, which Giorgio Franchetti restored to its former glory, with the help of the writer Gabriele D'Annunzio. In it he housed his magnificent art collection, which is open to the public today as a museum. The other Franchetti palace was the family's grand mansion next to the Accademia Bridge. The Franchettis asked the architect Camillo Boito to restore that building for them. Because Camillo was the brother of Arrigo Boito, Verdi's librettist, he, like the celebrated D'Annunzio, was part of a network of contacts who helped to advance Alberto Franchetti's theatrical career. In the music business, it was widely rumored that Franchetti used his wealth to guarantee sumptuous productions of his operas. His social connections may also explain why he could interest D'Annunzio in being his librettist. D'Annunzio loved power.

Franchetti and Puccini both also worked with the temperamental librettist Luigi Illica. When Puccini went to hear one of Franchetti's symphonies, he liked what he heard and let the composer know it. He also sent his congratulations on Franchetti's *Cristoforo Colombo,* which had its premiere in Genoa in 1892. Nevertheless, Franchetti offended Puccini by criticizing him during one of his lavish dinner parties, surely knowing that gossips would carry his remarks back to his rival. Ricordi also played his hand with great skill. Although Catalani was convinced that Ricordi favored Puccini above all others, the publisher sometimes seemed to prefer Franchetti, who could write the large-scale, imposing operas that Ricordi later urged Puccini to compose. Soon Puccini took a tougher line against

Franchetti and his "German school" (Puccini's term) and mocked him in letters, calling him "Il Barone" and "Il Baronissimo." Just as Puccini was trying to get the Italian public to accept *Edgar,* Franchetti, with Verdi's support, was working on new commissions and, it seemed, would always be a threat, especially after *Edgar* turned out badly.

CHAPTER FIVE

❦

Manon Lescaut: 1890–1893

Puccini CREATED *Manon Lescaut* during a running battle with five librettists and two families, his and Elvira's. Still wretchedly poor, he could barely pay the rent on the Milan apartment he had taken for her, Tonio, and himself. The flat was cold; they were often ill; and by 1890, because of family pressure, he and Elvira were about to separate again. He had also changed librettists, turning to Ruggero Leoncavallo in summer 1889 and abandoning Fontana, who had done so much to help him. More than once Fontana asked why he could not write *Manon Lescaut,* a subject he had suggested; later he was to ask the same question about *Tosca,* another of his ideas. But Puccini never used him again, although he had no satisfactory librettist and was struggling with one writer after another.

Michele and His Brother

As Puccini began this opera, all his personal problems continued to plague him. Although he and Elvira had attempted to deflect criticism by living apart for long periods, they were still considered rogues, with Tonio a blot on two clans' honor. Puccini's married sisters were still criticizing him, while Iginia, the nun, prayed constantly for his soul, then and for years to come. Although he tried to reconcile them to his situation, he evidently could not do so. Tonio was two before Puccini sent a photograph of him to Ramelde, the sister dearest to him, but even then he sent it to her husband, Raffaello Franceschini, not to her, and he asked him to show it to her. Ramelde and Franceschini could not accept Tonio in their family; they could not explain Tonio to their three small daughters, nor could they face neighbors who could easily have guessed who he was. Their actions, like those of others, originated in a middle-class code of conduct, for the Puccini sisters had married men who were successful in education, law, or government. They could not risk any scandal.

In 1891, after Ramelde refused to have Tonio in her home, Puccini railed: "*Lucchesi, lucchesi!* You always judge people from gossip . . . and without looking at the circumstances or the facts. Enough of that! It is urgent to settle this matter in the best way possible, without violence and without any extra shocks. Let Fate spin [her thread], and I am telling you that I have decided to make a new life." Even then, however, he and Elvira were separated, and Elvira could not keep Tonio with her because of pressure from her own family. Ramelde had asked Puccini to keep Tonio away from her, which he agreed to do. "I will fix things so the little boy shall not meet you," he wrote, adding, "If that should happen, I will persuade Elvira not to do things that would make me unhappy" (GP to RPF, end of April 1891, in A. Marchetti, pp. 160–161). This is not to say that Ramelde had abandoned her brother, for he had been sending her news when Tonio was ill, and he had told her how happy he was when she "recognized how violent certain of her ideas were" (GP to RPF, April 22, 1891, in A. Marchetti, pp. 159–160).

By this time Puccini no longer had his brother to lean on. Michele, in the midst of this ongoing crisis, had abandoned his studies at the Milan Conservatory and left for South America in October 1889. His reasons are not clear, for he had a good school record and his family's support. His 1884–1885 grades, reproduced in A. Marchetti's *Puccini com'era*, show several high marks, 8.75 (out of a possible 10) in the study of harmony and 8.00 and 8.50 in the history and philosophy of music. He also got 10s for conduct and constancy (*assiduità*). He had a job, helped Puccini, and was such a promising composer himself that some people in Milan claimed he had written part of *Edgar*. He did, though, have a volatile temperament; some family letters also suggest that he occasionally got into trouble, although nothing serious was ever mentioned. At the most, it was a question of unpaid bills or the use of prepaid correspondence postcards that his employer had bought.

As we have seen, the two brothers had shared apartments at several different times, until summer 1885. That was the very moment when Michele began criticizing his older brother for being "too interested" in

Elvira Gemignani, although no apparent conflict ever arose between them over her or anyone else. Even after Tonio was born, Puccini and Michele spent a summer together in Caprino Bergamasco and in Pizzameglio. Because Michele knew Fontana well, went to operas, and kept up friendships with such important people as Francesco Tamagno and Luigi Mancinelli, he was useful to Puccini; yet, for whatever reason, he left Italy, accompanied by Ulderigo Tabarracci, another Lucchese. (The complete account of Michele's life in South America appears in Arnaldo Marchetti's *Puccini com'era,* together with his letters.)

Michele's destination was Buenos Aires, which he described to his brother and his sister Ramelde as crowded and full of Italians, among them many Lucchesi whom they knew. At first Michele taught piano privately, but in the spring of 1890 he was offered a post as professor of music, singing, and Italian language in the town of Jujuy (Yuyuy), a remote place more than sixteen hundred miles from Buenos Aires and six thousand feet up in the Andes. There he also acted as a secretary to the recently arrived Italian consul. He had found work but hated living among "Indians and cretins," as he said, and was as lonely and isolated as anyone could be after years in cosmopolitan Milan. Then, unfortunately, he followed Puccini's model to the letter, giving piano lessons to a married woman and falling in love with her. Her husband, an important senator, learned of their affair, sent his wife away, and challenged Michele to a duel. When Michele shot him, the man fell as if he were dead, although he later recovered. After that, Michele had no choice but to flee, to Buenos Aires and then to Rio, where he found Tabarracci.

During Michele's absence, he and his brother corresponded regularly. Beginning in December 1889, their letters offer a trove of news about the opera business and about themselves. (Puccini's letters to Michele are in *Carteggi pucciniani.*) Discouraged about his own lack of success, Puccini told his brother that Mascagni had won the Sonzogno prize with *Cavalleria Rusticana.* Influenza struck Puccini three times, leaving him "a rag"; Tonio was waiting for his uncle to send him chocolate from America! In January 1890 Puccini told Michele he was working on *Manon Lescaut,* surely using Leoncavallo's libretto, and had composed *Crisantemi,* a string quartet written on the death of Prince Amadeo of Savoy, the son of Italy's ruling family. The title of this elegiac work refers to chrysanthemums, the "flowers of death" of Italian culture, which bloom in autumn, just in time for the Day of the Dead. Although Puccini was busy, he remained very hard up; and in February he asked Michele for money. Send it, no matter how unfavorable the exchange rate is, he begged. Michele, who had been in Argentina less than three months, said he could barely cover his own needs; but the desperate Puccini ordered him to spend as little as possible, save, send cash, and think about helping him to buy back the family home in Lucca.

As for himself, Puccini said he had little hope. In April he said he was broke, saddled with a rent so high that only a miracle could get him through the month. Sick of poverty, *la miseria,* as he called it, he also had to find a new place to live, having just been given an eviction notice for playing the piano at night. As always, he was composing between ten at night and three or four in the morning. As for the move, he was looking for a place outside Porta Monforte. On the family front, their sister Nitteti's husband had died, leaving her a widow with children; Dr. Cerù was demanding that Puccini repay his early loans with interest. The good doctor's anger over Elvira was one factor that led him to try to collect; but money was also an issue. Hearing that Puccini had earned a fortune from *Le Villi,* Dr. Cerù apparently did not know how poor he was, nor was he aware of the true nature of Ricordi's monthly payments. Since 1884 they had gone to Puccini not as fees or a regular salary, but as advances against future royalties. When money came in, Ricordi deducted part of those payments from Puccini's earnings.

That explains why Puccini kept telling Michele that he was "as broke as I can be" and said he did not know how to go on. He fell deeper in debt every month, and saw his market growing smaller because of theater closings and poor box office returns. He said if he could earn a living in Argentina, he was ready to join Michele. They would make out somehow. Again he asked his brother for money, then added, "I am ready, very, very ready, if you tell me to come," he wrote. But where would he get the money for the trip (GP to Michele, [1889–90], in Gara, pp. 33–41)?

Turmoil

At the beginning of April 1890, as Puccini struggled to save his career, he had not heard from Michele in about two months. Then came the day when he opened the *Corriere della Sera* and read that on March 12 Michele had died of yellow fever in Rio. He was twenty-seven. Puccini and his grief-stricken sisters exchanged letters over their loss, with him swearing that he was left shattered and sleepless. Ramelde also grieved deeply and had annual Masses said for Michele on what she called the saddest day of the year, the anniversary of his death. The news came at a time of crisis in Puccini's own household. At the end of March, he and Elvira separated, driven apart again by poverty and family pressure. She had a plan of her own: to take a furnished room in Milan and try to convince Gemignani to let Fosca live with her. But as Puccini said, it was a foolish dream. Gemignani refused, and Elvira had nowhere to turn but to her sister in Florence.

Tonio was left behind with Puccini, who had to find someone to care for him. At the same time, as we have seen, Puccini had to promise Ramelde she would never have to see the child. At any rate, she left for San Martino in Colle, where she often spent the summer. In the most generous gesture imaginable, Tomaide Puccini Gherardi agreed to keep Tonio in Lucca; Puccini also may have stayed with her while he worked on *Manon Lescaut,* which was scheduled to open during the next Carnival. He still had an enormous amount to do on it.

He had every intention of living alone for seven months, until November, when he expected to deliver the opera to Ricordi. According to his plan, he and Elvira would then be reunited, for he was passionately in love and concerned for her. One pleasant turn came when her mother asked Puccini to bring Tonio to her house. Finding that she liked her grandson, she invited him back. In June he arranged to spend part of a day with Elvira in his furnished room in San Martino, although she would have to leave that evening. Then, as always, they were afraid of Gemignani.

During that visit, she saw both Puccini and their son, whom a softened Ramelde brought over for the day. Elvira returned to Florence before nightfall. The next morning, though, Puccini's landlady told him that because Elvira was not his wife, he could never have her there again. So the long arm of Lucchese gossip had reached even San Martino. Nor were things better in Lucca, where he suspected Tomaide of destroying his letters to Elvira, which he had asked her to mail.

Puccini then planned to meet Elvira, Fosca, and Tonio in Viareggio, but he canceled the trip. Then Elvira and her husband discussed a settlement, but nothing came of that. As for Puccini, he pressed Elvira to try to get Fosca, at least for a visit; but he was speaking only of a visit, for he wanted to remain unencumbered until he finished *Manon Lescaut*. His other project at that time was a possible production of *Edgar* at the Teatro del Giglio in Lucca, but he feared Gemignani would cause a scandal that would ruin the opera. At this time, someone—perhaps her sister—had told Elvira that Puccini was about to end the relationship. That became her obsession, although he steadily denied that he was unfaithful. She insisted on face-to-face confrontations in Lucca, but he, genuinely alarmed, forbade her to come. If she came to Lucca, he said, he would leave; but she defied him. Through all this, he pleaded for time and peace of mind.

A Home in Torre del Lago

After a short business trip to Milan, Puccini began roaming the country-side around Lucca, looking for a cheap place to live. In that dire moment he returned to Torre del Lago, the village he had visited just after his mother's death. Having once found peace there, he again sought its strange isolation and primitive way of life. The natural beauty of Torre is owed in part to Lake Massaciuccoli and the Apuan Alps, which rise toward their northern peaks above the lake, their flanks dotted with mountain villages. At the end of the 1800s, when urban centers in Tuscany were profiting from tourists visiting their art treasures, the folk of Torre del Lago lived more or less as they had done in the Middle Ages. Stranded in the fens between the sea and the mountains, the village huddled in the middle of the Màcchia Lucchese, the Lucchese Scrubland, where trees and bushes run along behind the shoreline of the Tyrrhenian Sea. The Màcchia lies at the northernmost edge of the bleak land called the Tuscan Maremma. The 1897 edition of *Baedeker's Central Italy* warned against the health risks of the region when it described the rail line from Pisa to Rome: "Many places on this route are subject to malaria between the end of May and the end of October," and "the evil is very great." The Maremma itself was "a world of its own, consisting of forest and swamp, in summer poisoned by malaria." So was Lake Massaciuccoli, which had the swamps but had scrub growth and pines instead of forest. Although one had to go south of Pisa to experience the full grimness of the Maremma, the marshy Màcchia Lucchese and the adjacent Màcchia di Migliarino shared plenty of its "evil" nature. Still, the Màcchia had a haunting, desolate beauty, with its silence broken mostly by the squawks of birds. Fish and game abounded in the area, and in the autumn shots rang out from hunters' guns.

The village of Torre, sprawled across more than two square miles of land, lies in the marshes between the shallow, reedy lake and the sea. To the east, across Lake Massaciuccoli, stand the town of Massarossa and the hamlet and villa called "La Piaggetta," which belonged to Marchese Carlo Ginori-Lisci. Behind them the village of Quiesa perches in the foothills. Further on, there is Chiatri, a village Puccini had visited in his childhood. On that side of the lake the woods are clothed in chestnut trees, oaks, elms, and sycamores. In Puccini's day Torre del Lago's only road was a dirt track that led east from the La Spezia–Pisa road to the lake. Paths wound through groves of trees, connecting one cluster of humble houses to another. Many of the nearly destitute families lived in two-room huts cobbled of wood siding and roofed with marsh hay; only a few masonry buildings had been constructed. The Church of San Giuseppe had a small brick rectory; and close to the lake was the tower that gave the place its name. Once the gatekeeper's house of an estate, it stood guard not far from the shore.

Shortly before Puccini's arrival, Torre del Lago had attracted a small group of Tuscan artists, whose lives Simonetta Puccini has reviewed. Although many of their paintings are romantic, photographs of Torre del Lago taken in the early 1900s show scenes that could have been captured six hundred years earlier. After the marsh hay was harvested, the village women loaded hundreds of pounds of it onto wagons, then worked as dray animals by wrapping long leather reins around their waists and dragging the loads behind them. They often cooked on charcoal-burning braziers outside their doors, raising the scent of rosemary and laurel, the seasonings that they laid on fish or fowl. On Mondays they gathered on the bank of the reedy lake, hitched their long skirts into their belts, and stood knee-deep in the water to wash their clothes. Clean laundry was laid on the ground to dry. When Puccini moved there, Torre's only modern convenience was a north-south rail line, laid more than a mile from the lake. It provided access to Viareggio, Pisa, Genoa, and the world beyond.

One of the local artists, the painter Ferruccio Pagni, had settled in Torre in 1890. He described the day he first saw Puccini in the village.

One day in June 1891, I was sketching beside a path that ran along the shore of the lake, when I saw a cart with two men in it coming toward me. When they reached me, they stopped; they watched what I was doing [and] exchanged some remarks under their breath, then drove on. I watched them move away and went on with my work. Soon Count [Eugenio] Ottolini (Sor Ugenio) came along and said to me,

"Did you see those two men who came by a short time ago in the gig?"

"Yes. What about them?"

"Do you know who that younger, heavier man is?"

"No."

"It's Puccini, the composer of *Le Villi,* the opera that people went to hear last winter at the Verdi in Pisa." [Pagni and Marotti, p. 18]

Pagni soon heard that Puccini had rented part of a house from Venanzio Barsuglia, an overseer on a large estate. Within a week of that first visit, he and Elvira moved in, bringing along a piano and dozens of bundles. The move, however, failed to provide a solution to their problems. Seen in the context of his attempt to work alone and win seven months of peace, it has to be counted as a defeat for him and a victory for Elvira. All things considered, this wrenching event in a desperate time was no romantic flight to a love nest. Nor did Puccini jump quickly into the circle of local artists, for Pagni found him awkward and hesitant toward his new neighbors. Later, though, he made many friends in Torre, among them Pagni, his dear "Ferro." Like the others, Pagni learned to interpret Puccini's moods. He described the boisterous good humor that alternated with bouts of depression; and when Puccini became sad, he turned to his friends for help. Writing little notes to invite them over, he would say he was "bored"; but Pagni knew that meant he was sunk in melancholia. They always came to his aid. In fact, Puccini never hid his depressions, and even wrote to others about them, saying that he had been born carrying a heavy burden of melancholy.

Loving the area around Torre, Puccini came to believe that it was the most beautiful place in the world. In a frequently quoted letter, he described it as an earthly paradise, an ivory tower. From the earliest years of his stay, he filled many of his letters with news about hunting permits, guns, ammunition, duck blinds, and the hundreds of birds he brought down. At least twice he was caught poaching on others' territory. As his income grew, he also began buying boats, eventually graduating from small skiffs to inboard motors to a small yacht.

But as much as he loved it, the city-bred Elvira disliked the village and its people, whom she described as a hundred boors living in huts. As for her life with him, she said they did not have enough to eat, and he didn't "do a damned thing." Quite naturally, the native-born villagers mistrusted her, because of the gossip that had reached them from Lucca. To them, Elvira was an adulteress who had abandoned her husband and children. Superstitious as they were, some peasants said she had the evil eye and had laid a curse on them. She also alienated them by being somewhat demanding; and she compromised Puccini's relationships with some friends and colleagues. Faced with the village's collective hostility, she responded by staying in the house with Tonio and inviting her relatives for long visits. Her sister, Ida Bonturi Razzi, and the teenagers from their family eventually became a tremendous burden on Puccini, who resented their influence over Elvira and their meddling in his affairs. Still, even though Puccini disliked Elvira's clan, Beppe (Giuseppe) Razzi, Ida's husband, became a regular at Torre, after the composer and his friends founded the "Club La Bohème" in a hut near Puccini's house.

For Elvira, being isolated in a primitive fishing village was nothing short of punishment. As she sensed, she would have been far better off in Viareggio. In her worst moments her desolation resembled that of Giuseppina Strepponi, the retired prima donna who became Verdi's mistress, and, in 1859, his wife. Verdi often left Strepponi in his remote farmhouse in Sant'Agata while he went to Rome, Naples, Venice, and other cities to produce his operas. Sometimes she would leave when Verdi did, for she had money of her own and could go where she wanted. But she could also comfortably stay home, for rich as Verdi was, he left her with several servants in the house. Elvira's situation was far more difficult than Strepponi's, for she had no financial resources and few friends. Nor would Puccini take Elvira with him, at least in those early years. She struggled to keep the home together with Fosca, whom Gemignani allowed to come to Torre, and with Tonio, who remained with her until he was old enough to go to boarding school. Given her circumstances, Elvira's unhappiness is understandable.

Getting the Libretto Right

Puccini wrote in June 1890 to Tomaide that he had "gone back" to *Manon Lescaut* but was "out of luck," and "desperate" over the libretto, which he had to have "done over" (GP to TPG, in Gara, pp. 45–46). He had dismissed Leoncavallo after working with him in the previous summer and fall. This suggests that he acted on impulse in the spring of 1890, when he appealed to the dramatist Marco Praga for help. According to Praga's own account, he was playing cards in the Caffè Savini one evening when Puccini, a casual acquaintance, came in and asked if they could talk. As they strolled through the Galleria, Puccini abruptly asked him to write a libretto, although, as the dramatist protested, he had never written one before and was no poet. Undaunted, Puccini described the subject, *Manon Lescaut,* and begged him to write the scenario or plot and choose a poet to versify it. Praga turned to Domenico Oliva, a friend and fellow playwright.

The three worked together, even taking the scenario and Oliva's finished libretto to the Ricordi villa in Bellano, where they read it to Giulio Ricordi and Paolo Tosti, a popular composer-conductor. All found it effective, and Puccini prepared to go on. He spent several months with Elvira and Tonio in Vacallo, where Leoncavallo, now removed from the project, was the nearest neighbor. While there, he worked on two acts of Oliva's text and waited for the last two, which came in December. The collaboration soon failed, when Puccini demanded that Praga and Oliva eliminate one entire act, substitute another for it, and create a new, grand effect for the third act, which had originally been the scene in Geronte's house in Paris. It now had to be created out of whole cloth. With that, Praga had had enough. He abandoned the project, leaving Oliva alone to make the cuts and write new text to fit Puccini's scheme. But this collaboration too was doomed, for Puccini asked for more changes, then still more. At that point Oliva also gave up. (Praga's account is in Osborne, pp. 60–61; in Italian it is in Gara, pp. 42–45, together with some of Puccini's recollections of this period.)

With Leoncavallo, Praga, and Oliva out of the picture, Giulio Ricordi decided to have the libretto completely rewritten, and for that he turned to Giuseppe Giacosa, a distinguished poet, dramatist, and man of letters. Affectionately called "The Buddha" because of his big belly and his wisdom, Giacosa stood light years above many Milanese intellectuals of the time. In 1901 he would deliver the oration at the commemorative concert mounted by La Scala to honor Verdi. A close friend of Arrigo Boito, he was a senior member of Puccini's libretto team. Giacosa turned to the playwright-librettist Luigi Illica for help. Volatile, unpredictable, and sharp, Illica later provided scenarios and prose and poetic drafts for librettos. While both he and Giacosa contributed poetry to *Manon Lescaut,* much of the groundwork was Illica's. In June he, Giacosa, and Ricordi approved the final draft of the libretto, more or less as we know it, but Puccini also turned to Leoncavallo for help in August, when both were still in Vacallo (GP to Leoncavallo, [August 2, 1892], in Pintorno, letter 4). Puccini was still tinkering with the opera thirty years later, when he asked Giuseppe Adami, another librettist, to write one new line for the last act. So many people had worked on the text that it was printed without an author's name on the title page. Most credit, however, should go to Illica and Giacosa; Illica alone created the scene of the women's embarkation at Le Havre, the most moving moment in the opera, and Giacosa wrote the poetry.

The Premiere of *Manon Lescaut*

Puccini took time off to oversee the production of *Edgar* at the Teatro Grande in Brescia in 1892, during the late summer fair season. Meticulous as he was about work, he asked Emma Zilli, his leading soprano, to rehearse her role in Milan long before the first night, coaching it with Puccini's Lucchese friend and music copyist and editor, Carlo Carignani. In January 1892, during an earlier production of *Edgar,* Puccini met Giulio Gatti-Casazza, the future head of La Scala and then the Metropolitan Opera. The occasion saw the revised *Edgar* come to the Teatro Comunale in Ferrara, where Gatti's father was the president. Later Gatti remembered that meeting and wrote that Puccini "came to present the new version of one of his operas, *Edgar,* which had been given earlier at La Scala in four acts and which was given in three acts in Ferrara, where it had a remarkable success." Their friendship continued for thirty years (Gatti-Casazza, typed memoir of Puccini, written in 1924, Metropolitan Opera Archives).

Puccini finished *Manon Lescaut* in October 1892, and Ricordi wisely placed the premiere at the Teatro Regio in Turin, partly because *Edgar* had done very well there the previous spring. At that time Milan was out of the question, because Verdi's *Falstaff* would have its premiere at La Scala on February 9, 1893. With two important events so close together, Ricordi did not reach Turin until the day of the dress rehearsal of *Manon Lescaut;* but Puccini and Illica had been overseeing the production for weeks. As the composer had done before, he complained about the voices, which, he said, could hardly be heard. The tenor Giuseppe Cremonini was Des Grieux; Achille Moro, Lescaut; and Alessandro Polonini, Geronte. Alessandro Pomé conducted. The composer's remark, however, is scarcely credible, because Cremonini had a good reputation, and the Manon, who has to carry the opera, was Cesira Ferrani, a polished, versatile soprano.

A native of Turin, seven years younger than Puccini, Ferrani had made her debut in 1887 as Gilda and gone on to sing Elsa in *Lohengrin* and Suzel in Mascagni's *L'Amico Fritz.* Puccini had begun to correspond with her in July 1892, saying he was "very lucky" to have met her, asking her to "prepare for the tremendous battle" of *Manon Lescaut,* and telling her she had the ideal appearance, acting skill, and voice for the title role (GP to Ferrani, July 15, 1892, in Gara, pp. 74–75). Later that year she was learning Puccini's opera and studying Eva in *Die Meistersinger* at the same time. Soon after the premiere of *Manon Lescaut,* she was billed as a star in Buenos Aires and helped establish Puccini's reputation there. All in all, she sang this opera more than three hundred times, and the grateful composer acknowledged her achievement, writing her in 1899 to affirm that she was his "ideal Manon."

As Puccini wrote to Elvira, he realized long before the opening night of *Manon* that he had written something extraordinary, because people in the company had gone "mad" over his music. His triumph was complete on February 1, 1893: thirty curtain calls for him, and the tenor and soprano weeping with emotion as they all stood together onstage. The opera got very favorable reviews in important papers, with the critic of the *Corriere della Sera* in Milan describing the sold-out house, the excitement of the gala; the opera's artistic merit, music, and theatricality; and above all its "passion and melody." Others wrote of its strength and brilliance. For Puccini, his long wait was over, and he had won at last. The opera brought him a decoration from the king of Italy and took him to places where new productions were being mounted. Among these was Ham-

burg, where it was given with the composer present. Later it went to Buenos Aires, Paris, New York, and Milan. For many people this was their introduction to Puccini's music, and it was a score they loved on first
hearing.

Some Italians call it their favorite Puccini opera; others say "second."
But in 1948 the great bass Ezio Pinza said he liked it better than any
other opera. Singing with the Cincinnati Summer Opera, he was sitting
through rehearsal one day when he was not on call. Having interviewed
him once and spoken to him occasionally, I started to chat during a break.
We talked about his plans. Then I asked him what his favorite opera was.
Without a second's hesitation, he said, *"Manon."* Of course, I thought he
meant Massenet's opera, which we had recently seen in Cincinnati; but he
quickly set me straight. *"No! No! la* Manon *di Puccini,"* he shot back, and
started talking about how beautiful it was. He even sang some of the
tenor's music from the second act and said the opera had been a staple of
his youth. The opera's passion had won him over. *Manon Lescaut* transformed Puccini from an unrecognized composer into a respected Maestro
of full stature.

CHAPTER SIX

✦❧✦

La Bohème: *1893–1898*

Even BEFORE the premiere of *Manon Lescaut,* Puccini had been considering another French subject, Henry Murger's semiautobiographical story about life in the Latin Quarter in Paris. It became the source of *La Bohème;* but no one is sure about how he first came to this work, although, as I have said, it seems Fontana first suggested it to him. This is not to say that he was swept away, for at the beginning he sometimes doubted its merit and thought about abandoning it. Long after the project got under way, he seemed to prefer *La Lupa* by Giovanni Verga, the author of *Cavalleria Rusticana.* Quite naturally, his librettists and publisher were confused about his intentions. Luigi Illica, however, remained firmly convinced of the importance of *La Bohème.*

The Dispute with Leoncavallo

After the premiere of *Manon Lescaut,* Puccini and Illica left Turin for Milan. At some point, probably early in February 1893, the composer asked Illica to write a scenario based on Murger and the Bohemians. The original story had been published in installments in a French periodical, under the title *Scènes de Bohème.* Seeing how popular it was, Murger collaborated with Théodore Barrière to write a play called *La Vie de Bohème.* Then he used his characters again in a novel, *Scènes de la Vie de Bohème.* Illica may have read an Italian translation of it, but he may also have known the play. By mid-March, he had a well-tailored scenario ready. Because composers, librettists, and publishers traditionally tried to prevent their rivals from learning their plans, no announcement was made about it at the time.

Soon, though, Puccini's project erupted in a full-blown opera-business scandal over the rights to *La Bohème*. It began with an angry and well-pub-licized exchange between him and Leoncavallo. Once Puccini's close friend and collaborator, Leoncavallo had become famous with *Pagliacci,* which had had its premiere in 1892 at the Teatro Dal Verme in Milan. Widely traveled and sophisticated, he, like Catalani, Mascagni, and Franchetti, had become a serious rival of Puccini. Like Mascagni, he was a protégé of Casa Sonzogno. Puccini's letters to Ramelde show that he feared Leoncavallo and Franchetti more than any other rivals, especially after Catalani's death in 1893.

In March, during a chance encounter in the Galleria, Puccini and Leoncavallo went into a café to discuss their work. When Puccini said he was writing *La Bohème,* a stunned Leoncavallo responded by saying that he, too, was composing *La Bohème,* and that he was using his own libretto, the very one he had offered to Puccini some time before. On that occa-sion, Leoncavallo said, Puccini had shown no interest in the subject. An angry exchange followed, with each claiming the prior legal right to the story. Thinking about that conversation, Leoncavallo decided to turn to the press. News of his new *Bohème,* "taken from the novel of the same name by Murger," was published in the issue of March 20–21 of *Il Secolo,* the newspaper owned by Casa Sonzogno. The notice, really a shot across Ricordi's bow, stated that he had been working on his opera for several months. On March 21 a similar announcement about Puccini's *Bohème* ap-peared in *Corriere della Sera.*

In the *Secolo* of March 22–23, another announcement described the contract Leoncavallo had to compose the new opera. And it went further. "Maestro Puccini, to whom Maestro Leoncavallo spoke two days ago, telling him that he was composing *La Bohème,* confessed that he got the idea of writing *La Bohème* just a few days after he returned from Turin, and that he had spoken about it to Illica and Giacosa, who, according to him, have not yet finished the libretto. For that reason, it is confirmed be-yond dispute that Maestro Leoncavallo has the priority in this opera" (Girardi, *Giacomo Puccini,* pp. 113–114). Puccini shot back in the *Corriere della Sera,* saying that Leoncavallo's statement established his own good faith beyond all doubt, for it was certain that if Maestro Leoncavallo, "to whom I have been bound for many years by intense feelings of friendship, had told me earlier what he told me unexpectedly the other evening, then I would not have thought of composing *La Bohème*. Now, for reasons that are easily understood, I do not have the time to be as courteous as I might wish to be toward him as friend and musician. Anyway, what does this matter to Maestro Leoncavallo? Let him compose, I will compose. The audience will decide. . . . I only want to let it be known that I have been working seriously on my idea for about two months, that is, since the premiere of *Manon Lescaut* in Turin, and I have made no secret of that to anyone" (GP to *Corriere della Sera*, March 24, 1893, in Gara, pp. 81–82).

Quite a different story was told by Ferruccio Pagni and Guido Marotti. In *Puccini intimo* they said Leoncavallo had indeed offered Puccini his libretto of *La Vita di Bohème*, about a year before the controversy arose, but Puccini had turned it down without even looking at it. At that time, their account ran, Puccini said he had other projects in mind, and in any case he was not familiar with the Murger work, which Leoncavallo had used as a source. Nearly a year later, after reading the novel, he had decided to commission a scenario from Illica (cited in Weaver and S. Puccini, p. 147). From surviving correspondence, it is clear that Illica had been working on Puccini's project for some time, and that he had produced something good enough to be shown to the demanding Giacosa. Just this fact alone casts suspicion on Puccini's story, for it would have been almost impossible for Illica to have read the Murger story, digested it, and finished an acceptable sketch of such a complex work in just six weeks.

On March 22, just when news of the dispute reached the newspapers, Giacosa congratulated Illica on having created a theatrically valid scenario, although he felt the novel could never become an opera. By then Puccini, convinced of the opera's potential, asked Ricordi to inquire about acquiring the rights to Murger's work, a sure sign that he had not taken this step before. Had he secured the rights, he could have prevented Leoncavallo from writing his *Bohème*. But when Ricordi learned that Murger's novel was in the public domain, both men were free to use it; and two versions of the same opera were launched.

Keeping Illica in Check

As Illica correctly guessed from his earlier experience with Puccini, his job would not be easy, for he felt no one could predict what the composer might do. At Ricordi's suggestion, he had suggested new ideas to the composer at the end of 1892, but had found him impossible to please. Nevertheless, Ricordi insisted that Illica stay the course, which he did. But all was not well, for in January 1893, before Puccini had settled on *La Bohème,* the desperate librettist wrote to Ricordi again "about Puccini, with my usual frankness," complaining about how difficult it was to satisfy him. Not without humor, Illica appealed to God and Ricordi for help.

> Puccini acted toward me in a way that I don't even want to discuss. . . . You and I, searching for something and torturing our brains or inventing outlines [of plots] for Puccini, are making a serious mistake. Puccini spoke in confidence to one of his friends, [saying] he could get along without my librettos, and that [my libretto] *Le Nozze di Nane* [written for Gaetano Luporini, one of Catalani's students] is horrible trash; and that anyway *no one* understands him, because he is yearning for something . . . something . . . something . . . that . . . ! You will understand that this *"something,"* as he describes it, is very difficult to interpret.
>
> Thus I have to grope around in pitch darkness, looking here and there for this "something" that Puccini is yearning for, only to hear him say every time [in Tuscan dialect], *"Un mi piasce"* [I don't like it]; and [I run] the risk of ending up with a libretto that Puccini will have to set to music using the same system he used with *Manon,* with his lines of doggerel. [LI to GR, January 1893, in Gara, pp. 78–79]

Thus, Illica was quick to denounce Puccini's practice of composing musical lines or passages, then writing meaningless verses with the correct rhythm, rhyme, and accents, and asking his librettists to write words to fit them. Illica gave a prime example at the end of this letter.

He also compared Puccini unfavorably to other composers: "Today, with Verdi and Boito, their great artistic effort is directed toward using the music to convey the most complete truth and effectiveness of the words." Then came a catalogue of complaints about Puccini's character. "Please note that Puccini's vacillation is nothing new. Do you remember his enthusiasm for *Tosca?* And then what happened? Wasn't I the one who had to tell you that *Tosca* 'un gli piaceva più' [he no longer liked it]?" Puccini had indeed been enthusiastic about *Tosca,* then had turned it down. Then, as we shall see, after Ricordi assigned the libretto to Franchetti, he changed his mind about it again. In the end, however, Illica continued working with Puccini on *La Bohème,* although he begged Ricordi to force the composer to be more specific about his needs.

> Let Puccini explain himself clearly and well, because as things stand, I don't know where to turn to find which "something" is the "something" Puccini calls "something," but [he] doesn't know what that "something" is. Let him bring me an idea, a character, "something" of his, and we will make a libretto which, after you and I have seriously reviewed it, shall be handed over to Puccini, and—Holy God!—let Puccini set the words of the libretto to music, with the emotions that these words inspire and with [words] suitable to the characters in the libretto, and not—for example— when he has to express something about love, write out his music above [meaningless] words such as:
>> "Rats—satellites—sole [the fish]
>> Tallow—weighing scales—infant
>> Are children of love!"
>> [*"Topi—trabanti—sogliole*
>> *Sego—bilance—pargoli*
>> *Son figli dell'amor!"*]
>
> Forgive my complaints and my chatter, but Giulio Ricordi, like a good editor-father, must give the same love to his librettist-children as he gives to his composer-children. [Ibid., pp. 78–79].

If Ricordi had been able to change Puccini, he might have had his operas produced more quickly, to Casa Ricordi's advantage and the composer's. Puccini was already set in his ways, however, so Illica and Giacosa went on complaining about his vagueness and countless revisions (and reworking of scenes and lines already redone several times), while Ricordi protested about lost time. Nor could they ever persuade him to "explain himself clearly and well," as Illica begged him to do. In 1893, and for decades to come, his changing plans and inordinate demands for revisions reduced his librettists to despair and continued to irritate Ricordi. Of the librettists, only Fontana got off easily, for Puccini, a recent conservatory graduate when he and Fontana worked together, accepted much of what Fontana handed to him. All his other collaborators had problems: from Leoncavallo, Marco Praga, and Domenico Oliva through the dismayed Illica and the defeated Giacosa to Carlo Zangarini, Guelfo Civinini, and, finally, to the poets and dramatists who served Puccini for *La Rondine,* the

Trittico, and *Turandot*. His reputation as a demanding and even impossible colleague may have led his librettists to stall the work on *Turandot* so long that Puccini could not finish the opera.

Puccini soon returned to Torre del Lago and to work. He also bought a bicycle, which made it easy for him to get to Viareggio and the villages nearby. In July he wrote to Ricordi's employee Cesare Blanc about paying for the bicycle, which he had bought from a firm in Milan. Would Blanc make the monthly payments directly to the proprietor from the Ricordi office? Seventy lire the first month, then fifty a month after that; otherwise, the whole bill could be paid at the end of summer, when Puccini would be in Milan. It appears from this that he was still quite poor and was waiting for royalties from *Manon Lescaut*. A later letter confirms this, for even after the opera became popular, he was still in a tight spot, and still waiting. Because the bike was apparently to be paid out of Puccini's house account on Ricordi's ledgers, he was effectively using the firm as a bank. That means that Casa Ricordi considered him a promising composer, for not everyone enjoyed such privileges. For decades Verdi had had the publisher's employees handle similar matters for him; but Puccini was at the very start of his career. In his letter to Blanc he also asked about planned productions of *Manon Lescaut* and solicited his opinion about singers who might be suitable in upcoming performances. He was well, he said, and was working (GP to Blanc, July 18, 1893, in Gara, pp. 85–86).

Three weeks later he invited Illica to leave Milan, "that sewer of heat and humidity," and visit him in Torre. He wrote:

I am struggling with our characters. I am working, and having a good time. I'm killing vast numbers of birds while I wait to leave for Brescia, where [Emma] Zilli will amaze everyone with her verve . . . and kill off Manon before her time! [The conductor Alessandro] Pomé wrote to tell me that you might come to Lucca. In my house there are soft beds, chickens, geese, ducks, lambs, fleas, tables, chairs, guns, paintings, statues, shoes, velocipedes, pianos, sewing machines, clocks, a map of Paris, good [olive] oil, fish, three different qualities of wine (we don't drink water), cigars, hammocks, wife [a title Elvira could not claim], children, dogs, cats, rum, coffee, different kinds of pasta, a can of rotten sardines, peaches, figs, two outhouses, a eucalyptus, a well in the house, [and] a broom, all for you (except the wife). Come.

As an afterthought, he again expressed his concern about *La Bohème:* "I beg you, keep it fast, and easy to stage. Lighten up the stage action. [And take care with] the links between the scenes" (GP to LI, August 4, 1893, in Gara, pp. 87–88).

French local color is crucial to *Manon Lescaut,* for the action moves from a tavern in Amiens to a salon in Paris, then to the grim docks of Le Havre, and finally to a wilderness in the French colony of Louisiana, where Manon dies. Puccini's new project, with its tales of Bohemian life in the Latin Quarter, while geographically more circumscribed, is also rich in details and local color. Fortunately, Illica and Giacosa could provide them, but Puccini also contributed his part. *La Bohème* opens and closes in a dilapidated top-floor apartment shared by Marcello, a painter, and Rodolfo, a writer. Their best friends are Schaunard, a musician, and Colline, a philosopher. The plot is built around their lives and the lives of two women, Mimì and Musetta. The opera ends as Mimì dies in Rodolfo's shabby flat. Murger took all his characters from real people, his Latin Quarter friends, although he took some poetic license in adapting them for the stage. The characters are vividly drawn and not easily forgotten, but the true and beating heart of *La Bohème* is Paris itself, which Puccini captured onstage by recalling his own memories of "Bohemian life," his student days in Milan and his home turf, Lucca.

His "perfect Paris" of the nineteenth century has its garrets and rooftops, its streets, a café, and, in the third act, one of the city gates, where the four main characters meet as snow falls. Puccini's own experiences in Lucca and Milan are also found there, as Herbert Handt pointed out. In fact, Handt saw much of Puccini's native city in the opera. At Christmastime and at the big September holidays, the central square in Lucca resembles the Latin Quarter setting of the opera, for it is full of vendors' stalls and carts, "with all the local populace and children milling around" and people buying toys, candy, and local delicacies. Sometimes, Handt said, it is so mild in Lucca in December that people can sit outside the cafés, as the Bohemians do in the Latin Quarter scene. Even the milkmaids in Puccini's act 3 recall expressions one might hear in Lucca. "Where are you going?" asks one group of milkmaids in the opera, and the second answers, "To San Michele." That is an important gathering place in the city, the Piazza San Michele. The milkmaids' cry of *"Hopplà"* and other lines from their scene are "typical Tuscanisms," Handt said, in an article that goes on to describe the influence of Tuscany on the opera (Handt).

During that summer Illica and Giacosa both worked on the libretto, but in July Giacosa, who was being fed the text scene by scene, began to doubt his own ability to meet the deadlines imposed on him. "I don't have Illica's prodigious ease [in writing]; I can't go forward if I am not satisfied with what I have done" (GG to GR, July 28, 1893, in Gara, p. 89). Nor did the situation improve. "I am giving up," he wrote to Ricordi in a letter of October 6, saying he was completely defeated by the Latin Quarter scene, which is now the second act of the opera. He had other commitments: a playwright-poet with an international reputation as a man of letters, he was the Italian representative of the prestigious Società degli Autori, and he headed an organization that offered financial help to theater folk in need. This was the Associazione Teatrale di Mutuo Soccorso, of which Verdi was the honorary and ever-vigilant president. These duties and his own personal life took much of his time. Again he complained about the toll that *La Bohème* had taken on him, but far worse, he questioned whether the opera was actually worth the effort they were putting into it.

Failing to find any merit in the story, Giacosa faulted it for a lack of inner warmth and inspiration; it did nothing to "lift the spirit," he said. "I don't feel [anything for] it; I don't live in it; I cannot succeed in deceiving myself and cannot create for myself that imaginary reality without which you cannot begin anything." Having spent an entire week on the scene in act 2 in which Musetta slaps Alcindoro, her elderly admirer, Giacosa simply could not go on. He was looking for something serious and elevated, something moral, and found nothing. Thus his decision to withdraw from the project. Sure that Illica could manage it alone, he said he could no longer go on jotting down just anything so he could get paid (ibid.).

The opera he described as "this lyric comedy" had defeated him. Giacosa intimated that he was too old to handle the story, but he also blamed his own work method. So far as he went, he was right. But a far greater problem lay in the aesthetic abyss that separated him and Verdi and Boito from the world of Puccini and Illica. Giacosa, clearly hating what he was doing, described a hopelessness and chagrin that stand in sharp contrast to the joy Boito felt when he was writing Verdi's librettos. Apart from the fact that Giacosa lived in an elite aesthetic world, he was a revered intellectual, a man who stood shoulder to shoulder with Boito;

like him, he had been one of Verdi's houseguests, invited for long visits at Villa Verdi in Sant'Agata. He had sat at the venerable composer's dinner table and at his side in the courtyard of the villa on summer evenings. There he, Verdi, Boito, Verdi's wife, and Teresa Stolz ran through, acted, and even sang some scenes from Verdi's *Ernani*. But *La Bohème*, with its shabby Bohemians, was not *Ernani*, nor was it *Don Carlos* or *Aida*.

Giacosa had every right to weigh his situation against that of Boito, his close friend. Boito had just worked with Verdi on *Otello* and *Falstaff*, while he, Giacosa, was dealing every day with a story he disliked and characters he saw as superficial, even loutish. The characters were too young, and he could not capture that "bright and frivolous festiveness that is the essence of the creations of the young." Because nothing satisfied him, much of what he wrote did not satisfy Puccini either, and it is no wonder he decided not to continue. As Eugenio Gara wrote in *Carteggi pucciniani*, in the notes following this letter of resignation, Giacosa graphically described the problems Puccini's librettists always had while working on his operas. To Ricordi, the poet's withdrawal meant the loss of the prestige associated with the respected playwright. Then, of course, every delay meant money lost. Wanting to profit quickly from the success of *Manon Lescaut* and needing a viable opera and the cash it would bring in, he tried to persuade Giacosa to go on.

At the same time, Puccini himself also considered quitting. After going to Hamburg to oversee a production of *Manon Lescaut*, he frightened everyone by saying he had had enough of *La Bohème*. Lacking the support of Ricordi, who had gone to Paris with Verdi, he had also become discouraged by the long, fruitless wait for Giacosa's text. To Illica he wrote, "And how is *Bohème* going? . . . I am beginning to get fed up! In Milan I will find a way to work, if not on *Bohème*, then on something else that we two will pull together, all right? In the meantime, look into your phosphorescent brain cells [for a new subject]" (GP to LI, October 29, 1893, in Gara, p. 91). Illica lost no time in writing to Ricordi about Puccini's state of mind. "What!? Puccini is already tired of *La Bohème*? The other day Elvira had lunch with me here, and from her I learned—and I was not surprised— that Puccini has worked very little, very little, very little. But there is a huge difference between working very little and wanting to turn to another work, all the more if you think of how necessary swift conception and work are for *La Bohème*. I know very well that Puccini is like a watch that gets wound up and quickly runs down," he said, and begged Ricordi to keep Puccini on the job. It was a matter of their honor, Illica said, because Leoncavallo was proceeding with his version. "For heaven's sake, don't give in to Puccini. Puccini must write *La Bohème,* and what is more, he must write it quickly and do it well; then he will surely win that success that you and I are already sure will come" (LI to GR, [late October 1893], in Gara, p. 91). Like the able conciliator he was, Ricordi healed these breaches by persuading Puccini to go ahead. Giacosa, a great gentleman, also signed on again; but years passed before he could register anything like pleasure over the opera.

Puccini, who, as Elvira said, had actually done very little on *La Bohème,* started composing, but soon he left Torre to oversee the first Bologna production of *Manon Lescaut,* which was on the calendar for November. A big success, it was given eighteen times. November 9 marked the Rome premiere, which led the king of Italy to honor Puccini with a decoration, *Commendatore dell'Ordine della Corona d'Italia.* The composer spent December in Milan, having made an important change in *Manon Lescaut.* His revised first-act finale was heard later that month at the Teatro Coccia in Novara, a safe place to try it out. In fact, Illica had suggested this change, protesting to Ricordi in October that the original ending simply did not work. "[We could] cut the final ensemble and replace it with some exchange between Lescaut and Geronte that then could clarify the [action of the] second act" (LI to GR, c. October 20, 1893, in Gara, p. 92).

On January 21, 1894, *Manon Lescaut* had its first performance at the Teatro San Carlo in Naples, again with the revised finale. Here composers from northern Italy often faced hostile audiences and claque-mounted organized opposition; but Puccini, who had seen *Le Villi* fail there, could congratulate himself on racking up a success. Fortunately, he had decided to oversee the Naples *Manon Lescaut* himself, having gone there with Elvira. They stayed at the Hotel Europa e Oriente and had a chance to see the city, which Puccini found extraordinary. Most of his time, though, was devoted to the rehearsals. One newspaper described him: shouting until he had no voice left, gesturing, and doing the work of four men as he coached his singers. In the cast were Eva Tetrazzini, the Spanish tenor Fernando Valero, and the baritone Arturo Pessina, under the conductor Vincenzo Lombardi.

After the event, the jubilant composer wrote to tell Illica that his new scene for act 1 had not only gone well but been encored. He stayed with the production through three performances before returning to Milan. In all, the opera was given twenty times that season. While in Naples, he gained a valuable and trusted friend in Carlo Clausetti, Ricordi's agent, a composer and publicist who remained fiercely loyal to Puccini for many years.

If Naples brought satisfaction, Puccini faced quite another outcome in Milan when *Manon Lescaut* opened at La Scala. He described the singers to Clausetti as a "pack of dogs" who turned the February run into what he saw as rank failure. The opera looked and sounded like a "stagnant Dead Sea," he said, describing it as so dull that it seemed like something "heard from behind a wall." Lacking enthusiasm, the singers dampened the action; the women sang flat. The composer described Olga Olghine's Manon as "positively bad" and added that the audience hissed her, especially in the second act, "which she ruined for me." Tieste Wilmant was Lescaut, "passable, but wrong for La Scala"; and the "excellent" tenor Giuseppe Cremonini had too weak a voice for that big house. The soprano and tenor were later replaced, but the damage was done. Although the opera stayed on the boards, the composer saw it as a failure, and, worse, a failure in Italy's most important opera house. This sent Puccini into an emotional tailspin. Often miserable in the winter in Milan, he told Clausetti he was flattened by *"sfiducia,"* a loss of confidence, and *"abbattimento,"* a depression (GP to CC, February 16, 1894, in Gara, pp. 97–98). In March, while Puccini was still fighting depression and struggling with his tormented librettists, he received a note from Toscanini, the conductor who was later to provide significant support for many of his operas. In his note he invited Puccini to Pisa, where he was to conduct the upcoming season. The composer accepted.

Even before the Milan production of *Manon Lescaut,* the year had begun badly on another front, with a disgruntled Illica again complaining to Ricordi about Puccini and *La Bohème.* "Do you really think that when we have put this whole Latin Quarter scene together, Puccini will be satisfied with it? Permit me to say I doubt it. There's no one as blind as one who will not see, and there is no man more impossible to satisfy than one who enjoys making others work so he can get out of working himself" (LI to GR, January 5, 1894, in Gara, p. 96). Among other blocks to progress were

Puccini's indolence and his hunting trips, which he took alone, with Raffaello Franceschini, his brother-in-law, and with Marchese Riccardo Ginori-Lisci. At that time Illica, also busy on other projects, was collaborating with Franchetti on the libretto of *Tosca.*

Tempers flared later, when Illica, whose dramatic instincts were very strong and often on the mark, sent Ricordi another bitter letter about Puccini's willfulness as they tried to work out the last act of *La Bohème.* Illica felt they had drifted too far from Murger in not having the Separation Scene between Mimì and Rodolfo; but Puccini had no interest in the idea. Illica felt instinctively that eliminating the beauty of their reconciliation meant a huge loss for the drama. "So Puccini really dislikes the way we resolved the problem on Sunday evening. He wants to start [the scene in the last act] with Mimì in bed and Rodolfo writing, seated at the little table, with a burned candle stub to light the stage. That means Rodolfo and Mimì have never been separated! Well, with this we really no longer have *La Bohème;* and beyond that, this is no longer Murger's Mimì! We have a meeting in an attic apartment between a journalist-poet and a little dressmaker. They fall in love, they argue, and then the little dressmaker dies. It is a pitiful story, but it is not *La Bohème!* The love story is a tear-jerker (and romantic), but Murger's Mimì is more complex than that!" He urged Ricordi to force Puccini to accept his plan: Rodolfo and Mimì should break up; Mimì should find a new lover, who gives her silk and velvet dresses; and when she knows she is dying of consumption, she comes back to a "desolate and cold attic apartment, just so she can die in Rodolfo's arms. . . . Forgive my griping, but that Puccini frightens me so much." Placing blame squarely on the composer, he concluded, "The truth must come out; and Giacosa and I are not the only two ugly ducklings [in this situation]" (LI to GR, [February 1894], in Gara, pp. 99–100). Illica was right, and Puccini eventually agreed that he had been wrong. The lovers' separation makes their reunion all the more dramatic. On other occasions Illica lost his battles, but he never stopped fighting.

Progress was also interrupted when Puccini left Milan in mid-March, again to go hunting. In Lucca he also took part in the ceremonies to mark the burial of Catalani's ashes in their native city. Next came an important personal appearance at the Teatro Nuovo in Pisa, where Toscanini was conducting *Manon Lescaut.* At that time Toscanini had been conducting for eight years. Born in Parma, he had made his debut in a sensational *Aida* in the summer of 1886 in Rio de Janeiro when he was only eighteen. Then the "boy wonder" returned to Italy, where he built his reputation gradually. When they met in Pisa, they naturally were not well acquainted, although they had certainly met and may have even have worked together earlier, when Toscanini conducted *Le Villi* at the Teatro Grande in Brescia.

The conductor was still grieving for Catalani, his closest friend. In Pisa *Manon Lescaut* would share the program with Verdi's *Otello*, which Toscanini had never conducted before. Often an advocate of new works, the conductor expressed a genuine interest in Puccini, and the two men soon began a correspondence that reveals much about their strange, tormented relationship. Over the next thirty years, moments of alienation and fierce hostility alternated with fresh reconciliation, as Toscanini rose to become the most powerful conductor and music director in the world. He helped Puccini by scheduling and promoting several of the operas he liked; but on the other hand, he may have harmed the chances of other Puccini works, the *Trittico* among them. In spite of many arguments and fallings-out, the bond between them lasted until Puccini's death.

On April 13 Puccini was on his way to Munich, Vienna, and Budapest to promote his opera. Then he was briefly in Milan, took a short trip to Torre, and went to Florence, where *Manon Lescaut* got a big ovation in the Teatro Pagliano on May 5, again with Eva Tetrazzini in the title role and Giuseppe Borgatti as Des Grieux. He then left for London for the first production of *Manon Lescaut* at Covent Garden. It opened the season, with a cast that included the unsatisfactory Olghine, Umberto Beduschi as Des Grieux, and Antonio Pini-Corsi as Lescaut. A "very great success," it attracted the attention of George Bernard Shaw, who declared Puccini the man most likely to be Verdi's successor. By May 25 Puccini was back in Milan, thinking about a proposed production of one of his works in Lucca. Then, as always, he had such an unholy fear of bad productions in his native city that letters to his brother-in-law and others touch on this subject. While he was away, Illica was busy in Naples; also there were Giordano and Franchetti. Giacosa had again taken up the libretto of *La Bohème*.

A Detour in Sicily for *La Lupa*

Even while Puccini struggled with *Bohème,* he was working seriously on an opera called *La Lupa,* based on a story by Giovanni Verga. His interest in that project dated to spring 1893. In this story, Verga, the author of *Cavalleria Rusticana,* created a vivid character in Mara, the "She-Wolf" of the title, the protagonist of a sex-and-blood tale. In spite of, or perhaps because of, some similarity to *Cavalleria Rusticana,* the work initially appealed to Puccini, but as he studied it all progress stalled. Wanting to discuss the plot and characters with the author, he decided to go to Sicily, where Verga lived, and also made a side trip to Malta. Reporting to Giulio Ricordi about his visit, he said he had taken photographs of local characters and farmhouses but had not heard any Sicilian music. Meeting Verga several times, Puccini discussed the action and motivation and almost reached an agreement about use of the Sicilian story, but he came away discouraged by the unattractive characters.

During the return trip, his doubts became certainty. On shipboard, he met Wagner's stepdaughter, Blandine von Bülow, who had acquired a title by marrying Count Biagio Gravina in the 1880s. When Puccini discussed *La Lupa* with her, she advised him against it, perhaps because the story seemed immoral. With that, he decided to wait to learn the fate of a play based on Verga's story, but soon afterward he gave up the project.

Back to *La Bohème*

His indecision and his eventual decision not to write *La Lupa* threw Ricordi into a fit of despair. Apologizing on July 13 for the "lost time," Puccini promised to throw himself "body and soul"—*a corpo morto*—into *Bohème.* His words, however, were far from reassuring, for he said he had been working on it "for two days, with goodwill." Of course, his mention of "two days" was guaranteed to discourage the publisher, who wanted his composers to dedicate months and years, not two days, to their projects. Puccini clearly knew he was causing problems, for he begged Ricordi to send him a word of forgiveness and absolution that would put his mind to rest. In short, he asked for a letter "that will not condemn my inconstancy, which I would call *belated understanding.* But better late than never." Claiming that Illica's sketch of the scene at the gate of Paris in *La Bohème* left him cold, he said, "I don't like it much, or not at all" (GP to GR, July 13, 1894, in Adami, pp. 93–94).

This delay over *La Lupa* struck at the very heart of the Ricordi operation, and at a time when Giulio Ricordi was facing furious competition with Sonzogno, who had come out in full cry. Catalani's *Loreley,* published by Ricordi, had had its premiere in 1890, the same year that Sonzogno brought out Mascagni's enormously popular *Cavalleria Rusticana;* Mascagni's *L'Amico Fritz* followed in 1891, and *I Rantzau* in 1892. These operas made him a formidable threat to the Ricordi composers, but he was not Sonzogno's only asset, for Leoncavallo had joined the Sonzogno list with his popular *Pagliacci* and, as everyone knew, he was composing his own *Bohème,* which would rival Ricordi's products. In 1892 Ricordi brought out Catalani's *La Wally* and Franchetti's *Cristoforo Colombo,* a "ceremonial piece," which Franchetti's planned *Tosca* was supposed to follow. Thus, Casa Ricordi could not afford any further delay or financial loss, but just at this time Puccini's changes of direction threatened to cause the firm real harm.

When the disappointed and "sad" Ricordi learned that Puccini had dropped *La Lupa,* he replied by return mail, saying the news did not surprise him. Although he regretted the many lost months, he was happy about *Bohème.* Nevertheless, he begged Puccini to get back to work at once. Soon, though, he had to send his composer some very bad news: Illica was about to quit work on *Bohème* because the composer had treated him so shabbily; as Illica said, he shoved him aside like a dog. And again Ricordi raised the issue of how much time had been lost. In the event, Puccini was not quite honest with Ricordi, for although he threw out the words "Illica or another librettist" in writing to the publisher, he failed to say that he had actually begun negotiations with someone else: Gabriele D'Annunzio. Unwilling to make the contact himself, he asked Carlo Clausetti, Ricordi's agent in Naples, to act on his behalf. He then confessed that he had not had the courage to mention this to Ricordi. He wrote, "You have to work on this. . . . For years and years, I've thought of possessing some subtly original thing from Italy's foremost genius. You explain my genre to him. Poetry, poetry, affection, lovers, meat [*carne*], searing and almost surprising drama, and a rocket sent up at the end" (GP to CC, July 18, 1894, in Gara, pp. 103–104). This was the first of Puccini's overtures to D'Annunzio. At first a young poet, novelist, and dramatist, he later emerged as his country's leading literary figure and earned the honorific *Il Vate d'Italia,* the Bard of Italy.

At that moment, though, Puccini's main worry had to be Illica, whom Ricordi had just brought up to date on the situation. Understandably, the librettist was furious about *La Lupa* and about the composer's unremitting criticism of his ideas for *La Bohème.* With considerable guile, Puccini then wrote to Illica, saying he did "not understand" why the librettist was so irritated. He was searching his brain to find the reason for this reaction. "Didn't we agree on everything?" he asked, although he surely knew the answer. He had already asked Ricordi to tell the librettist about his objections to two critical scenes; but he insisted that Illica's reaction was "surprising" and "strange." He went on with his complaints: "When he came here, we were in perfect agreement—and he knew about *La Lupa*—and he deplored the fact that I was not doing *La Bohème,* and he said he would always stand behind me in everything. Now that I've come back to him, he is amusing himself by putting on airs; and anyway, if he says I have cast him aside, whose fault is it? All I needed was a work that was what it should be, that is logical, tight, interesting, and balanced. But right now, nothing of all this. Should I have to accept Illica's gospel blindly?" Wanting the scene with Musetta as he had "discovered" it, he rejected Illica's suggestions about Mimì's death, and he still hated the scene at the gate of Paris, where he wanted to add "some melodramatic element" and something that would give him the chance to compose something lyrical. And again he repeated his criticism of Illica's plan for the scene: "I don't like it much." He really wanted to have his say about it (GP to GR, July 21, 1894, in Gara, pp. 104–105).

Some relief came when Ricordi again persuaded the injured librettist to go on with the work. Seeking to bring the two men together, Ricordi asked Illica to come to his office. Whether Illica failed to receive the letter, or whether he just wanted to teach Puccini a lesson, we will never know; but ten o'clock came and went, and Illica did not appear. Thus, Ricordi had to write him again, sending a messenger to ask him to come at one-thirty. "Let it be Roman-style boxing or English boxing, but we have to put an end to this, once and for all." Illica came. Trying to be fair, Ricordi sometimes supported Puccini's position and at other times declared Illica right. But he was firm in saying that they must "finish all this today." As peacemaker, he appealed for "perfect harmony." But, as he well knew, Illica would "have to sweat it out"; months of conflict lay ahead. At the same time, Illica was juggling Franchetti's projects and the creation of a libretto of *Iris,* which Mascagni later set.

After such a hectic season, Ricordi badly needed a vacation, which he took at the spa in Levico, north of Verona. His patience paid off in August, when Illica delivered a complete libretto, one that Puccini approved. With the opening of the 1894–1895 season not far away, Puccini began steady work on *La Bohème* in Torre. But he also needed a place to relax, so his "second home" became a café that was housed in a shack near the lake. Patched together out of slab timbers and scrap lumber, it was roofed with marsh hay. Two sides had large panels that could be opened in summer for ventilation. The proprietor, Giovanni Gragnani, was nicknamed Blackbird Legs, *Stinchi di merlo.* He served wine, bread, salami, and other salted meats, and let the local artists, peasants, and fishermen play *scopa* and *briscola,* among other legal and illegal card games. Crude practical jokes became the daily fare. After Gragnani departed Torre for Brazil, he left behind a relative, Arnaldo, who later helped Puccini with little errands. In 1896 the café was christened the Club La Bohème, and an absurd set of rules was drawn up by the composer and his friends. The members should swear and drink well, and eat better; the president could act as conciliator but had to stop the treasurer from collecting dues whenever possible; the treasurer was allowed to abscond with the money; the room should be lighted by an oil lamp, but candles could be used if the oil ran out; all legal gambling was prohibited; silence was forbidden; wise men were not allowed; and grouches, professorial types, and a number of hapless people were not admitted or, if there, could be thrown out by any member.

Eventually, an old upright piano was installed, presumably for Puccini, but in truth the "members" only played card games, talked, and drank. Puccini helped to furnish it in summer 1896, asking Clausetti to send him used items such as painted vases, blinds, and wall hangings or rugs. Early and late, Puccini fled to it, using it as a secure refuge from the problems he had at home. Above all, the Club La Bohème became recognized as his headquarters, a place where he met neighbors and treated them as equals, something the much more reserved Verdi never did in Sant'Agata. Puccini was always a man of the people, freely available during his visits to

Gragnani's bar and, later, the Club La Bohème. Because he always composed at night, he could spend whole days at the club, meeting almost everyone in that tiny community. According to many accounts, he also took several club members home with him at night. They chatted and played cards while he worked. They repaid him with loyalty and even with love.

One very solid example of how generously Puccini treated his neighbors dates from the summer of 1894, when he helped a man from Torre who wanted to supplement his income by making and selling tomato paste, which is called *conserva*. Going far, far out of his way to do a favor, Puccini asked his Milanese friend Riccardo Redaelli to buy a machine the man could use. If all had gone smoothly, the matter might have ended there, but when the processor arrived, Puccini saw old tomato seeds and skins in it and realized it had been used. Then he and his neighbor discovered that it did not work. Asking Redaelli to get a refund for it, he said that if the seller would not give him one, he would ask Casa Ricordi to take care of it. Truly concerned about this fiasco, Puccini hated to see the disappointment of his acquaintance, "a poor man" who had "suffered a loss" and was "disillusioned" by the outcome (GP to Redaelli, August 2, 1894, in Gara, pp. 106–107). In another effort for others, he spent about three months in the spring of 1895 searching for a bicycle for Franceschini, going to every shop in Milan, examining all the models, and writing long progress reports to Ramelde's husband. When the bike was delivered to Franceschini with a broken wheel, he made a huge effort to have it sent back to Milan and get it repaired and returned in good order.

By this time Puccini was actually working hard on the opera, as he wrote to Illica, saying he was quite pleased with the libretto. In September he reported to Ricordi that it was truly original and that the last act was "very, very beautiful" (GP to GR, September 7, 1894, in Adami, pp. 94–95). Later disputes, however, arose over details. That autumn Ricordi, who had gone to Paris, found himself quite overwhelmed by commitments to Verdi and *Otello*, which was to be given in French. Verdi, who would turn eighty-one in a few days, was scheduling rehearsals from noon until evening. He nevertheless found time to ask Ricordi about Puccini's work. And Ricordi, in turn, asked Puccini to send Verdi a birthday wish. It would be very much appreciated, he said.

As the old year ended and the new one began, Puccini, who was back in Milan, in his old apartment at Via Solferino 27, complained to Ramelde about the bitter cold and the snow, which was three feet deep. His apartment, though, was warm; and he amused himself with his recently delivered American parlor organ. Although work on the new opera claimed most of his attention, he also took it upon himself to send a message of goodwill to an impresario in Parma, where *Manon Lescaut* was about to be given. This was something Ricordi would normally have done; but the composer bared his soul a bit, saying that although he hoped for the best, he was afraid. The Parma audience was intelligent, but it also had the reputation of being the most demanding and unruly in Italy. As for the orchestra, which was directed by A. Canti, he was not worried. "I am tranquil," he said, trusting in the "best elements" in the production (GP to Gerbelli, December 12, 1894, NYPLPA, Music Division, Wanda Toscanini Horowitz Donation).

By the beginning of 1895 Puccini, Giacosa, Illica, and Ricordi had agreed that *La Bohème* was fully workable. The composer stayed with the new opera steadily in January, although his most serious composition was done later that year, after months of further work with his librettists. Thanks chiefly to Illica, the Latin Quarter act and the third-act "Barrière d'Enfer" took on lives of their own. In fact, it would be hard to overstate Illica's importance in the creation of this opera. In *The Tenth Muse*, Patrick J. Smith, who emphasized the influence of French dramatists and librettists on Italian writers, credited Illica and his "emphasis on novelty of setting" with much of the success of *La Bohème*. He wrote, "Illica also took over the French practice—theretofore rare in the Italian theatre—of providing copious, detailed stage directions and historical justifications in the libretto itself extending to the genre elements he wanted in the setting. . . . In the best of Illica's work these elements mitigate or outweigh the standard love plot, or, as in *Bohème*, combine with it to make such an ineradicable whole that the opera has become symbolic of 'artist life,' even to those artists who know that it is photographed through rose-tinted lenses and gauze scrims, but who think that this must be the way they live" (Smith, p. 358).

But if Illica proved himself again and again, the desperate Giacosa continued to cause problems. In March Puccini demanded to have the revised last act as soon as possible, although he knew Giacosa was still troubled by act 3. At this time the composer went to Livorno, where *Manon Lescaut* was being given at the Teatro degli Avvalorati. Finding that Mascagni, the announced conductor, was busy elsewhere, he had to deal with an incompetent substitute and a production that was in disorder. Shouting until his voice gave out, he coached the cast and prepared the orchestra. In spite of the successful opening night, he left Livorno deflated and shocked: no friend or family member had come for the opera or sent him good wishes. As he wrote angrily to Ramelde, they all lived within easy reach of the theater, and they knew he was there because his visit had been covered in the newspapers. In the same letter he confessed that he was exhausted by the many productions of the opera (GP to RPF, late March 1895, in A. Marchetti, pp. 197–200). Further problems arose in June, while Giacosa struggled with *Bohème's* act 3. Troubled by personal and professional commitments, he swore to Ricordi that he could not go on. Yes, he could finish that act, he said, but only if he did not have to rework it "for the twentieth time." All the "reworking, touching up, adding, correcting, cutting, pasting together again, pumping it up on the right, and paring it down on the left" had drained him. "I have already redone this blessed libretto three times, from start to finish, *three times,* and certain pieces I have done four or five times. . . . Will it really be finished? Or do I have to start again at the beginning?" (GG to GR, June 25, 1895, in Gara, pp. 114–115).

At the end of the month, Puccini retreated to a summer home Ramelde had found in the woods near Pescia. It is likely that she or some friend or acquaintance arranged for him to use this villa or a few rooms in it, because his royalties from *Manon Lescaut* would never have covered such an extravagance at that time. He described Villa Castellaccio to Illica: forty rooms, a garden, and a creek. The librettist, Ricordi, and Fosca visited him that summer, while work continued on *La Bohème.* By August, though, he was bored with life in this isolated place, which he eventually grew to hate. Although he longed to return to Torre, he stayed on until October, finishing act 2 on July 23 and act 3 on September 18. Four days later he began the last act, still complaining that it was too long. Ricordi thought that the last act was too short, but in the end he also recommended removing 150 or even 200 lines from the whole text. The final revisions, made by Illica, took out some horseplay among the Bohemians and other passages Puccini considered "useless."

Until late November the composer stayed at home in Torre, exchanging letters with Illica about last-minute changes, some of them important.

By then Ricordi had arranged to present the premiere in Turin, although Puccini would have preferred Rome or Naples. The composer's star had certainly risen, but he worried that summer about not being well enough known, and specifically about getting enough publicity in the Milanese newspapers. Successful as he had been with *Manon Lescaut,* he resented the fact that the press, which regularly covered Mascagni, Leoncavallo, Giordano, and others, never wrote about him. As he lamented to Clausetti, journalists did not even refer to him as one of the new operatic composers, although he claimed to have launched the "new school" with *Le Villi.* The "school" became known as verismo. Now he had to stand by and see Mascagni hailed as its founder. An injustice had been done. This is not to say that Puccini held personal grudges against all his competitors, for although he had his feuds with Leoncavallo and Franchetti, he had a long friendship with Mascagni and affectionately referred to Giordano as "a good boy" whose success with *Andrea Chénier* made him truly happy.

The Premiere of *La Bohème*

Puccini finished the orchestration on December 10, even though some changes remained to be made, and left for Turin in the first week of January 1896. With Illica at his side, he began overseeing rehearsals. Pleased with Toscanini, he was dismayed to learn that his Marcello would be Tieste Wilmant, one of the "pack of dogs" from the *Manon Lescaut* at La Scala. Among the trustworthy cast members were Cesira Ferrani, the soprano; Camilla Pasini, the excellent Musetta; and Pini-Corsi. Rodolfo was sung by Evan Gorga. Sage advice came in Ricordi's letters to Illica. Don't let anyone overwork the singers by making them sing early rehearsals in full voice, for they would have to do that later. "Throats are not made of steel," he warned. Worried about the staging of so complex an opera, he also begged his team to pay strict attention to detail in the crowded Latin Quarter. He had also noticed a tiny change that was necessary in the third-act Marcello-Rodolfo duet. All was done as the publisher wished; and Puccini described himself as working like a dog to inspire his cast.

The world premiere was given on February 1, with an audience that included royalty, noble families, and several rival composers, among them Mascagni and Franchetti, a favorite son in Turin. The opera won the public slowly, with the singers and Puccini taking three curtain calls and the composer taking one solo bow. The Latin Quarter scene, only moderately successful, was interrupted by applause only once, near the end. Then two barely earned bows for the composer and soloists meant bad news. After act 3, five curtain calls; only two after act 4. All was far from well, as Puccini knew, for he remembered overhearing people in the corridors saying, "Poor Puccini!" and "This time he's made a mistake!" He told Arnaldo Fraccaroli, who would one day be his biographer, that he felt almost sad enough to cry.

A sleepless night followed, and the next day brought very bad reviews in the Turin papers. Perhaps the most frequently quoted review was written by Carlo Bersezio, who predicted that the opera would not survive, a view that was shared by an important theatrical agent, Carlo D'Ormeville, who wielded power in Milan. Another writer denounced Puccini for abdicating his position as a leader of Italian composers, while another compared the finale of the Latin Quarter scene to operetta. On the other hand, some critics from Milan and other cities found *Bohème* a vast improvement over his earlier operas. Musically clear and refined, it moved swiftly and used contrast effectively, and was, as one writer said, "Very, very good." Ricordi, who had seen far worse reviews in his time, called *La Bohème* a new and daring art form that few could understand; and, as he added, the audience had a good time and found it moving. In fact, the audience had such "a good time" that this initial production ran for twenty-four performances, all sold out.

Ricordi, from his seat of nearly absolute power, was able to get the singers he wanted for most other productions, the first of which was only weeks away. After a brief stop in Milan, Puccini left for Rome, where the opera was presented at the Teatro Argentina on February 23, under the baton of Edoardo Mascheroni, one of the great conductors of his day. The audience, cold at first, turned wildly enthusiastic about the last two acts, making the evening a success. In Rome the most important singers were the women. Ricordi, who had heard the rehearsals for that production in Milan, called Angelica Pandolfini extraordinary, and even better than Ferrani, the creator of the role. Rosina Storchio, a favorite of Ricordi and Puccini, was the Musetta. Another important *Bohème* was planned for the Teatro Massimo in Palermo, in Sicily, in April, where *Manon Lescaut* had also been added to the program. Preparing to oversee those productions himself, Puccini was revising part of *La Bohème,* particularly the finale, which he felt was cold, "a glacier," and adding something for the baritone role of Schaunard, who had too little to sing.

As the composer prepared to leave for Sicily, he confessed to Ricordi that he was completely broke and needed an advance to cover the trip; he then told Clausetti that if he had to pay for the ticket himself, it would mean financial disaster. Successful but not yet secure, he was expecting ongoing income from *Manon Lescaut* and had not yet received any royalties from *La Bohème*. The publisher sent his statements and checks every six months, not as the operas were produced; and Puccini had evidently used whatever he had earned in the previous pay period.

With the advance in hand, he left Torre for Palermo in March, stopping briefly at the Teatro San Carlo in Naples, where another *Bohème* was in rehearsal. Clausetti and the impresario protested when Puccini made an abrupt, unannounced departure before the first night. He soon explained himself, however. Afraid of the storm of publicity, he was afraid of being tagged a relentless self-promoter like Leoncavallo. As it turned out, he may have been wise to leave, for in February some critics had felt that Ricordi's big, insistent publicity machine had harmed *Bohème* in Turin. On this issue Puccini was torn: he wanted publicity and had complained to Ricordi that he did not get enough of it; but, on the other hand, he thought it might harm his career in the long run. And, of course, early and late, he was very shy. Peace with Clausetti was restored after the San Carlo management took in nine thousand lire in ticket sales for the opera.

Ricordi's publicity had also paved the way for him in Palermo, for when his boat arrived from Naples he was met by a boatload of theater people who welcomed him royally in the harbor. He leapt into rehearsals at once, happy about having a good, dependable cast and an inspired conductor, Leopoldo Mugnone, whom he particularly liked and, at that point, preferred to Toscanini. The conductor, he said, made "a real creation" out of his opera. The first night turned into an astonishing victory when a near riot followed the last act. Even after many curtain calls, and even after the singers had left the stage, the audience stayed on, cheering and shouting until the principals, some already in street clothes, repeated the final scene. This was the largest and noisiest demonstration Puccini had ever seen in the theater.

With Palermo behind him, Puccini returned to Torre and then went on to Milan. From there he wrote to Clausetti about the great Neapolitan actor and playwright Edoardo Scarpetta, to whom he had sent a "splendid" signed photograph of himself. In return, he had asked Scarpetta to send one of his own that Puccini could add to his personal collection. He also asked Clausetti to go to a studio in Naples and pick up the proofs of two portraits, *"Elvira's and mine."* He underlined those words (GP to CC, May 28, 1896, in Tollett and Harman Collection). Exchanges such as this bear witness to the composer's new status as a national celebrity who was often asked for autographs and photographs. Some went to theatrical colleagues such as Scarpetta; but at the top of Puccini's list were nobles and members of royal families. Among these is an autographed photograph Puccini signed in Torre del Lago on September 14, 1897, to "Princess Lady Jenny di Belmonte, Homage from Giacomo Puccini" (private collection). Then, as always, he respected titled personages, holding the Italian royals, the Savoias, in particular affection. The grant from Queen Margherita had helped to make possible his studies in Milan, and the Savoias' loyalty to him lasted from his early years until the end of his life, when the king, queen, and court applauded him from their royal box at the Teatro Costanzi.

After the trip to Naples and Palermo, Puccini waited for news from Buenos Aires, where *Bohème* was being given in June. Soon afterward, he received an offer of twenty thousand lire if he would go to Argentina, an offer he did not accept at that time, although he did make the trip many years later. That summer in Torre he and Elvira were still living in the house rented from Count Grottanelli, having left Venanzio Barsuglia's place some time earlier; but Puccini was already talking (though talking only) about building a villa of his own there. Always passionate about houses, he also managed eventually to buy his old family home in Lucca, which had been sold after Albina's death, in a complicated mortgage-loan arrangement. Puccini had promised himself and his sisters that he would get the house back, and he did. Ramelde and her husband oversaw most renovations and found tenants; but when they could not manage the chores, the composer found himself losing money by paying taxes on the building while no one was living there. He also paid for repairs. Alfredo Caselli kept the account ledgers in Lucca, while Ramelde and Franceschini monitored affairs from their home in Pescia. The composer often asked about the condition of the old Puccini house, and he complained when it was not properly maintained.

Monitoring further productions of *Bohème,* he worried about Leoncavallo's version, which had its premiere in Venice. After a friend had told him how good his rival's libretto was, Puccini became afraid it would be given worldwide, while his operas would be seen only in Italy. Of course, Leoncavallo's work never presented a serious challenge to his own, but he would not realize that until later. After its premiere, he sounded a note of jubilation as he played on Leoncavallo's name in a poem to Ramelde: the Lion *(Leone)* and the Horse *(Cavallo)* had reached the stage, and had failed; only one *Bohème* (Puccini's own) remained standing. His rival's opera had sunk in the Venetian lagoon.

As 1897 began, Puccini announced his travel plans: Paris, Brussels, and London. Productions of *Bohème* were also planned for Berlin and Vienna. His primary job that spring was the first *Bohème* at La Scala, scheduled for April, with Mugnone conducting and an excellent cast. Angelica Pandolfini and Camilla Pasini had sung the women's roles before, and Fernando De Lucia was Rodolfo. By April 17 he and Tito Ricordi were in Manchester, the city Tito's father had chosen for the first English *Bohème* because *Manon Lescaut* had been received so indifferently in London in 1894. The composer looked sophisticated and handsome in a photograph he signed in Manchester on April 22 (Sotheby's May 1990 catalogue); but he hated England, with its suffocating smoke, cold, rain, and fog. Just fifty years earlier, Verdi had reacted to the English climate in the same way. When he was in London in 1847, preparing the first production of *I Masnadieri,* Verdi and an Italian colleague dreaded going outdoors, believing that the coal smoke would turn their faces black.

Puccini brightened considerably after the successful production of his opera, which the Carl Rosa Company gave in English as *The Bohemians* at the Comedy Theatre. Afterward he looked "radiant with the recollection of genuine Lancashire feeling" (*Sunday Times,* cited in Carner, third ed., p. 104); however, when he wrote to Ramelde, he complained about fog that was the color of dirt and said that the English drank a lot of whiskey. He confessed to his sister that he was overweight by several kilos, but he was nevertheless in the best of health, though dismayed by streaks of gray he saw in his hair (GP to RPF, April 17, and May 11, 1897, in A. Marchetti, pp. 225–227). Returning from England, he could say that his new opera had been enormously successful in Manchester, Glasgow, and Edinburgh.

In May he and Elvira went to Venice, where *Bohème* was being given at the Teatro Rossini, and he planned a trip to Berlin in June for the first production of it there. But most of the summer would be spent on a new project, *Tosca,* and a short vacation. At first, he fixed on Bagni di Lucca, a place he knew well; it was cheap, he said, and near enough to Torre to permit him to run home, if necessary. Next under consideration was San Pellegrino. In a May letter to Ramelde he mentioned his dream of spending part of the summer in Celle, the Puccinis' ancestral village; but, as he said, he could not bear the solitude, the bad beds, and the distance from a telegraph office. With this brief vacation, he could take time off from his travels on behalf of *Bohème.* It proved more successful every month, opening the new seasons in Vienna and at Covent Garden in London. Not everyone was won by it, though, for many criticized it as a "weeper" or "tearjerker" backed by trivial music. Mahler, among others, took a violent dislike to Puccini's work. Nor did the controversy over it die out. Decades later, the composer Benjamin Britten found the music cheap and empty.

For more than a hundred years, though, audiences have loved this opera, and singers have enjoyed performing in it. One prominent fan is Plácido Domingo, who analyzed *Bohème* in an article he wrote in 2002. Praising its "almost universal appeal," he said it "combines meltingly beautiful music with a very realistic love story of everyday young people." Puccini is "a genius" at using the power of his music to make "love at first sight" completely believable in act 1. Of the finale of the last act, Domingo said, "I defy even the most cynical listener not to be touched by Mimi's reminiscing . . . and by their friends' concern for her." He finds her death so "absolutely shattering" that he admits to having a lump in his throat and tears in his eyes. Overall, the opera has "a rare fusion of light and dark, as much buoyant and bright as foreboding and tragic" (Domingo).

The opera became Puccini's never-fail signature work. Quite simply, *La Bohème* is a masterpiece.

CHAPTER SEVEN

✥

Tosca: *1887–1900*

A FTER the troubled gestation of *Manon Lescaut* and *La Bohème,* Giulio Ricordi might have hoped for an easier time with *Tosca;* but he did not get it. First he had to deal with Victorien Sardou, the French playwright who had written *La Tosca* and held the rights to it. The play proved attractive to opera composers because of its vivid characters, some of whom Sardou took from historical figures, as Deborah Burton's fascinating research on the "originals" has proved. Ricordi also had to balance the needs of his composers, Alberto Franchetti and Puccini. Three librettists were also in play. Ferdinando Fontana, the poet of Puccini's first two texts, was again hurt and angry at being shut out of the project. It was unfair, he said, for in 1889 he had been the very first to propose *Tosca* to Puccini and had even corresponded with Sardou about the project (FF to LI, [undated, after August 9, 1895], in Gara, p. 32n.1). Together he and Puccini had seen Sarah Bernhardt in *La Tosca,* once in Milan, once in Turin. But all Fontana's protests went unanswered after Ricordi found better librettists in Illica and Giacosa.

"What Difficulty with This Signora Tosca!"

In fact, Puccini had been staying with Fontana and his wife in Caprino Bergamasco on the day he first wrote to Ricordi about *Tosca.* At that moment, he and Carlo Carignani were correcting the score of *Edgar.* "After two or three days of lazing around in the country and resting up after all the overwork I've suffered through, I realize my desire to work has come to life again, livelier than ever, rather than leaving me. I am thinking about *Tosca!* I beg you to take the necessary steps to get Sardou's permission for it before you give up on the idea, something that would make me terribly sad, because I see in this *Tosca* the opera I need, one with no overblown proportions, no elaborate spectacle [*spettacolo decorativo*], nor will it call for the usual excessive amount of music" (GP to GR, May 7, 1889, in Gara, pp. 31–32). If Ricordi was disappointed to learn that Puccini was again looking for something small and simple, he kept his chagrin to himself and began the process of getting the rights for his composer.

As his negotiator Ricordi chose Emanuele Muzio. Then living in Paris, Muzio oversaw Verdi's interests there. Whatever else he was, the conservative Muzio was no fan of Sardou. In 1887, just before the premiere of *La Tosca,* Muzio had written to Verdi, speculating on whether it would be full of the "usual artificial stunts [*le solite fichelles*]" or "whether [Sardou] has really created an original work" (Muzio to Verdi, November 13, 1887, in Vetro, *L'allievo di Verdi, Emanuele Muzio*, p. 236). Muzio had evidently met Sardou through the professional association of authors and composers in Paris. In fact, *La Tosca* actually reached the stage, and was very successful, chiefly because of Bernhardt, who played the title role. Muzio already knew Puccini's work. As we have seen, he criticized *Le Villi* from a study of the score. After seeing the opera in Rome at the beginning of 1888, he sent a friend these impressions. "It seems to me that there is too much music in this opera, [given] its subject, and it is not appropriate, excepting in the fantastic parts. There is no sentiment, and where there is any, it sounds like Gounod. In short, it is music that does not awaken the emotions, and it gets lost in symphonic descriptions, and the characters don't know what to do onstage" (Muzio to [Carlo D'Ormeville?], January 30, 1888, in Vetro, *L'allievo di Verdi, Emanuele Muzio*, p. 238).

In late spring 1889 Muzio negotiated with Sardou for *La Tosca.* His assignment: "To get permission to do the libretto of *Tosca* for Puccini." He often saw Sardou on Fridays at the office of the Société des Auteurs et Compositeurs, and he may have mentioned it there. In any case, Sardou sent him a telegram saying he was asking the head of the Société how to handle Ricordi's request. "[Sardou] will want money," Muzio warned Ricordi. One day later, in the offices of the Société, the director read him a letter from Sardou. Muzio described it as "full of complaints over the bad reception his *Tosca* got in Italy and particularly in Milan, where the press abused him, showing no deference to him and no respect." Then Muzio went on: "Sardou is above all a businessman, or rather, in my eyes, a real merchant. He is not very inclined to let anyone make an Italian libretto out of his *Tosca,* because one day or another, a French composer may want to make a French opera out of it. However, he would like to know how much Puccini would propose to pay him. He does not want to dictate the conditions, but he will consider the offer. [It] should be in cash, and [include] some [ongoing] interest in the rights; and he wants to know which Italian [theaters] will be given the score; [he is] keeping the author's rights for France for himself" (Muzio to GR, June 21, 1889, in Vetro, *L'allievo di Verdi,* p. 249). Muzio warned that Puccini was not the only composer interested in *Tosca.* Among others were Mario Costa and "another Neapolitan," whose name Sardou said he did not remember. "I believe he will choose Puccini above the others, but watch out, because he won't give it away for a few thousand francs; he will want to be paid a lot. The treaty of Berne guarantees him the rights for *Tosca* in Italy. Because I read in [the journal] *L'Événement* that Musset's heirs wanted to sue over Puccini's *Edgar,* I asked [about that], and [was told that] Musset is in public domain in Italy. I will give Sardou's agent whatever answer you send me, and if necessary, I will go to Marly-le-Roi [to visit Sardou in the country]" (ibid.).

In the summer of 1889 Muzio was also negotiating with Sardou for the rights to *Théodora,* which the conductor Marino Mancinelli, the older brother of Luigi, wanted for himself or for some unnamed composer. No Italian composer, however, ever seems to have used it, although Xavier Léroux's version was performed in Monte Carlo in 1907. At the end of the 1880s, Puccini had a vested interest in Marino Mancinelli, whom he wanted to see as the leading conductor at La Scala, replacing Faccio, who was ill. When Marino was not chosen, Puccini lost an important ally in Milan, where his works often got a hostile reception. But Milan was not an issue for him at the time, for Sardou soon lost interest in Puccini, who got busy on *Bohème* with Illica, who was complaining about Puccini at every step, even as Giacosa was describing his experience as "the Puccini torture." At that time, Puccini had a contract to write two new operas for Ricordi.

Franchetti's *Tosca*

Sardou proved difficult, but finally Ricordi reached an agreement on the financial terms and could ask Illica to write the scenario of *Tosca*. Early in 1894 he also commissioned the libretto from him and transferred Puccini's rights to Franchetti, who had just had a big success with *Cristoforo Colombo*. As we have seen, Puccini and Franchetti had a complicated relationship even before the 1890s, and there remained in Puccini a sense of his own unworthiness. Even when *Bohème* was on the programs of the world's greatest theaters, he seemed surprised to be so famous. In 1897 he marveled to Ramelde that he had come so far, given the fact that he had once been defined as the man who aspired to emulate Franchetti.

In October 1894 Ricordi, Illica, and Franchetti visited Sardou in Paris. While there they also heard from Verdi, then eighty-one, who was in the city to supervise *Otello*. He weighed in by saying he liked *Tosca* and might have composed it himself, had he not been so old. Encouraged by that, Illica began sending Franchetti the opera, one act at a time, although from the start, the librettist found the play unsuitable for opera. Nevertheless, everything went smoothly until Franchetti began to demand major revisions. Illica found a way to keep the two composers at work, telling Puccini about the progress of *Tosca* and Franchetti about *Bohème*. January 1895 had hardly begun when the librettist exploded to Ricordi: "What difficulty with this Signora Tosca!" Franchetti was then composing the first act and asking for changes in the second. But Illica warned Ricordi not to say anything, because he knew Franchetti would rush to his apartment and "tear everything apart" (LI to GR, January 12, 1895, in Gara, pp. 113–114).

There are several accounts of how Ricordi got Franchetti to surrender *Tosca* to Puccini, but the truth may never be known. Some say Ricordi convinced him the story was too violent and coarse for an opera. That was also Illica's opinion of *Tosca*, if not Ricordi's, and the shocked Giacosa, too, found it gross. However, the American scholar Deborah Burton, the author of recent studies of these events, found Franchetti decided against *Tosca* because he remained unconvinced of its merit and did not "feel the music" in the drama. In the Casa Ricordi Archives, Burton also found a letter from Giulio Ricordi to Franchetti in which Ricordi expresses his annoyance with Franchetti for having backed out of the project. According to a family tradition that Cody Franchetti mentioned to me in a telephone interview in 1998, Franchetti told his children he willingly gave up *Tosca* to his rival. In a grand gesture that sounds just like him, he shrugged it away, saying to Ricordi, "Give it to Puccini. He has more time than I have."

The controversy does not end there. After the premiere of Puccini's *Tosca,* people began saying that the beginning of the first act was actually Franchetti's music. According to another rumor, everything up to the Sacristan's entrance in act 1 was Franchetti's. Arnold Franchetti also claimed this when he spoke to the American impresario Willy Anthony Waters, an artistic director of the Greater Miami Opera. Recently Waters described his preparations for a new production of Alberto Franchetti's *Cristoforo Colombo* for the 1992 Columbus anniversary celebration in Miami.

> [Arnold] Franchetti, a composer in his own right, recalled that his father indeed told him that Puccini "stole" the rights to *Tosca* from him, with Ricordi's help. Apparently, Ricordi convinced [Alberto] Franchetti that *Tosca* was not for him, calling it too dramatic, too bloody; that Franchetti was too much of an aristocrat to write music such as *Tosca* required. [Arnold] Franchetti also told me that *all* the music leading up to the Sacristan's entrance was written by his father. I questioned the veracity of his statement, having been shown no physical evidence in support of his claim, until I studied the score [of *Cristoforo Colombo*]. In the last act, during Colombo's mad scene shortly before his death, Franchetti wrote a five-chord motif, which is *exactly* that of the Scarpia motif, voiced in basically the same way and beginning with B-flat major, although the mood is mournful instead of sinister. *Colombo* bowed in 1892. *Tosca* [reached the stage] in 1900. Draw your own conclusion!" [Waters to *Opera News,* April 2000]

The idea that Puccini might have taken something from Franchetti might not be worth consideration, save for the fact that the opening page of the autograph score of *Tosca* has only the chords of the Scarpia motif on it, and nothing else. These begin the section that some say Puccini took from Franchetti. William Ashbrook, who examined it and many other Puccini scores in the Ricordi archive in Milan, said that page bears the date "January 1898" (Ashbrook, *The Operas of Puccini,* p. 72). The rest of the score, beginning with the first act, takes up on the next page.

Burton, when I interviewed her in 2002, found a number of flaws in this claim. First, she said, Franchetti's music is in a quite different style from Puccini's. Second, if Puccini had borrowed all of the music up to the Sacristan's entrance, as some say, why does his autograph stop after the Scarpia chords? But even if the material had been borrowed, she says, it is used in a Puccinian way: this opening motive is essential to the large-scale structure of *Tosca*. It appears at the endpoints of both act 1 and act 2 and is part of the deeper musical structure as well. Also, the motive is based on the whole tone scale, which Puccini used in many works, including *Manon Lescaut, Butterfly,* and *Fanciulla*. However, the most convincing piece of evidence is that Puccini wrote this autograph in the same month that he thanked Don Pietro Panichelli for having informed him of the pitch of the Vatican's largest bell, the "campanone," a very low E. Burton believes that this information led Puccini to choose the pitches B-flat, A-flat, and E for his opening Prelude.

The professional rivalry of Franchetti and Puccini would be set aside, however, when they talked about automobiles. At the turn of the century, Franchetti, the president of the Italian Automobile Club, had a Mercedes and a Renault and was scouring Europe for a car that could reach the un-heard-of speed of fifty-four miles an hour. He had also infected both Giordano and Puccini with "automobile fever," as Puccini described it. They all went frequently to the automobile show Franchetti mounted in May 1901 in Milan's Public Gardens. Both he and Puccini drove; and the Franchettis, being daring adventurers and explorers, drove hard and far.

Puccini's *Tosca* at Last

Ricordi may have handed the libretto to Puccini in Milan, on the same day that Franchetti gave it up; but the composer told Father Dante Del Fiorentino that he actually came to Torre del Lago to deliver it in person. Whatever the events, Puccini wrote to his friend Carlo Clausetti, "I will do *Tosca,* an extraordinary libretto by Illica, in 3 acts, Sardou is enthusiastic about the libretto" (GP to CC, August 9, 1895, in Gara, pp. 116–118). At that moment, much of Illica's work lay ahead; he and Puccini would argue over countless revisions. The composer also had second thoughts after he saw Bernhardt in *La Tosca* in Florence; but Ricordi reassured him, saying that Illica's libretto was more effective than the original drama, and that Bernhardt had been ill when she played in Florence. Ricordi, who had seen her in Milan, described her as "splendid." Giacosa began to write the poetic text in mid-December. But in the spring of 1896, he criticized it because it had too many duets and Scarpia had two boring monologues, one at the end of act 1 and another as the next act opens. Although he raised one objection after another, he remained on the job, setting aside a play of his own to do so. Giacosa, though, believed Puccini did not really want to write the opera.

In February 1897 Puccini's main concern was *Bohème,* which was being produced at La Scala and would, as we have seen, have its first performance in England in the spring. With Tito Ricordi, Giulio's son, he traveled to Paris, Belgium, and London on his way to Manchester. And then, as he said, he had to get back to Torre del Lago and pay attention to *Tosca*. However, in May he and Elvira went to Venice, where Toscanini conducted Puccini's *La Bohème* in the Teatro Rossini, while the Teatro La Fenice had Leoncavallo's *La Bohème* on its schedule. In June Puccini supervised the rehearsals for the first German-language performance of the opera in Berlin; he did the same in Vienna, where it was given at the Theater an der Wien. But he stayed in Torre del Lago for much of the spring, summer, and autumn. His health was good, his teeth bad. By this time, he and Elvira had Fosca with them, while Tonio was in boarding school. Although he said he was working, he also got in some hunting. November found him taking a short trip to Rome, where he studied the sounds of various church bells for *Tosca* and solicited help on the religious aspects of the opera from Don Pietro Panichelli, a priest mentioned earlier.

As the first pages of the autograph score show, Puccini began to orchestrate *Tosca* in January 1898; but that month *Bohème* was produced in Parma, where Puccini oversaw rehearsals, then returned for the first night to face Italy's most capricious and demanding audience. The opera was a success. In Turin Toscanini, whom the composer hailed as the "sublime and incomparable commander," was conducting a reprise of *Bohème* (GP to AT, card, January 17, 1898, NYPLPA, Music Division, Wanda Toscanini Horowitz Donation).

In February Puccini went to Paris to negotiate personally for the premiere of *La Bohème* at the Opéra Comique. It was to be given in French. He was also planning the world première of *Tosca*. In March Puccini wrote to ask Toscanini to help Carlo Angeloni, his former composition professor from the Istituto Musicale in Lucca; in that letter he also mentioned having Toscanini conduct the first *Tosca*. At that time Toscanini was directing a program of forty-eight concerts for the Turin Exposition of 1898. In correspondence that shows how much effort Puccini spent on such appeals for friends, he wrote:

Dear Toscanini, I have had a letter from my old teacher from Lucca, Cavalier Carlo Angeloni, a very (really) distinguished Maestro of counterpoint and composer of sacred music, asking for help with a *Stabat Mater* that he composed for chorus and orchestra. This Maestro Angeloni would like to have this *Stabat* performed during the concerts for the Exposition. (Are they performing sacred music?) Believe me, Angeloni really is a true and authentic and distinguished composer for the church. If you are willing to do so, and if you can manage to do this favor, I will be so grateful to you. I beg you to answer me with just a line. If you are not opposed to this idea of mine, I will have the score sent to you so you can see it and decide. Dear handsome Little Arturo [*Caro Arturetto bello*], when can we see each other in Milan? I am going to Paris [again] at the beginning of April, because they are to give *Bohème* at the Comique. *Tosca* is coming along well; please remember that you have to be the man who deflowers her [*che tu devi essere il suo sverginatore*]. Many affectionate greetings, and don't be lazy, answer me right away about this matter of the *Stabat* that I am interested in. [GP to AT, March 11, 1898, NYPLPA, Music Division, Wanda Toscanini Horowitz Donation]

In another note, also sent to Toscanini in Turin, Puccini took up Angeloni's cause yet again (GP to AT, card, undated, NYPLPA, Music Division, Wanda Toscanini Horowitz Donation). In the years that followed, he often tried to help his old Maestro and Carlo Carignani and many, many others. This and dozens of similar letters in his correspondence, like his letters about the tomato-processing machine and the bicycle, show how hard he tried to help people. But he was ready to help even those he hardly knew. In these matters he remained generous all his life.

With Elvira and Fosca he returned to Paris in April to prepare the cast and oversee the *Bohème* rehearsals. The visit, which began well, grew difficult when Puccini turned moody and angry. He lost weight, cursed fate for keeping him away from Torre, and swore over the opera company's foot-dragging; the progress of the production was "as slow as turtles" and "as slow as a snail." He called his experience a *Via Crucis*. The arrival of Illica, Luigi Pieri, and Caselli lifted everyone's spirits briefly. Illica sent Ricordi bits of gossip about Franchetti and news of the rehearsals: the French-language version worked very well; the orchestra was ineffective in the Latin Quarter scene; the set was spectacular. The first night was June 13. Although it went well, the opera got mixed reviews; but by that time, it was so popular that what the critics said did not matter. After he got home, Puccini learned that the box office receipts matched any ever recorded at the Comique. Although the audience loved the opera, the French critics did not. Mentioning Puccini's debts to Verdi and Massenet, they found it banal and stuffed with cheap effects.

Puccini, who had been longing to leave for the country, soon set out for Torre. He also had plans for yet another home. Writing to Ramelde in May 1897, he had asked her to look into the possibilities in Chiatri, a remote village he remembered from his boyhood visits with Don Roderigo Biagini. Dante Del Fiorentino, who served as an altar boy in Chiatri in the summer, described its twelve families, two hundred sheep, ten cows, chickens, and parish church. While Puccini was staying there, he went to Mass with his extended family, including Elvira's sister and brother-in-law, Ida Bonturi Razzi and Beppe Razzi, a couple whom the composer saw as the most dangerous of Elvira's troublemaking relatives. Del Fiorentino remembered them as an astonishingly sophisticated group of city-dwellers—the women beautifully dressed and Razzi wearing a long-bushy beard—all sitting apart from the local peasants. Another man who joined Puccini at Mass that summer was Carlo Carignani. Quite naturally, the composer and his entourage attracted so much attention that Father Chelini, the priest, had to call his parishioners to order, saying: "Good people, please remember the Blessed Sacrament is on the altar, and not elsewhere" (Del Fiorentino, pp. 99–100). Because Puccini soon began construction of a large villa in Chiatri, Del Fiorentino may have been right in believing he wrote part of *Tosca* in that village. Even after the villa was finished, he continued work on it, hiring a prominent Florentine architect to add a balcony to the facade and create a large terrace outside the main entrance. In fact, he loved Chiatri so much that he once ordered a hundred postcards of his house to use for correspondence.

Later in the summer of 1898, while the villa in Chiatri was being built, Puccini rented Villa Mansi in Monsagrati, a mountain village in the municipality of Pescaglia, not far from Celle. Like Villa Castellaccio in Pescia, it was a place he soon came to hate. Defeated by the stifling heat, he slept during the day because there was nothing else to do; and he worked all night, as he always had done. During this summer critical for the creation of *Tosca,* he changed some lines in the libretto, added others, and finally omitted whole numbers that he found superfluous. Thus he cut *Tosca* to the bone, leaving three strong characters trapped in an airless, violent, tightly wound melodrama that had little room for lyricism. Illica and Giacosa quite rightly complained about that. William Ashbrook described the music as "telegraphic, highly charged, sensuous," and saw Puccini as a portraitist who proved his mastery in *Tosca.* Cavaradossi, Tosca, and Scarpia come alive as complex, believable figures: Cavaradossi, an artist and "man of taste"; Tosca, with her "abundant temperament"; and Scarpia, the aristocrat, sardonic, a "connoisseur of evil." The Sacristan, while not a full-scale portrait, is at least a miniature, "an avaricious hypocrite." By honing these characters and writing music "in character" for each, Puccini created a gallery of people as real as reality itself (Ashbrook, "Puccini as Portraitist").

Creating such a tight work as *Tosca* proved extremely hard for Puccini. Working at the end of 1898, he wrote to Ramelde from Milan that he was "busting his balls" on the opera. "I am in the house, working almost all the time. *Tosca* is immensely difficult; and who knows whether I can get her off the ground" (GP to RPF, end of December 1898, in A. Marchetti, pp. 236–237). Before the end of the year, he summed up his complaints: he was progressing slowly, because that was his way; he had a cold; the weather was terrible; and most of the time Milan got on his nerves. Longing to be in Torre, he said, "For me, the country is a necessity, something urgent, as when you are desperate to go to the bathroom, and there are people there and you cannot go. . . . Torre is ideal for me, and you don't feel that: so much the better for me, because I can have it all for myself." He wanted to be alone there, and added a list of friends he would gladly keep out. Apologizing for writing such a scattered letter, he admitted that his writing was as nervous and irregular as his thoughts (GP to RPF, December 28, 1898, in A. Marchetti, pp. 237–238). Ten days later, he again said he could not bear Milan and told Franceschini it made him vomit (GP to RF, January 7, 1899, in A. Marchetti, pp. 239–240).

In January 1899 Puccini returned to Paris to discuss his progress with

Sardou. They talked mainly about details of the action and the setting of the last scene, which Sardou wanted to inflate with grand effects and Puccini wanted subdued and subtle. The playwright's approval was necessary, though, for he had once believed that Puccini was not capable of writing *Tosca;* on another occasion he had called Giacosa an idiot. In the end, though, Sardou put his seal on the project, leaving Puccini free to return to Italy. He looked forward to Torre del Lago and "uninterrupted work," which meant the cancellation of a planned trip to London. Everyone involved was under such pressure that Ricordi, fearing Puccini would not finish on time, added his own lines to the last act duet and sent it to Illica for a final touch. With luck, they expected the score of *Tosca* to be in the publisher's hands that autumn; but again the project was interrupted when Ricordi saw Puccini's act 3 and hated it. He described his objections in a long letter, prefacing his criticism with a long declaration of affection for Puccini. To Ricordi the act seemed so flat, fragmentary, and scattered that it would wipe away all memory of the high drama of act 2, Puccini's "masterpiece." Later he decided he liked it.

In fact, the problem was not new, for all opera composers face the peculiar problem of how to handle the third or last act. Rossini had railed about it. As Verdi put it, the composer had to convince the audience that the act 2 finale was not the end of the opera, because another act would follow. And by Ricordi's standards, Puccini had not solved the problem, for he thought act 3 of *Tosca* was weak enough to kill the whole evening. He particularly objected to the soprano-tenor duet, where, to his dismay, he found music that Puccini had cut from *Edgar.* Suitable for a peasant from the Tyrol, Ricordi said, it was wrong for a Roman hero. Where, he railed, was Puccini's inspiration? Where was his imagination? By return mail, Puccini put up a strong defense and stood by his choices. He had created the fragmented effect by shortening lines and disliked the idea of a long aria for the tenor. He wanted it realistic, not operatic.

But he profoundly regretted the incident. Never, Puccini said, absolutely never in their long association had they disagreed so strongly on anything; but he was convinced that if Ricordi looked at the act again, he would change his mind. The composer also offered to go to Milan, sit down at the piano with Ricordi, and play and sing the act for him. In the end, Puccini got his way, chiefly because, as both men knew, they had no time to make major changes. Under other circumstances, Ricordi's troubling letter about the third act might have remained private; but after the premiere of *Tosca,* his reservations became the talk of Milan. But at this stage the opera still was not finished, for more work lay ahead. The words to the Shepherd's Song were added at the end of the year. In December the composer could tell Don Panichelli that he believed the opera would have a great success—if no noisy demonstration wrecked the first night. By the end of the month Puccini was settled in the Hotel Quirinale and was in rehearsal at the Teatro Costanzi. With a cynicism worthy of Scarpia himself, he described *Tosca* to Ramelde as a *zibaldone,* "my new hodgepodge." As Marchetti shows, he later called it "a vile opera" and *"quella puttana di Roma,"* "that Roman whore" (A. Marchetti, pp. 243–244).

Nor was *Tosca* his only concern in 1899: one of his short pieces was played that year, for what may have been the first time. This was *"Scossa elettrica,"* the "Electric Shock March," written for a celebration that the city of Como mounted to honor Alessandro Volta, the inventor of the electric battery, who taught at the university there. Although Puccini's little march may have been commissioned as early as 1896, it was first played by a band for the Volta tribute, during an international conference of telegraph operators. Mario Morini, writing in *"Un omaggio di Puccini a Volta,"* noted that the march was published in *I telegrafisti a Volta.* (Recently it was resurrected by Charles Yates, a scholar from San Diego State University. After discovering a piano version of it in a library in Lucca, he arranged for it to be heard again. Thus, in July 2001 the work was played by a wind ensemble at the University of North Texas in Denton.)

The *Tosca* Premiere

For all Ricordi's attempts to give *Tosca* a worthy premiere, it had a wild baptism. He had chosen to present the opera in Rome's Teatro Costanzi at the very peak of the Holy Year celebrations of 1899–1900. Pope Leo XIII, following the example of his predecessors, had designated the period a Universal Jubilee, which began on Christmas Eve 1899 with the opening of the Holy or Jubilee Doors of the great churches. Catholic pilgrims could earn a plenary indulgence if they confessed, received Holy Communion, and visited the city's four major basilicas, Saint Peter, Saint Paul Outside the Walls, Saint John Lateran, and Santa Maria Maggiore. They must also visit three other basilicas, to complete the mystical number of seven; and all had to lay offerings at the feet of the pope, who appeared often to give the apostolic blessing. While in Rome, the pilgrims had to pray for (among other graces) the triumph of the Church, the expunging of errors, peace among Christian rulers, and the prosperity of Christianity. At one point in history, a Holy Year had attracted more than two million pilgrims to Rome; in 1899, with the turn of the century at hand, even greater participation was expected. Hotels and *pensioni* were full; the streets were crowded. This upsurge of religious fervor, however, had also set off Italy's many anticlerical factions, including the anarchists, who threatened mayhem.

Because Leo's bull declaring the Holy Year had been published in May 1899, Ricordi knew perfectly well what he was doing in placing *Tosca* in Rome in that season. As anyone might have anticipated, its premiere, on January 14, 1900, was chaotic. Leopoldo Mugnone conducted; Hariclea Darclée sang the title role; the tenor Emilio De Marchi was Cavaradossi; and Eugenio Giraldoni was Scarpia. Giulio Ricordi had sent Tito, his son, from Milan to oversee the staging, and Puccini oversaw all the rehearsals. Everyone in the Costanzi was nervous about a threatened anarchist bombing, which might well come in the wake of the strikes, bread riots, and other violent events that had plagued Italy for years. Nor were their concerns groundless, for Mugnone had actually survived a bombing in a theater in Barcelona. Anarchists were active everywhere, and later in 1900 one of them assassinated Umberto I, king of Italy.

At the Costanzi, the curtain had just gone up when a loud disturbance broke out in the rear of the auditorium and the foyer. When someone shouted, "Bring down the curtain!" Mugnone, who had been told to strike up the Royal March in an emergency, panicked and stopped the orchestra. It soon became clear that the uproar was owed to latecomers trying to get in, while people in the theater tried to hush them and keep them out. Finally, when everyone was seated, the curtain went up again, and the performance began. Many Roman dignitaries attended, although Queen Margherita arrived late and missed the first act. In the audience, a contingent of Puccini's colleagues and rivals included Franchetti, Mascagni, Francesco Cilea, and Ildebrando Pizzetti. Although Ricordi feared they might wreck the first night, they apparently behaved themselves.

Given the circumstances, it was rather a miracle that *Tosca* survived, although many voices were raised against its violence and sadism. As Vincent Seligman noted, it included a torture scene, an attempted rape, an assassination by knife, an execution by shooting, and a suicide. Yet several numbers were encored, and Puccini took many curtain calls. The critics, those same critics Puccini had blamed for criticizing Mascagni, wrote mixed reviews, with one faulting the long, wordy second act, and another finding, just as Illica and Giacosa had, that the rush of action prevented flights of lyric beauty. The music lost the battle, one writer said. More outspoken reviewers deplored the sexuality, while some found self-plagiarism of ideas from *Manon Lescaut,* though few could have discovered the music from *Edgar* that Puccini had buried in the last act. Another critic railed about "three hours of noise." The writers who found fault with the libretto sent Illica into a fury. In an angry letter he denounced Puccini for treating his librettists badly and acting as if they were his servants (LI to GP, January 15, 1900, in Gara, pp. 192–194). All in all, the press was unfavorable. Nothing, however, has kept *Tosca* from being a popular favorite, although criticism of it has never really died down. The American scholar Joseph Kerman, writing in *Opera as Drama,* branded *Tosca* "a shabby little shocker"; he denounced Puccini's music as "second-rate stuff" and accused him of coarseness and cynicism. "Talent, craft, and pretentiousness," Kerman said, were no substitute for spirit. The composer also made a "shrill" demand for emotion, even when the action of his operas did not warrant it (Kerman, pp. 189–205, passim).

After the premiere Puccini returned to Torre. Ill that winter, he apologized to Toscanini for not being able to come to the rehearsals of an unnamed opera the conductor was preparing, although, as he said, he hoped to be well enough to attend the first night (GP to AT, December 1899 or January 1900, NYPLPA, Wanda Toscanini Horowitz Donation). He was, however, able to attend the rehearsals of *Tosca,* which was scheduled for March at La Scala. Toscanini had opened the 1899–1900 season there on December 26 with the first Italian *Siegfried,* then had scheduled a reprise of *Otello* with Tamagno and Emma Carelli. *Lohengrin* followed. In February, when *Tosca* rehearsals began, the company had to deal with the financial problems that faced the management.

Both Puccini and Toscanini had worked under the impresario Luigi Piontelli, a former contrabass player who had taken over Turin, Pisa, and La Scala; Toscanini had run several seasons for him. Verdi, though, had criticized Piontelli as "a bad impresario"; at one point he had threatened not to produce the world premiere of *Falstaff* at La Scala if Piontelli was still in charge. Hating his "discourteous and uncivil manners," Verdi said, "I would not set foot in his house." That said, one must say that Toscanini saw in the impresario "a second father" and close friend. In 1892–1893, it had taken all Ricordi's skills as a conciliator to get Verdi to relent so *Falstaff* could go onstage in Milan; now, seven years later, Ricordi again had to intervene, this time in a dispute with Piontelli over *Tosca*. The plain fact is this: the impresario refused to schedule rehearsals that the cast needed, although the first night was only about three weeks away. In the end, Puccini and Toscanini had to give up several piano rehearsals, because the management simply did not have the money to pay for them (GP to AT, February 23, 1900, NYPLPA, Music Division, Wanda Toscanini Horowitz Donation). In spite of the problems, Puccini assured Primo Levi that everything was going smoothly and that the performance would be "superb."

After the premiere, he wrote of its success and full houses (letters of March 14 and April 3, 1900, in Gara, pp. 195–196). Because many March productions at La Scala had had too few performances to establish themselves with the audience, Puccini begged Toscanini to schedule six extra performances, knowing that a longer run would be better for him and the opera (GP to AT, February 23, 1900, NYPLPA, Music Division, Wanda Toscanini Horowitz Donation). In the Milan cast were Darclée as Tosca, the great Giuseppe Borgatti as Cavaradossi, and again Giraldoni as Scarpia.

Puccini also attended the first London *Tosca,* at Covent Garden with the celebrated Croatian soprano Milka Ternina in the title role and Antonio Scotti as Scarpia. Both sang these roles at the Metropolitan Opera in 1901, with Cremonini as Mario. Much later, Emilio De Gogorza, the patrician baritone who married Emma Eames, described Ternina to the Philadelphia critic Max De Schauensee as "the sort of person who seemed to cross the stage in three strides, riveting you with her blazing eyes." It is no wonder Puccini liked her in the role. Other popular Toscas of his era were Eames, Lina Cavalieri, Geraldine Farrar, and Claudia Muzio.

When the opera returned to Milan in 1908, Puccini could again send good news to Carlo Clausetti: "*Tosca* here has full houses and is a great success. At the first performance there was panic, but as soon as the chaff had disappeared, a strong and incisive interpretation by Toscanini came to the surface, with a competent stage production" (GP to CC, January 5, 1908, in unidentified autograph dealer's inventory sheet). In Vienna the composer discovered Maria Jeritza, who became one of the greatest Toscas of the century. De Schauensee called Jeritza "the most thrilling Tosca in my experience," and said when she finished "Vissi d'arte," she was kneeling on the stage, with mascara "coursing down her cheeks in two black streams, as many in the audience wept with her." He also said that after she killed Scarpia, "her fear of Scarpia's corpse was so vivid that I often was afraid I might see the body move" (De Schauensee). Jeritza also became known for singing "Vissi d'arte" while lying prone on the stage. Having tripped once while trying to evade Scarpia, she fell and sang the aria without getting up. Seeing what a success it was, she continued to do this.

Naturally, each singer creates his or her own character out of personal conviction. Much has been written about Jeritza's Tosca, as if all her stage business burst forth spontaneously; but Helen Noble, in Life with the Met, showed how contrived her portrayal was. From the very moment of her act 2 entrance, Jeritza was carefully removing her hairpins, one by one, so she could pull the last one out during the struggle with Scarpia. Taking her famous fall from the couch, she would shake her head just once, making "the great mass of gorgeous, gleaming golden hair" tumble down over her shoulders. As Noble recalled, the audience always "oh'ed" and "ah'ed," with few understanding that Jeritza had planned it all. A different, very intellectual kind of planning went into the character created by the Italian baritone Cesare Bardelli, who sang Scarpia more than 950 times. The finest Scarpia I ever saw, he made the arch-villain so smooth and fascinating that no one could suspect that a brutal sadist crouched within. The veteran Venetian critic Mario Messinis, reviewing Bardelli's Scarpia at the Teatro La Fenice, placed it among the "best we have ever had occasion to hear in the theater," and "just what Puccini imagined." Birgit Nilsson called Bardelli "my greatest Scarpia." Without a powerful Scarpia, the opera cannot succeed.

As was his custom, Puccini oversaw several important productions of Tosca himself; but at the beginning of 1900, he was also busy with Villa Puccini, his new house in Torre del Lago. Like the villa in Chiatri, it was made possible by royalties from Manon Lescaut and La Bohème, which were gradually making him rich. His lifestyle, however, had never changed, for he and Elvira lived very simply for years in an old villa in Torre and in his old apartment in the unpretentious building at Via Solferino 27 in Milan. Now he could build a place of his own, choosing a site in Torre that was just a few feet from the shore of Lake Massaciuccoli. The house is certainly comfortable and was ideally situated for him, but it is by no means luxurious, although he took great care with decorating it. In February his first order of business was finding decorative wood and plaster details for the ceilings and walls, and he asked the painter Plinio Nomellini to add frescoes later. (The house, which is now a Puccini museum, has a large salon where Puccini composed, a study, a kitchen, a small room for his guns, and other service quarters downstairs; on the second floor are bedrooms of modest size. The original dining room has been made into a small chapel where he, Elvira, and their son, Tonio, are buried.) His concern with the house, however, did not prevent him from looking for a subject for a new opera. Even before *Tosca* reached the stage, Puccini was prodding Clausetti and others to find something new and great, and something to captivate the audience with its novelty. Eventually, he found that work himself in the play *Madame Butterfly*.

CHAPTER EIGHT

❧

Madama Butterfly: *1900–1906*

O F ALL THE OPERAS of Puccini's maturity, perhaps none remained at greater risk than *Madama Butterfly*, first in the years before its premiere, then in the course of his many revisions of it. As a result, much of his original idea has been lost. The opera also nearly foundered in the storms of the composer's turbulent private life. Puccini, injured twice in automobile accidents, escaped with minor bruises in the spring of 1902, but he was almost killed in a serious crash a year later. A long, painful recovery followed, but during it he also had to deal with his newly diagnosed diabetes. Other crises arose out of Puccini's long affair with a young woman from the Piedmont. First he was forced to break off this relationship because of Elvira's well-founded jealousy and the pressure brought by his publisher, librettist, sisters, and friends. Then he had to face the woman herself, a furious rejected lover who threatened him with lawsuits and public exposure. All these distractions cast a shadow over the creation of *Butterfly*, before and after its catastrophic premiere in 1904.

The East and Beyond

In London in 1900 for the first English *Tosca*, Puccini saw David Belasco's play *Madame Butterfly*, but not with the famous American actress Blanche Bates, who had taken the title role in New York City. The direct source of the drama, John Luther Long's short story "Madame Butterfly," had been published in 1898, but nothing suggests that Puccini was familiar with it. Belasco, like Long, told of an American naval officer stationed in Nagasaki. After an arranged marriage to a fifteen-year-old Japanese geisha, he sets up housekeeping. Cio-Cio-San, believing that she is "Mrs.

Pinkerton," is cut off from her own religion and people; after their son is born, she tries to become truly American. Pinkerton, on the other hand, sees the marriage as a temporary arrangement that will end when he returns to the United States and takes a "true American woman" as his wife.

Historically, this was a moment when public fascination in the West with things Japanese and Chinese had become a near mania, although popular Orientalism in art dated back to the start of the nineteenth century and peaked between 1850 and 1890. One American adventurer in that mysterious world was Ernest Fenollosa, who lived and died in Japan and inspired Ezra Pound to edit his tract, *The Chinese Written Character as a Medium for Poetry.* Of Fenollosa, Pound said, "To him the exotic was always a means of fructification." The same could be said of Puccini, who chose Oriental subjects for *Butterfly* and *Turandot;* even *La Fanciulla del West* was exotic in its own way, although it was not set in Asia. Another foreigner who plunged into Oriental culture was Lafcadio Hearn, the Greek-born American journalist who eventually took a Japanese name, Yakumo Koizumo. His many books on the East began appearing in 1894 and 1895 and were translated into European languages, introducing many to Japan and its people.

Among the tales to come from this little-understood place was Pierre Loti's novel *Madame Chrysanthème,* the first big narrative with a plot similar to that of *Madama Butterfly.* A westerner and exploiter of Japan, Loti wrote of a naval officer who was in some ways the forerunner of other foreign men in later operas, plays, fiction, and even a recent Broadway musical, *Miss Saigon,* which is derived directly from Puccini's opera. In the works of Loti and other Europeans, the heroes' basic disrespect for Asian women and their culture is fundamental to the plots. The officer in Loti's tale also wants to marry a Japanese woman, but he intends to stay with her only for the length of his assignment. Unlike Butterfly, Loti's Madame Chrysanthème, called O-kiku-san, is a crass opportunist, more than a match for the man who bought her on the marriage market. As he prepares to leave, both feel relief. She returns to her former profession, while he goes back to his life in the West. This novel, published in 1887, was the source of an 1893 opera by the French composer André Messager. Whatever her virtues and failings, Madame Chrysanthème served as a model for Long's Cio-Cio-San and Madame Butterfly.

Pietro Mascagni, who wrote *Iris* to Illica's libretto, also sought authenticity, doing research on Eastern instruments in a museum in Fiesole, near Florence, and presenting a brilliant rendering of the "Oriental moments" in his score. *Iris* had its premiere at the Teatro Costanzi in Rome on November 22, 1898, with Puccini and Toscanini in the audience. Although the evening almost ended in fiasco, it revealed the protagonist in her strange innocence and tragic beauty and put Mascagni's gorgeous orchestration on full display. It also demonstrated the weakness of a sordid tale.

The plot of *Iris*, taken from a fable, is similar to the ancient Korean folktale "Shim Chung, the Blind Man's Daughter," chiefly in the abuse both protagonists suffer. Like Shim Chung, Iris is abducted from her home and thrown into a dangerous, hostile environment. Both women are mere sex objects to the men around them; both are threatened with rape and otherwise abused physically and emotionally; but the two stories have very different endings. Shim Chung, a model of filial devotion, marries a king and is reunited with her blind father; in the last scene rulers and subjects rejoice. Iris's life ends tragically when her father rejects her, throwing filth at her when he sees her exhibited as a prostitute in a public place. Like Madame Butterfly, Iris commits suicide. Because Mascagni wrote *Iris* under a contract with Ricordi, it set him and Puccini in direct competition under the same publisher, at a time when cutthroat rivalries ruled the opera business. Much to Puccini's credit, he found merit in *Iris*, although he could see its dramatic flaws, and he felt the critics had treated Mascagni badly. When Toscanini conducted *Iris* at La Scala, it fared rather better than it had at its premiere, although even there it fell short of success. It did, however, remain popular among Italians and Italian-Americans well into the twentieth century. (Several years ago, a solid production of it at the Mosque Theatre in Newark, New Jersey, showed how affecting it is.)

Puccini's experience with Mascagni's opera may have led him to Belasco's play, even as it taught him what issues to avoid. Six years later, *Madama Butterfly* followed *Iris*, overtaking Mascagni on the Oriental front. Ricordi learned of the composer's interest in November 1900, and when he did, he remained unenthusiastic, thinking it a poor choice even after Puccini made his case. A delay ensued during negotiations for the performing rights to the drama.

While Puccini waited, he again became infected with what he called his *"mal di calcinaccio,"* his "mortar disease," or love of buildings. It drove him to make further improvements to the old Puccini family home in Lucca, which he intended to rent out. He also continued supervising the last touches on his new villa in Torre del Lago, even choosing the fabrics. In a 1900 letter to Alfredo Caselli, a much-loved childhood friend who knew the place as well as he did, Puccini reveled in the pleasures it had to offer:

> TORRE DEL LAGO: Supreme bliss, paradise, Eden, the empyrean, "Ivory Tower," a refuge for the spirit, kingdom, 120 inhabitants, 12 houses. A peaceful place, with splendid scrubland running down to the sea, populated with deer, boars, hares, rabbits, pheasants, woodcocks, blackbirds, finches, and swallows. Immense swamp. Luxurious and extraordinary sunsets. The air bad in summer, splendid in spring and autumn. Dominant winds in the summer, the mistral [from the northwest], in the winter the *grecale* [from the northeast] or the *libeccio* [from the southeast]. In addition to the 120 inhabitants mentioned above, there are the navigable canals, the troglodite huts made of marsh hay; the many coots, whistlers, grebes, and digging birds that are certainly smarter than the inhabitants, because it is hard to get close to them. They say that in the pinewoods there is also a rare animal called the Antilisca. For information about it, you may ask Giacomo Puccini. [GP to Caselli, (July 1900), in Gara, p. 201]

He invited others to hunt the imaginary Antilisca, with predictable results.

Happily settled in his new house in August 1900, he told Ricordi it was comfortable, quiet, and free of mosquitoes, with zinc screens on all the windows. As he worked on the house, he went on studying possible subjects and even visited Emile Zola in Paris to discuss *La faute de l'Abbé Mouret.* Quite naturally, he kept in constant contact with Illica. Many other novels and plays came under scrutiny at this time, among them Carlo Goldoni's *La Locandiera* and Alphonse Daudet's *Tartarin de Tarascon,* which the newspapers reported that he was composing. Still strangely insecure about his fame, he wrote to Caselli about his friendships with celebrities of his time. "I am the friend of Zola, Sardou, Daudet. Whoever would have said that—eh?—about the third-rate organist from Mutigliano?" (GP to Caselli, [undated], in A. Marchetti, p. 229n.5).

Naturally, things did not go smoothly, for a problem arose when Illica heard that Puccini was considering asking Gabriele D'Annunzio to write a libretto for him. The composer denied it at once. Then he and Illica tackled the old subject of Marie Antoinette, which was again put aside because settings with the French Revolution had become too commonplace. Puccini also supervised productions of his operas, as he had done since 1893, sometimes rehearsing them for weeks or—more rarely—simply appearing in time for first nights, sitting in a box and taking bows onstage. He followed the fortunes of *Tosca* from Genoa to Bologna in 1900 and to Palermo and other theaters the next year, then to his home territory, Livorno, in 1902.

A real fiasco, however, occurred at the end of 1900, with a disastrous *Bohème* that handed him a smacking defeat at La Scala. The tenor Enrico Caruso, singing in that theater for the first time, was ill and had to have his first act aria transposed down. Emma Carelli, the Mimì, was out of character, crudely made up, and badly costumed. On that disgraceful opening night, *Bohème* got no applause at all, with act after act ending in silence. After act 3, when Puccini could bear no more, he fled the theater, too stunned to wait for the end. The next evening he left for Torre del Lago, where, as he said, he could "breathe better air." Before leaving, however, he wrote to explain himself to Toscanini: "Last evening I left at the beginning of the last act, and so I did not speak to you as I would have wished. Forgive me, I was too saddened over last evening's outcome. I beg you to take care with the second performance [*Ti raccomando la seconda recita*], above all Carelli, for her costume and makeup. Tell her to present the character as Murger perceived and realized her, and not to slow down the whole thing as if she were tired. I have only to thank you for the care you took for my opera. So I hope that the second performance will be livelier throughout, and that Caruso can show what he is worth. Will you have another rehearsal?" (GP to AT, December 27, 1900, NYPLPA, Music Division, Wanda Toscanini Horowitz Donation).

The fiasco of *Bohème* at La Scala laid the composer open to criticism at a time when Ricordi was worrying about how slowly he composed and Illica was faulting him for not working hard enough. Having complained about the amount of time Puccini wasted in hunting, the librettist now mentioned the public's perception of him as lazy. A comparison with Mascagni was inevitable. Puccini, however, defended himself, saying he was a hard worker, but in confidence he wrote to Ramelde, admitting that

he was "obscenely lazy." At that time he did not know that he was diabetic. His perceived "laziness" may have been caused by his illness.

Verdi's Death and Puccini's Future

Puccini stood in an aura of glory at the beginning of 1901, when he won
undisputed recognition as Verdi's successor. On January 27 Verdi died in
his hotel suite in Milan; his death plunged Italy into national mourning.
Because he had stipulated in his will that he wanted none of the "usual
rites" after his death, a simple service was read on January 30 in the
Church of San Marco in Milan. He was then buried in the Cimitero
Monumentale. On February 1 Toscanini conducted a grand concert, the
"Commemorazione di Giuseppe Verdi," at La Scala. Among the artists were
Francesco Tamagno, Enrico Caruso, Giuseppe Borgatti, and Emma Carelli; and the orator for the evening was Giuseppe Giacosa, Puccini's librettist. Although most of his discourse was a dignified homage to Verdi,
he also exhorted the composers of the next generation, many of whom
were in the audience. "And you Italian musicians, you must gather in the
legacy of the hero we have buried. Plough not in his furrow but in the
same field that he opened [for you]. . . . Gather in the sacred legacy. He
will rejoice at the applause that will greet every new triumph of Italian art
in this theater" (Giacosa).

On February 27 Verdi and his wife were reburied in the chapel of the
Casa di Riposo per Musicisti, the home for aged, poor musicians that he
had built as a supreme act of charity. That event became an enormous celebration, with about three hundred thousand people turning out along
the route of the funeral procession, and Toscanini conducting a chorus of
eight hundred voices in "Va, pensiero" from Verdi's *Nabucco*. Puccini had
an official role in the church service and in the reburial in the Casa di
Riposo, because Cesare Riccioni, the mayor of Viareggio, asked him to
represent the municipality. Accepting the honor, he responded, describing
Verdi as "the purest, shining glory of Italy" and saying that, for the good
of Italy, he hoped others would "imitate and carry on the virtues of the
man and the artist" (GP to Riccioni, [probably January 28, 1901], in
Pintorno, letter 74). With that, Verdi was truly buried, and Puccini had
few real rivals for the title of successor. Still, in his modesty, Puccini was
reluctant to use the words "Verdi's successor" in describing himself, but

he did so at least once, then added the word "naughty" (GP to SS, June 22, 1906, in Seligman, pp. 80–81).

After the 1901 ceremonies for Verdi, Puccini took up the challenge of *Butterfly,* which was so different from everything he had written. As he and Illica began the libretto, he researched original Japanese music and even asked Madame Hisako Oyama, the wife of the Japanese minister in Rome, to help him find authentic melodies. She gave him recordings and an album of songs, which Puccini later said he used in the opera. In an article in *Opera News,* Duiti Miyasawa identified several themes Puccini chose. Among them are Butterfly's entrance, from a Nagauta long-song; "Kimi-ga-yo," the Japanese national anthem; "Sakura," a cherry blossom festival song; "Oedo-Nihonbashi," played at the wedding and in the second act; "Miya-san," also heard in act 2; and "Honen-bushi," a harvest song (Miyasawa, "Madama Butterfly's Original Melodies").

The composer later discussed Japanese music with the great soprano Tamaki Miura, who would sing more than two thousand performances of *Butterfly,* beginning in 1914. She met him and Tonio in Rome, then visited in Torre del Lago, where Puccini showed her his Oriental artworks and sang some Japanese music. He also spoke of his choice of subjects, saying, "I compose only to a successful and sensational drama; it is the best way to catch success." Miura, perhaps the most authentic Butterfly of her time, sang the role in Europe and America; she appeared with the Boston and Chicago companies, as well as the San Carlo Opera, where she was engaged from 1923 to 1926 (Miyasawa, "Tamaki Miura and Puccini"). Miura also taught the role to Hizi Koyke, who made it her signature role in the United States.

In 1902 the composer may also have seen the famous actress Sada Yokko (known in Italy as Sada Jacco) in Milan, for Illica urged him to go to one of her performances. The wife of Otojiro Kawakami, an actor, she collaborated with him on a collection called *La Musique Japonaise.* With his love of exoticism, Puccini showed imagination in his use of these themes and "Oriental" music of his own creation. Particularly impressive was his re-creation of nature, which seemed to flow freely out of the "dawn interlude" that had proved so popular in *Tosca.* Nature also figured in his consideration of *La Locandiera,* where, as he told Illica, he could imagine writing about spring, gardens, greenery, bushes, and flowers. All this came out of his own passion for natural things; but it also strongly suggests the works of the poet Giovanni Pascoli, one of many living literary figures in Puccini's creative sphere.

Giovanni Pascoli in Puccini's Land

"If you want to understand my music, you have to understand Pascoli," Puccini once said. Three years older than Puccini, the poet had been born in the Romagna, but Tuscany was his adopted home. Like Puccini, Pascoli was an *"orfano di padre,"* a boy whose father was dead. The elder Pascoli, his town's mayor, was murdered in 1867 in mysterious circumstances, shot dead on the road by unidentified assassins. As boys and men, Puccini and Pascoli were passionately attached to their mothers and sisters. Pascoli's sisters, Ida and Maria, much like the Puccini girls, were sent to board in a convent of Augustinian nuns. However, neither took the vows, and Pascoli set up a household for himself and them.

In 1884 he came into Puccini's orbit when he took teaching posts in Massa di Carrara, Pisa, and Livorno; and in 1895 Pascoli and his sister Maria moved to the mountain hamlet of Castelvecchio di Barga, now called Castelvecchio Pascoli, in the province of Lucca. Located in the wild region called the Garfagnana, this village clings to the crags above the Serchio River. Pascoli became nationally famous in the spring and summer of 1903 with the publication of *I Canti di Castelvecchio,* a classic that had a little dictionary of Lucchese dialect terms sold with it. The revised edition that followed in 1905 contained additional nature poems. So popular is this work in Italy that a new, critical edition was published in 2001. Pascoli and Puccini shared several close mutual friends in the Caselli family of Lucca. Alfredo Caselli, whom Puccini loved and trusted, owned a shop and the Caffè Buon Gusto on Via Fillungo in Lucca. The Lucchesi called it the Caffè da Carluccio, after Alfredo's father. Pascoli dedicated poems to Alfredo, who first introduced him to Puccini, and also wrote often to Alfonso Caselli, Alfredo's brother. In 1903 Pascoli wrote to Alfonso, "I am writing birdsong, so beautiful!" In another letter, he described odes to crickets, frogs, and grasshoppers; and he wrote about the Tuscan woods, so beloved by Puccini. Meeting in Barga, Bagni di Lucca, and especially in Caselli's café, Pascoli and Puccini exchanged ideas and were photographed together. Del Fiorentino described both as retiring and shy, and said Puccini venerated Pascoli because he remained humble and modest, even in the face of his fame.

Two other poets, Giosuè Carducci and Gabriele D'Annunzio, were also emphatic in their esteem for Pascoli. His first book, *Myricae*, is a volume of radiant lyrics celebrating nature and the simple, rural life that he and Puccini loved. In 1894 the third edition made him famous almost overnight. Its very title, *Myricae*, evokes the scattered shrubs that are found on Tuscan beaches, for *"myricae"* is the Latin name of the tamarisk. The theme of the first poem recalls the title of Puccini's *Crisantemi*, a string quartet, for its subject is All Souls' Day, the Day of the Dead, with its rituals of mourning, and the dark cypresses of Tuscany; it ends with "O Mother! Heaven pours out its tears darkly, above the cemetery." In other poems, holiday mornings ring with church bells clanging in the air.

Pascoli wrote about washerwomen, seamstresses, nuns, beggars; mothers and children who have died; dawn, day, noon in the village tavern, sunset, evening, night, woodlands and flowing springs, crows and swallows, robins, blackcaps, nightingales, bees, roses, periwinkles, ivy, trees; fire, wind, rain, storms, the beach; the seasons, owls, laurel trees, and skylarks—in short, all things Puccini cared about. In search of old forms, he even fell back on madrigals and the ancient Tuscan *rispetto*, and he rhapsodized about the Tyrrhenian Sea.

In 1901 Pascoli emerged for the first time as a librettist, having written an *azione scenica*, or brief music drama, called *Il Sogno di Rosetta*. The composer was Carlo Mussinelli, a musician from Barga, where the little work was performed. His next libretto was for an opera, *L'Anno Mille*, a tale of the millennium written for the composer Renzo Bossi. It was never performed. Not surprisingly, one rumor had him writing a libretto, perhaps *L'Anno Mille*, for Puccini. In 1904 came the first of his *Poemi Italici*, his Italian poems, which were followed by his *Poemi Conviviali*.

In these early years of the twentieth century, Puccini and Pascoli were two of Italy's most respected creative artists. In a recent article in the *Corriere della Sera*, Giovanni Raboni examined the relationship between Pascoli, whose art Puccini understood and loved, and D'Annunzio, with whom he could not work. In another article on the same page, the poet Edoardo Sanguineti mentioned Puccini's relationship to Pascoli. "In the first half of the twentieth century, whole generations grew up being

taught a belief in tears that flow easily, the emotions, and the sentimentalism that Pascoli stood for in poetry and Puccini in music" (*Corriere della
Sera,* September 23, 2000, p. 33). But far beyond sentiment, they loved nature, little people, and little things. Both suffered when nature was vio-
lated. In the 1920s a heartbroken Puccini wrote to Giuseppe Adami, his librettist, about having to cut down twelve pine trees near his villa in
Viareggio. He was doing it, he said, "to get more air and to satisfy Elvira,
[who complains] about the humidity. My heart is weeping" (GP to GA,
[1923?], in Adami, p. 292). Here Puccini speaks with Pascoli's voice.

The Affair with Corinna

Sometime in 1899 or 1900, Puccini fell in love with Corinna, a young
teacher or law docent from Turin. In the Puccini literature, she is
identified only by her first name. Corinna was unmarried and in her twenties. He was past forty, and under the law he was free to marry. The two
may have met casually on a train; but one account has Puccini flirting
with her on the station platform in Pisa and becoming her lover soon afterward. Throughout this passionate relationship, they met whenever
they could and originally saw each other regularly in and around Viareggio, his "second hometown," as he called it in 1900 in a letter to Ferruccio Pagni. Later, he took a house for her near Torre. Regretting the on-
set of old age, he complained of life with the grim Elvira. Living with her
had never been easy, and even Illica, who rarely saw her, said she got on
his nerves. Corinna, with her youth and optimism, offered Puccini a welcome respite from that. Because both took this long relationship seriously,
she even seems to have believed he would marry her. During one crisis he
even decided to leave Elvira for her, because, as he said, she offered him
love and inspiration.

Elvira admitted to people such as Ramelde and Illica that she had
known about Corinna as early as 1900. When Ramelde scolded her
brother about his lover, he admitted his guilt rather awkwardly, saying
that although he had brought his troubles on himself, another factor was
Elvira's conflict with Gemignani, which had contributed to what he called
her "illness," presumably her nerves. Even after seventeen years of separation, she was still Gemignani's wife. Puccini wrote to his sister about a
possible "divorce," which they could not get in Catholic Italy, but Elvira

may have sought an annulment instead. Reassuring Ramelde, he said that if Elvira became free, he would marry her. In the end, however, Gemignani balked. In this ugly situation, chance meetings with Gemignani were so unpleasant that Elvira had a friend report on his comings and goings, so she and Puccini could avoid seeing him in Lucca. All this took its toll on her, leaving her sick and "a wreck," as Puccini said.

Some relief came in the summer of 1901, when they took a vacation with Fosca and Tonio in Cutigliano, a village in the mountains east of the Serchio Valley and Pascoli's Garfagnana. From there, the composer could drive around the province, revisit scenes of his boyhood, and spend time with people he had not seen for more than twenty years. Elvira's spirits rose briefly but did not improve. He confided his despair to Illica, saying that his "unenviable" life had to change. It did not; and when they returned to Torre, Puccini and Corinna began meeting again. Apart from his situation with Elvira, he was also profoundly lonely after Fosca married Salvatore Leonardi, a theatrical agent and impresario, and moved to Milan. As Puccini wrote, he missed her dreadfully and found life with Elvira thoroughly depressing. "You, Fosca, left a huge void when you left, and the life we two live is simply terrible!" And in another letter to her he wrote, "I would like to see you here sometimes. Come, even if for a few hours, to lend a little of your kindness and good nature to the sad atmosphere in my house" (GP to FGL, August 1902 and August 8, 1902, both in Gara, p. 223).

Gossip about Corinna eventually reached Ricordi, who worried about scandal ending the career of his most important composer. As he told Illica, he was praying to God, Heaven, and Divine Providence to save the situation before "the Puccini tragedy" ruined them all (GR to LI, undated, in Gara, p. 254n.1). His prayers went unanswered then, as did those of Elvira, Ramelde, and Puccini's sister Iginia, the Augustinian nun Sister Giulia Enrichetta, who mustered the other nuns in rounds of prayers for Puccini's body and soul. These matters appeared not to bother him, for although he swore to Ramelde that he was "getting over" Corinna, he continued seeing her.

Not surprisingly, Elvira tried to find out everything about her rival, although she might have accepted Puccini infidelities as did many wives and companions of men of all walks of life. In spring 1902 she learned that "La Signorina" arrived in Viareggio in the evenings, met Puccini, and left before noon the next day. Desperate, Elvira waged her campaign by appealing for help to Puccini's Lucchese friend Guido Vandini, Illica, and family members. She went on hunger strikes, sometimes refusing to eat for two days at a time. But all in vain, for nothing could keep Puccini at home. Del Fiorentino, who asked Count Eugenio Ottolini about Puccini's love affairs, said the count described Corinna as "that pretty little schoolteacher from Turin." Puccini, he said, had invited her first to Viareggio, then, fearing Elvira's wrath, had followed Ferruccio Pagni's advice and arranged to have her travel by carriage to a remote place in the woods near the hamlet of Migliarino, about three miles south of Torre. There, in a cluster of houses called Chiesaccia, he found a secure place for their meetings.

Each time Corinna came, he told Elvira he was going hunting near Migliarino. She, always suspicious and on the prowl for his real or imagined women, went to Chiesaccia one day, but arrived too late to catch the lovers together. Puccini had left, and Corinna was leaving. Elvira ran in front of the horses and carriage in a narrow country lane and began poking Corinna with an umbrella. In the ensuing uproar, the coachman whipped his horse and drove away, the sudden commotion throwing Elvira into a ditch. Ottolini described the scene that followed Puccini's arrival at home: Elvira attacked him with fists and fingernails, forcing him to run to the bedroom, where he tried in vain to lock the door. When the fight was over, he was left with bloody scratches all over his face. The next day, he joked about them to his cronies, saying he had fallen into a bramble bush (Del Fiorentino, pp. 77–79).

Steady pressure over Corinna built up for about three years, with this young woman clearly important to the composer's emotional life. Then two events brought matters to a head on a single February night in 1903: Puccini was nearly killed in a car crash that left him immobilized for months; and within hours Gemignani died, leaving Elvira free to marry. Under Italian law, ten months had to pass before the widow Gemignani could remarry; and in those ten months, Puccini was constantly under siege.

The *Butterfly* Libretto

Against the backdrop of his romantic attachment to Corinna, Puccini began to compose *Butterfly*. In spite of his initial enthusiasm for the Belasco play, he seemed somewhat uncertain about how to handle it; but by August 1900 he admitted that he was thinking about it all the time, as he waited for permission to use it. He was bored, had nothing to do, and described himself as a laborer without a job. Soon, however, he was busy. Virtually from the moment he began working on *Butterfly,* the composer argued with Illica and Giacosa about its characters and structure, exhausting them in the process. Ricordi was again called into service as a peacemaker, as Puccini fumbled with his second, third, and fourth thoughts and veered one way and another as he tried to get the libretto he wanted. As before, the arguments exacerbated the deterioration of their relationships and delayed the opera's completion.

As Puccini told Illica, he was completely taken with the idea of *Butterfly.* Some early confusion arose, however, when the two men were using different sources. Illica worked from Long's story, while the composer drew on the play, which he said was better. The last two acts of the opera come from Belasco. Eventually, after Puccini had acquired the operatic rights to both, he agreed that Illica's first act, taken from the story, was brilliant. According to the original plan, the opera was to have three scenes, the first and the third in the house Pinkerton provided for Butterfly, the second showing a meeting between Butterfly and Pinkerton's American wife at the consulate. Illica favored the contrast this arrangement provided between the Oriental way of life and the Consul's villa in the "European Concession." At first, Puccini liked the Consulate Scene, saying it was too impressive to be left out. Giacosa, again assigned the job of turning Illica's drama into poetry, began work on *Butterfly* in summer 1901, with unremitting pressure brought by Puccini. Racing ahead with his ideas, Puccini had even begun to think of the intermezzo and the Humming Chorus. As soon as he received act 1, he began asking Giacosa for the rest of the libretto and for changes in the existing text. By spring 1902 Puccini was criticizing the first scenes of Giacosa's act 2, while the infuriated librettist took his case to Ricordi, complaining about the wide-ranging revisions Puccini had asked for. These included the entire love duet of act 1 and an overhaul of most of act 2 at a time when he had not even begun act 3. November brought a new request for "radical changes."

At that point the Consulate Scene filled the entire middle of the opera. Then Puccini suddenly decided to drop it, saying it would lead him straight into a fiasco. Instead, he wanted to reshape the work as a two-act opera, both acts to take place in Butterfly's house. That, he said, would work, although the second act would last an hour and a half! At first Illica stood up for his convictions, defending the Consulate Scene as "modern" and having "everything." It even had a reappearance of the remorseful tenor, with a reunion between Sharpless and Pinkerton, at the end of which the remorseful Pinkerton flees. The act also had the meeting between Cio-Cio-San and Kate Pinkerton. Puccini listened, but would not budge. Over Illica's and Giacosa's protests, the act was dropped, although some parts were moved to the last act, where Pinkerton, Sharpless, and Kate appear.

When 1903 began, Puccini was still in Torre del Lago, trying to solve problems in the scene with Butterfly and Kate in the garden. As he often did, he wanted it shortened, because he could not afford to have a minor character take up large blocks of stage time. At loggerheads over his cherished idea, he met Giacosa and Illica in Milan. By then Giacosa, a seasoned veteran of the theater, was convinced that the long second act would ruin the opera. As he said again and again, it was a disaster. No audience would stand for it, at least in an Italian opera. He begged Puccini to bring down the curtain after Butterfly's vigil; but Puccini refused and clung to his two-act scheme. After a heated exchange and angry letters, Giacosa quit. Puccini then felt abandoned and complained that everything was falling apart. He sent Illica the bad news. "All in all, almost a complete break with him," Puccini said, but he answered another of Giacosa's angry letters. It seemed that their collaboration had ended.

The Crash

Toward the end of February 1903, Puccini prepared to leave Milan for Lucca and Torre del Lago. Uneasy about the trip, he decided to take the car, but he wrote to Illica that he hoped God would see him through. He had every reason to be worried, for he had had an accident only eight months earlier, when he slid into a ditch near Lucca. He and Guido Vandini, his passenger, had suffered bruises and scratches, but neither was seriously injured. Since then, he had driven without incident. On the twenty-fifth, Puccini and Elvira decided to go to Lucca, to see friends and perhaps take care of personal business. What they did during the day is not clear, but they had dinner with Alfredo Caselli. By the time they were ready to leave, it was so late that their host urged them to stay overnight, but for whatever reason, Puccini declined. He, Elvira, Tonio, and their chauffeur left the city; and before they had gone far, their car overturned on a country road. The story released by Ricordi was this: Puccini and "those closest to him" spent time with friends and stayed late, chatting. (Another account even named the restaurant where they had eaten and the time they left Lucca.) Their friends begged them not to go on. It was very cold and dark when Puccini started home, with Elvira and Tonio in the car and the chauffeur driving.

In his biography of Puccini, Del Fiorentino told another story, one that he heard from people in his family. According to them, Puccini and Elvira had not only visited with friends in Lucca but had also stopped to see her husband, Narciso Gemignani, who, people said, was dying. "Now Gemignani was seriously ill and near the end of his life. All this, of course, was true. Now the rumor-mongers said that Elvira had gone to see him, hoping that he would change his will and leave this world without bitterness. So she had driven with Puccini to Lucca, but as soon as they reached Gemignani's house, they were set upon by a host of [his] angry relatives, all intent upon seeing that the will was written in their favor. They barred the door and refused to let Elvira in, and asked her why she was not cringing with shame for all the harm she had done to her husband." After she was turned away, she and Puccini set out for Torre (Del Fiorentino, p. 7).

The truth may never be known, but Del Fiorentino's account is at least as believable as the version released by Ricordi. No one knows whether Elvira managed to see her husband that day, or whether she saw her oldest son, then or at any other time. Accounts of her relationship with Renato are missing from biographies of the composer. Whatever the circumstances, Puccini decided to make a dangerous trip from Lucca to Torre del Lago on a foggy, pitch-dark night. In 1903 very few people would have risked driving at night in the fog with low-wattage headlights. His route led through the countryside on narrow, twisting, unpaved roads that were then scarcely better than mule tracks.

The facts of the crash are clear: the weather was bad, and when Puccini's driver got to the hamlet of Vignola di San Macario, about three miles outside Lucca, he failed to negotiate a curve by a bridge and ran off the road. The car plunged about sixteen yards down a small gully by the bridge and turned over in a field. Fortunately, one villager saw what happened. And a physician, astonished to hear the sound of a motor on such a bad night, looked out his window and realized that the car had crashed. Dr. Sbragia lit a lantern and ran; several farmers, also carrying lanterns, joined him. They found Elvira and Tonio bruised and shaken but not seriously hurt. The driver, who, like them, had been thrown from the car, lay on the grass, crying out in pain. His leg was broken at the thigh. But the searchers could not find Puccini, even though they called out to him, which might make us think that he was unconscious. Finally he was found under the overturned car; he lay in a little hollow; and that probably had saved him from being crushed by the vehicle. The car hung over him, resting on the trunk of a tree that it had hit and brought down. He was in a state of shock. At first he could not speak, and when he began to recover his senses, he realized that he had injured his right leg. After Puccini was moved to a nearby home a surgeon from Lucca, Dr. Guarnieri, arrived. Both Dr. Sbragia and Dr. Guarieri saw that two parts of the fractured leg were out of line, and there was bleeding. Both urged Puccini to go to the hospital in Lucca, but he refused. The next day a stretcher was laid in a wagon, so he could be moved to the lakeshore villa of Marchese Carlo Ginori-Lisci, his friend. From there Puccini was taken by boat across Lake Massaciuccoli to Torre del Lago.

Whatever the circumstances of the accident, its association with the date of Narciso Gemignani's death is clear. Elvira's husband died the next day, on February 26, only a few hours after the crash that almost cost Puccini his life. Michele Girardi claims that Gemignani, a relentless womanizer, died from injuries he got when an angry husband attacked him (Girardi, *Giacomo Puccini,* p. 50). As soon as newspaper accounts of the crash appeared, telegrams began to pour in, about three hundred in all. Among them were good wishes from the king of Italy, whom Puccini had met. Cabinet ministers and many Italian and French impresarios also wrote, as did Mascagni, who was in San Francisco. Nothing, however, came from Franchetti, "Il Baronissimo."

Three days after the crash, Dr. Guarnieri and a specialist from Florence visited Puccini in Torre and began supervising his long, painful recovery. First he was immobilized in a cast, then he graduated to an orthopedic device, then to crutches. In the months that followed, this restless patient smoked thirty cigarettes a day. Confined to bed for more than a month, he grew so thin that his legs shriveled; he was put on a high-calorie diet. Next he suffered from edema. Pain kept him awake, and at night he could hear the two sections of bone grinding together when he moved. During the course of treatment, he found he was diabetic. After his physicians reset the leg, he consulted with another doctor, who came down from Genoa to examine him. Then an X ray showed that his leg would need at least three months more to heal. Unable to move, he could not even sit at his old upright piano. Finally, when Puccini began feeling better, he ordered a grand piano delivered and worked several hours a day. He sent this good news to Giacosa, who had by then agreed to help this invalid and make the final corrections in the libretto. Later he graduated from a metal brace to a wheelchair, crutches, two canes, and one walking stick, which he used for years.

Most troubling to him was the fact that Ricordi did not send him a letter for months after the accident, although he did communicate occasionally by telegram. Then came Ricordi's accusatory letter of May 31, with its blanket denunciation of Puccini's sexual behavior and his affair with Corinna. Not knowing that the composer was diabetic, he even suspected that syphilis caused his illness. That, he feared, would lead to the paresis that had killed Donizetti (GR to GP, May 31, 1903, in Gara, pp. 240–241). Puccini took this scouring as a well-meant reproach from his surrogate father, but he protested to Illica that Ricordi had got everything wrong. Corinna was not a whore; and he did not have venereal disease. Soon he was back in his publisher's good graces, chiefly because he swore to give up Corinna. Nevertheless, his relationship with Ricordi changed after these events.

Puccini's health gradually improved. He spent part of the summer in the quiet mountain village of Boscolungo Abetone, north of Bagni di Lucca and Cutigliano, about seventy miles from Lucca. The 1895 Baedeker described Boscolungo as a popular center for hikers, located in a "fine forest" near the watershed between the Adriatic and the Tyrrhenian seas. Puccini loved his little villa there and told Fosca everyone envied him for it. He furnished the house with large pieces brought up from Chiatri, and he bought an upright piano, a sign his leg was better.

The Settlement with Corinna

Puccini, an invalid, was hounded by Elvira, Ricordi, and his sisters, all demanding that he stop seeing Corinna and marry Elvira. That spring he agreed to use Luigi Pieri, an old friend, and two attorneys—one of them was Carlo Nasi—as his intermediaries in persuading Corinna to accept his decision gracefully. That she would not do. Even Illica found himself caught in this tangle. Finally, a clause was added to the agreement with Corinna that stipulated that Puccini would publicly announce his imminent marriage to Elvira. This was added so Corinna would not feel so injured, for she evidently had expected Puccini to marry her instead.

The negotiations took at least nine months; and when Corinna realized that Puccini really intended to leave her, she wrote him a long letter threatening legal action and swearing to use his love letters against him. As Elvira described the situation in a later letter, Puccini even risked going to prison over this young woman and became so frightened that he considered moving to Switzerland (EBP to GP, March 25, 1909, in A. Marchetti, pp. 356–365). In November 1903 Corinna demanded a personal meeting with him; and it was this meeting that Elvira was trying to prevent when she wrote to Ricordi for help. The following are two of her letters to him. The initial capital letters in my translation reflect Elvira's use of "He," "Him," and "You." She refers to Puccini as "Egli" and "Lui," and to Ricordi as "Ella," the formal usage.

Sunday evening
[probably written from Torre del Lago]

Dearest Sig[nor] Giulio

Just this moment I learned that while I was in Milan, He [Puccini] wrote to the woman from Turin [Corinna], begging her to stop her legal action and come to a direct understanding with Him. Now I am clear about the reason for the letter that woman wrote! I have not yet said anything to Him, so as not to cause trouble for the person who told me this, and it seems that was also Carignani's advice! The best thing would be for You to summon Him to Milan as quickly as possible, because here He only becomes [more and more] convinced that He is right [*qui non fa che montargli la testa*]. And You had faith in all the proposals He made at the station! Believe me, Sig. Giulio, to be sure about Giacomo, You have to get that perfidious, big troublemaker [*quel perfido bazzone*] away from Him.

Again, many apologies and thanks for everything You are doing in this ugly business. Together with my most cordial good wishes, [I send] eternal gratitude from Elvira. [EBG to GR, undated, The Pierpont Morgan Library, New York]

Torre December 6, 1903

Dearest Sig Giulio

I know that Giacomo has written to Nasi to ask his advice about whether to agree to have a face-to-face meeting with the woman from Turin, I think that the attorney will be smart enough to tell Him not to do this, but in any case, I think that it would not be a bad idea if You warn [Nasi] to write to Giacomo, telling Him not to bother any further with this, leaving Him to settle this matter. Don't You think I have the right idea? Because sometimes Nasi, not knowing the character of that individual [Corinna], could let Him get carried away [*lasciarsi prendere*], all the more since He is saying that the sole purpose of this face-to-face meeting would be to try to settle this thing amicably, and not to lose money [*non sacrificar denari*], because in His naïveté, He believes that woman would be affected by His words!! His [Nasi's] [or your, Ricordi's] telegram of yesterday calmed Him down a little, but that is what was needed to convince Him not to write [to her]!!

I apologize for the continuing annoyance, and send You a cordial handshake from your Elvira. [EBG to GR, December 6, 1903, The Pierpont Morgan Library, New York]

Clearly desperate to stop Puccini from seeing Corinna again, Elvira took this circuitous route in asking for help: Ricordi should write to Nasi so the attorney would, in turn, write to Puccini—and this at a time when she and Puccini were together in their home every day. In a sense, this was a last-minute appeal, for at this point the ten months that she had to wait before marrying again would end in about two weeks. That was when she and Puccini's sisters wanted the marriage to take place. Even in this situation, and with Elvira, Ricordi, and Nasi trying to stop him, Puccini did meet Corinna again, perhaps in Viareggio, Torre, or Chiesaccia.

Elvira described to Ramelde the violent aftermath of that meeting. After Corinna went home, Puccini argued with Elvira and even gave her a punch. The next day Puccini was out hunting when Caselli came to the house, giving this unhappy woman a chance to confide in him. She also begged Ramelde to come to Torre as quickly as possible, because Puccini apparently argued less with her when guests were in the house. Elvira concluded the letter by saying, "In my present situation, knowing that someone is thinking kindly of me and feels pity for me lifts my sad, sad spirit a bit!" (EBG to RPF, in A. Marchetti, p. 286). Through it all, it was evident, not the least to Elvira, that Puccini loved Corinna.

The matter seemed settled when he agreed to announce his upcoming marriage to Elvira. A document was drawn up for both to sign. Under its terms, he would marry Elvira on a given day, and Corinna would make no further trouble, for which she would receive a substantial settlement. At the height of the battle, Puccini, profoundly depressed, complained to Illica, saying that he was friendless and alone because no one loved him.

The Bonds of Marriage

As soon as Elvira's waiting period ended, she and Puccini were married. On January 3, 1904, Cesare Riccioni, the mayor of Viareggio, conducted the civil rite in their house. The witnesses were Giuseppe Razzi, Elvira's brother-in-law, and Dr. Rodolfo Giacchi, the municipal physician in Torre. Then the couple married in a religious ceremony in the parish church in Torre del Lago. To guard against any chance invasion of their privacy, they had asked the diocese for a dispensation from the reading or publication of the marriage banns. Puccini also asked Father Giuseppe Michelucci, the parish priest, to marry them at ten o'clock at night. The curtains were pulled over the nave windows to prevent anyone from seeing a light in the church at that odd hour or stumbling in on them.

In the register the entry read: "Maestro Giacomo Puccini, son of Michele and Albina Magi, and Elvira Bonturi, widow of Narciso Gemignani, born in Lucca and residing in this parish, having obtained the dispensation from the three canonical banns, not being impeded by criminal records and having no canonical impediment now existing against the valid and lawful celebration of their marriage, having been questioned [by the priest], and their [declarations] having been received, were by me here, subscribed the third of January 1904, united in the holy bonds of Matrimony in the presence of two witnesses, Dr. Rodolfo Giacchi and Giuseppe Razzi" (Del Fiorentino, p. 114). Father Michelucci later told Del

Fiorentino that Puccini gave him a generous donation after the ceremony, saying, "This is to thank you, for you have made me very happy." With this rite, Puccini fulfilled his legal obligation to Elvira and satisfied his sisters, but perhaps not himself. The next day he sent a bitter, scattered letter to Ramelde, asking, "Now are you calm?" He added, "Iginia will be glad," as if he had lived through a shotgun marriage (GP to RPF, January 4, 1904, in A. Marchetti, p. 290).

The Howling Fiasco of *Butterfly*

One day after the wedding, Puccini left to prepare the premiere of *Butterfly* in Milan. At his side were Giacosa and Illica, who had continued working with him. Rehearsals went smoothly, with Cleofonte Campanini conducting. Giovanni Zenatello was Pinkerton, and Giuseppe De Luca sang Sharpless (a role he often repeated during a long career, including one memorable performance in Newark, New Jersey, near the end of his life). Rosina Storchio, whom the composer had chosen, took the all-important title role. No newcomer to Milan, the soprano had made her debut at the Teatro Dal Verme in 1892 and had sung in *Werther* at La Scala three years later. With dependable singers, a competent conductor, a very good orchestra, faithfully executed settings and costumes, a successful dress rehearsal, and a sold-out house, Puccini felt confident enough to invite twelve friends and relatives as his guests. On February 17, 1904, with the opening a few hours away, he sent a note to Storchio, congratulating her on her interpretation and anticipating a triumphant first night. Neither he nor any of his collaborators could have predicted the disaster that followed.

The composer, disbelieving and in shock, watched *Madama Butterfly* go down as one of the classic fiascoes in the history of opera. It began badly, when people recognized fragments of melody they had heard before, favorite phrases that they could even hum. They compared it to *Manon Lescaut* and *Bohème*, whispering complaints about "old stuff." Puccini took two curtain calls, but only two, after the love duet and the act 1 curtain, a very bad sign. Worse, when he came from backstage leaning on a cane, people laughed. Gradually whistles and shouts of protest overwhelmed the scattered applause, causing long stretches during which the singers could not hear the orchestra. "Butterfly is pregnant," one man shouted when a breeze swelled Storchio's kimono. Giacosa, who had begged Puccini to create a three-act opera, saw that he was right. As Butterfly and Suzuki begin their vigil, applause broke out, for people thought the act had ended. They shouted "Encore" and cried for Puccini to take a bow. He did not, and the Humming Chorus and the Interlude followed. Humming choruses were always risky, as Verdi had discovered in Venice in 1851, when he tried to get the male chorus to hum during part of the storm scene in *Rigoletto*. Verdi got through, and *Rigoletto* was a hit. Puccini was unfortunate, because shouts and whistles broke out as soon as the humming began; the audience had had enough. As one critic said, the long orchestral piece delayed the action and started the long downhill slide to the end. At several points, Storchio was crying onstage when she could not hear the orchestra. Ramelde wrote home, saying she could not imagine how the performers got through it, because she had not heard a note of the last scenes and had fled the theater as soon as the curtain came down. Given the history of fiascoes in Italy, Puccini was lucky to get to the end of the show.

One review, perhaps written by Ricordi himself, described the catastrophe. "Groans, roars, moos, laughs, bellows, sneers, the usual cries for encores that were intended to inflame the audience even more—that, in brief, is how the public at La Scala welcomed the new opera by Maestro Giacomo Puccini. After this pandemonium, during which almost nothing could be heard, people walked out of the theater, as contented as lambs! Never have we seen so many happy faces . . . in the lobby. . . . The show in the [audience] was as well-organized as the one onstage, beginning just as the curtain went up." Ricordi and the composer believed the demonstration had been staged by jealous rivals who had waited years to bring him down. Puccini described the evening as a virtual lynching; but he believed in the opera, which he described to Ramelde as "daisies thrown to swine" (GP to RPF, February 28, 1904, in A. Marchetti, p. 296).

Other reviews, however, were mixed; some were even balanced. In general, the critics praised Puccini's skill as a composer but blamed the fiasco on his lack of originality. In every opera his main characters were alike. The opera was fragmentary, a patchwork of earlier works. It lacked coherence; the scenes were "snapshots." Again they blasted his sentimentality and accused him of having created another tearjerker. It was small, an "operetta." That accusation had been hurled at Puccini before. Where, one critic asked, was Puccini's growth? Where were the larger themes, the daunting challenges? Where was the moral message? It was time for him to write something more coherent and more complex. Ricordi soon began saying the same things.

Sipping from what he called "the bitter cup," Puccini raged against despicable, heartless, unfeeling "cowards, pigs, and cretins"; the "cruel" Milanese audience; and the critics, who were "dogs." But he swore to God and the angels that he cared more about *Butterfly* than about his earlier works, and that he had poured sincere emotion into it (GP to AB and LI, February 1904, in Gara, pp. 264–266.)

Pascoli: "The Little Butterfly Will Fly Again"

As letters and telegrams of condolence poured in, one of the first to console him was from Pascoli, who sent a poem to "Our dear, great Maestro":

> The little butterfly will fly.
> Her wings are covered with dust
> and drops of water,
> drops of blood, teardrops.
> Fly, fly, little butterfly,
> you who wept from your heart
> and made your bard [il tuo cantore] weep.
> Sing, sing, little butterfly,
> you call out in your dreams,
> with your little voice,
> as fragile as sleep,
> as sweet as a shadow
> as gentle as the tomb,
> under the bamboo trees
> in Nagasaki and Cefù. [Pascoli to GP, A. Marchetti, pp. 296, 299n.3]

Puccini thanked Pascoli, saying that he, too, was sure the fragile creature would fly again.

On the morning after the ill-fated premiere, Puccini, Illica, and Giacosa sent the directors of La Scala a brief note, saying that, with Ricordi's full approval, they were withdrawing the score and asking that all further performances be canceled. Ricordi refunded the rental fees; then he and Tito held a conference with Puccini and the librettists about saving the opera. Giacosa, who agreed to make the necessary cuts and changes, began sending them to Puccini within days, so that the first act and much of the second were finished by the end of the month. Puccini's extensive revisions made it a three-act opera, the work Giacosa had long argued for. Next, Ricordi had to find a theater that would produce it—not an easy task after such a clamorous failure. Then Tito Ricordi suggested giving it in the Teatro Grande in Brescia, where Puccini's operas had always been welcome.

Butterfly had its first resoundingly good performance there on May 24, 1904, with Campanini again conducting. Butterfly was Salomea Krusceniski, who lent weight to her role with an Aida voice, a voice much heavier than Storchio's. Krusceniski also had a personal tie to Puccini, for she married one of his staunchest supporters, Cesare Riccioni, the mayor of Viareggio. Zenatello was again Pinkerton, much more comfortable than he had been in Milan. Discussing *Butterfly* in New York in the 1940s, Zenatello said Puccini had to transpose down the act 1 love duet because the La Scala version lay too high for him. With its revisions, its solid cast and conductor, and a sympathetic audience, the opera was a hit, a "colossal" success, as Illica said. The presence of Boito lent additional luster to the event. Seven numbers were repeated; the critical second and third performances went as well as the first; and a long engagement followed. Puccini learned that the last night had a sold-out audience, one greater than any the Grande had ever seen.

Long before the end of the run, he left for Acqui Terme, a spa northwest of Genoa, where he treated his diabetes, took mud baths, slept, and complained because all the women were over sixty. August and part of September were spent at Boscolungo Abetone. The success of *Butterfly* in Brescia left him with new burdens: monitoring productions of it to see it produced as he wished; keeping his earlier works alive; and finding a new subject, for without it the flow of royalties would dry up. Another serious concern was Ricordi's attitude toward him, which he thought had changed.

The Composer in Crisis

On March 2, 1904, "an ugly day" a mere two weeks after the *Butterfly* fiasco, a battered Puccini complained to Illica about his "damned swine of a life." Unable to put a single note of music on paper, he felt sure his audience had deserted him: "And also they are fed up with my sugary music now" (GP to LI, in Gara, pp. 265–266). Although written in a moment of sheer despair, his phrase *"mia musica zuccherata"* illuminates a moment of self-analysis and scrutiny about his work. Beginning with *Manon Lescaut,* few professional critics had seriously questioned his skill in composition and orchestration, but several never stopped hounding him about the size and scope of his operas; and as he read the bad reviews of *Butterfly,* he took their attacks very personally. Whenever his "wound" started to heal, he said, some reviewer would stick his "dirty fingers" in it.

At about that same time, Ricordi began doubting Puccini's ability to grow. By 1904 their all-important professional collaboration had survived for twenty years, with the publisher backing his composer with all the authority and power of the three-generation-old firm. Equally important to both, and certainly to Puccini, was their friendship. In one unguarded moment, the usually distant and reserved publisher even admitted to having developed a real affection for his protégé, while Puccini almost found a surrogate father in him. Ricordi's attitude changed, however, after the crisis over Corinna and the fiasco of *Butterfly.* True, theaters began to ask for it after the Brescia production. By spring 1905 it had been seen in Buenos Aires and was scheduled to return there; it was also on the programs of the Teatro Dal Verme in Milan, the Comunale in Bologna, and the Regio in Turin. Ricordi certainly had no reason to give up on it, nor could he ignore the projected box office figures. None of this, however, stopped him from defending his aesthetic positions and urging Puccini to try something more ambitious. As the owner since the 1880s of the Luccas' firm and its imposing list of foreign composers, Wagner among others, Ricordi inevitably compared them with Puccini; and, for the first time, he seemed to turn against the "little weepers," and especially *Butterfly.*

His demeanor shocked Puccini, who confided his dismay to Illica in 1905. "I knew about Sig. Giulio's lack of faith in *Butterfly,* but I didn't know it was this bad. . . . [He liked it] right through the rehearsals at La Scala.

Now that he has changed his mind, and changed his mind about all my work, calling everything I have done 'little sketches' [*bozzetti*], this is truly discouraging and demoralizing for me" (GP to LI, March 3, 1905, in Gara, p. 288). But in the end not even this crisis could push Puccini toward a work that did not convince him. He refused to consider "patchworks [*centoni*]" or what he referred to as "the so-called grand operas" and the "*operone,*" the big opera Ricordi wanted. This conflict accounts in part for the fact that Puccini spent frantic years, from 1904 to 1908, reading plays, novels, and short stories and going to the theater whenever he could. On the cusp of change, he veered toward the future, then—almost against his will—turned back to the past. He looked to Illica and *Maria Antonietta,* but was also pushing for Gorky and reading the novellas of Tolstoy and Turgenev.

Longing to change course entirely and write three short one-act operas, he found Ricordi absolutely opposed to something so expensive to cast and produce. In the event, years passed during which the composer seemed unable to satisfy anyone, least of all himself. Some long-standing Lucchese friendships became strained, some ruptured, and others were patched together again. The decades-long friendship with Mascagni ended. Even the loyal Illica felt unsure of himself when he wrote to ask Ricordi, "Who knows whether Puccini, with a change of librettist, might find what he wants, dreams of, hopes for, and vainly seeks?" (LI to GR, [May 1905], in Gara, pp. 294–295). In fact, Puccini had already begun to contact other librettists, D'Annunzio among them, beginning in 1900. In 1904 he became interested in the works of a busy contemporary writer, Valentino Soldani. Writing to Soldani about his frantic search for material, he described himself as nervous and sleepless, longing to find something like *Bohème,* with comic and tragic elements but with less sweet sentimentality. Or if not that, then something great, new, and packed with emotion. With his "mind in flames" and his "soul gone astray," he began to consider Soldani's *Margherita da Cortona,* which might have made a perfect subject for him, in spite of his reservations about medieval subjects.

Margherita was a Tuscan penitent and mystic, born in 1247. She bore an illegitimate child, a son. At one point, she also married. Nine years after her child's birth, she sought asylum among the Franciscans in Cortona, where she lived a life of expiation, tended the friars' kitchen garden, cared for her little black-and-white mongrel dog, nursed the sick, and founded a hospital and a religious order called the Poor Little Women, Le Poverelle. Her ecstatic visions led many people to see her as a holy figure, and she was canonized in 1728. Buried in Cortona, she was adored in Tuscany. Puccini found her a woman of passionate faith; her story resembles in many ways that of his later Suor Angelica. In that opera the nun, Sister Angelica, had an illegitimate child, a son. As a penitent, she tended a garden in a convent setting, had transcendent visions, and was redeemed in the end. The message of *Margherita da Cortona* also looks toward *La Fanciulla del West,* with its message of human redemption.

Urging Soldani to "put in more visions" and pay more attention to miracles in the story, Puccini worked with him on this project for more than a year. He liked the first act and the setting but disliked the finale, he said. Writing in December 1905, he encouraged Soldani by saying he was satisfied. "All in all, we've got most of it." In Milan later that month, he said he was so nervous that he felt like a sailboat harried by the south wind called the *libeccio,* because he saw everything around him as false and dishonest. "The fact is that [when I am] here, I am sick in body and soul," discouraged by the length and size of *Maria Antonietta,* yet somehow taken with its tragedy and the story of the French Revolution. Nevertheless, he had not forgotten "my dear 1200s and Margherita" (GP to Soldani, December 15 and 30, 1905, in Gara, pp. 308–309).

Soon after New Year's Day 1906, he confessed to Soldani that *Maria Antonietta* was about to go up in smoke; in one of his next letters, he swore that the sun was setting forever on that project, and in another he swore that he had definitely decided against it the previous night. Back to *Margherita da Cortona;* he poured out more than a dozen suggestions for the libretto: more exposure for the chorus, more drama, a more intense moment of reconciliation. Six days later he warned Soldani that the drama and characters did not work. Having told his librettist, "We've got most of it," he wrote twenty days later to say, "We've not got it." Railing about many scenes, he declared, "I cannot start thinking about Margherita again," and yet he went on.

For *Margherita da Cortona* he said he wanted something very simple, the kind of thing he saw in the architecture and frescoes of the 1200s, and instead Soldani gave him a wordy libretto and the "usual" and well-worn panoply of medieval life with characters that "were asleep." Two days later he sent off a list of things that should be changed. After reading the first act to get several friends' reactions, another round of suggestions was fired off. Then, wracked by nervous tension, he felt miserable over what Soldani had done. Above all, he dreaded seeing the project fail, because he had "dreamed about this Margherita for so long," seeing her as someone who would save him, a "mirage I could keep in sight." It was "really sad," but in the next sentence he wrote, "But I am not in despair! No! This or something else will pop up" (GP to Soldani, January 1906, in Gara, pp. 310–316). Promising to visit Soldani in Florence, he dropped *Margherita da Cortona* after fifteen months of work. He may, however, have had this Tuscan penitent in mind years later, when he wrote *Suor Angelica*. One month after dumping Soldani, he turned again to D'Annunzio, but there, too, his hopes were dashed. As Illica often complained, the composer wanted "something," but did not know what that "something" was. Eugenio Gara, the editor of *Carteggi pucciniani,* said it best: He had to find something different. But how, but where?

London and Sybil Seligman

In autumn 1904 Puccini left for England, where *Manon Lescaut* was to open the season at Covent Garden in October with Rina Giachetti in the title role, Caruso as Des Grieux, and Campanini conducting. *Tosca* followed. Both were real triumphs. Puccini was honored at a gala at the Savoy Hotel, where he always stayed. During this visit, he began a friendship that lasted for the rest of his life. Sybil Seligman, to whom the composer Paolo Tosti introduced him, was the wife of a London banker and the mother of a young son. She invited Puccini to dinner; and his acceptance, dated October 22, 1904, is the earliest letter from him that Vincent Seligman, Sybil's son, found in his mother's collection. It is one of more than seven hundred that the composer wrote during his intense personal association with this elegant, intelligent, beautiful woman. Gradually, Puccini found welcome emotional release in the flood of their letters, finding in Sybil the perfect confidante. As he sometimes said, she was the only person who understood him. Even in occasionally awkward English translations, these letters reveal a Puccini who emerges in no other correspondence.

According to Violet Schiff, Sybil's sister, Sybil and Puccini had a brief, early sexual relationship that soon turned platonic, because Sybil would not risk a scandal that would wreck her reputation, end her marriage, and perhaps cut her off from her son. Hers was the turn-of-the-century sphere of the Schiffs, the Warburgs, the Eberstadt sisters, Otto Kahn, and Lady De Grey, people who lived for society, art, and music, wintered in Nice, Monte Carlo, and St. Moritz, and spent the summers in Italy. However, Puccini saw Sybil not as a social butterfly but as a wise, sincere, trustworthy friend. She also helped him professionally. An amateur singer and a trained musician, an active theater enthusiast and opera lover, she reported on singers and scouted for plays that might not otherwise have come to his attention. Even some of their earliest letters are about "the search." In autumn 1905 he thanked her for calling his attention to Rudyard Kipling's *The Light That Failed,* a play taken from the novel of the same name. Although he said he had no interest in many works she proposed, works such as *Mérimée, Anna Karenina, The Last Days of Pompeii,* and *Enoch Arden,* he seriously considered others. She was particularly helpful when he began studying Belasco's *The Girl of the Golden West.* One year after their first meeting, he fondly recalled their "unforgettable" days in London and the "sweetness of your character, the walks in the Park, the melodiousness of your voice, and your radiant beauty," and missed her "charming and delightful company" (GP to SS, November 5, 1905, in Seligman, p. 69).

The Continuing Fortunes of *Butterfly*

Madama Butterfly was first heard at Covent Garden in the summer season of 1905; and Puccini agreed to oversee its return that autumn, when it would have Rina Giachetti, Giovanni Zenatello, and Mario Sammarco in the cast. From London he wrote to Toscanini, who was then in Bologna directing a strange season that included everything from *Hänsel und Gretel* to a landmark *Siegfried* (with Giuseppe Borgatti) and *Butterfly.* In a letter written from the Savoy on October 12, he reported on the earlier London production and his current one and spoke of his hopes for the upcoming *Butterfly* in Bologna.

Carissimo Toscanini, I am very unhappy to have to tell you that it is impossible for me to come to Bologna when *Butterfly* is produced there! Here things are going slowly; imagine that we have not yet even begun rehearsals! The opera really had a big success here in July, and we all expect that it will go well and hopefully will be sung better. You know how things are rushed in these Italian seasons abroad, so to get a good performance, we need rehearsals and [more] rehearsals; and I would never let anything contaminate the chances for a good outcome; so now there is a delay, and it will take days before everything can go as it should. The premiere here will not be given before Monday, a week from now. How can I manage to come there in time? Even you will understand this; but I am calm. You know how much esteem I feel for you, so that I entrust the opera to you and feel secure and tranquil with it in your hands.

Be careful to get the [right] effect in the third act, with the lanterns that flicker out when the sun rises at the first moment of dawn, as if they had run out of oil, because all the intermezzo or half of the descriptive prelude must be played. You must also play the scene with the baritone in the second act [*"Aria Imperatore"*], quickly [*con agitazione*]. [Puccini later removed this aria from the opera.]

If by chance the date for the first performance should be changed, I beg you to let me know. Addio, dear Arturo; when the performances are under way, I will come to hear you, and I will certainly admire you once more. Please care about me [*voglimi bene*]. Your affectionate Giacomo Puccini. [GP to AT, October 12, 1905, NYPLPA, Music Division, Wanda Toscanini Horowitz Donation]

The *"Aria Imperatore"* appeared in Giacosa's text and in the original score in the scene when Sharpless goes to Butterfly's house. She tells him that should Pinkerton abandon her, she could imagine standing on a crowded street with their son in her arms. Then "warriors will pass by with the Emperor." The ruler will stop, and in his grace, will make her child a Prince of the Realm.

His next letter, also on Savoy Hotel letterhead, is undated. "Dear Toscanini, Two words about the staging. Last scene, when Suzuki closes [the house], the stage must become completely dark, with few [lights from the footlights]; and when the baby enters through the door that leads outside [*porta d'uscita*], an intense ray of sunshine will come [from there], strong, and a broad shaft of light, within the orbit of which the entire final scene will take place. Addio, affectionate greetings, Giacomo Puccini" (GP to AT, undated [October 1905], NYPLPA, Music Division, Wanda Toscanini Horowitz Donation). And on October 24 Puccini had more to say about the aria in a telegram to Toscanini. "I will be there Friday; I believe effective tempo for the *"Aria Imperatore"* almost *agitato* good quick great impression end of the piece" (GP to AT, telegram, October 24, 1905, NYPLPA, Music Division, Wanda Toscanini Horowitz Donation). As this correspondence shows, the composer remained on the alert even when he could count on a great conductor.

Reaching Bologna in time to oversee the rehearsals for *Butterfly,* he stayed at the Hotel Baglioni. In the theater he struggled to get his effects, a difficult job because he disliked the singers, even Krusceniski, who had sung so well in the "redeemed" *Butterfly* in Brescia. "I had to fight like anything in Bologna, but it was a real success," he wrote to Sybil. "Toscanini conducted marvelously, the rest were good, but not more than good" (GP to SS, October 30, 1905, in Seligman, p. 69).

However, he was not quite honest with her, because the audience for the first performance had been quite cool, a fact he mentioned in his next letter to Toscanini. He wrote from the Baglioni, perhaps even hours after the curtain came down.

"Dear Toscanini, Again a million thanks for all the intelligence and heart you poured into my *Butt[erfly]*. I hope that the audience's severe and unjust judgment (or at least the far from serene [judgment]) will change during the next performances, and I beg you to tell me about it in Milan, Via Verdi 4. I hope things will change, and then I will come back again from Torre del Lago to enjoy your splendid interpretation. About Turin [in 1906], even if the little tenor [Emilio De Marchi] did not do a bad job, I insist that he be changed, this is a little artist who does not wreck things, but he adds nothing in terms of effectiveness, whether with his voice or with his physical appearance in the role. Greetings [from] Elvira and your affectionate Giacomo Puccini" (GP to AT, October 30, 1905, NYPLPA, Music Division, Wanda Toscanini Horowitz Donation.)

Later that night, again from Bologna, he sent Toscanini his revisions and cuts for the opera. "Dear Toscanini, I would make another cut, in the toilette, from page 309 at the 9th bar at the last chord [he added a musical example] I would place a long rest, and Suzuki dresses Butt[erfly]'s hair in a bit of a hurry, and I would go on to page 315 [another musical example]. What do you think about it? Like this, and also by making the Imperial cut [cutting the *'Aria Imperatore'*], it seems to me that the act runs more smoothly. I beg you to send me news of the second performance. Your

G. Puccini" (GP to AT, October 30, 1905, NYPLPA, Music Division, Wanda Toscanini Horowitz Donation). Puccini often asked Toscanini's opinion about his scores, so this letter was not unusual.

Although he had originally planned to go to Turin, where Toscanini was conducting the first production of *Butterfly* in the recently restored Teatro Regio, he decided against the trip, because he had "had second thoughts" and was afraid his presence might turn the audience against the opera. People were right in not judging the opera on the first night, he added, but he had suffered too much over their "just reservations" about it, their *giuste riserve* (GP to AT, January 1, 1906, NYPLPA, Music Division, Wanda Toscanini Horowitz Donation). Although he sometimes feared failure, most productions of *Butterfly* went well enough, at least after the first performance, and the opera found its place in the repertory. Puccini saw *Butterfly* return in triumph to Milan on October 12, 1905, under the baton of Tullio Serafin. The audience at the Teatro Dal Verme was so enthusiastic that Butterfly's entrance, sung by Angelica Pandolfini, had to be encored—fifteen curtain calls for her, and more for the tenor, Edoardo Garbin.

Puccini at that moment was still spending most of his time on *Maria Antonietta* and hounding Illica about it. He had ample support from the librettist, who described the opera as "So Puccinian! And so strong at the same time! So grandiose, so much an *operone* [a big opera] in its settings, and so humanly gentle, and so feminine!" Puccini, also convinced of its potential, leapt ahead from questions about the plot to matters of casting, asking Illica whether they should set the first act in Vienna or at the Trianon, and whether insurmountable problems would follow when they tried to find a soprano to sing the title role. But he was also burdened by doubts: the baritone role was too thin; the last scenes were perhaps not beautiful enough; they might not be effective. "I am eating my soul," Puccini wrote, and Ricordi, in Milan, was "eating a lobe of his liver because of us" (GP to LI, November 11, 1905, in Gara, p. 302). Dozens of letters about *Maria Antonietta* were exchanged over the years.

In autumn 1906 the first French *Butterfly* went badly in Paris, where Albert Carré and his wife, Marguerite, a soprano, wanted cuts and extensive revisions made. As Puccini had confided to Sybil in July, Ricordi was against these changes, feeling that it was beneath the composer's dignity to make them. But Madame Carré had a virtual monopoly on the leading role in France; Puccini thus did what she requested so he could get his opera performed at the Opéra Comique. During this visit, he heard Debussy's *Pelléas et Mélisande,* which he described to Ricordi as having "extraordinary harmonic qualities and diaphanous sensations in the instrumentation [*senzazioni diafane strumentali*]. It is truly interesting, in spite of its somber color, as monotonous as a Franciscan's habit. The subject is interesting" (GP to GR, November 15, 1906, in Adami, pp. 159–160).

Since its productions in Brescia and Paris, *Butterfly* has remained a staple of the repertory. Year after year, it, *Bohème,* and *Tosca* earned very large royalties for the composer and for Casa Ricordi. By any standard, Puccini was rich, and his operas were astoundingly successful.

CHAPTER NINE

~~✎✎~~

The International Celebrity at Home and Abroad: 1905–1908

AFTER HIS FIRST modest travels in Europe in the 1880s, Puccini covered thousands of miles in Italy, France, England, Belgium, Holland, Switzerland, Germany, Austria, Hungary, Malta, Egypt, and South and North America. He accepted most of the invitations he received, save those from Russia. Many trips involved productions of his operas, with a good number planned around festivals of his works; but he also traveled to go hunting in the Tuscan Maremma, Lombardy, France, and even South America. He visited automobile shows, boat shows, an air show, and the Venice Biennale, where his friend Plinio Nomellini was exhibiting his paintings. Given the extraordinary strength needed for keeping to this schedule, it is remarkable that he accomplished so much, given his diabetes, about which he often complained, and after 1903 his disability from the automobile accident. Nothing stopped him, for he continued to accept invitations and take curtain calls when he was still on crutches, when he had to use two canes, and finally when he could manage with one. To all outward appearances, this sophisticated, elegant man was sure of himself, the epitome of success, a sophisticated, elegant man of nearly fifty, the owner of several large villas, expensive cars, boats, and fine clothes. Inwardly, however, he seemed emotionally drained and appeared to be looking to escape an artistic dead end.

He did, however, compose a work for a charitable institution in 1905, when he was invited by the head of Verdi's home for aged musicians, the Casa di Riposo per Musicisti, to preside over the premiere of his *Requiem a tre voci,* on the anniversary of Verdi's death. In a letter to Nomellini, the composer described this work as "a little Requiem that leaves a sorrowful impression," something to be played "for Verdi's old folks" (GP to Nomellini, [undated], Koch Collection, Pierpont Morgan Library, New York). By January 1906 the Casa Verdi, which had had only nine people living there when it opened, was sheltering forty-eight retired musicians. In addition to writing the Requiem, Puccini helped the institution in his own way by sending game that he shot on his hunting trips. Among his contributions to the Casa Verdi dining tables were sides of deer and wild boar (article in *L'Illustrazione Italiana,* January 28, 1906, cited in Lopez, p. 91).

Puccini also composed his *"Ecce Sacerdos"* for Benedetto Lorenzelli, the archbishop of Lucca, in 1905. Much later, the piece figured in another rite, when Puccini's future biographer Dante Del Fiorentino was ordained into the priesthood in the cathedral of San Martino in Lucca, just before World War I. Ever loyal to Puccini, his idol, he chose to put that *"Ecce Sacerdos"* on the musical program for his first Mass, which he celebrated with his family in Quiesa, their village.

After going to Bologna in autumn 1905, Puccini returned to Milan, Torre, and his all-too-familiar search for a new subject. After rejecting an unidentified English story and something taken from Dante, he went hunting in the Maremma, but, as we have seen, began soliciting Soldani in 1906. He had also told Illica of his hopes for a comic opera. In his own words, he *"needed something,"* and he could no longer go on. Still, he vetoed anything that smacked of Ricordi's preferences. Finally, the publisher, exasperated over his stubbornness, almost canceled one of their meetings, something he had never done before. One month later Ricordi suggested that Puccini write something quickly, perhaps an operetta. Briefly tempted by the idea of tossing something off while he traveled, Puccini thought about turning out "about twenty pieces" that would be a huge hit on the operetta stage outside Italy, particularly in London. When nothing came of this, he again took up *Maria Antonietta,* only to drop it once more as frighteningly big. With that, Illica gave up. This was all a farce, the librettist told Ricordi; Puccini had no common sense; he had gone crazy; he liked plays with marionettes, not characters. At the end of the year Illica went further, saying, "Either he's finished, or he's a coward" (LI to GR, [November 1905], in Gara, pp. 303–304).

Montevideo and Buenos Aires

Few people outside the opera business and Italian literary circles would have known about his struggle; and it was the international celebrity — not the desperate composer — whom the Argentine newspaper *La Prensa* invited to Buenos Aires for a summer season in 1905. The audience already knew something about him, for Toscanini had conducted *Manon Lescaut* and *Tosca* there and in Montevideo and had returned in 1904 with the successful *Butterfly,* featuring Storchio and Garbin. The occasion for the 1905 trip was a full-scale Puccini festival, with five operas, including *Edgar,* for which he prepared the definitive edition, although he still felt the opera was a failure. Puccini seemed astonished when he received the invitation to go to Buenos Aires. As he told Ramelde's husband, *La Prensa* would give him a flat fee of twenty thousand lire and cover all the expenses of the trip, treating him like a prince. He told Tomaide he would get fifty thousand francs, plus two round-trip tickets. To Illica he described two round-trip tickets in first class, a luxurious apartment in the newspaper's building, and a benefit evening that would bring him forty or fifty thousand lire. He would also be able to hunt and take tours of the region — a wonderful opportunity, he said, except for the banquets he hated and the speeches in his honor. As he planned the trip, he also considered going on to Rio, where he could earn even more from another benefit performance.

In early June Puccini and Elvira were on board the transatlantic liner *Savoia,* nearing the city of Las Palmas on Grand Canary Island. The seas were so rough, he said, that his inkwell had rolled off a table and into the sea. Nevertheless, he was at work, reading — against all odds — about what he called the "life and miracles" of Marie Antoinette, the heroine of the opera he had sworn never to compose. The seasick Elvira stayed in bed, ate dry biscuits, and wanted to get off at Grand Canary and wait for him to return; but she did not. The sea voyage had been a disaster for her, Puccini reported to Ricordi on June 24, one day after arriving in Buenos Aires. In Montevideo he was greeted by people in small boats in the harbor and crowds and bands in the city; he had to attend events in his honor at the Ateneo, a literary society, and at the Circolo Italiano. Argentina had given him such a magnificent welcome that he was worn out, he said. Their apartment, service, and food were "princely," but he dreaded the seventy-two banquets that lay ahead. All the newspapers printed "monstrously big" photographs of him, and he was inundated with requests for autographs (GP to GR, June 24, 1905, in Pintorno, letter 110). At the Teatro de la Opera, *Manon Lescaut* had been given in May with Rina Giachetti in the title role. Then came the hugely successful *Butterfly* with Storchio and Zenatello, then *Tosca,* with Giachetti, Giuseppe Anselmi, and Eugenio Giraldoni in his signature role of Scarpia. During the second performance of *Bohème,* Puccini made his first public appearance in the theater and took curtain calls with the cast, which had Giachetti paired with Anselmi and Adamo Didur. Puccini also oversaw rehearsals of *Edgar* with Giannina Russ, Giachetti, and Zenatello. It went onstage on July 8 and achieved no more than a modest success. Leopoldo Mugnone, who was then one of Puccini's favorite conductors, directed the season. In spite of all the glory, he was homesick for Torre.

He and Elvira returned to Italy in time to exult over the October production of *Butterfly* at the Dal Verme in Milan; then he went hunting as the guest of two noblemen, the Counts Della Gherardesca, who lived in Bòlgheri Castle, south of Livorno. They intended to sweep the marshes near Castagneto Marittimo (Marina di Castagneto), a seaside village (GP to Pietro Panichelli, [November 1905], in Gara, pp. 302–303). By the end of the month, though, he was back in Torre, admitting that he had bagged nothing. With more requests for autographs and photographs pouring in from South America, he confided to Nitteti and Ramelde that he had fifty unanswered letters on his desk. Always courteous to his fans, he was also especially helpful to aspiring composers who asked his opinion of their music. One good example is his answer to a South American admirer, when he sent a musical quotation from *La Bohème* to a Signor Mola, who had sent Puccini some of his compositions and asked his opinion of them. Saying that he had studied them carefully, he generously wrote, "This is truly a noble effort for someone who is just beginning in the difficult field of Art. I am happy about [your music] and I urge you to persevere in your studies" (GP to Sig. Mola, August 5, 1905, Sotheby Catalogue, May 17, 1990.) In the summer of 1907 he sent off a letter of recommendation to Maestro Giuseppe Martucci to help a young woman, the daughter of an army officer, who wanted to study violin at the Conservatory of San

Pietro a Majella in Naples. These are but a few of the dozens he wrote, apart from the many *raccomandazioni* he made in conversations with colleagues. As Italians would say, he was a busy *raccomandatore*.

Puccini's long, determined effort to help Ervin Lendvai, a young Hungarian composer and conductor, went on for years as he offered advice, criticism of Lendvai's compositions, letters of recommendation, and even money. All this moved Lendvai quickly into the circles of Puccini's family and friends. Born in 1882, Lendvai met Puccini in Milan in 1905. Living in an apartment at Via Solferino 1, he was physically close to his Maestro, at least until Puccini moved to Via Verdi 4. Ervino, as the composer called him, tried to arrange for performances of *Butterfly* in Budapest in the late winter and early spring of 1906; but Puccini was scheduled to travel to Palermo, and to Nice for the Puccini Festival at the theater in the Municipal Casino. Using the young musician as his intermediary, he inquired about more convenient performance dates and financial terms, things Lendvai could arrange when he went home to Budapest.

All was settled, and Puccini went to Hungary in May. *Butterfly* had what he described to Cesare Riccioni as "an immense, astonishing success" with "40 curtain calls" (GP to CR, card, May 13–14, 1906, in Pintorno, letter 122). Puccini also fell in love with Lendvai's sister, Blanke, probably while he was in Budapest. They corresponded for many years, while the furious Elvira kept track of their letters and reproached her husband about them. On his way home, he stopped in Austria to see Richard Strauss's *Salome,* which he described on a postcard to Lendvai as "the most extraordinary thing, terrible cacophony [*cacofonica terribilmente*], there are some very beautiful feelings in the orchestra, but in the end it wears you out. It is a spectacle that is very interesting" (GP to EL, card, May 17, 1906, in Pintorno, letter 124).

The day after he arrived back in Milan, the composer set out for London, where three of his operas were to be given at Covent Garden. He sent his report to Lendvai, "a triumph," he wrote. He returned to Italy and, for a time, was comfortable in Torre del Lago; then he was off to Paris to attend to preliminary negotiations for *Butterfly*. He spent July and August at Abetone, then returned to Paris and corresponded with Lendvai from there. At that time the young composer wanted to see *Butterfly* staged in Berlin, where he was working; but Puccini and Ricordi both vetoed that idea, fearing that it would be produced in a small theater rather than in the Imperial Theater. In 1907 he wrote a detailed criticism of one of Lendvai's compositions, praising the first part of it and telling him how to correct the errors that cropped up in later passages. In an undated letter, also in Pintorno's book, he recommended him to a nobleman in Rome at a time when Lendvai had gone there to give some of his symphonic works in concert. For more than fifteen years he sent affectionate letters to this young friend, never failing in his concern for him, and he continued to help him for a year or two beyond that.

Again, the Seligmans

Puccini's success in Nice in March 1906 marked a high point in his career up to then. In February Sybil, her husband, and her son went to Nice, as they often did in winter. Puccini and Elvira arrived on March 8 and stayed in the Hotel Royal. He was there to oversee rehearsals of *Tosca* and *Manon Lescaut* in the theater of the Casino Municipale. During his visit the Circolo Artistico Italiano offered a magnificent banquet in his honor, with tributes and speeches, followed by a concert of his music. Vincent Seligman, still a boy, left vivid descriptions of his first dinner with the Puccinis at the Café de Paris, then later luncheons, and an evening at the opera when *Tosca* was given.

I can see him now, strolling up and down the Promenade des Anglais in that leisurely manner that was so characteristic of him; indeed, so slow was his progress that it could hardly be called walking at all, for every few yards, he would come to a complete standstill, pausing to light one of his eternal cigarettes, or to think over some point in the conversation that interested or amused him. I remember, too, a curious trick which he had, when searching for a word or an idea that eluded him, of clicking his fingers with a gesture of comical despair and a rueful smile, rather like someone trying unsuccessfully to catch a fly. He took considerable care of his personal appearance and was invariably well dressed, although—unlike many other musicians—he avoided sartorial eccentricities or exaggerations; for some reason, I always picture him at that time dressed in a dark blue suit with white stripes, with light gloves and a walking stick—a reminder of his automobile accident—in his hand, and his soft hat, which he often wore indoors, cocked at a slightly jaunty angle. But more clearly than anything else do I remember the look of indulgent affection in his

large brown eyes, and the rare sweetness of his frank smile—and yet, even
when he was in his happiest and jolliest mood, there always seemed to
lurk at the corners of his mouth a hint of melancholy, if not of actual suffering—the look that one sometimes sees on the faces of the blind.
[Seligman, pp. 72–73]

In Elvira the boy saw a more troubled figure. "At that time, she was still
a very handsome woman, although built on rather generous lines, with,
in particular, very large hands and feet, which may perhaps have ac-
counted for the fact that Giacomo was apt to refer to her jokingly as his
'policeman.' Her temper always appeared to be a trifle uncertain; and her
voice, which she was apt to raise over the most trifling matter, quickly became harsh and discordant. The fact was that I was more than a little
afraid of her; and it was only after a severe internal struggle that I could
bring myself to raise my face to hers to be kissed." In fairness, he added
that Elvira was unfailingly kind to him (Seligman, p. 74). However, the
fact that Puccini called Elvira his "policeman" in a conversation with people he had known for only a short while tells us something about his relationship to his wife at that point. Vincent believed that Puccini found
peace in the "tranquil atmosphere" of the Seligman house, a peace "he
could not always find in his own home." Then and later, Elvira's abrasive
character stood in stark contrast to that of the woman Puccini called "beloved and unforgettable Sybil."

By March 26 the composer was back in Torre del Lago; in April he
confided his worst fears to Sybil: "I'm having a wretched time; I think that
even Signor Giulio's feelings toward me have changed" (GP to SS, April 6,
1906, in Seligman, p. 77). And again, later that month, he brooded: "Signor
Giulio is no longer easy to deal with and won't pay attention to anything.
He seems to me to have altered toward me too" (GP to SS, April 10, 1906,
in Seligman, p. 77–78). In these letters, Puccini sounds troubled and even a
bit frightened. Having depended on Ricordi from the very first hour of his
career, he would certainly be at risk should he fall out of favor. And Puccini, sensitive to Ricordi's moods, knew that any change in his attitude
might have dire consequences, because no one else in the opera business
could guarantee a composer more than Ricordi could.

Sybil, ever mindful of Puccini's needs, had had fresh flowers delivered
to Torre del Lago in March, so he would find them there when he got

home from Nice. Earlier she had sent a stole to Elvira, and soon an expensive letter case and purse came for him; in June 1906 she sent an ornate cushion and a picnic basket. An enthralled Puccini responded by sending Sybil his photograph, and he wrote, "It seems to me that you are the person who has come the nearest to understanding my character. . . . A thousand affectionate thoughts for that exquisite and beautiful creature who is the best friend I have" (GP to SS, April 6, 1906, in Seligman, p. 77). Within weeks Puccini returned to London and to Sybil. When he left, he said, he felt as if his "heart were being torn asunder"; he was looking toward the summer, when he could invite the Seligmans to Abetone. Writing to Sybil from his home in Chiatri in July, he described his "famous villa," which was in a wild, hard-to-reach area, about twelve hundred feet up in the mountains, with a magnificent view of the sea and Lake Massaciuccoli. August found Sybil and her two sons visiting the Puccinis in Abetone; in September they all went to Chiatri. By then, this solidly founded friendship had become a constant in the composer's life.

Giacosa's Illness and Death

A persistent concern in 1905 and 1906 was Giacosa's illness, which stunned everyone working in "the Puccini factory." Illica, aware that the composer and all his projects were in peril, minced no words in a letter to Ricordi. After the success of *Butterfly* at the Dal Verme, he said, Puccini had fallen back again into his "full-blown disease of doubts and fears;" Illica, too, had given up. "Giacosa gave us a secure refuge! 'Fine! Giacosa will take care of it!' or 'But Giacosa will do it!' And these few words were enough to get us all back on the right road. . . . Now, it's good-bye to everything" (LI to GR, [November 1905], in Gara, pp. 301–302). Giacosa had gone to Karlsbad in August to take the waters, but failing health had forced him back to Italy; and at the beginning of November he was virtually given up for lost. At that point, Illica said that the idea that Giacosa might die was beyond imagining. He was still planning ahead for *Maria Antonietta,* "so Puccinian, and so strong, so grandiose." Puccini, however, took a dark view of his career at this moment. To Salvatore Leonardi, Fosca's husband, the composer admitted that his "new opera" did not exist. After Giacosa became too ill to work, he said, everyone stopped talking about it. "Will we go back to it? If I find three one-act works that suit me, I'll put

M.A. off until later." He did not find the one-act operas then, but he did set that big opera aside (GP to SL, November 23, 1905, in Gara, pp. 304–305).

In January 1906 his first concern was an important production of *Butterfly* in Naples. As it was being planned, Puccini had discussed the production at Casa Ricordi and had heard about it from the Neapolitan impresario Roberto De Sanna. Then he wrote to Clausetti.

> Dear Carlo, Together with your letter, I received [a] telegram from De Sanna, in which he says that he would postpone everything until February, and he suggests Garbin or [Fiorello] Giraud [as Pinkerton]. I spoke to Tito; he told me that is fine. I sent a telegram to Roberto [saying] "I accept Garbin in preference to Giraud, but also the latter can do it, if necessary." And I think that postponing everything until February is better, [when] all this uproar has died down, there will be a free, calm period for my badly mistreated *Butterfly* [*la mia tartassata Butterfly*]. Tell [the conductor] Ettore Panizza (I forgot to answer him) that the "Uh" of the chorus can be changed into an "Ah," but I would not cut anything from the backstage chorus music when they follow the Bonze offstage. Ciao, and a hug, G. Puccini. [GP to CC, January 11, 1906, Tollett and Harman Collection]

The composer then added a postscript. "I have read De Sanna's telegram again, where he says, 'Send me a telegram if we can get Garbin.' Tito, reading the telegram, interpreted it to mean 'If Ricordi agrees or approves.' But when I read it again, it seemed to me that he means 'Can Ricordi get Garbin?' Now Garbin is in Venice. When does he finish? And where is the other one [Giraud]? Tomorrow I will see Tito (he is impossible to find), and I will have him approve the most [acceptable] interpreter, and I will let you know. Ciao. Your P" (ibid.). This letter and dozens like it show the composer's scrupulous attention to detail, not just for the premieres of his works, but for every important production; Naples was particularly so because of the prestige of the San Carlo. By the beginning of 1906 Garbin, who had sung in the world premiere of Verdi's *Falstaff* at La Scala in 1893, had clearly won Puccini's confidence, first by singing the opera in the successful performances in Buenos Aires in 1904, then by his effort in the brilliant Milanese *Butterfly* at the Teatro Dal Verme. Giraud, on the other hand, had sung the world premiere of Leoncavallo's *Pagliacci* in 1892. In any case, both were competent professionals, which was lucky for the composer, because the opera, which the impresario could not postpone, was given late in January. Writing from Naples to Nitteti about its success, Puccini said that it had been "a truly great triumph" (GP to NP, January 26, 1906, in Adami, p. 164).

In mid-June Puccini sent Lendvai his plans for a trip to New York and to the Metropolitan for the following January and February. Giacosa died late that summer, and by then the composer had agreed to work with D'Annunzio, although their projects, the librettos of *Parisina,* which Mascagni later set, and *La Rosa di Cipro,* came to nothing. For all the luscious adjectives and expressions of mutual admiration, D'Annunzio found he could never satisfy Puccini, even though he tried discussing their problems when they met. In August he was flattering the composer with "I'll always be your friend," and "I'll come to applaud your operas in the future." But their hopes were dead; and this failed collaboration left D'Annunzio angry and disappointed, for he felt Puccini had failed to mature and was not a serious artist. To their mutual friend Camillo Bondi he wrote, "He [Puccini] came here to confess to me that he needs 'some light, little thing he can set to music in a few months, between one trip and another.'—So that's not art, it's commerce" (GD to Bondi, August 31, 1906, in Bernardoni, p. 19).

Of course it was commerce: Ricordi was in the business of promoting operas and composers and selling or renting out scores. At that time he needed to add something to his catalogue, because he had been selling *Madama Butterfly* for more than two years, with no new Puccini opera in sight. As far as Ricordi was concerned, the composer was wasting valuable time, as he had done in the 1890s. He might just as well write "some light, little thing" as do nothing; and that is probably why he suggested an operetta. Nevertheless, Ricordi can only have been disappointed when Puccini said his collaboration with D'Annunzio had gone up in smoke. The publisher certainly understood Puccini, perhaps better than any of his colleagues, and he respected his determination to have his works sung well and staged properly. But from the publisher's point of view, his failure to find a new subject was dismaying, and all that travel kept him from his desk for too long. Except for a few very important productions, the trips were a loss for a publisher who needed new material. When Puccini did work, his effort sometimes seemed desultory and unfocused. Ricordi chafed, Illica chafed, but Puccini found nothing. He had held out the carrot of Oscar Wilde's *Florentine Tragedy* to Illica just before Giacosa died, but neither it nor their other projects became operas. Among other rejected subjects were *Maria Antonietta,* Wilde, and *Conchita,* based on Pierre Louÿs's *La femme et le pantin.*

Family Matters

Puccini and Elvira became grandparents when Fosca and Salvatore Leonardi had their first child, Franca. In 1905 a second daughter followed. She was called "Little Elvira" and was the baby Puccini adored. A third child, Antonio, followed later. When she grew up, Little Elvira Leonardi became the famous Milanese fashion designer "Biki," who reigned supreme in her atelier and whose clients included Milanese noblewomen, film stars, Maria Callas, and Toscanini's daughters and granddaughter. I met Biki in Milan in the spring of 1956, introduced to her by Callas, whom I was interviewing for *Opera News.* Biki's recollections of Puccini and Elvira provide intimate glimpses of them in her home and theirs. She called Puccini "Tato"; he was the doting grandfather, Elvira the severe family matriarch. Born in Milan, Little Elvira grew up in Fosca's large, elegant apartment on the most fashionable corner in the city, where the narrow, ancient Via Morone joins Via Alessandro Manzoni. Fosca and her husband rented from the powerful Crespi family. (Much later, Fosca married into the Crespis.) Across the street from her apartment was the Hotel Continental, where many famous singers lived or stayed, and where Puccini occasionally checked in for brief visits. His new winter residence in Milan was an apartment in the building at Via Verdi 4, a block from Fosca's place. This was Milan's most fashionable neighborhood; its most famous private residence was the Alessandro Manzoni house, a veritable shrine.

Fosca's close friendship with the Toscaninis—Carla Toscanini, the conductor's wife, was Fosca's best friend—brought Little Elvira together with the Toscanini children, Wally, Wanda, and Walter, who became her lifelong friends. Wally and Little Elvira were particularly close. The Toscaninis lived on Via Durini, just a few blocks from Via Morone, so the two families' children were able to visit back and forth. They had the same tutors and went to dancing school with another boy, Gian Carlo Menotti, whose family had moved to Milan from Cadegliano, in the province of

Varese. Later Little Elvira described Fosca's apartment in the palazzo in
Via Morone as a "worldly" home, where conversations about music and
art were commonplace and artists and art critics and musicians came and
went regularly. Before World War I, she said, Italy was a place of great cultural ferment, a country where innovations and ideas from beyond the
Alps constantly came into conflict with tradition.

Even as a very small child, Little Elvira spent part of the summer in
Puccini's villa in Torre del Lago. Later the Leonardis had their own villa in
Viareggio. This meant that Little Elvira spent a lot of time with her
grandparents, first at Torre, where she visited with her sister Franca and
later alone, then after World War I in the new Puccini villa in Viareggio.
During the winter, whole days of Puccini's life in Milan were spent visit-
ing Fosca and her children, as they all went back and forth between the
Leonardis' home and his.

Puccini's most important professional commitment at that time was
the Paris *Butterfly*, mentioned in the previous chapter. Sending Sybil his
news, he said it had been put off, and that he had go back to Paris in mid-
October. "As for *Conchita*, I'm now getting back into it a bit. Because I
have some ideas about changing it, which I will discuss with the Vicar
[Vaucaire] in Paris. But I am still trying to get to know Wilde's play [*A Florentine Tragedy*]. I still have sugar [from diabetes], but not too much; nevertheless, I stay on my diet. But I don't feel too bad." He concluded the letter with expressions of concern for her health, saying he would answer a
letter from her son Vincent, and sending regards to her husband (GP to
SS, October 3, 1906, Tollett and Harman Collection).

Renato Gemignani

Just after Little Elvira was born, Puccini showed his concern for yet another member of the family, Renato Gemignani, the second child and first
son of Elvira and Narciso. About two years old when Elvira left to join
Puccini in Milan, he had been raised by Gemignani, while Elvira and Puccini effectively raised Fosca after Gemignani agreed to let her live with
them.

Little is known about Elvira's relationship with Renato (to say nothing
of any acquaintance Puccini may have had with him) from 1886 until
1906. As Puccini had written to Ramelde fifteen years earlier, Elvira had

chosen between her two little boys, and had chosen his, not Gemignani's. As a result, Renato was first put in the care of relatives and servants; he probably began school in Lucca and later attended some upper school as a boarder. It is even possible that he grew up without seeing his mother, given the bitterness Gemignani harbored toward his wife, although it seems much more likely that Elvira kept in touch with him somehow. As we have seen, Narciso Gemignani died in 1903. In 1904, when Elvira and Puccini married, Renato would have become Puccini's stepson, had he still been a minor. But even if he had reached his majority, Puccini would have felt some responsibility for him.

Whatever the circumstances, in 1906 Puccini was staying at the Londres in Paris when he wrote to Clausetti about getting help for Renato. To be specific, he was trying to persuade a minister in the royal government in Rome to help him. Renato had entered some competition, perhaps for a government post, perhaps for a teaching job. And Puccini supported and tried to help him. To Clausetti he wrote, "Dear Carlo, Some time ago I referred Mr. Renato Gemignani of Lucca to Minister Gianturco; and His Excellency kindly answered, saying he would attend to it. Now that this young man has finished the examinations in the competition in Rome, a reminder must be sent [to the minister]. Do you want to write it? Probably the minister is there, or certainly his wife is there. Do it; Elvira, too, asks this of you. Thanks" (GP to CC, around November 14, 1906, Tollett and Harmon Collection). Again one must remark on how generous Puccini was in sending such letters, and how diligently he followed them up. This concern for others was one of the most attractive traits of his character. In this same letter he sent Clausetti the news about his work. "The piano is at the port. [Illegible] will go around the 10th and [illegible] the tour well. In America the tour [of *Butterfly*] is going splendidly. In New York, a huge success. Here [in Paris] *Bohème* has almost reached its 200th performance, with an admirable production" (ibid.).

New York and the Metropolitan Opera

Puccini wrote to Sybil on November 14 about the triumphant *Butterfly* tour in the United States. Produced by Henry Savage and overseen for part of its itinerary by Tito Ricordi, the opera, given in English, was scheduled to run for six months, with eight performances a week. When the tour ended, more than two hundred performances had been tallied up. "After Washington, Baltimore, and Boston, now New York — good," Puccini exulted (GP to SS, November 14, 1906, in Seligman, p. 96). The composer, who always followed American news, read stories about Caruso's arrest in the "Monkey House" episode in the Central Park Zoo, where a woman had accused him of making a sexual advance. Commiserating with the tenor over the scandal, Puccini sent good wishes, saying he hoped he would survive "this ugly farce," be exonerated, and emerge "gloriously triumphant" from it all (GP to Caruso, November 23, 1906, The Pierpont Morgan Library, New York). His vindication was particularly important to Puccini, because Caruso and Puccini would be working together at the Met in January and February 1907.

Otto H. Kahn, the banker who had joined the Met's board of directors in 1903, had carried out his ambitious plans for the organization. As a board member, and later as the chairman and executive director, he was so identified with the Met that reporters joked about his initials, O.H.K., saying that they stood for "Opera House Kahn." His first important responsibility with the board had been to find a new general manager to replace the ailing Heinrich Conried; but when he invited Puccini to New York for the company's premiere of *Manon Lescaut,* the old regime was still in place. Not until June 1907 did Kahn approach Giulio Gatti-Casazza about the position; not until 1908 did Gatti arrive in New York, followed by Toscanini, who had been the leading conductor at La Scala since 1898. Kahn had negotiated Puccini's engagement through Count Enrico di San Martino Valperga, the head of the Accademia di Santa Cecilia in Rome; and after Puccini accepted, the company representatives could announce plans for a kind of Puccini festival at the Met.

By November Puccini had his schedule in place, and a month later he was ready to leave. On a cold, wintry day, the whole village of Torre del Lago turned out to see him and Elvira off to Paris and New York. As a crowd milled around the tiny train station, many gave him letters for relatives in *"L'America,"* and one old man brought a sausage for Puccini to deliver to an uncle in Argentina. Others brought sentimental poems. The mayor made a speech; then the train pulled in. After a mountain of baggage was loaded, the composer and his entourage got into their carriage and left.

He and Elvira sailed in January 1907, on the *S.S. Kaiserin Auguste Victo-*

ria. To his delight, he found that the Met had reserved a luxurious suite for him, with a salon, bedroom, and bath that were lighted by seventy electric bulbs. Impressed by the huge ship, he sent Ramelde a marvelous letter describing it: twenty-five thousand tons, forty thousand horsepower. It had salons, little sitting rooms, a winter garden with flowers and "colossal" live palm trees, two restaurants, a beer hall, a gym with wooden, electric-powered horses, a band and two little orchestras, two on-board daily newspapers, hot and cold water twenty-four hours a day, electric cigarette lighters, and an electric heating system. He worried about the seagulls and other birds that followed the ship: two thousand miles from land, and where did those "poor birds" sleep? (GP to RPF, January 14, 1907, in A. Marchetti, p. 326).

Even in the middle of the Atlantic, he missed Torre del Lago. "A plain, little corner in my kitchen, with the smell of beef cooking, is worth more than all this! My beautiful Torre! And Chiatri, too!" He was already planning the garden he would plant in front of his house. On the day he wrote this letter, he was in his underwear, trying to amuse Elvira, who was less seasick than she had been on the way to South America, but stayed in bed just the same (ibid.). According to the terms of his agreement with the Metropolitan Opera, Puccini was to oversee the last rehearsals of *Manon Lescaut,* but he missed these after heavy seas made for a slow crossing. On January 17 the fogbound liner had to drop anchor off the coast of Sandy Hook, New Jersey. The next day was spent between quarantine and Hoboken. For a moment, it seemed he might not even get to the Met for the first *Manon* that night; but just before five in the afternoon on that dank winter day, the *Auguste Victoria* steamed into her berth in the Hudson River.

A covey of reporters and Met representatives had been at the pier since early that morning. As soon as Puccini landed, they surrounded him and made him give a press conference before he and Elvira were whisked away to their hotel. Evidently impressed with his bearing and his expensive suit, one reporter wrote that he was "very different from some of the Italian maestros who have visited New York." At seven, they were in their suite at the Hotel Astor, where a maid laid out the composer's evening clothes, and soon he was slipping into a chair in the general manager's box in the great red-and-gold auditorium. Impressed by the fully sold-out

Puccini as a youth in
Lucca. *Opera News*.

Puccini as a young man,
in a rare photo from his
family. *Opera News*.

Giulio Ricordi, Puccini's
publisher, mentor, and
friend. *Opera News*.

Elvira Bonturi Gemignani,
Puccini's mistress and,
later, his wife. *Opera News*.

Puccini with his librettists Giuseppe Giacosa and (right) Luigi Illica. *Opera News*.

Puccini at the door of his villa at Boscolungo Abetone, in a 1906 snapshot signed to Maurice Vaucaire, his collaborator on *Conchita*. "*Boscolungo, agosto [1]906, All'amico M.ce Vaucaire, con affetto, Giacomo Puccini.*" Tollett and Harman Collection.

Elvira and Puccini in the garden at Torre del Lago.
Opera News.

Puccini steering a boatload of friends on Lake Massaciuccoli. *Opera News*.

In Egypt in 1908, with Puccini (on camel) and Elvira (in car). *Opera News*.

Puccini and Arturo Toscanini in Paris, where they planned the Metropolitan
Opera premiere of *La Fanciulla del West*. *Opera News*.

La Fanciulla del West in rehearsal at the Met, 1910. *Opera News*.

Puccini with Antonio,
his son. Studio portrait,
1920s. Metropolitan
Opera Archives.

Puccini and "Little Elvira" Leonardi, his step-granddaughter, in yachting clothes. Credit: *Opera News*.

Puccini in 1913. Signed portrait postcard. Tollett and Harman Collection.

Puccini in the 1920s. Engraved
portrait, Bleistift-Bildnis Nr. 137,
by Kunstanstalt Stengel & Co.,
Dresden. Tollett and Harman
Collection.

Giacomo Puccini a Celle (Pesca,
26 ottobre 1924

Puccini's visit to his family's ancestral home in Celle, on October 26, 1924, a
month before his death. Puccini is standing, sixth from right, hands in pockets.
Opera News.

house, Puccini experienced what he called an evening almost beyond description.

People saw him for the first time after the lights came up at the end of the first act. Then the applause erupted, and the orchestra struck up a brassy fanfare in his honor. That launched a ten-minute ovation—"Extraordinary," he said—during which he took six bows from his box. Then Caruso and Antonio Scotti persuaded him to come backstage during the second act and take bows from the stage. He got seven calls, he said. At the end of the third act, he stayed in his seat, applauding the singers and orchestra while the audience applauded him and shouted. Through that ovation he tried to remain serious and composed, he said, and not to act like a clown, as Mascagni and Leoncavallo had. Later he stood at the door of the box to chat in Italian or French with people who had looked for him in the corridor; and after the last act and more applause, he took four more solo bows. As for the singers, he raved about Lina Cavalieri, calling her "the best," full of temperament, and truly moving. Her voice carried more than he had ever imagined it could. As for Caruso, he was extraordinary, as usual; Scotti, very, very good; and the orchestra very lively and subtle.

Even the critics were impressed, with Richard Aldrich of the *New York Times* describing the opera as the only "unqualified success" of that season and a work likely to remain in the repertory. *Manon Lescaut* "has a remarkable flow of melody, and the score has the transparency and unfailing charm by which Puccini is raised above his fellows in the contemporaneous Italian school." His style, so marked and identifiable, included making the orchestra "the life blood of the whole drama." Aldrich, who heard the Met orchestra often, found it melodious and expressive. In sum, the opera has "much variety and piquancy, and much dramatic warmth" (review in Seltsam, p. 172).

Puccini soon began exploring New York, although he later admitted he could not see as much as he wished. He especially appreciated the energy and the bustle of the place; and, with his childlike enthusiasm for anything mechanical, he discovered a trove of machines and gadgets. As he told Ramelde, he was living in the very heart of the city, which he particularly liked in the evening when the streetlights came on; he was impressed by the beautiful buildings, some very high, with twenty-five or thirty stories. Nevertheless, he said he preferred London and Paris. Life in New York was horribly expensive; the dollars flew away, and he was particularly upset about tips. As for American women, he said, "How many women! And how many of them look for me and want to see me! Even an old man could find one, if he wished! And what figures the women have here, what big behinds, and what hair! It's enough to make the Leaning Tower of Pisa stand up straight!" As he wrote that, Elvira was already asleep, otherwise, he said, he could not have put it on paper. "She is always as jealous as Otello [*Otelleggia sempre*], but I get away with everything. Don't tell anyone, and tear up this letter" (GP to RPF, early February 1907, in A. Marchetti, p. 329).

As Marchetti wryly remarked, Puccini rarely got away with his adventures. Del Fiorentino, who heard many stories from Puccini's cronies and some from the composer himself, said the furiously jealous Elvira watched him every moment they were together. One day she made a scene during a rehearsal when she suddenly realized he had been courting a young woman associated with the Met and had given her a ring. Outraged, she ordered him to go to the woman's box and get the ring back at once, otherwise she would get it back herself. After the mortified Puccini retrieved the ring, a bitter private exchange with Elvira followed.

On another occasion, she was ill with the flu on the night when he was the guest of honor at a reception at the Met. She made Caruso swear to police her husband's activities and keep him away from her rival. It was dawn when Puccini got back to the Astor, and he checked to be sure she was still asleep before he went to bed himself. The moment he was still, she began going through his clothing—pockets, linings, and trouser cuffs included. When she searched his top hat, she found a note from the woman tucked behind the inside band. Del Fiorentino said Puccini told this story himself, cursing his fate and swearing that Elvira was a mind reader, a medium, or a witch. In New York her suspicions were probably aroused by the widely circulated rumor that Puccini was having an affair with Lina Cavalieri. In any case, he continued to flirt with women, and Elvira's jealous scenes went on.

When she was not there, he spent many days in the opera house, renewing old friendships and making new ones as he prepared *Madama Butterfly,* scheduled for February 11. He could not get enough rehearsal time, he said. The ailing Conried, soon to be replaced, offered no help at all, and the singers had had no coaching on movement and action. The conductor, Arturo Vigna, was barely competent, and many subtle moments in the score were lost in the huge auditorium. Caruso and Scotti were often with him during rehearsals, Caruso cast as Pinkerton and Scotti as the American consul. Geraldine Farrar was Butterfly, and Louise Homer, Suzuki. The rehearsals moved from upstairs rooms to the main stage, closely monitored by the composer. Tension often ran high, sometimes over Farrar's long-established habit of singing in half-voice. The Italians, many of whom were happy to sing out for the composer, accused her of cheating. As for Puccini, he wanted to hear her in full voice, because then and later he found her voice too small for the house. Farrar, a star who was at least as popular as Caruso, later said the Italians resented her, but tempers never flared openly. For her part, she wanted Caruso and Scotti to pay more attention; but they, having sung their roles in London, were casual about them. They obviously felt more comfortable than she did, although she would never have admitted that.

I first met Farrar in the early 1950s, when she came to the *Opera News* office, every inch the retired prima donna, carrying an expensive purse and wearing a long fur coat. Later I interviewed her in "Fair Haven," her home near Ridgefield, Connecticut, and also corresponded with her about Otto Kahn. In these later years of her life, she looked the part of the mistress of a country estate: tweed skirt, silk blouse, and carefully set hair, busy with the American Red Cross and worried about local schools and community projects. Discussing the first Metropolitan Opera *Butterfly,* she spoke of problems that arose during rehearsals. Long before Puccini's arrival, Farrar had spent weeks in her suite in the Hotel Netherland, preparing the role with a Japanese actress. Both would put on kimonos and obis, slip their feet into Japanese tabis, and get out their fans. Farrar learned bows, hand gestures, facial expressions, and the right way to kneel; she had even shaved her eyebrows and penciled in a thin line.

All her careful study meant that Puccini was dealing with a very well prepared, headstrong diva convinced that she knew everything about his opera. After rehearsals began, he told her what he wanted her to do and said he expected her to obey him. Disagreements followed when she did not. Farrar resented his bossiness and even hated the sound of his voice, most of all when he spoke to other Italians. From descriptions of the young Puccini directing rehearsals in Italy, we know how passionate he could be about them, and when he was truly upset, which was rarely, he shouted, stomped his feet, and sweated—everything that would have offended Farrar. She also felt the composer was not hard enough on Caruso and Scotti, who, she thought, came to rehearsals merely as a gesture to Puccini, while she was struggling to master a very challenging role. She also complained about Homer, who had just given birth to twins; all she thought about was whether her babies were being properly fed while she was away from home. Farrar recalled that Puccini had his own list of complaints, because he had to do all the direction himself. Convinced that the management had scheduled too few rehearsals, he was troubled because Vigna, the conductor, could not maintain discipline in the orchestra. Caruso, he said, was too lazy and self-satisfied to learn anything. Nevertheless, he admitted that the tenor's voice was magnificent.

Caruso also served as the ideal guide to show Puccini around New York. After rehearsals, he, Scotti, and the composer would window-shop, looking at the most expensive clothes and the biggest cars. Although Puccini told Ramelde he was tired and glad to get in bed after the rehearsals, sometimes he was free at night, chiefly because Elvira always went to bed early, while he always stayed up until two, three, or four in the morning. With Caruso, Scotti, and their hangers-on, he would go downtown to Little Italy to join members of the Sisca family or eat with singers at Del Pezzo's restaurant on Thirty-fourth Street. "Sor Gennaro" Del Pezzo, the owner, had become the confidant of many singers from the Met and other companies.

The Siscas, Caruso's best friends in New York, were an important clan of Italian-American physicians and publishers. The head of this family, Marziale Sisca, published the widely read Italian magazine *La Follia,* to which Caruso contributed his caricatures for many years. Alessandro Sisca, under the pen name Riccardo Cordiferro, wrote the words to the popular song *"Core 'ngrato,"* which Caruso recorded; he also edited *La Follia.* Puccini, Caruso, and the Siscas would sit around tables heavy with Italian specialties as crowds of curious onlookers peered through the windows. After dinner the men moved to a back room for a game of *scopa.* Caruso, whom everyone feared as a veritable wizard at cards, often hit winning streaks that cleaned out every wallet. However, his card-playing friends finally worked out a scheme to beat him by bribing Del Pezzo to put an inconspicuous mirror behind Caruso's chair. Of course, the tenor began to lose, but the other men let him win often enough so he would not become suspicious. Not until Puccini was back in Europe did he take pity on Caruso and tell him about the trick they had played on him.

The Met honored Puccini with a formal banquet at the Hotel St. Regis on the evening of January 27. Plans for the event had been made by five members of the board's Executive Committee, among them Conried, Kahn, and Rawlins Cottenet, the man who later helped to negotiate the contracts of Gatti-Casazza and Toscanini (minutes of the Executive Committee, Metropolitan Opera Company, January 15, 1907, Metropolitan Opera Archives).

On the day of the dress rehearsal of *Madama Butterfly,* the theater was filled with invited guests. One of the most recognizable was David Belasco, the playwright and producer who had written and produced *Madame Butterfly* as a play in 1900. He was dressed in his full "Bishop of Broadway" black suit and the white clerical collar he always wore. Farrar remembered that many brought their lunch with them and had "that new fad," a Thermos bottle, tucked into their lunch boxes. They were allowed to eat during the rehearsal, so they would not miss a note of the music. *Madama Butterfly,* given at the Metropolitan on February 11, was a hit there and in Philadelphia, where the Met performed better than in New York, Puccini thought. Again Aldrich, writing in the *New York Times,* hailed him, saying *Butterfly* was given under "brilliant and favorable circumstances." Surprisingly, Scotti and Caruso were singled out for having achieved "perfection"; but Farrar and Homer got only a mention in the review. Puccini's "fine Italian hand" was responsible for bringing this "refined and beautiful" work to the Met. In this, his most highly polished score, he had perfectly matched music to action (review in Seltsam, p. 173).

Writing to Tito, Puccini said the critics and public liked the first performance, but he did not. It lacked the poetry he had put into it; Farrar had sung flat and had too small a voice for the Met's large space. Going on to other things, he said he had given up the idea of going to see Niagara Falls. He had, however, seen several plays, and had also convinced himself that *Conchita* could never become an opera. He simply did not believe in it, nor had he received any encouragement when important people in New York sat through a reading of part of the libretto. The whole world was waiting for his next opera, he said, and he needed one. He wanted to go forward, for he had grown as an artist. Yet he felt stymied by not having a good, workable drama for his next work, nor had he found anything in New York, although he had seen three Belasco plays, among them *The Girl of the Golden West.*

Home and Away Again

Puccini and Elvira sailed for Europe at the end of February. In mid-March, again in Torre del Lago, he wrote to Clausetti, not about *Conchita,* but about his new idea: three one-act operas taken from three scenes from Gorky. By May he had stopped talking about those and was focusing on two possibilities, one new and one already overly familiar: "an American girl of the West" and "the revolution with M. Antoinette." And to Lendvai, he sounded positively jubilant at having two operas instead of none. By August, writing to Giulio Ricordi from Boscolungo Abetone, he could say, "We've got it! The *Girl* promises to become a second *Bohème,* but stronger, more daring, and broader. I have an idea for a grandiose scenario, an open space in the great California forest, with colossal trees, but 8 or 10 horses will be needed" (GP to GR, August 26, 1907, in Gara, p. 353). Illica worked again on *Maria Antonietta,* "or, rather, *L'Austriaca,*" as he now called the opera, but Puccini, who hated the first act of it, sent his librettist a very nasty letter. An angry exchange followed, with both men drawing Ricordi into their dispute. As for Puccini, the old restlessness still possessed him: in July he was in Torre del Lago, in August in Boscolungo Abetone, and in September in Torre del Lago, then in Chiatri, where he worked with a new librettist, Carlo Zangarini, on *La Fanciulla del West.* Finally, he settled in Torre, where he remained until well into December. As he wrote to Toscanini, he could not go to Milan at once but hoped to get there in a few days. Referring to a well-publicized *Tosca* at La Scala, he wrote, "It's not necessary for me to be there, but it was just for the pleasure of hearing it performed at La Scala, and your conducting. I hope to get there in time for a rehearsal with scenery (GP to AT, December 15, 1907, NYPLPA, Music Division, Wanda Toscanini Horowitz Donation). As he wrote to Sybil, the theater was "incredibly full, and [it was] a splendid performance, especially the orchestra, and the mise-en-scène was magnificent." He had already been told that *Butterfly* was playing to full houses—*teatroni*—in Vienna, Berlin, Prague, and Madrid (GP to SS, [January 8, 1908], in Seligman, pp. 151–152). Much of that autumn was spent on the libretto of *La Fanciulla del West,* which he was eager to finish. In several letters to Sybil he complained about Zangarini's slow pace and lack of skill. "I feel like blowing my brains out—Zangarini is keeping me waiting," he wrote as he got ready to spend Christmas in Milan (GP to SS, December 23, 1907, in Seligman, p. 151). The problem continued, and an exasperated Puccini finally decided to give the librettist a deadline for producing something acceptable.

The Egyptian Jaunt

Early in 1908 Puccini and Elvira again planned to travel, this time to Naples and across the Mediterranean to Egypt. During the trip he wrote several times to Fosca, describing his experiences. In Naples, before sailing, he saw *Salome* again, this time conducted by Richard Strauss. "It was a success, but I don't believe it convinced anyone," he wrote. "Strauss conducted, and, as required, he won respect and even acclaim. [Gemma] Bellincioni, in spite of the extreme circumstances, acted artistically and danced very effectively" (GP to FL, February 2, 1908, in Gara, p. 364). After the performance, Puccini visited with Strauss, Bellincioni, the composer Martucci, and the famed Neapolitan journalist Matilde Serao. Satisfied because he was treated royally, he then set out for Egypt on the steamship *Heliopolis.* On February 4, during the outbound journey from Italy, he composed a poem for Caruso. In scatological schoolboy doggerel that suggests an eight-year-old trying out his new vocabulary during recess, Puccini hails his tenor. However, the verses have a certain value in what they reveal about the composer, and because Puccini clearly wanted Caruso to sing Dick Johnson in *La Fanciulla del West.* It reads:

> Pyrrhus, the schoolboy,
> [son of] an Etruscan mother,
> Showed off his behind,
> Bending over, head down.
> So without you,
> Egypt [will be] unpleasant,

Like fried [fish]
Without a lemon.
Oh, you who stink
All over,
Why don't you spit
Before you eat?
You had that poem,
Full of sun.
Tears of sorrow fall,
Because I am unhappy
At not seeing you
All the time in Florence,
Nor see you sitting down later
On a coverlet,
And instead of [going] down to the river,
Which is black and dirty,
You bring your light
Without blushing.
You sing
Everything well.
Pious women
Throw themselves at your feet.
And I, on the other hand,
Am going to the Pharaoh's El Dorado
With a listless woman [Elvira].
I'm going for pleasure;
I'm going for fun.
[My] trunk is empty
And changing color.
[I'm not getting any sex.]
You call yourself Johnson
And Ramerrez.
You shall see
How well I will
Take care of you.
It will be a role
Filled with love,

The finale will be
A card game;
But in the third act,
They want to kill you,
But to go crazy,
I want you to be the King.
This is the story
Of that matter,
Which I,
Without giving myself airs,
Will write for you.
My regards to Peccia
My regards to Buzzi [Buzzi-Peccia, his old companion from his student
    days],
And all the scum
Who love me.
Ciao, Your Puccini. [February 4, 1908, Enrico Caruso Museum of
    America, Inc., Cav. Aldo Mancusi]

Written on the stationery of the *Heliopolis,* the nonsense rhyme delivered
a clear message: Caruso would be Dick Johnson.

Three days later, Puccini sent good news to Carlo Clausetti, saying that
he had "arrived in Alexandria in great shape." While there, he stayed at
the Grand Continental Hotel, and went to the opera to see "a good
Cruscenisca [*sic*] *Butt*[*erfly*]." Again the soprano was Salomea Krusceniski,
who had starred in the opera in Brescia and had sung it in Bologna. With
another rhyme, Puccini teasingly described a meeting with friends in the
hotel, and matched "*gli amici in coro*" with "*ed io con gran decoro*" ("[my]
friends in chorus" and "I with much decorum"); among these was Riccioni from Viareggio, Krusceniski's husband. Next, Puccini said, he would
go to see the Nile, dressed like a character from Verdi's *Aida:* "Soon I will
head for that river, filled with Verdian passion, dressed in a toga like
Ramfis [*in Aida*]." He closed with this: "If you find any shit, step in it, because it will bring you good luck!" (GP to CC, February 7, 1908, Tollett
and Harman Collection). He sent Toscanini a serious, simple greeting
that same day (GP to AT, card, February 7, 1908, NYPLPA, Music Division, Wanda Toscanini Horowitz Donation).

The tone of his letter to Clausetti suggests that Puccini was enjoying himself in Egypt, in spite of being stuck with what he called a "listless" female companion. He and Elvira went on to Cairo. Writing to Fosca, he described the weather there as "ugly, cloudy, cold," but told her of a pleasant boat trip on the Nile, where by chance he met several acquaintances. He and Elvira were planning side trips to the pyramids, to Heliopolis, Luxor, and Aswan; he was dining with friends one night and had been invited to lunch by an Italian diplomat. But he complained about Elvira, who was tired and out of sorts. A week later, when the weather improved, he wrote again to Fosca with news of their trip to Luxor, where they stayed at the beautiful Winter Palace Hotel, "very chic and expensive," he remarked. He had seen the temple of Karnak and the tombs of the kings. The couple reached the valley by carriage, then mounted donkeys. The tombs were "50 or 60 meters below ground, and to go there, you have to pass through a barren, desolate, treeless landscape, through gullies in the mountains, which have very strange shapes. These tombs are impressive, magnificent. The Nile is beautiful, the sky clear, the sunsets splendid. Hot like summer in the daytime, a little chilly in the morning." Lack of time had kept them from visiting Aswan (GP to FL, February 15, 1908, in Gara, pp. 365–366).

In good humor he sent Ramelde a long list of the sights he had seen.

The pyramids, camels, palm trees, turbans, sunsets, sarcophagi, mummies, scarabs, colossuses, columns, the tombs of the kings; the feluccas on the Nile, which are nothing but a larger Freddana [a type of Italian boat]; the fez, tarboosh, black-skinned people, brown-skinned people, veiled women, sun, yellow sands, ostriches, Englishmen, museums; portals like those in *Aida*, Ramses I, II, III, etc.; fertile mud, cataracts, mosques, flies, hotels, the valley of the Nile, the ibis, buffaloes, irritating street vendors, the smell of fat, the minarets, Coptic churches, the Madonna's tree, [Thomas] Cook's steamers, cats, sugar cane, cotton, acacias, sycamores, Turkish coffee, bands with pipes and big drums, processions, the bazaar, belly dancers, crows, black falcons, dancing women, dervishes, Levantines, Bedouins, the Khedive, Thebes, cigarettes, hookahs, hashish, baksheesh, the sphinxes, the immense [god] Ftà, Isis, Osiris. It has all busted my balls, and I am leaving on the 20th to get a rest. Ciao from your Egyptian swine [*tuo Egittrogolo*]. [GP to RPF, February 18, 1908, in A. Marchetti, p. 340]

(He often referred jokingly to Ramelde and her husband and even some friends with the nickname *Trogolo,* which actually means a feeding trough for hogs.)

Sailing again on the *Heliopolis,* Puccini and Elvira returned home through Naples, where he stopped to talk business with Clausetti. When Puccini got back to Milan, his good humor vanished, blown away in the struggle to get a finished libretto from Zangarini. On February 28 he sent off a blast to Clausetti: "The 3rd act that I read is something infuriating! You must have seen it! I dreamed of a great, tragic house, a cathedral; and instead they spit out a miserable hut! Believe me, I am so discouraged, because in Casa R[icordi] no one understands anything, and they go right on, either with great indifference or incompetence. You lighten up the 2 [preceding] acts from the point of view of language, and tell me your general impression. But even in the 2 acts, you won't find any poetry at all, neither lofty nor low. Ciao, your G. Puccini" (GP to CC, February 28, 1908, Tollett and Harman Collection).

On that unpromising but familiar note, *La Fanciulla del West* got under way. But there were happier moments that raised his spirits that spring. In Rome in March for performances of *Butterfly* at the Teatro Costanzi, he was the guest of honor at a banquet, which he described to Luigi Pieri, his old friend from Lucca. "Banquet for 200 guests and more; more than 100 others were turned down for lack of space. [Among those] present were the mayor of Rome, the prefect, the minister, the press, [he lists many other guests], senators, deputies, artists from the French and Spanish Academies. The Pope was not there because he didn't have a gondola to bring him over [a reference to Pius X, who had been the revered patriarch of Venice before becoming pope]. Speeches (not by me, naturally). Tuesday, a gala with the King and Queen. Wednesday I leave for Torre. I am well; the weather is divine; an enchanting visit. *Butterfly* very, very good, as far as the voices are concerned; superb, [indeed] unique settings. A good orchestra, but [Leopoldo] Mugnone plays loud and speeds up the tempos, and forces me to hear a *Butterfly* that would otherwise have been ideal (between you and me)" (GP to LP, March 30, 1908, in Gara, p. 367).

For the rest of the year, Puccini divided his time among Torre del Lago, Milan, Chiatri, and Boscolungo Abetone. For more than a month he had intestinal flu; then he worried about Giuditta and Ginetta Ricordi, Giulio's wife and daughter, who were also ill. At the same time, he was keeping a watchful eye on his possessions, his decoys and his "offshore properties," as he called them, including his duck blind in the lake. At the end of September he sent a note to Antonio Bettolacci, whom he had glimpsed outside his house earlier that day. "I wanted to see you to tell you that yesterday in the mud around the hut on the little island [in Lake Massaciuccoli] I found a rope with iron weights on it . . . a rope for tying up ducks. So someone went in while I was away. I beg you to tell the guard to watch out and, when [I am hunting, and] he passes by, he should come close and call out to me, and I will answer and stand up, and then he will see me" (GP to Bettolacci, September 28, 1908, Tollett and Harman Collection).

The subject of property came up again when Edoardo De Fonseca, a publisher, wanted a piece about Puccini's houses. Puccini sent him this: "Dear Edoardo, I made photographs of the interior and exterior [of the house at Torre], and as soon as they are ready, I'll send them to you. About the short note, there are problems. What can I tell you? They all begin the usual way: low estimates and final expenses that are three times higher. Torre del Lago was an old tower of the 1300s, then it became a house for the [estate] watchmen for [Duke Carlo Ludovico], then it belonged to Don Carlos, and now it is mine. Chiatri was an old villa . . . that I restored, with an estimate of 30,000 [lire]. It cost me more than 100,000!! I bought Abetone when it was half finished. The architect Camillo Bondi oversaw the work as I finished it. The architect for the balcony was Castellucci from Florence" (GP to De Fonseca, November 29, 1908, in The Pierpont Morgan Library, New York). Puccini sent his song *"Casa mia, casa mia"* with this note to Fonseca.

That autumn of 1908 marked the departure of Gatti-Casazza and Toscanini for New York and the Metropolitan, where Gatti was to be general manager and Toscanini a leading conductor. Their contracts, like Puccini's, had been arranged by Otto Kahn and negotiated through Count di San Martino Valperga. Toscanini had to arrive in the city for the autumn rehearsals of the orchestra; as he was leaving Milan, he received a card of good wishes from Puccini. "Have a good trip and a good stay in America," he wrote, as he also sent regards to Gatti, the "good-natured" man "with the frown" (GP to AT, undated card, NYPLPA, Music Division, Wanda Toscanini Horowitz Donation). Gatti and Toscanini would produce his next opera.

CHAPTER TEN

◦◦◦

La Fanciulla del West *and Beyond:*
1908–1913

SEEING PUCCINI'S huge personal success in New York, Otto Kahn and others at the Met considered asking him to do something else for the company. First, however, they had to install Giulio Gatti-Casazza as the new general manager, whose contract Kahn and other board members had negotiated in Paris in July 1907. His tenure began in 1908, with three-year contracts for him and Toscanini. Gatti, with the support of Kahn and the Board of Directors, transformed the Met in the twenty-seven years that he ran the company, giving the first American performances of fifty-two operas and eighteen world premieres. The most important was Puccini's *La Fanciulla del West.*

Belasco Revisited: The Play and the Libretto

In New York in 1907, Puccini had visited David Belasco and seen three of his plays, *The Music Master, Rose of the Rancho,* and finally *The Girl of the Golden West.* Then in the third year of its existence, it had played at the Belasco Theatre and had moved to the Academy of Music. One sensational effect of the production was a moving panorama, achieved by a long painted backdrop mounted on window shade-like rollers. They seemed to take the audience along the path to the miners' camp on Cloudy Mountain; the lights then dimmed as the scene changed to the Polka Saloon. Even more impressive was the scene at Minnie's cabin, with the blizzard created by thirty-two stagehands operating wind and snow machines. Although Puccini had grown far too sophisticated to be taken in by such spectacular effects, the evening awakened a response in him. He was, after all, a lover of nature and a sworn enemy of civilization, a man who hated pavements, palaces, top hats, trains, and all trappings of urban life. Thus, he realized there might be some promise in an opera set in the grand California forest, but he was not yet convinced that *The Girl* was right for him. His first taste of the Far West had come in Milan in 1890, with Buffalo Bill Cody's traveling show and its Indians, buffaloes, sharpshooters, and authentic scenes of the North American frontier. In New York seventeen years later, he was still interested in that world, even though he wrote to tell Ricordi he had found no thoroughly convincing subjects in the city. "There is nothing possible, or, rather, nothing complete. In Belasco I found moments, but nothing finished, solid, complete. I like the atmosphere of the West, but in all the plays that I've seen, I liked only a few scenes here and there. There is never a simple line, it is all muddled and sometimes in bad taste, old stuff." In closing, he said that worry over his future had left him nervous and in very bad humor (GP to GR, February 18, 1907, in Gara, pp. 339–341).

Before leaving New York, however, he did talk to Belasco about a possible future collaboration. If he had not found a play that satisfied him, he had at least heard something new when Belasco's pit orchestra struck up "Wait for the Wagon," "Camptown Races," "Old Dan Tucker," "O Susanna," and other American tunes. They were played in a potpourri intermezzo between acts of *The Girl*. In a fascinating essay in *Puccini*, a volume edited by Virgilio Bernardoni, Allan W. Atlas describes finding the original music materials for Belasco's *Girl of the Golden West* in the William Wallace Furst collection in the Music Division of the New York Public Library for the Performing Arts. These include a version of "Old Dog Tray, or Echoes from Home"—not Stephen Foster's song, but the arrangement Furst had made for the actor playing Jake Wallace. Wallace sang this "Old Dog Tray" to a banjo accompaniment in act 1 of the play, a scene Puccini later recreated very effectively in the opera. As his source for the song in the opera he used a "Festive Sun Dance of the Zunis," which had been collected by a writer from San Francisco and published in 1904 in a collection of Native American music. Atlas believes Puccini had this volume, *Traditional Songs of the Zuni*, although he has also discovered other transcriptions of Zuni music from that period that the composer might have known (Atlas, *"Belasco e Puccini,"* in Bernardoni, pp. 211–244).

The Belasco play owed much to Bret Harte, for its heroine was a composite of his fictional women. One was Miggles, who in 1853 had operated the Polka Saloon in Marysville, California. She became Minnie Falconer in Belasco's *The Girl*, giving Puccini an exceptionally strong female title character, his most authentic heroine. Like many women of the American pioneer venture, Minnie became the iconic earth mother of the American consciousness. In 1910 millions of Americans could have recognized their grandmothers in her, women who told marvelous tales about themselves. A daughter of the 1840s and 1850s, Minnie had a Virginia or North Carolina background, as her name indicates. In California she lived in a society where men farmed, hunted, and looked for gold. Girls and women worked, and not just as housewives. They tended one-room grocery stores, taverns, and saloons; they carried guns when they went to the spring for water; they shot mountain lions and copperheads; they guarded their virtue as a prized asset; and when they married, they got twenty-five-cent gold pieces for wedding gifts. Belasco, who knew that culture well, could recreate Minnie's beauty, Ramerrez's style, and the miners' gritty, miserable lives, their disease, homesickness, and depression.

One thing is certain: Puccini saw something in Belasco's Far West, for as he was about to leave New York he hinted to reporters that he might write an opera about it. From home he wrote to Sybil, on April 15, 1907, and her enthusiasm may ultimately have tipped him toward *The Girl of the Golden West*. First she found a copy of the play, then she had it translated into Italian. By the first week in July 1907, she had sent him the first two acts, and even before he read the rest of it, he wrote to say he would do the opera. But he hated the translation; he asked her for the original, although he certainly worked from an Italian text that summer and sent it to Giulio Ricordi. He also asked George Maxwell, Ricordi's New York agent, to secure the rights from Belasco, while keeping *Maria Antonietta* in reserve. Whenever Ricordi accused him of going to sleep on the job or growing cold toward "the West," Puccini would mention "some good things" in the play, especially the scene in which Minnie teaches the miners. Then he asked Sybil to send him American music, which he said he needed for creating atmosphere. Helpful as always, Sybil had it in his hands within days. Along with other material came a book of American Indian songs, almost certainly the one Atlas discovered. Although Puccini liked Belasco's second act, he immediately worked out a sketch of the play's third and fourth acts, which he combined to create the last scene of the opera. Then came the search for a new librettist, for the dependable Illica-Giacosa team no longer existed. Giacosa was dead, and Illica, still working on *Maria Antonietta,* would never accept a collaborator for *The Girl,* Puccini said. And had not Illica said it was time for Puccini to find someone new? In the summer of 1907 Tito Ricordi suggested Carlo Zangarini, a thirty-three-year-old, English-speaking dramatist whose mother had been born in Colorado. He seemed the perfect choice, but after their collaboration on *Fanciulla* went sour, Puccini referred to the librettist contemptuously as "a present from Savoia," his nickname for Tito, whom he grew to dislike.

In August Sybil and her son visited Torre del Lago, then went to Abetone with Puccini and Elvira for the rest of the summer. Vincent Seligman remembered the composer as restless, talking and thinking only of *The Girl.* After they left, he moved to Chiatri to work with Zangarini— not that the work moved along, for the librettist dragged. Soon, though, he could report to Sybil that the first act was almost finished, although other work interrupted their progress. At one point Puccini, who had been unable to go to Berlin and Prague for two immensely successful productions of *Butterfly,* decided to direct rehearsals of it in Vienna. Things there went badly. Lonely and sad, he longed to get back to Italy and his "dear" *Girl;* but first he had to struggle with an unsuitable cast, in which only Selma Kurz, the Butterfly, satisfied him. In spite of his reservations, his opera did a sell-out business, and soon he heard about new productions of it in many German cities and in Spain. His other operas were also in demand, and sheet music sales were strong. Writing to Sybil in November, he said he adored *The Girl,* the first two acts of which Zangarini had finished. Particularly enthusiastic about the "magnificent" last scene in the California forest, he thought it would be "marvelous." While waiting for act 3, he went to Genoa for *Butterfly,* hunted in Sardinia and around Torre, worked in Milan rehearsing *Tosca* at La Scala, and oversaw another *Butterfly* in Rome. Jubilantly, he announced that 250 performances of his operas had been given that year. By the first week in January 1908, news of the splendid *Tosca* was offset by slow progress on the *Girl* libretto, for Zangarini was clearly not working out. Puccini, dissatisfied with his slow pace, his language, and his inability to create strong characters, delivered an ultimatum: if he did not receive the whole libretto by mid-month, another librettist would be called in. He got the book on time and found it truly beautiful, "not fully built, but the foundations have been laid." On April 7 Puccini wrote to Lendvai that he was working on the American opera and called it "a magnificent subject." However, he asked Zangarini to make dozens of changes, as he always had done; and with that, the libretto stalled again. Losing patience, Puccini told Zangarini that he would have to work with a collaborator. Zangarini balked; but when Ricordi summoned the firm's lawyers, he gave in, and Guelfo Civinini was in place by the first week in May. Civinini was a journalist from Livorno who also wrote poetry, which brought him onto the team. But at that point Puccini was ill in Milan, so they worked by exchanging letters.

In one of these, the composer mentioned the word "redemption" for the first time in connection with the opera. That, in the end, became its overriding theme and message. Drawing parallels between Puccini and Wagner, Michele Girardi brilliantly associates the importance of redemption in *La Fanciulla del West* with that in *Parsifal,* Puccini's favorite Wagner work. Mosco Carner had already compared *Fanciulla* to *Walküre,* because both have elements in common: the "savage" heroines who love their horses, and episodes in which the wind blows open the door of the house. As Girardi adds, Sieglinde and Siegmund embrace just as Minnie and Johnson do. Writing of *Tristan und Isolde,* he also discusses the use of the "Tristan Chord" in Puccini's score, calling it a kind of thematic reference to Wagner's opera. Johnson's wound is related to Tristan's wound, both men having been injured by "impotent rivals," Rance and Melot. And as Tristan is run through after he kisses Isolde, so Johnson is shot after he declares his love for Minnie. Girardi pairs *Fanciulla* and *Tristan,* "two 'fables' that are apparently so different" (Girardi, *Giacomo Puccini,* pp. 292–293).

Closeted with Puccini in Torre, Civinini worked under killing pressure, even as Puccini began to worry about the opera's size and sweep. In Chiatri for part of the summer, he told Sybil it was proving to be much more difficult than he had imagined, and he had lost his way, at least temporarily. The next day, wrestling with the first act, he told Clausetti he was taking small steps but was moving ahead (GP to CC, June 23, 1908, in Gara, p. 368). Then he complained to Ricordi about his librettists (plural), who were a disaster, a sign that Civinini had not saved the day, and that Zangarini had been called back.

Again, he described the opera as "tremendously difficult." He even confided in Lendvai, to whom he sent a gift of a hundred francs: "I am here, and I am working a little, not much, and not as well as I would wish." He was also sad (GP to EL, July 12, 1908, in Pintorno, letter 154). The very next day, however, he reassured Ricordi, saying he was "well" and "working." But in Abetone in August, he told Civinini he was sick, the weather was terrible, he could not work, and his house was full of guests, with someone even sleeping on a sofa. Desperate to escape, he needed Chiatri, or Torre, or Viareggio, anywhere but Abetone. Nor did things improve. Finally at home at the end of summer, he was still in bad humor. Nothing had gone well; and he had even ruined his photographs, including a whole roll that he had snapped of Pascoli during a visit with the poet. He did, however, find the strength to revise the last act of *The Girl,* which Civinini described as entirely Puccini's work. The composer's effort was necessary because the last act of Belasco's play depended largely on scenic effects, so he had to supply his own scenario for a finale.

"The Most Tragic Days of My Life"

Having been out of sorts much of the summer, Puccini planned to see Dr. Grocco, but within a week he faced turmoil at home. Through four decades of his relationship with Elvira, two constants ruled their lives: his flirtations and his few affairs with other women, and her wild jealousy over his real sexual adventures and those she merely imagined. Even Vincent Seligman, who hardly knew her, mentioned her "uncertain temper" and "violently jealous disposition," while women closer to Puccini's household had greater reason to fear her. Ramelde warned her brother that Elvira would ruin him, and, as he later said, she was right. As we have seen, two of their arguments over Corinna ended in physical violence, with Elvira hitting him in the face and scratching him, and, in another dispute, Puccini punching her. When angry, she did strike out, attacking Corinna with a big umbrella, one that Seligman had seen and called "worthy of Sarah Gamp." He had been told she used it against women she saw as possible threats.

In fact, Puccini suffered for decades from Elvira's constant policing. Her aggressive attitude and what he called her "sick jealousy" set her utterly apart from other long-suffering wives of wandering husbands. They tolerated their men's casual affairs and long-standing relationships with mistresses, but she did not. Even Elvira's little granddaughter realized that her grandmother listened behind his study doors when he talked with friends. She went through his clothes, spied on him when he left the house, and asked others to report on him; she threatened to cause scenes in public. She monitored incoming and outgoing correspondence, checking on what he wrote and even opening his letters. In 1907 Puccini told Ervin Lendvai that she had destroyed all of Blanke's photographs and letters. That was no surprise to Lendvai, who wrote that he had "always known" that Elvira, whom he had gotten to know in Milan, was very jealous, and that she would "one day" cause "a big earthquake" in Puccini's house; and that is what she did. While Puccini was busy with *La Fanciulla del West,* she drove an innocent young woman to suicide and almost drove her husband to suicide as well. (Extensive accounts of these events are given in Vincent Seligman's book and in Arnaldo Marchetti's *Puccini com'era.*)

In 1902 Elvira had convinced herself that whenever she became suspicious of Puccini, her suspicions were well founded. And sometimes she had been proved right. In August or September 1908, she began accusing Puccini of having an affair with Doria Manfredi, one of their servants. Doria, a village girl, had worked at the villa for more than five years, having been added to the staff after Puccini's car crash. She had been just sixteen when she started there, one of six children of a poor widow, Emilia Manfredi; over the years of the girl's service as a nurse, housemaid, and occasional cook at Villa Puccini, she remained respectful and devoted, satisfying everyone. Vincent Seligman remembered her as the willing and industrious maid who had helped him and his mother in Chiatri and Torre. The whole household revolved around Doria, he said.

As for Elvira's suspicions, Del Fiorentino, who heard a lot of home truths and gossip in Torre del Lago, said she became angry that summer after Doria started doing the ironing at night. It was reasonable for a housemaid to iron then, because daytime temperatures reached around ninety degrees; but Elvira saw this as Doria's scheme to stay near Puccini, who always composed at night. According to Del Fiorentino, she told the maid to iron during the day or take the clothes to her own home; and for a while, Doria obeyed. However, when she began again ironing at night, Elvira started her regular spying. Finally came the moment when she claimed to have caught Doria and Puccini stepping out into the garden together. A less tormented woman might have thought nothing of that; but she, after weeks of surveillance, believed they were going outside to make love. As Puccini said, Elvira later swore she had caught them having sex; and in one letter of December 1908, he described her obsession about his having sex with women—not Doria, but other women—in the garden.

When Elvira first began accusing Doria and Puccini, she hurled a torrent of abuse against them and called Doria a slut. According to Del Fiorentino, she drove the girl out of the house at midnight, sending her home. There the girl found her mother still at work, mending a suit and trying to beat the heat. Puccini, left alone with his wife, swore that he had never touched Doria, but she did not believe him. Early in October, Elvira, who was still calling the girl a whore, gave her formal notice. Under other circumstances, the episode should have ended there, with a private dispute over domestic help resolved after the mistress fired the servant; but Elvira's jealousy grew into rage and near-madness. Like a woman possessed, she kept up her barrage through October, November, December, and far into January 1909, telling everyone she knew that Doria was Puccini's mistress. The scandal raced through the village, then around Lake Massaciuccoli, and on to Viareggio and Lucca. Pro-Puccini and anti-Puccini factions arose, with many believing him guilty.

Puccini wrote many letters about this episode, none more moving than those to Sybil. Still in Torre, he described himself as sad and desperate to escape, but lacking the courage to leave. Work on *La Fanciulla del West* had "completely dried up" (GP to SS, October 4, 1908, in Seligman, p. 166). This letter was hardly in the mail when he fled to Paris and took a room at the Hotel Bellevue because life in Torre had become unbearable. Later, he would have to return to "that Hell" out of force of habit, he said; but he stayed away, desperate enough to consider suicide. As he told Sybil, he had "lovingly fingered" his revolver (GP to SS, [October 1908], in Seligman, 166–167). A quick trip to London and visits with her lifted his spirits briefly, but by the end of the month he had returned to Italy and moved into the Hotel Regina in Milan. There he hoped to meet Tonio. Although he thought about Minnie and *Fanciulla,* he had perhaps stopped working because he was taking Veronal (barbital) to get to sleep, and it stole away his most productive time, the hours of night (GP to SS, October 30, 1908, in Seligman, 168).

On October 26, 1908, he wrote to Doria to say how saddened he was to see Elvira slandering her; on November 21 he wrote to Emilia Manfredi, swearing that her daughter was pure and that he was innocent. He was again in Torre the week before Christmas, trying to make peace with Elvira and begging her to put the incident behind her. To Sybil he wrote, "I can write more freely today because Elvira has gone to Lucca, where her mother is ill. It's a ghastly, horrible life, enough to drive one to suicide." He said he was working so slowly that he doubted he could ever finish *Fanciulla*. "Perhaps I shall be finished first. . . . Elvira's persecution continues unabated; she has been to see the priest to get him to talk to [Doria's] mother, and is doing everything she can to drive her out of the village. I've seen the poor girl secretly once or twice, and the sight is enough to make one cry. . . . My spirit rebels against all this brutality, and I have to stay on in the midst of it!! If only it hadn't been for my work, which keeps me here, I should have gone away, and perhaps forever. But I lack the courage to take action, as you know." Doria was ill. He was ill, and he despaired for the new opera (GP to SS, December 20, 1908, in Seligman, pp. 168–169).

After visiting her mother in Lucca, Elvira came home, still angry, and Puccini became more desperate. At least twice he visited the Manfredi brothers, who had once been his hunting and fishing pals, to reassure them and Doria's mother about his innocence.

One item of professional correspondence from this period is his letter congratulating Toscanini on his triumphs at the Met. He intended to go to Milan only for *Manon Lescaut,* he wrote, and he reaffirmed his commitment to *La Fanciulla del West* (GP to AT, December 29, 1908, NYPLPA, Music Division, Wanda Toscanini Horowitz Donation). As he well knew, he needed the new opera, because even a Roman critic sympathetic to him had described *Bohème* in a national newspaper as that "too often given or too often performed opera by Puccini," further eroding his confidence in himself. The composer believed that people were tired of his operas. But in Torre del Lago that December, opera was rarely on his mind.

Elvira continued to hurl false accusations at Doria long after she was fired, and she defamed and criticized her in conversations with many people in Torre. On Christmas Day, she confronted Doria, perhaps after Mass, with others nearby, then attacked her again in public in January

1909, calling her by an assortment of offensive names and threatening her life.

Puccini's accounts of these distressing events are found in letters to Sybil and others. In Torre in early January, he was trying to work on the opera but was bitterly unhappy, with Elvira constantly spying on him. He no longer wanted to live, and above all, he did not want to live with her. He thought of going away to make a new life somewhere else, to escape what he called a "prison atmosphere" that was killing him. But where would he go? Accustomed to the comfort of his home, he would not know what to do (GP to SS, [January 4, 1909], in Seligman, p. 169). If Elvira would only leave, he said, he would stay there alone, composing and hunting. In other letters, he told Sybil about the contretemps that followed, saying that Doria was facing "a Hell in her own home, and dishonor outside, with Elvira's insults ringing in her ears." He said Elvira even prevented the girl from taking walks in the village and told tales about her all over Torre—to Doria's mother, her relatives, who lived next door to Villa Puccini, the priest, and others. Everyone told her to calm down, but she would not listen. Then she finally promised Puccini that she would do so, but that very night he found her outside the villa, dressed in his clothes and trying to catch him with a lover.

So paralyzed was he that he said nothing to her about this grotesque, shocking episode. Instead, he left the next day for Rome and checked into the Hotel Quirinale, where he could count on the management for respect and Tosti and his wife for moral support. He continued writing to Sybil from Rome. Elvira, who had planned to leave for Milan when he left Torre, stayed at home for three more days, doing everything she could to harm Doria. Again she confronted Emilia Manfredi, calling her daughter a whore, and repeating her claim that Doria and Puccini had had trysts in the dark outside the villa. She lied to one of the Manfredi uncles about letters the two had supposedly exchanged. Rodolfo, the girl's brother, believing Elvira's story, wrote to Puccini, threatening to kill him for defiling an innocent girl (GP to SS, February 6, 1909, in Seligman, pp. 171–173). Elvira had given him the details of their affair, he said.

Doria was in fact under suspicion in her own home and in the village from early October on; after Elvira's attacks in January, she refused to leave her mother's house. On one of the last days of her life, she wrote a suicide note to her family, swearing that she was innocent and begging them to take revenge on Elvira and spare Puccini. He had never harmed her, she said. Del Fiorentino said Doria went to the local pharmacy and bought a bottle of corrosive sublimate, mercuric chloride, which was used as an antiseptic and disinfectant. Dispensed in tablets, it was packaged in a glass container with skull and crossbones on the label and marked "Poison." On January 23 she swallowed three sublimate tablets and began having stomach cramps. Dr. Rodolfo Giacchi, the municipal physician, rushed to the house and tried to save her.

Puccini, still at the Quirinale in Rome, learned about the poison that day, probably by telegram. "I'm in the depths of despair," he wrote frantically to Sybil, saying he was ruined. Certain that Doria would die, he said, "I am done for," and added that the Manfredis were bringing a legal action against Elvira, who had fled to Milan. "It's the end of my family life, the end of Torre del Lago, the end of everything," he despaired. "I am really weary of life, which has become an intolerable burden. It's impossible to forecast the consequences of this ghastly tragedy. Oh, God! What a dreadful misfortune this is!" (GP to SS, January 27, 1909, in Seligman, pp. 169–170).

When Doria died, on the twenty-eighth, after five days of atrocious suffering, Puccini was notified at once. Learning the news, he wrote to Sybil. "It's the end of everything. . . . Feel for me. I am utterly broken" (GP to SS, January 28, 1909, in Seligman, p. 170). According to gossip in Torre, Doria had died after a botched abortion. Everyone there had turned against him, and the Manfredis indeed had decided to sue Elvira. If she went back there, she would be lynched. With Tosti and his wife, Berthe, to console him, he weighed his own situation and kept in touch with his lawyers. And he told Ricordi to settle Elvira's affairs, for he "never, never" wanted to have anything more to do with her.

Then came the news that the authorities had ordered Dr. Giacchi to perform an autopsy in the presence of witnesses. It was established that Doria was a virgin. With that, the Manfredis added further charges against Elvira. As Puccini said, they intended to accuse her of being directly responsible for her suicide. He wrote to Ramelde about his confusion, saying he had not yet recovered from the terrible blow. He had no idea why he was in Rome, and did not know what he was thinking or doing. "If I, too, could die, I would be happy." And about Doria, "poor little girl, so good, so affectionate toward me—and to end like this! It is horrible, unjustly horrible" (GP to RPF, early February 1909, in A. Marchetti, pp. 349–350).

In the flood of publicity, Doria's suicide was reported in national and international papers, in stories so prominent that even Lendvai wrote from Berlin, "My God, the whole world is reading about this very strange story" (EL to GP, February 12, 1909, in A. Marchetti, pp. 352–355). He begged Puccini to join him in Berlin and offered to find him an apartment. Illica thought Puccini should go to New York to finish *Fanciulla*. Because of its American subject, no one would think it strange to see him there. He also felt that if Puccini put an ocean between himself and Elvira, he would not give in to what Illica called his "weakness" and be reconciled with her (LI to GP, [beginning of March 1909], in A. Marchetti, p. 355). At that moment, though, reconciliation seemed impossible, for Elvira blamed Puccini for everything. Through all this, he depended chiefly on the counsel of Carlo Nasi, who had served him well in settling the matter with Corinna in 1903. Nasi went to Torre two days after Doria died to interview Dr. Giacchi and Antonio Bettolacci, who also wrote to Elvira. Too optimistic by far, he felt the Manfredis would drop their legal action within weeks or months, but said Elvira could never return to Torre. Puccini would be welcome eventually, but he should stay in Rome as long as possible. Nasi also went to Milan to arrange the legal separation, because, as he said, Puccini could not "go on living every day with that poison" (CN to GP, January 31, 1909, in A. Marchetti, pp. 345–349). Puccini spent almost a month at the Hotel Quirinale, in despair over the continuing attention Doria's death got in the press. Finally, he took refuge in the Maremma and he went hunting in Capalbio.

On February 23 he returned to Torre, staying in the villa with some of his nieces. Tonio soon joined them; but Puccini remained depressed and unable to work. In March he wrote to Sybil that his life was "finished, done for [and] I only want to die." He cried; he could not sleep; he could not get Doria out of his mind and claimed that he saw her face before him all the time. Still outraged because Elvira was saying she had caught him having sex with the girl, he wrote: "The most infamous lies!! I defy anyone to say they ever saw me give Doria even an innocent caress. She was so persecuted that she preferred to die—and her strength and her courage were great" (GP to SS, March 6, 1909, in Seligman, p. 174). Flattened by influenza, he called on two of his sisters to care for him.

Soon came the first sign that he was wavering about a legal separation: he told Sybil that although he insisted on one, he did not intend to make it permanent. Both money and emotional ties with Elvira and Tonio may have figured in his decision, for at one point she was asking for a very large settlement; and in another letter Puccini said she and her lawyers even wanted to take Torre away from him. He also felt he would eventually be forced to settle with the Manfredis, to whom he had already offered money. Soon he was dividing his time between Torre and the Grand Hôtel de la Ville in Milan, where he could see Tonio. Elvira, whom he refused to meet at first, was absolutely unrepentant. Then their meeting in Milan proved useless, as did his written pleas. Unleashing a torrent of abuse and accusation in March, she called him "a great egotist" and "heartless," saying everything was his fault, "not my fault, but yours." Again and again she denied any responsibility. "For too long, you have made me your victim; you have always trampled on my kind and loving feelings for you, always offending me, the loving wife and passionate lover that I have always been. If there is a God, He will have to make you pay for the way you made me suffer, and you too will be punished, and then you will regret the evil you have done to me, but it will be too late. With your egotism, you have destroyed a family and have caused very serious events, and if it is true that we pay for everything in the world that we do, you will pay. . . . You will end up alone and abandoned by everyone. Your theory that money can buy everything is wrong, because you cannot buy affection and the certainty of having loving people around you." These few lines can only suggest the virulence of Elvira's long attack on her husband (EBP to GP, March 25, 1909, in A. Marchetti, pp. 356–365).

In all these months of torment, Puccini had one moment of professional satisfaction, in March with the huge success of *Manon Lescaut* at La Scala. The performance and staging were splendid, he said, and it was the biggest hit of the season. *La Fanciulla del West,* however, lay untouched until mid-April. He and Elvira met several times, all encounters ending with exchanges of angry words. Finding her as violent as ever, he refused her demand that they meet in Switzerland, in the presence of witnesses. Instead, he left for London in May to spend time with Sybil; he then went to Paris in June to meet Gatti-Casazza to discuss the Met's plans for *Manon Lescaut,* in which Lina Cavalieri was to sing. Going to the theater almost every night, he saw ballets and operas; then he spoke of getting back to "Mademoiselle Minnie," a sign he had begun again to think about *La Fanciulla del West.*

In early June he was again at the Grand Hôtel de la Ville in Milan, where he and Elvira finally met. Although he sharply criticized the advice her lawyers had given her, he mentioned reconciliation and said he intended to return to her, but only if he could work and live a peaceful, orderly life (GP to EBP, [June 12 or 15, 1909], Pierpont Morgan Library, New York). He also told Sybil about an eventual reconciliation and complained about greedy, incompetent lawyers.

Puccini returned to Torre to wait for news about the Manfredis' suit. On July 6 the court in Pisa heard the case, but Elvira did not appear. When the verdict was read, she was found guilty of defamation of character, libel, and menace to life and limb, and was condemned to five months and five days in prison, a fine of seven hundred lire, and all costs—a much stiffer sentence than anyone had expected. Worse, the story was again carried by all Italian papers and by the foreign press. And still Elvira railed at him for not doing enough to stop the trial. Did he want to see her go to prison? With that, he agreed to reconcile with her and left for the Grand Hotel in Bagni di Lucca, expecting to meet her and Tonio there.

The fact that he had his piano moved to his hotel speaks volumes for his hopes in such a moment. This was a good omen for *Fanciulla.* A bad omen for his future came with the thousand Sanitas brand cigarettes that he asked Alfredo Vandini, a longtime friend, to send him. He also ordered cigarettes from Sybil and directly from the national monopoly in Rome. Settled in Bagni, he worried about Tonio, who was ill in Milan. Elvira, desperate over the court's sentence, wrote him another of her violent, angry letters, saying she could not appeal without telling the truth about him and the Manfredis, who were blackmailers. Doria's mother, she claimed, was the most evil of all. Elvira's attorneys filed her appeal on July 21, saying what Puccini had suspected: Elvira's sister and others in her family—her "entourage," as he called them—had misled her by saying he was in love with Doria. Elvira pleaded guilty to libel but denied the defamation charge. Finally, after months of correspondence and negotiations involving her attorneys and Bettolacci, Puccini went to Pisa himself. His settlement with the Manfredis cost him twelve thousand lire, but they withdrew the suit. At the beginning of October, more than a year after Elvira first accused Doria and her husband, the court nullified the action.

Puccini's separation from Elvira had by that point ended on his terms, after the sentence was pronounced. They reconciled in Bagni di Lucca in July, with Tonio as a buffer between them. Again the composer confided in Sybil, saying he hoped his life might be now less unpleasant. He wanted to get back to work, but soon found how hard that would be, because *La Fanciulla del West* was terrible. However, he felt it had begun to take on life and strength at last. With his peace of mind still shattered, he held off work until August, and even then progress was sometimes slow. Nor was music his only concern, because sometime that summer he sold his villa at Boscolungo Abetone, though he would spend time at the resort later.

The year of turmoil had obviously taken its toll on him. After Franz Kafka and Max Brod saw Puccini among the celebrity spectators at an air show in Brescia, Kafka reported in a Prague newspaper that the composer "had a drinker's nose" (Hoelterhoff, pp. 157–158). In fairness, I must add that no one else has ever suggested that Puccini, a diabetic, had a problem with alcohol. An early fan of aviation, he had gone to the show in Brescia to see Louis Blériot, Europe's most famous airman. In July 1909 Blériot became the first person to fly across the English Channel. Back home in October, Puccini told Guido Vandini his life was tranquil at last, and said he wanted to forget the bitter days he had lived through. However, as his later letters to Elvira prove, he reminded her of the tragedy of Doria Manfredi often enough to keep it alive.

La Fanciulla at Last

Staying in Torre through September and October 1909, Puccini almost finished the second act and planned to finish the whole job in about a year. By November he was busy with act 3. Occasionally he had to pay attention to other business—for example, he took two weeks off to rehearse *Butterfly* in Brussels. His health was good, and Elvira was being fairly reasonable, although her old obsession erupted that autumn when she became jealous of Sybil, "taking our friendship amiss," as Puccini regretfully wrote his English friend in October 1909. Just before Christmas he described himself to Sybil: driven by work and happy with Minnie; but he asked, "Am I alive? I don't know myself." He had Minnie, he said, and the rest was "emptiness" (GP to SS, December 23, 1909, in Seligman, pp. 187–188). New Year's Day 1910 found him still working hard, keeping to his schedule, and feeling the opera was actually very good. Never too busy to help someone with a letter of recommendation, he asked the management at the Théâtre de la Monnaie in Brussels to engage Ettore Panizza, whom he had heard conduct in Naples. By April 9 he had finished his opera.

In June Puccini went to Paris for Gatti's and Otto Kahn's Met engagement at the Théâtre du Châtelet, mentioned earlier. The company, complete with soloists, technicians, and press agents but without orchestra (local forces would be recruited), had sailed from New York on the *George Washington* and the *Kaiser Wilhelm II*. The season started with a rare public dress rehearsal of *Aida* with Emmy Destinn, Caruso, and Homer, Toscanini conducting. On the program as well were *Otello, Falstaff, Cavalleria Rusticana, Pagliacci,* and *Manon Lescaut.* The Met also gave a benefit for the survivors of a French submarine disaster. Everyone, including Puccini, had expected Cavalieri to sing the title role in *Manon Lescaut,* but when she fell ill, an ideal replacement was found in the young Spanish soprano Lucrezia Bori, who went on to a long career at the Met. Caruso sang Des Grieux, and Pasquale Amato was Lescaut. Writing to Sybil about the rehearsals, Caruso said the "chauvinistic" French doubted whether it could survive, given the popularity of Massenet's *Manon.* But "we all got down to work," and the opera did very well. Puccini described it to Ricordi as a "unique performance," and later could congratulate himself on its huge box office returns.

At that same time, the Opéra Comique had fully sold out a series made up of *Tosca* with Farrar and Scotti, *Bohème,* and *Butterfly.* The management said Puccini's operas sold more quickly than those of any other composer. Respected and admired, he basked in the attention, becoming embarrassed only when people pointed to him in cafés. At the Renaissance Theater after the dress rehearsal of a play, Queen Margherita stopped him in the lobby and chatted. All this added up to a smashing success, something never before seen in Paris, Puccini said, and something he could never have imagined.

While there, he signed his contract for *Fanciulla* at the Met. An earlier verbal agreement had been reached when Gatti-Casazza had visited Puccini in Torre. The final typed document, dated June 9, 1910, reads:

> Today an agreement has been reached between the Metropolitan Opera Company of New York and Maestro Giacomo Puccini, who lives in Torre del Lago, as follows:
>
> 1. Maestro Giacomo Puccini commits himself to come to New York in the months of November and December 1910, to stay for four consecutive weeks. It is agreed that, excepting for a case of *force majeur,* the first performance of *La Fanciulla del West* will take place on December 6, 1910, and the Maestro must be in New York two weeks before the opera is performed.
>
> 2. In these four weeks, Maestro Giacomo Puccini will attend the performances of his operas and will oversee the staging of *La Fanciulla del West.*
>
> 3. The Metropolitan Opera Company commits itself to paying Maestro G. Puccini the sum of 20,000 lire, that is to say, "twenty thousand lire," plus the round trip from Milan for the Maestro and his wife, plus [the expenses of] his entire stay of four weeks in New York.
>
> 4. The sum of 20,000 lire shall be paid to the Maestro at the rate of 5,000 lire a week at the end of each week.
>
> 5. *Place to stay* means: 1 salon, 1 bedroom, 1 bath, and meals, as well as taxis.
>
> 6. During these four weeks, Maestro G. Puccini commits himself to being completely at the disposition of the Metropolitan Opera Company for the agreed-upon work described above, and without the consent of the Metropolitan Opera Company, he cannot attend any performance of his operas, whether in concert form or in the theatre [other than those produced by the Metropolitan Opera].
>
> 7. All these conditions were accepted by mutual agreement, and they are in force from the moment both parties sign.
>
> METROPOLITAN OPERA COMPANY
> [Signature] Giacomo Puccini
> General Manager

In his haste, he signed on the wrong line. And Gatti did not sign at all (original in the Metropolitan Opera Archives).

Having just heard Toscanini's interpretation of *Manon Lescaut* in Paris, he wrote him about it as soon as he got back to Milan. Ricordi was preparing a new score of the opera, and Puccini needed the conductor's help.

"Dearest Arturo, Casa Ricordi has finally decided to print the orchestra score of *Manon.* A copy, which you will want to see, will be sent to you. Believe me, you could do me no greater favor. In this way, after you have corrected the timbres and the ligatures that will be useful for the strings, etc. etc., I will finally be able to have *the definitive Manon,* and free her from the anarchy that has tied her up. In my soul, I have full confidence in what you do, and in the goodness of your soul; I hope to see you soon. Many good wishes to Signora Carla and a warm handshake from your affectionate G. Puccini" (GP to AT, June 23, 1910, NYPLPA, Music Division, Wanda Toscanini Horowitz Donation).

On July 18 Puccini wrote from Torre to the conductor Ettore Panizza to answer questions about an orchestration, a good example of his care in instructing conductors how to handle his music and following up on the details. The conductor was in London. "Dear Panizza, I will check, but I think I put in the middle '*mi*' only for the second trumpet, because the high note interfered with the *diminuendo* of the [sung line], and so I would leave the '*mi*' in, but only for the trumpet. Anyway, one trumpet makes plenty of noise [*ha suono abbondante*] to fill out the chord. I am happy the first act is finished, and I am certain it will come out well and be faithful to my intentions. Thanks for everything. How are things going at Covent Garden? Will they do *Manon?* Ciao. Affectionate greetings from Giacomo Puccini" (GP to EP, July 18, 1910, Tollett and Harman Collection).

Then he turned his attention back to *Fanciulla.* With *Manon Lescaut* in Toscanini's hands, he could get on with the orchestration, which he finished at midnight on July 27. "The opera is finished," he informed Ricordi, adding, "Praise God!" With Carignani at his side, he celebrated closure "of a work that is not small" (GP to GR, July 28, 1910, in Adami, p. 181). He told Sybil it was his best opera. Later the same day, he went back to *Manon* and wrote again to Toscanini. "Dear Arturo, Tell me, are those little changes for *Manon* still in your hands? I would need them, because it is to be given right away in Lucca. I am expecting to meet you in Viareggio. I have here the scores of the first and second acts and part of the third. I am doing the last scene, and then, God willing, I have finished" (GP to AT, July 28, 1909, NYPLPA, Music Division, Wanda Toscanini Horowitz Donation).

August was a particularly busy month in Torre, with Carignani at the villa copying the score of *La Fanciulla del West,* while final conferences with Toscanini settled questions of music and staging. Family also mattered, for as soon as the two maestros left, Ramelde and two of her daughters came to stay, spending their days taking warm seabaths in Bagni di Torre and Viareggio. Puccini, who was waiting for the delivery of a new automobile, went swimming with them, then took time to escort them and Elvira to the theater in Lucca. Always worried about productions of his operas there, he awaited the upcoming *Manon Lescaut*, which was planned as part of the city's big autumn holiday and fair season. In mid-August, he wrote directly to Guido Vandini, who was in charge of the production, saying that when the theater received the *Manon* scores from Ricordi, he would come to Lucca to go over the material himself.

Finally, in September, he, Elvira, and Antonio took a vacation in Lausanne, staying at the Grand Hotel de la Paix. While they were there, Puccini went to Simplon to watch a competition for the first flight over the Alps. Writing to Ramelde, he described an early trial run by the Peruvian Jorge Chavez, who circled up the valley to reach a height of twenty-four hundred meters before spiraling down again. "It was truly beautiful to see this great bird against the background of the glaciers"; but the flight was "incredibly dangerous," he said. In fact, he had seen a remarkable feat of aviation by a true pioneer (GP to RPF, September 20, 1910, in A. Marchetti, pp. 384–387).

After a short stay in Torre, he returned to Milan, where another problem arose over the score of *Manon*. Toscanini wanted Puccini to make a correction to the score; but he said he could not make it. He had explained his problem to Toscanini's wife, he said. "I don't have the score here, and I don't remember the configuration of the notes. You put it in," he offered. This meant, in effect, that Toscanini's corrections became part of the definitive edition. Then Puccini added, "I am very sorry you could not come with us to Simplon." Apparently, he had hoped the Toscaninis would join them on their vacation (GP to AT, September 18, 1910, NYPLPA, Music Division, Wanda Toscanini Horowitz Donation).

A Triumph in New York

At the Met, Toscanini oversaw the first three weeks of rehearsals of *La Fanciulla del West*, which would be in his hands until the composer arrived. This left a nervous Puccini waiting for news; and when it came, he was clearly relieved. He wrote to Toscanini from Milan: "Dearest Arturo, You cannot imagine how happy I was to have your telegram about the good reading of the opera. I had been waiting for it for three or four days, and in my heart, that wait worried me a bit. Now I am tranquil and happy, and I thank you so much for having kept your promise to me so quickly. So Tonio and I will leave, it seems, on November 9; Tito will also leave with me. I can't wait for the moment I can be near you, not so much because of my own self-interest, but to be with you, whom I love and esteem so much. Give my regards to Gatti, and we'll see each other again soon. Affectionately, Giacomo Puccini" (GP to AT, October 28, 1910, NYPLPA, Music Division, Wanda Toscanini Horowitz Donation). In fact, Toscanini liked *Fanciulla del West* very much, as Walfredo Toscanini told me in 2002. Walfredo remembered his grandfather calling it a "great symphonic poem."

When Puccini sailed for New York, a resentful Elvira was left behind in Milan, apparently because Puccini said he was punishing her for the anguish she had caused him over Doria. Tonio and Tito Ricordi sailed with him on the *George Washington,* and again the Met provided him with a suite fit for royalty. Writing to Albina Franceschini, Ramelde and Raffaello's daughter, he described his quarters: four large, brilliantly lighted rooms with bath, thick carpets, huge windows with silk curtains, mirrors, sofas, closets with interior lighting, desks, and two card tables. The suite even had a breakfast room, and he had been assigned two valet-waiters to tend to his every need. The liner, a floating palace of thirty-six thousand tons, was more than six hundred feet long. "Colossal! As big as the pyramids!" He read, took walks around the deck, played cards, drank, slept, read the shipboard papers, and took photographs. Ahead, he said, was the famous premiere (GP to Albina Franceschini, November 12, 1910, in A. Marchetti, pp. 388–389). His hotel was huge, and he was treated like a prince, with the Met even paying for his meals. Reporters followed him everywhere and quoted his remarks on the opera, and one described him as rich and the most successful of all modern composers, a man with an income of fifteen thousand dollars a week during the opera season.

His New York visit surpassed even his stay in Paris. With the Met's press department and Otto Kahn's own public relations man priming the newspapers every day, an enormous wave of publicity promoted Puccini and the opera. The tickets went quickly, even with prices that had been doubled for the nonsubscription premiere. The cheapest seat was $3, the most expensive was $10; but scalpers were selling them at many times their original price, as much as $150. In an attempt to stop them, the box office staff tried to get everyone to sign the back of his or ticket, so it could be countersigned at the door. Such an elaborate scheme, however, could not work, and it was soon abandoned.

At the same time, the Met's Board of Directors was doing everything possible to make the composer happy. They asked for two extra performances of *Fanciulla,* planned a reception for him after the premiere, and gave him Henry Frick's box that night (minutes of the Board of Directors of the Metropolitan Opera Company, November 22, 1910, Metropolitan Opera Archives). Puccini also knew he could rely on Toscanini, who had rehearsed the orchestra to perfection, and Belasco, who coached the singers until they acted like Broadway professionals. Accustomed to appearing as ancient Egyptians, Druids, and figures from Renaissance courts, they found it difficult to see themselves as ordinary men and women from California. Additionally, the difficult score, tricky staging, and special effects taxed the whole company. Then there were the animals: Puccini, who had once told Ricordi he wanted eight or ten horses onstage, got only eight, but they caused problems in the crowded final scene. Still, he felt confident about the opera. Caruso was magnificent in the role that had, after all, been written for him; and Amato was an admirable Jack Rance. Only Emmy Destinn, the Czech soprano, seemed somewhat dull in rehearsals, but Puccini liked her. On the whole, everything was going splendidly.

In *The Golden Age of Opera* Robert Tuggle recaptures the atmosphere of the rehearsals. In his book is an account by a writer for the *Sun,* who described the morning of December 5 in the Met auditorium. Toscanini was at the conductor's desk, with his nose almost touching the score as he made corrections. Puccini, sitting quietly, had on a derby hat, brown suit, and red tie. A little group of associates gathered around him. Belasco, with his own entourage, often "blasted" away with his criticisms of the staging and the lights. A missed cue in act 2 set off pandemonium. Caruso, in a brown business suit, could barely be heard, because he was trying to save his voice for that night's *Aida.* He did, however, go through all the exhausting action of the second act, through many repeats of the scene in which Minnie drags him in from the porch, and later, when he had to climb a ladder to the loft of her house. Destinn, on the other hand, sang and acted her role fully. At one in the afternoon, they began the act again, but without Caruso. Toscanini sang Johnson's music! Puccini, who sat through this with an unlighted cigarette dangling from his lips, went once to speak to Toscanini about the score. Then the company began act 3, with Belasco making them go over and over the scene with Johnson. None of the Italians could throw a lasso! (Tuggle, pp. 65–69).

On December 10, the night of the premiere, the Met offered a gala of unparalleled extravagance. The auditorium was hung with American and Italian flags, and bouquets decorated the boxes. Puccini, alone in his box, said the audience held its judgment for most of the first act, stunning him when an hour and five minutes passed with no applause. But at the end of the act, a big demonstration swept the theater, with fourteen curtain calls, and Puccini, Toscanini, and even Belasco taking bows with the singers. Nineteen more followed after act 2, with more solo bows for the composer. After the fifth call, Gatti-Casazza came onstage to give Puccini a silver wreath from Otto Kahn and the Board of Directors. At the end, the audience demanded another fourteen bows. "Applause. The whole evening was a hurricane of applause," according to the *Sun.* The night ran on and on, with a reception following the performance. Finally, Puccini, Tonio, and Toscanini went to an Italian restaurant for dinner at two in the morning. The next day Puccini stayed in bed until four.

On another day he accompanied the troupe to Philadelphia for a performance that may have gone even better than the premiere. The Met also gave *Fanciulla* at the Brooklyn Academy of Music.

The critical reception for *Fanciulla* was mixed. Richard Aldrich wrote in the *New York Times:* "It was the first time that a new work by one of the most distinguished and popular composers had had its first representation in New York, and it is not likely that any finer or more authoritative presentation of this most difficult opera will be given on the other side of the water." He went on to praise Puccini for undertaking something that might well have been impossible a few years earlier. He sometimes used a "rapid and staccato vocal utterance" and "broad points or broad sketches of color, thematic fragments, quickly shifting, kaleidoscopic harmonies." The music hurried along after the action and tried to keep pace with the spoken word. Then Puccini would write pages and pages in "a broader style, a lyric movement of psychologizing, when the music is given more opportunity to rise to its true task of expressing emotion or passion or sentiment. Here voices may likewise also find a broad *arioso,* in phrases that at least have melodic outline and shapeliness." Aldrich said the score reflected the new directions in Puccini's development. With new harmonies and dissonance, he was speaking in a different language, and anyone who knew him only from *La Bohème* might not recognize him in *Fanciulla,* because he had come so far in fifteen years. Toscanini's conducting was a "masterpiece." Destinn rose to the occasion and acted well. Caruso was at his best, in a role that suited him better than many other, more famous parts. Amato brought Jack Rance to vivid life, and the chorus was "especially good" (review in Seltsam, p. 225).

Others wrote less balanced reviews, with some accusing Puccini of burdening Belasco's characters with too much Latin emotion and making them unbelievable. Some mentioned his debt to Debussy, but few said much about his splendid orchestration. Some gratuitous criticism centered on the "absurdity" of having "cowboys" singing in Italian. Overlooking the power of Minnie, Johnson, and Rance, Ravel later praised Puccini for making the orchestra the protagonist. (Stravinsky, on the other hand, decades later called *Fanciulla* "a horse opera, extraordinarily right for television, with a Marshal Dillon and professional Indians" like those hired to perform in hotels in Santa Fe.) Critics have slammed Belasco for stealing Sardou's plot for *Tosca* and throwing it down in a California setting. Accusations of plagiarism and self-plagiarism have also flown. But this criticism is far too narrow, for the plot and characters of *Fanciulla* are "taken from" *Tosca* no more than from *Il Trovatore* or any other drama in which two men love the same woman. The excitement of the card game awakened a response in some; but the scene with the American Indians drew an unfavorable response. One critic passed over the touching lullaby that Wowkle sings to her illegitimate child and took aim at Minnie for wanting Billy Jackrabbit and Wowkle to marry—as if well-meaning women of the 1850s never gave that kind of advice to lovers who had a child!

Surprisingly, none of the American writers seemed moved by the clear moral message about redemption, not Belasco's message, but Puccini's, which gives this drama such substance. In the play Minnie reads parts of Joe Miller's joke book to the miners; in the opera she reads from the Bible, then explains the text, which is taken from the Fifty-first Psalm. The Psalm begins: "Have mercy upon me, O God, according to thy loving kindness; according unto the multitude of thy tender mercies, blot out my transgressions." Minnie's passage in the opera, taken from later verses, reads:

> "Wash me, and I shall be whiter than snow.
> Create in me a clean heart,
> And renew a right spirit
> Within me." *(She breaks off.)*
> Boys, that means the road to redemption
> Is open to every sinner in the world.
> May you all hold in your hearts
> This supreme truth about love.

Minnie's Lesson Scene remains a sublime moment that can stand with Puccini's finest, perhaps because he understood how real his characters were. The composer, in his profound simplicity and Tuscan earthiness, breathed life into the characters of *Fanciulla*. The opera is especially moving when it is sung and acted naturally, as it was by Eleanor Steber and Mario Del Monaco in Chicago; or by Leontyne Price or Dorothy Kirsten and Richard Tucker, or Barbara Daniels and Plácido Domingo in New York. In my view, it is Puccini's finest opera.

At the time of the *Fanciulla* premiere, no one—apart from a few critics—could deny Puccini his victory. The Met Archives records show the box office returns for opening night as $20,270, reflecting the gala's inflated ticket prices. The next performance brought in $7,303, while the third, in Philadelphia, brought $14,831. As a gesture of thanks to the Toscaninis, Puccini went to Tiffany's and bought a sterling silver candelabra for their dinner table. To Belasco he gave a copy of the score of *Fanciulla* with a dedication: *"A David Belasco al collaboratore all'amico con animo grato offre Giacomo Puccini, New York 10.12.10"* ("To David Belasco, to the collaborator, to the friend, with a grateful heart, offered [by] Giacomo Puccini, New York 10 December 1910") (author's collection).

As he left for Italy, Puccini seemed filled with genuine regret, although he was longing for Torre. On board the *Lusitania,* he slept through part of the ship's New Year's Eve party, then sat down at three in the morning on New Year's Day to write a sad letter to Carla Toscanini.

Dearest Signora Carla, Here we are, close to land. We were very indifferent toward the [old] year's end. I was sleepy; Tonio was pensive, perhaps thinking wistfully of his life in New York; down in the salon, all the English people and Americans were drinking and shouting while the music played: I was sleepy and fell asleep on a sofa until midnight. Now it is three in the morning, and I cannot sleep; I am turning over and over in the bed, helped by the gentle rolling of the ship. I think over and over again about past days, about the rehearsals, the "premiere," the lights of New York. Now it is all over, but in my heart, I still have a great, strong feeling of affection for all of you! And it will always be there! You were so good and kind to me, so sweet and concerned. Toscanini [was] such a patient and affectionate friend! My mind is full of thoughts of you two; and I envy you, [for] I would also love to be like you, who have your family together [*come voi, colla vostra famiglia unita*], with your children who love you so much, with friends who surround you and believe in you. Unfortunately, I feel alone in the world, and I am always sad because of that, and yet I have always tried to love people; but no one has ever understood me, that is, people have always taken me wrong [*sono stato sempre male interpretato*]. Now it is too late; I am too old, unfortunately too old. Please go on being my friends; at least [I will have] good and intelligent people, people who tolerate me and understand me [*persone buone che mi tollerino e che mi capiscono*]. So thank you for everything you have done for me, and believe in my unending gratitude and affection. [GP to CT, January 1, 1911, NYPLPA, Music Division, Wanda Toscanini Horowitz Donation]

Two weeks later, he wrote directly to Toscanini from Milan.

Dearest Arturo, Thank you for your telegram. I am happy to see that *The Girl* is doing well, and I am pleased about that. As for [the planned first Italian production in] Rome, I spoke to Sig. Riccieri, insisting on having [Cecilia] Gagliardi, whom they have engaged. However, people tell me that she is not the vibrant artist that we need. [She has a] beautiful and warm voice, just the same. I know nothing of the two [women who are singing] the Girl in Chicago and Boston. Tito sent a telegram to Casa [Ricordi] to say that he was very, very happy about the rehearsals in Boston. To sum up, I do not know what to do, and I cannot decide anything about Rome. We need you to come forward with your authority in the business of the [soprano], so we don't find ourselves stuck with an artist who is not really one. I am all right, and you? I am sure you have a lot to do for [the American premiere of Dukas's *Ariane et Barbe-Bleu*]." [GP to AT, January 14, 1911, NYPLPA, Music Division, Wanda Toscanini Horowitz Donation]

The Dukas work was given at the Met with Farrar and Léon Rothier, Toscanini conducting. Puccini, familiar with the work, disliked it.

At home in Torre, he reminisced about New York in another moving letter to Toscanini.

> Dearest Arturo, in the silence of this place, I am thinking and remembering the days I spent near you while we two prepared *Fanciulla* together! Now that time of my life is also over, and my memory of it, though it is a happy one, is also tinged with some sadness: the beautiful moments fly by too quickly. When you get back [to Italy], how happy I would be, were I able to tell you that I have found a new libretto! And I am thinking about it and looking for it all the time, but also looking in vain. Everyone offers them to me, but none of them strike me as right; how hard it is, and I am in a hurry! I know that my opera continues to do well, it would not do otherwise, as it is performed! I beg you to give my regards to Destinn, and scold her a bit because she has not sent me her photograph, as she promised, and the same to dearest Caruso and Amato. Endless regards to Signora Carla, and to all your and my good friends in New York. P.S. I am waiting for the revision to the tenor's aria in the second act, as I said in my telegram to you. I too have added something to it, but it will not be like yours: you already have lived through the trial by fire. I filled out the final scene with choruses and added a little something ([Minnie's and Johnson's] outburst and the chorus), I think it will be better like this. About Rome, what do you think about the [soprano]? Have you seen Tito? I hear that in Milan [Eugenia] Burzio did very well in [Pacini's] *Saffo*. I asked about Gagliardi, but I am afraid she will not take direction very well [*che sia poco malleabile*]. [GP to AT, February 1, 1911, NYPLPA, Music Division, Wanda Toscanini Horowitz Donation]

The Triumphs of *Fanciulla*

After the Met premiere, the opera was given in Chicago by the Chicago-Philadelphia Opera Company, with Carolina White as Minnie and Amedeo Bassi as Johnson. In Boston, Carmen Melis sang Minnie, a role she later repeated in Europe. Puccini, always concerned about the ongoing fate of his operas, foresaw many of the problems in producing *Fanciulla,* and he followed the opera from city to city to guarantee high standards of performance. Where theaters, stages, and orchestra pits were smaller than the Met's, adjustments had to be made to sets, action, and sound. And, of course, European audiences did not know Belasco's play as Americans did, so the plot had to be made clear with good diction. Knowing all this, he worked tirelessly to get the public to accept what was, in effect, a novelty: an opera from the New World, with a score rich in "exotic" music and American songs, a score that critics called "new," or at least new for him, and a happy ending. With its authentic Western settings and requirements for top-ranking singers and credible acting, *Fanciulla* was expensive to produce and rehearse. It could never be given on the cheap.

As Puccini and Toscanini were planning the all-important Rome premiere, the first performance of the opera in Italy, they faced as unexpected crisis when Caruso became ill. Puccini wrote about this on March 23.

Dear Arturo, Caruso's illness makes me think seriously about Rome. Tell me what you would think about doing, if Caruso could not come. And give me advice about the woman [the soprano]. I'm desperate [*non so dove battermi la testa*]: Gagliardi will sing *Aida,* and because of that, she cannot sing *Fanciulla.* There is [Eugenia] Burzio, but she doesn't seem to me to have the strong voice she once had, even though I didn't dislike her in *Saffo.* There is [Livia] Berlendi, but she is a bit too much of a mezzo-soprano, and then I don't think she has as fresh a voice as she once had. There is [Ernestina] Poli-Randaccio, and I don't know her: I know that she shouted [Mascagni's] *Amica* two years ago. All in all, I worry constantly about this production in Rome. Ricordi writes to tell me to arrange everything with you, as regards the [soprano] as well as the tenor; and without Caruso, will you come to Rome [to conduct the opera]? Please write me something about this; even if you're very, very busy, please find a moment to write and give me advice. If you can't (big lazy fellow), give Maxwell instructions so he can tell me everything. I saw Sig[no]ra Carla and the little girls [Wally and Wanda Toscanini], and they are very, very well. Many affectionate greetings, and waiting to read something from you as soon as possible. I give you a hug [*ti abbraccio*]. Your, Giacomo Puccini. [GP to AT,

March 23, 1911, NYPLPA, Music Division, Wanda Toscanini Horowitz Donation]

Although he wrote this letter on Torre del Lago letterhead, he asked Toscanini to send his answer to Milan.

In April he went to Monte Carlo with Elvira for the motorboat races. Then it was back to Milan, to get ready to leave for London. When Covent Garden put *Fanciulla* on the program for May, he agreed to oversee the rehearsals, and he took Elvira with him. They stayed at the Savoy, and by May 9 he was working, although very slowly. The conductor was Cleofonte Campanini. Destinn and Bassi repeated their roles, and the baritone was Dinh Gilly. As Puccini wrote to Guido Vandini, he had a big job ahead, with twenty-four performances of his works on the program. On the tenth, "old Melba" appeared in *Bohème* with Bassi as Rodolfo and Mario Sammarco as Marcello (GP to GV, May 9, 1911, in Pintorno, letter 178). Then, as the composer feared, *Fanciulla* was delayed, not reaching the stage until May 29. This meant he had to stay in London longer than he had anticipated. After London, Puccini had to think about Rome and the premiere at the Teatro Costanzi. Toscanini, who would conduct, was already there.

Having seen the opera in two major productions, Puccini now had second thoughts about parts of it. Asking Toscanini to enter his revisions into the score, he wrote, "Dear Arturo, This follows upon my telegram. I hear that *Falstaff* went very well. People tell me that there are mistakes in the parts and in the orchestral score [of *Fanciulla*]. In spite of all my recommendations, they were not able to make all the corrections they should have done. You'll have to be patient. Listen: I made a cut in the last act that is all right: from page 309, from the 12th bar, to the 9th bar of page 310, giving Minnie: *'Ah!'* And I am thinking of making one or two in the first act: [in the] Indian Scene, after *'Va via di qua,'* go to Minnie's: *'ora via'* and that means [go to] the final explosion [*allo scoppio finale*]; and another little cut in the Mail Scene; but I will tell you about these after I have had advice from you" (GP to AT, June 1, 1911, NYPLPA, Music Division, Wanda Toscanini Horowitz Donation).

Another letter in this same collection probably dates from 1911, for Puccini wrote to Toscanini from his hotel to say he and Elvira had had a horrible drive to Rome, plagued by sun and dust. These were the days when ladies wore floor-length dusters and broad-brimmed hats with veils. Puccini, who particularly loved speed and the air blowing in his face, kept the top down whenever possible. By the time they got to Rome, Elvira had a toothache and, he said, was "swollen up like a Zeppelin" (GP to AT, undated but probably from early June 1911, NYPLPA, Music Division, Wanda Toscanini Horowitz Donation). He seems to have written this letter as soon as he reached his hotel.

The first Italian performance of *Fanciulla* took place at the Teatro Costanzi on June 12, 1911, with Toscanini conducting. Burzio was Minnie, and Amato again was Rance. After the first performances, Bassi, who was Johnson, went to London, leaving the young Giovanni Martinelli to take over the role. The first night was an important gala that celebrated the fiftieth anniversary of the Kingdom of Italy. Afterward the composer was decorated as Grand'Ufficiale della Corona d'Italia. The Roman public liked the opera. The critics seemed startled by it, although many wrote favorable reviews. In *Carteggi pucciniani,* Eugenio Gara, who included many long excerpts from the papers, remarked that the critics came with preconceived ideas about Puccini as the prisoner of his lower-middle-class sentimentality and were simply unprepared for what they heard. The critic of *Il Giornale d'Italia,* whose cheap attack on *Bohème* had so offended the composer earlier, wrote glowing praise of the "new" Puccini and his "exquisite" and "robust" new work. He was "modern," and the reviewer recognized in him a composer who had never before seemed so strong. Other reviews hailed Puccini's courage in creating such a brilliant palette of colors; there was no modern advance that he had not used to advantage. The reviewer for *Il Messaggero* was another who wrote of "modern techniques." Other newspapers recognized his larger understanding of his art, while the *Corriere della Sera,* sometimes Puccini's adversary, welcomed his mastery of his genius and his art. Primo Levi took another tack, saying the characters were too small for the grand music Puccini gave them. His score was worthy of Alexander the Great, Caesar, Waterloo, or the San Francisco earthquake, but it ill suited Minnie, Johnson, Rance, and the miners. In short, the opera suffered from elephantiasis.

Puccini took these reviews very personally, especially after finally writing the "big opera" that Giulio Ricordi had long wanted, and asked

Clausetti to help him draft a letter to the critic of the *Messaggero*. In this correspondence, he set forth his defense and creed, saying that all composers, from Verdi to Mascagni, had grown, for better or worse. It was a question of self-renewal or death. Convinced of the originality of *Fanciulla*, he felt he could no longer be accused of copying from his earlier works. He also promised that once he found a subject for his next opera, he would follow the new path, because he did not want to be left behind.

At that moment, and for much of the next two years, Puccini's job was to keep *Fanciulla* alive, although he did not go to Buenos Aires, where it was first given in July 1911. His next important assignment for the opera was in August in the Teatro Grande in Brescia, where he had racked up many triumphs; but in the event, he was miserable. Staying at the Hotel d'Italie, he wrote to Antonio Bettolacci: "I arrived here at 10 and found your letter. I'm in a very big hurry as I write to you, and I am so nervous I can't even describe it. I will tell you when we meet; and anyway I don't want to write because I don't trust even myself. I hope to be in Torre about the 25th, and I will leave for Lucca right away, and then I get the [new] boat in Varazze. . . . Here they have an orchestra of dogs. Let's hope it comes out well. Oh, it is absurd [in] this theater (and in the provinces, too) in this season. Ciao, your Giacomo" (GP to AB, August 19, 1911, NYPLPA, Music Division, Special Collections). His complaints about the company, however, cannot be reconciled with what the Grande offered. He had a fine cast, with Carmen Melis as Minnie, Martinelli as Johnson, and the baritone Domenico Viglione-Borghese — "my sheriff," as Puccini called him — as Rance. The superbly prepared conductor was Giorgio Polacco, and the orchestra one he had worked with in the past.

After this, Puccini could get his boat and relax. Dante Del Fiorentino said he called that boat *Minnie* and raced it far and wide on Lake Massaciuccoli. "The tremendous explosion of the engines brought the villagers to their doors . . . as the boat skimmed across the lake [and] startled the birds from the marshy hedges. Tonio adored it, and Giacomo loved nothing better than to order [his hunting companion and occasional employee] Nicche to get the boat ready; then he would go speeding across Lake Massaciuccoli's calm blue waters to Viareggio, by way of the canal of Burlamacca" (Del Fiorentino, p. 149). Once Puccini in his motorboat hit a rowboat full of his relatives, but no one was hurt, and local fishermen saved everyone. The composer's main concern that summer was *Fanciulla,* not boats, for he was already looking toward other productions of his opera.

In July he had a letter from the soprano Emma Carelli, asking him to let her sing Minnie at the San Carlo in Naples. He would not, because he did not think she could do it, but lacked the courage to tell her so. Shifting the responsibility, he asked Clausetti to deal with her. "I didn't want to write her what I think, because I'm just not able to. I'm confiding this to you, because she will come to you. I told her that De Sanna has other *ideas* that I cannot fail to take into consideration, and that I would, however, in spite of that, write to my Clausetti. So be ready; this is just for your information, because she will speak to you about the Costanzi (and other performances). Tell her that . . . nothing concrete has been decided about that project. Warmest regards and tear up this letter" (GP to CC, July 20, 1911, Tollett and Harman Collection). Clausetti did not destroy the letter, and Carelli did not sing Minnie in that *Fanciulla.*

Puccini attended an English-language production of *Fanciulla* in Liverpool in October. This was his first experience of seeing the opera produced "with reduced dimensions," the modified version that might make the opera suitable for small theaters and companies with reduced budgets. Cured of "elephantiasis," *Fanciulla* might have a brighter future. In fact, Tito Ricordi wanted to circulate what Puccini called the "little score," the reduction that Ettore Panizza had prepared, but Puccini loved the full version and wanted it for the upcoming production in Monte Carlo, because of the size of the orchestra and theater there. In Naples for the December production at the San Carlo, he attracted the attention of press and public. As he told Sybil, the opera went very well, although he hated Mugnone's dragging tempos, which sucked the life out of the music.

In Budapest in February 1912, *Fanciulla* was given in full scale and in Hungarian, with its composer treated like visiting royalty, although he was wretchedly unhappy. The guest of honor at a dinner offered by the mayor and city council, he could hardly protest about the unacceptable conditions in the opera house. After a week in the city, he still had not heard his baritone, who was ill, wanted to rehearse at home, and said he would come to the theater only for the final rehearsals. Finally, another man came in as a substitute, but when Puccini found him wholly unsatisfactory, he was dismissed, and the original artist was called back. Complaining that he was dealing with "dogs," Puccini told Tito Ricordi that the orchestra, scenery, and chorus passed muster, the soprano was an "absolute disaster," and the tenor was good. A "long Via Crucis" lay ahead. He was fighting "a storm at sea" because the baritone, still ill at home, had not even agreed to appear at the pre–dress rehearsal. He was old, Puccini said, afraid of the role, and offended by the composer's criticism. The whole company was mired in intrigue. "And after so much work, here we are on the night before the first performance, without a baritone" (GP to TR, February 19, 1912, in Pintorno, letter 182).

Not even Puccini's heavy schedule in Budapest kept him from his daily search for something new. He had considered *Hanneles Himmelfahrt,* a play by Gerhart Hauptmann, but set it aside, objecting to Hannele, "that girl in bed, and those (beautiful and fine) apparitions." *Anima Allegra,* adapted from a play by the brothers Joaquin and Serafin Álvarez Quintero, also bogged down after he objected to the translation he was using. Even though he had said he wanted nothing more to do with Luigi Motta, the translator, Motta did in fact, have a hand in the text. Giuseppe Adami, thrust into the breach, had been told to create a more workable second act. As things stood, though, the story was almost worthless (GP to TR, February 12, 1912, in Pintorno, letter 180). Work on it went forward.

Friendship with Margit Vészi

At some time, probably in 1912, Puccini met the Hungarian writer Margit Vészi, with whom he corresponded as a friend and confidant for many years. This young woman, born in 1885, was just one year older than Puccini's son; and she may have been a friend of Ervin Lendvai, who was living in Berlin at that time. She lived in Berlin during the winter, at 24 Hardenbergerstrasse, Charlottenburg. The composer's first note to her, however, suggests they had originally met in Tuscany, for Vészi was in Puccini's "backyard" that season, staying in Villa Parodini in the seaside town of Levanto, just up the coast from Torre del Lago. This resort attracted other artists and writers, among them at least two who later wrote librettos for Puccini. That August he sent her a postcard from Karlsbad, where he was taking the cure for his diabetes, on which he wrote, "I forgive you for Viareggio. I will leave on the thirty-first. I will be in Viareggio on the third, in Milan for a few hours on the 2. Greetings from your very devoted G. Puccini" (GP to MV, postcard, August 28, 1912, Pierpont Morgan Library, New York). From this it seems that they planned to meet.

In Berlin the following spring, he saw Vészi again and wrote to her from the Hotel Eden, inviting her to go to the opera with him the next evening. "Dearest Margherita, Do you want to come to *Rosenkavalier* at the Opera tomorrow evening? I would be very happy to spend some time with you. If you want to come, I will expect you between 7 and 7:30. Many cordial greetings, G. Puccini" (GP to MV, March 23, 1913, Pierpont Morgan Library, New York).

Only a few days later, he wrote her a long letter that reeks of depression. It was Saturday afternoon at three, and he was writing on the letterhead of the Caffè Biffi in Milan's Galleria Vittorio Emanuele. In it he also shows his ambivalence about his affair with Josephine von Stängel, his new mistress. (This romance is discussed in greater detail in the next chapter; it continued for many years.)

This letter to Margit reads:

Dear Signora, I have landed again in this Milan, for which I care so little, and where life has absolutely no attractions for me; and my useless life [*la inutile vita mia*] finds a treacherous moment of rest here, as if it were lying in a coffin. My mind is black today!! I would like to be able to fly to your studio and speak to you, for I feel my spirit would find an echo in yours. I know you have understood me so well. You are the only person who knows how to weigh me, down to the last milligram. You have an intuition about me and about all the strange nuances of my temperament. I think you know them, and because of this, I want so much to be near you. I feel like a baby who's rocked by its mother [*un bambino cullato dalla sua mamma*]; and you know that, and take care of my smallest desires, my smallest whims. And for my art, which comes so much from the soul, I really need a guide, a spirit who will understand me, and you could be this counselor [*consigliere*]. But alas, we are so far apart, and it is hard for us to be together! And I am going off to my Torre, to think about the *nothing* that surrounds me and weighs upon my spirit and stands in my way.— Strange to be blocked by nothing; but that's the way it is. Nothing, nothing in my heart for *anything*.

And then in Stuttgart [where Josephine von Stängel lived], *nothing* or rather less than *nothing*. I left more empty than before, and now I am dragging this chain along, thinking that I will certainly break it. Dear Margit, I remember everything about you. Perhaps you will laugh. What does that matter? I cherish my memory [*mio souvenir*] and I caress it in my mind. Try again to find me a subject that will make me weep with joy and with sadness. . . . Your very devoted Giacomo Puccini. [GP to MV, April 5, 1913, Pierpont Morgan Library, New York]

Again in Torre, he told Margit how unhappy he was.

Dearest Signora, I'm still the same. I'd like to come back to life, but I cannot. I think it's too late now. No more of that! Let's go on and carry our loads, like beasts of burden. The lady of the hour [von Stängel] is just the same, and I don't know what to do. I go on; at least it gives me a moment of relief to know that I have someone who thinks of me with her awful German heart and mind [*con cuore e mente Tedescucci*], which are nonetheless good and sincere. I am not throwing my whole self into this, no, I put up with it.

My family life is terribly boring, and when I can, I live here, boring myself, and writing preludes at the piano, with the pedal down, without having any place to put my music. However, I read a lot, and I am looking for things, and this, too, is a kind of sport. Write to me and console me, but don't write any hints about what I have told you. My wife is here now, and she has the bad habit of investigating everything on my desk. But don't forget me, for heaven's sake, write to me. *I Conte di Gleichen* won't do for me. It is too romantic and old-fashioned. Are you coming here or not? You speak of our seeing each other in Berlin in the autumn. Write me, then, and send me a word that will lift my spirits. Don't mention [von Stängel] and other annoyances! Remember me as much as I remember you. What sweet moments I spent with you. And yet they were innocent! But how dear they were! Addio, my dear, many good and affectionate greetings from your, G. Puccini. [GP to MV, May 5, 1913, The Pierpont Morgan Library, New York]

(Some letters appear to be missing from this correspondence, for others survive, dated 1923.)

Among musical matters, *Fanciulla* remained his main concern, and he asked Tito about casting the production at La Scala and especially the one in Florence, where, he felt, he had been treated shabbily in the past. *"Since Bohème* and *Manon* (eons ago) I have never had a decent performance

there, never, absolutely never. I *don't want Fanciulla* to be a trashy production," he said, adding, "I insist, I insist on having a conductor who knows
the opera and has a good hand and the guts to stand up to them and their
stinginess, which works against art. I would be very, very unhappy if
Fanciulla were not given with all possible honor [*onorissimo*]. . . . Florence
is my *capital,* and this controversy goes back fifteen years. You don't know
about that; I do. I heard all about *Butterfly* there, and the news about the
poor production and the poor reception got back to Lucca. So now be
strong, as you are when you want to be." Otherwise, Puccini said, he
would veto the production, because neither he nor Ricordi needed the
two thousand or three thousand lire the score rental to Florence would
bring in (GP to TR, February 19, 1912, in Pintorno, letter 182). In the
event, he need not have worried, for Gilda Dalla Rizza sang such a lively
Minnie that Puccini often planned to cast her in important productions
and, in 1921, gave her the highest praise, saying, "At last, I've seen my
fanciulla." He may also have had her in mind when he wrote *La Rondine,*
the premiere of which she sang in Monte Carlo. (However, the American
scholar Charles Mintzer, author of *Rosa Raisa,* says that Puccini originally
wanted Raisa as Magda.) Dalla Rizza, as intelligent as she was daring, had
blistering diction and a voice with a marked vibrato that let her wring
emotion out of any phrase. Once heard, she could never be forgotten.
Puccini's letters to her reflect outspoken admiration for this strong
woman. Her experience with him and her views on *Rondine* appear in
chapter 11.

In April in Monte Carlo, *Fanciulla* went magnificently, with Puccini
lending luster to the gala, which he described as "colossal." The cast included Poli-Randaccio, Martinelli, and Viglione-Borghese. One month
later, it was produced in Paris in Italian. Puccini reached the Hotel West-
minster so early that he sat in on the first orchestra reading, then stayed
until the end of May, with Elvira, Tonio, and Fosca for moral support.
Conducted by Tullio Serafin, the production had Carmen Melis (later replaced by Poli-Randaccio), Caruso, and Titta Ruffo (replaced by Viglione-
Borghese) as the principals. As expected, it was very popular.

Then it was time for Puccini to take another look at *Anima Allegra.*
Studying it in Torre that summer, he again found it disappointing. Almost
desperate with chagrin, he wrote to Tito Ricordi. "It is sad that I have to
pass the time gazing at my own navel, and [especially] for me, as I am con-

sumed by my need to hurry and by my thirst for work. I, who have already done something that was *alive*, must inflict on myself a feeble thing such as *Anima Allegra!* And yet, if nothing else develops, I will have to try this stupid, insipid little thing [*questa cosuccia slavata*] by the Quinteros, if I don't want to end up like something preserved in vinegar. [But it] is the best stupid little thing among all I have looked for and found; but it won't work as it is, and Adami tells me he will clean it up. . . . . If things go on like this, Puccini's works will be written by his biographers!" (GP to TR, probably June 1912, in Pintorno, letter 186). His greatest pleasure that year was his new yacht, the *Cio-Cio-San* as he called it, which had come from New York to the Italian Riviera. Planning for its maiden voyage, he wanted to have Tonio with him when he took it out on the Sea of Varazze and went on to Viareggio and Torre.

Although Puccini may not have gone to Genoa for the autumn performances of *Fanciulla,* he did write a thank-you letter to Carmen Melis, who again was largely responsible for its success; and he recommended its conductor, Icilio Nini-Bellucci, for the production at the Teatro Sociale in Mantua. A much more important performance followed at the Opéra in Marseilles, where it was given in November in French as *La Fille du Far-West,* the success of which would lead to other productions in France. The translation was by Maurice Vaucaire, who had struggled with Puccini over *Conchita.* Minnie was the wildly popular Jane Morlet, who had made her debut six years before. The audience went crazy over it, a local newspaper reported.

At Covent Garden in 1912, *Manon, Bohème, Tosca, Butterfly,* and *Fanciulla* were offered in one festive season. Puccini also oversaw the rehearsals at La Scala, where *Fanciulla* got a mixed reception on December 29. It did, however, run for thirteen performances, with Tullio Serafin conducting and Poli-Randaccio, Martinelli, and Carlo Galeffi in the leading roles. In Berlin for the March 1913 production, Puccini was again given a big personal demonstration; he had also arranged for the opera to be given in twenty theaters in Germany. The reviews, however, showed that the German critics had not understood the opera or Puccini's attempt to venture down new paths. When it returned to the Costanzi in Rome that year, he stayed home. After the first Vienna production, which took place in October, Puccini was decorated with the Star of the Order of Franz Josef. (In 1915 *Fanciulla* would also be given at the Teatro Verdi in Pisa, the city where the teenaged Puccini had first heard the *Aida* that had, as he said, opened a musical window for him. There, as in Florence and Lucca, the audience greeted him as a native son.)

Grief

Although Puccini sailed from one artistic triumph to another from 1911 to 1913, he also faced grave professional problems and profound sorrow, especially in 1912. Effectively hobbled in his search for new material, he had no opera even in the planning stage. As we have seen, he had appealed to many people, even to Margit Vészi, for help in finding a subject. Then Ramelde, his favorite sister and the only member of the family in whom he could easily confide, fell ill in August 1911. Puccini sent loving letters to her from Brescia while he was there for *Fanciulla,* then followed her condition all that winter. Worried that she never took care of herself, he preached to her, saying she must get X rays, change doctors, see Dr. Grocco in Torre or Lucca, and get treated in Viareggio. Writing from Budapest, he begged her not to give up. Finally Ramelde, who may have had cancer, agreed to have surgery in Bologna. After the operation, Puccini and Elvira visited her in the hospital. Like her daughters and her husband, they expected her to recover, but she did not. Just past fifty, she died in April 1912. Puccini, who had always been fond of Ramelde's three daughters, remained especially close to Albina Franceschini Del Panta. Many letters from him to Albina are found in Arnaldo Marchetti's fascinating *Puccini com'era.* Loyal to Puccini to the end, she helped him get the family's old coat of arms, so he could display it in his house in Viareggio. After he died, Albina was chiefly responsible for founding the museum in their ancestral home in Celle; and, as I have said, it was she who welcomed Licia Albanese and other celebrity guests there.

Giulio Ricordi's illness and death also proved absolutely devastating to the composer. In January 1912 Puccini had asked Ricordi's advice about collaborators for *Anima Allegra.* Again in early February, seeing it as a three-act opera, he asked for an opinion on Adami and Zangarini; then he went ahead with it. By that point, however, Ricordi was ill. "How bad I feel for poor Signor Giulio," the composer wrote to Tito. Ricordi died on June 6, 1912, leaving Puccini lost and adrift without his mentor, friend, and publisher, the man whose judgment he most trusted, the man who had dominated every aspect of his career. "You simply can't imagine how grieved I am at his death!" Puccini wrote to Sybil. He now mourned two of the people closest to him, Ramelde and Ricordi; and he wore a black silk mourning band on his sleeve (as he is shown in a strange photographic portrait of 1912, used as the frontispiece in this book). Puccini sent this portrait of himself to Margit Vészi. Because he described himself as "carrying a large burden of melancholy" even in normal times, he grieved deeply over these personal losses.

Even in this trying period, Puccini still managed to think about helping others. In July 1912, about a month after Giulio's death, he wrote to Ervin Lendvai, encouraging him to send him a manuscript of a symphony that the young Hungarian had just composed. Lendvai did so; Puccini examined it, and at the end of August he congratulated the young composer on what seemed to him to be a truly great work. He wished him well, and later tried to get his work played.

The "New" Casa Ricordi

With Giulio dead, everything at Casa Ricordi was in Tito's hands. For Puccini, this was not good news. In one of his last letters to Giulio, he had complained that Tito never answered his letters. Soon more serious disputes arose, and he told Sybil he might leave the firm. For the first time, Tito tried to force him to sign a contract for a new opera even before he had decided what he would compose. Because this was something Giulio had never required, the offended composer protested. In Giulio's era everything had been done with a handshake, and the new businesslike practices troubled him. Another immediate problem was Tito's lively interest in Francesco Zandonai, his protégé, whose opera *Conchita* had its world premiere at the Teatro Dal Verme in Milan on October 14. It was based on the subject Puccini had rejected. Surprisingly, it did well, although Puccini dismissed its good reviews as puffed-up publicity. Still, all the clout of the Ricordi name was behind Zandonai, whose *Francesca da Rimini* Tito would assiduously promote in 1914.

In this same period Puccini had mortifying criticism leveled at him by two young colleagues, the composer Ildebrando Pizzetti and the critic Fausto Torrefranca. Pizzetti's essay "Giacomo Puccini" was published first in a periodical in 1910 then again in 1914 in a small volume of his collected writings. In it he laced into Puccini's bourgeois taste and cheap sentimentalism, although he had some good things to say about *Butterfly*. Surprisingly, Pizzetti changed his mind after Puccini died. At the end of World War II, he made a kind of public endorsement of him, calling him the greatest and most influential opera composer of his era. By then Puccini was a national idol, and the years had apparently mellowed Pizzetti somewhat. However, when I interviewed him for *Opera News* in his Rome apartment in 1963, he seemed tense over what still seemed to be his mixed feelings about Puccini, and he was even reluctant to discuss him. At the end of the afternoon, Pizzetti autographed a copy of his *Musicisti contemporanei* for me and referred only briefly to what he had written about Puccini.

In 1912 Torrefranca was a young critic who published *Giacomo Puccini e l'opera internazionale* in Turin. In addition to Torrefranca's general fault-finding, he called Puccini lazy as a man and artist, as lazy as a student who has to be dragged into school. Instead of searching for the new, Puccini worked cautiously. A "Bohemian epicure," he got through life by recycling his old musical and dramatic ideas and serving up "refried" versions of his earlier works. Stealing from his own operas, he also assimilated the work of other composers, French, Russian, German—even his Italian colleagues. His operas had been "consecrated by success" and validated by those who followed current fads, Torrefranca said. "He is not a musician; he does not create art."

Although many believed Torrefranca's attack unwarranted, it provided ammunition to Puccini's enemies in the press and may have influenced Tito Ricordi as well. In January 1913 Puccini told Sybil that Tito was being more impossible than ever, and that he was actually his enemy, "or at least the enemy of my music." Ricordi's rival publishers were also a threat, as were rival composers. In 1911 Mascagni, who had seen his *Isabeau* through its premiere in Buenos Aires, was well along with *Parisina,* in collaboration with D'Annunzio. It was scheduled for La Scala. Ermanno Wolf-Ferrari gave *I Gioielli della Madonna* in Berlin. Italo Montemezzi was composing *L'Amore dei Tre Re,* which would come to La Scala in the spring of 1913. Through much of this time, Puccini had nothing, although he had worked on several projects.

CHAPTER ELEVEN

~❧~

La Rondine, *War, and* Il Trittico:
1913–1920

AFTER GIULIO RICORDI died, Puccini again picked up Oscar Wilde's *Florentine Tragedy,* which he had set aside earlier at Ricordi's insistence. He turned again to Sybil, "my Guardian Angel," asking her to contact Wilde's literary executor about the rights. Illica, he said, was already working on a new first act, which they would need to make up a full evening in the theater. If it worked, this would be his next opera. The rights were available, although a French composer, Antoine Mariotte, had asked for a nonexclusive agreement with time limits. Puccini could use the play. Within two months, though, he had abandoned it, perhaps because Illica disliked it. When Puccini wrote to Sybil about the Wilde piece, he was staying at Osborne Haus in Karlsbad, getting treatment for his diabetes. He had stopped taking sedatives, he said, after she warned him of the danger of addiction.

A New Relationship

In 1911 Puccini had fallen in love again, this time with Baroness Josephine von Stängel, a handsome, wealthy German aristocrat whom he met in Viareggio that summer. Their affair lasted at least six years. Although the composer was still exchanging love letters with Blanke Lendvai that autumn, he seemed fully committed to von Stängel. Arnaldo Marchetti, who published three of her passionate letters to the composer, described the baroness as a native of Bissing, near Munich. Del Fiorentino said her husband was a captain in the German army. When she and Puccini first met, she was thirty-four, the mother of two small daughters, and separated from her husband. Her nicknames for Puccini were Giacomucci and Mucci; he called her Josi or Busci. If her letters reflect her true nature, she was a nearly ideal companion for him, warm, tender, affectionate, funny, and optimistic. She loved theater and music, especially his operas. Her father, also an opera fan, encouraged their affair. To Puccini, who angrily reproached Elvira for failing to understand him and sneering "whenever the word 'art' is spoken," Josi offered welcome psychological support. They were very much in love; and in one outpouring, she said she went to the neighborhood chapel and prayed, thanking God for him.

Pagni and Marotti describe Puccini visiting her just as he had done with Corinna, except that in 1911 he had an easier time of it, racing from Torre through the Burlamacca Canal and around to Viareggio in his motorboat, the *Ricochet*. Because he kept the boat in a dockyard there, Elvira could not object. Nor could she complain when he came home from these excursions, whistling and joking. He spent two or three hours with Josi every day before she returned to Munich. Taking precautions, he had her address her letters to General Delivery in Viareggio or to a secret post office box he kept there. He visited her in Munich in June 1912 and again in August, staying in the Hotel Marienbad, and he may also have taken her to Karlsbad. They went to Bayreuth together for *Parsifal;* he registered under an assumed name. Because he was so famous, his true identity was soon discovered. Then, after someone noticed him in the theater, Cosima Wagner asked to be introduced, but he kept up the masquerade: No, he was not Giacomo Puccini.

He and Josi may well have been together in the winter as well. Although he had reservations about their affair, he continued it. In June 1913 he returned to Munich; then she came to Italy for her usual summer visit. In 1914 he rented Villa Motta on Via Cristoforo Colombo in Viareggio. They picnicked under the pine trees in the famous *pineta,* where she spread a table for him and made him so comfortable that he even wrote to his niece Albina about the beauty of the pines. Actually, he had an excuse for staying at the resort, for Adami was in the nearby Pensione Mimosa. This villa in Viareggio may be the place Josi described in a letter as "your pretty house," where they had been "a little couple, sitting in front of the fireplace while *Butterfly* played on the phonograph"; but Puccini may even have invited her to Torre while Elvira was in Milan. If so, he ran the greatest possible risk, for his womanizing and Elvira's jealousy had wrought havoc in their lives before.

Then, after the war began, Josi wrote to say she would come back just after Easter 1915. But Italy, which had been neutral, joined the Allied Powers in May. From that moment, Josi was an enemy alien. That did not stop Puccini from buying land in the *pineta* and telling her he would build a small villa on it, a house she believed would be their private place. As he confided to Tito, he told no one in his family about buying the land, which cost him so dearly that he had to ask Casa Ricordi for twenty-five thousand lire to make the purchase price. At the same time, he was griping to his niece about having a "mountain" of obligations and "no money!"

As we learn from Josi's letters, she intended to bring divorce proceedings against her husband and had decided to leave her daughters with her father-in-law. Her attorney said she could live wherever she wished, so she planned to move to Viareggio. Like Corinna, she may even have hoped Puccini would marry her, divorcing Elvira to do so. Alberto Franchetti and many other Italians got divorces in Germany or other countries where they were available to foreigners. But after May 1915, when Italy entered the war, Josi could no longer travel to Italy, nor could she correspond with Puccini through regular channels, so they had to exchange letters through a friend in neutral Switzerland. They continued meeting in Lugano, a beautiful lakeside resort in the Ticino canton, where Josi managed to establish a residence. One writer said that she brought her daughters with her and lived on money Puccini sent. He went up from Milan to be with her, ostensibly going to Switzerland on business; but for about two years he went there to see Josi, in the teeth of Elvira's suspicions about his trips—and, as it happened, in the teeth of the Italian authorities' conviction that Josi was a German spy. Each time, Puccini had to invent an excuse for going to see her. In mid-November 1915, he and Josi planned a three-day visit, but he could not convince Elvira that he had to go to Lugano. Desperate, he turned to Riccardo Schnabl Rossi for help. A close friend, Schnabl lived part of the year in a villa near Magione, on Lake Trasimeno in Umbria, but he traveled all over Europe and even to South America. Simonetta Puccini, who scrupulously transcribed and edited the

Puccini-Schnabl letters, described him as the composer's interpreter and sometime assistant in Austria and Germany, and the translator of *Hanneles Himmelfahrt*.

Puccini planned to have Schnabl send him an invitation to visit at his villa. Instead of going there, Puccini would travel to Lugano, and Schnabl would send telegrams and letters to Elvira—the telegrams to be signed with Puccini's name, the letters from Puccini himself, who would send them to Schnabl. Schnabl was then to forward them, so they would have a postmark from his town. This scheme and another like it came to naught (GP to RSR, November 1915, in S. Puccini, *Giacomo Puccini Lettere*, pp. 48–50).

It was perhaps inevitable that Elvira would cause a scene about Josi, which she did in autumn 1917. When the Italian consul there realized that the composer was meeting a German woman in the city, he refused to give him further visas. Del Fiorentino said the consul even threatened to have him arrested if he tried to cross the Swiss border again. The situation turned uglier when Elvira found the consul's envelope and, armed with her inquisitorial skills, was able to wring the truth out of her husband. As always, she was on the watch: seventeen years after his affair with Corinna, and seven years after Doria Manfredi's suicide, she mistrusted him so much that she opened all his mail and, as he said, might travel a hundred miles or more to spy on him. She truly was, as Puccini said, a policeman. In some ways, he was effectively her prisoner, at least emotionally, but they were really prisoners of each other. A modern counselor might say that both were enablers. For all their problems, however, they loved each other, and Puccini remained with Elvira through the most difficult moments of their lives, when he might easily have left her.

After the war, Del Fiorentino said, Puccini settled Josi in a hotel in Casalecchio di Reno, a small town near Bologna, and sent her money. The parish priest there understood that the composer was supporting this "poor widow," and apparently people left her alone. After the war, when Del Fiorentino was assigned to the parish in Torre, he won the composer's confidence and visited with him almost every day. Finally Puccini raised the problem of "the German woman."

One evening, when he was sitting at the piano, he suddenly pulled *La Tedesca's* [Josi's] latest letter from his pocket and asked me to read it.

"Yes, please read it, *Gonnellone.* I want your advice," he said, and for perhaps three minutes he remained there with his hands resting quietly on the keys, without looking up. In the letter she asked for 10,000 lire to open a hotel in Bologna.

"Shall I send it to her?" he asked.

"No," I said. "What good will it do?"

For the moment he was convinced. . . . [Then he said], "When I think of the beautiful moments she gave me, it seems to me I have no right to be deaf to her plea."

In the end, Puccini, who said Josi had promised to return the money when her business grew successful, realized that he would lose his "investment." With that he sent her a gift of five thousand lire. However, after the parish priest of Casalecchio told Puccini that the "poor widow" had become the mistress of an Italian army officer, the friendship ended (Del Fiorentino, pp. 169–171).

I Due Zoccoletti

Marie Louise de la Ramée, who wrote under the pseudonym Ouida, was English, a native of Bury St. Edmunds, and a popular novelist—known to the inhabitants of five continents, as Vincent Seligman described her. Ouida had lived near Puccini as an expatriate in a cottage in Massarosa, a town below Chiatri and just above Quiesa and La Piaggetta. She died in Viareggio in 1908. Three years later, Puccini first expressed an interest in her novel *Two Little Wooden Shoes,* but he put it aside when *Fanciulla* claimed most of his time. He also worried about legal issues involving proprietary rights to Ouida's work; later he tried in vain to interest Illica in writing a libretto based on it. Illica declined, but Puccini kept the project in the back of his mind. Then came another failed attempt at collaboration with D'Annunzio, whom Puccini visited at his villa in Arcachon during a stay in Marseilles. The poet proposed a piece on the Children's Crusade, *La Crociata degli Innocenti,* a subject that later inspired Gian Carlo Menotti but failed to interest Puccini, who wrote to Sybil at the beginning of the year that D'Annunzio had given birth to "a small, shapeless monstrosity, unable to walk or live!" (GP to SS, January 27, 1913, in Seligman, pp. 226–227). Discouraged and "in despair," he kept trying to get a response from D'Annunzio when both were in Paris, but again nothing came of the effort. D'Annunzio had no time to meet him and did not answer his calls.

Then he turned back to Ouida, although he had other subjects in mind at that same time. In spring 1914 he confided to Sybil his hopes about *Two Little Wooden Shoes,* saying he had chosen the work for its grace and poetry. He also wrote about this story to his Hungarian friend Margit Vészi: "*I have found the libretto*—with an entirely different kind of concept—a little thing, full of flowers, of little sorrows, of children's cries, of the laments of small spirits: the *2 Zoccoletti* by Ouida." He went on to say that he did not share her enthusiasm for *La Violaine,* which she had suggested; he also told her about problems he was having with his leg (GP to MV, March 17, 1914, in Sotheby's catalogue, *Fine Printed and Manuscript Music,* sale of May 17, 1990).

Puccini had been ill during the winter. In Milan in January 1914 a bout of influenza kept him in bed for four days and left him weak and a semi-invalid. He spent much of February in Capalbio in the Maremma, an unhealthy spot, where the damp climate kept everyone on watch. While there, he got sciatica. These ailments struck just as he was under heavy fire from the anti-Puccini faction in Paris, where critics and composers were protesting the predominance of his works in the repertory. As he wrote to Baron Angelo Eisner-Eisenhof, his "honorary agent" in Vienna, the Champs-Elysées Theater was to open with a Puccini opera, against the will of his French rivals and critics. The conspiracy—the *camorra,* he called it—to keep his works off the French stage had become a threat to him and Casa Ricordi, and he expected to spend six days in Paris defending himself against the "war that people are waging against me" (GP to AE, February 28, 1914, in Gara, p. 419–420). When the moment came, though, he was not well enough to go, so Tito went in his place, though he accomplished nothing. A useless effort, Puccini complained, retreating to Torre.

As always, he was looking for suitable fodder for his poets, but he apparently remained committed to *Two Little Wooden Shoes.* When Puccini wrote to Schnabl in 1914, it was one of three subjects he had in mind. Another was the drama *La Houppelande* by Didier Gold, which had first captured his imagination when he saw the play at the Théâtre Marigny in Paris. Calling the drama by its French name and adding the Italian title *Il*

Tabarro, Puccini first described it to Illica as "almost—and really—Grand Guignol. But that doesn't make any difference. I like it, and it seems very effective to me" (GP to LI, February 9, 1913, in Gara, p. 410). At the same time, he kept trying to get the rights to *Two Little Wooden Shoes* and announced in the *Corriere della Sera* that he would write an opera based on it. Soon he read in *Il Giornale d'Italia* that Mascagni was also using the same subject. So be it, he said, and took this possible rivalry as a promise of good luck.

In one letter to Adami, Puccini described his attempts to find who owned the rights to *Two Little Wooden Shoes.* His search had begun with Ouida's publisher in London and ended in Viareggio with the executor of her will. Even after he learned that the copyright extended to 1958, he remained confident about the project, giving Adami specific instructions about the libretto. He was to "polish it up again" and "think about it" (GP to GA, April 3, 1914, in Adami, p. 188). Captivated by Ouida's story, Puccini told Eisner that it was absolutely necessary for him to get the rights to it, in spite of Mascagni's attempts to grab them. However, he could not sign a contract with the Austrian publisher Herzmansky-Doblinger. "Unless I have the absolute, exclusive right, I cannot sign any contract; that would mean I am selling something that is not mine." (GP to AE, May 3, 1914, in Gara, p. 424–425). When the librettist Alfred Willner suggested they could get around the copyright laws by changing the text, Puccini said he would be sued and would either have to pay a huge settlement or be forbidden to set it to music, in case others came forward. Still, the lure of a solid contract was surely tempting: Willner, representing Herzmansky-Doblinger, came to Torre with a check for two hundred thousand Austrian kronen, but the composer stood fast. "*Addio,* big contract!" he said; but he did try to resolve the rights issues between the Austrians and Ricordi.

Then the creditors of Ouida's estate entered the fray and asked the prefect of Viareggio to adjudicate the matter. Pulling rank, Puccini had his lawyer appeal directly to the prefect, but to no avail. The rights, whatever they were, would be sold at public auction. When the sale finally took place, in mid-March 1915, Ricordi's representative acquired the rights for the Milanese firm, and Tito ceded them to Puccini. He worked on the libretto of *I Due Zoccoletti* in the summer of 1915 with Adami, who spent his mid-August holiday in Torre, but at the end of October he was still struggling with the third act. At one point, he even begged Tito to go over the libretto with Adami and put him "on the right road." By then, however, he had grown cold on Ouida's tale, although he had made some musical sketches for it. In the end, he gave it up. Bébée and her wooden shoes joined Saint Margaret of Cortona, Conchita, Hannele, and other heroines on the list of Puccini's abandoned projects. Mascagni, who finally acquired the rights, called his opera *Lodoletta*. Like *Anima Allegra,* composed by Franco Vittadini, it eventually made its way into the major theaters.

The Composition of *La Rondine*

Long before dropping *I Due Zoccoletti,* Puccini had begun another project. In his 1913 travels for *Fanciulla,* he went to Vienna in October, when it was produced at the Hofoper. As Mosco Carner believed, this event marked the "nadir" of the composer's relationship with Tito Ricordi. Not only did Tito fail to go to Vienna himself, but he also refused to let Clausetti go; he then neglected to send the obligatory telegram of congratulations after the first night. During this visit Puccini was approached by the directors of the Karltheater, who asked him to write a new work for them. As in the past, the fee, the choice of subject, and the production of a satisfactory libretto presented obstacles; and no serious agreement about the work was reached until later. According to the contract, Puccini would compose an operetta, which would have its world premiere in Vienna; but soon after he read the libretto sent by the management, he decided against that idea. To Eisner he wrote, "But no operetta; anything but that!" (GP to AE, July 26, 1914, in Gara, pp. 426–427). He commissioned the libretto from Adami, who used a revised text to create an Italian version of the German scenario, which would become *La Rondine*.

Drastic revisions left Puccini satisfied with the first act and unhappy over the rest. Adami, like all of his predecessors, complained about Puccini's demands, but he was far more accommodating than Illica or Giacosa had been, and he truly loved Puccini, in spite of his volatile moods. In one undated letter Puccini expressed enthusiasm and found the work "truly interesting and full of delicate charm." However, he worried about the third act, which he wanted to be "great, enthralling, moving. It has to be the theatrical *heart* of the work, where all the force of sound may pour out." Because this letter mentions Baron Eisner and Puccini's attempt to find Ouida's heirs in London, it is perhaps the composer's first about *Rondine* (GP to GA, undated, in Adami, p. 188).

At the end of September 1914, thoroughly dissatisfied with the second act, he wrote to Adami, "I'm not saying that it is ugly, sloppy, anti-theatrical. No, I'm not saying that." He summed up the situation when he said he found it "not very beautiful, not very polished and refined, not super-theatrical, as it should be." It lacked energy and all the emotions and colors that made a drama stageworthy. "The second act will not do, and that is that! Let's find another setting, something more alive, more varied, and with a better color. . . . Because of the sensation of weariness that drags my soul down when I work, I feel our business is not working out. I don't enjoy it; I don't laugh; I am not interested in it. We need something else in this rotten world, dear Beppino! We need a second act. And let's do it, because we have time. We'll keep the main episodes; but we have to create them again from the start and make them new and enjoyable. Excuse this diatribe, which is not directed at you, but rather at me" (GP to GA, September 25, 1914, in Adami, pp. 189–190). All of this, of course, is vintage Puccini. He had made his point, and Adami went back to work. For most of November, still on an emotional roller coaster, he would protest his despair on one day, boast of good spirits the next, and again start begging Adami not to turn his hair white over the project. He signed one letter to Adami in a dire moment, "Your great, unhappy, almost ex-[collaborator], G. Puccini."

His gloomy state of mind meant he had not done much on the opera; instead, he had started to hunt coots and woodcocks. The weather was nearly ideal, warm and clear, with splendid sunny days that put him in better humor. As his letters show, he was moving forward, although he still spent part of his time hunting and racing around in his new Lancia, which he drove so fast that the rush of air hurt his eyes. *"I am also going to Viareggio. Everything is fine,"* he added, which meant that he was seeing Josi (GP to GA, November 18, 1914, in Adami, 193–194). Five and six days later, he was rethinking two of the characters in *La Rondine* and asking for new, major revisions. The third act would not do, because parts of it were not credible. He particularly took offense at the idea that Ruggero was so naïve that he was not aware of Magda's past. After all, he had picked her up in a dance hall. "Where did he find Magda, maybe in a monastery? And then this great love of his falls apart in a second when he finds out who she is? Anyone who sees and hears this drama will not find it convincing and will think the ending is almost illogical." At that point, the composer felt *La Rondine* could never be successful, because the second act was "not very lively" and the third was "useless, dead. . . . *La Rondine* is absolute trash [*una solenne porcheria*]!" (GP to GA, November 19, 1914, in Adami, pp. 194–195).

Little Elvira Becomes Bicchi

Over the years, Fosca brought her children to Torre and left Little Elvira, her second daughter, for long visits with her grandparents. By the summer of 1912, she had grown to be a spirited, beautiful seven-year-old, with her dark hair and green eyes. Puccini also loved Franca, of course, bragged about her to friends, and often had her as his guest; but Little Elvira had special privileges. Even when she was small, he had taken her hunting or boating on the lake, and as she grew older, they went farther. He also taught her a lot about art. Speaking later about her childhood, she said she always felt the strong pull of art in Puccini's villa, which she called "the Magic Place" where she felt safe and could find understanding and love. Somewhat in awe of Grandmother Elvira, she described her as "tall and severe," an intelligent woman with a strong will. Puccini was then a handsome man with "a proud expression" and a thick mustache that had not yet turned gray. He was a susceptible and adoring grandfather who, she said, lived for music and beautiful women, "good wine and hunting, and the quiet woods around Lake Massaciuccoli" (Blignaut, p. 11). All through her childhood, he would let her stand behind the door of his studio, so she could listen as he composed. Sometimes he left the door ajar so she could peek in. Over and over again, Grandmother Elvira would chase her away, saying, "You're always hanging around Grandfather! Don't you get bored at listening to so much music?" Little Elvira never answered back. She said it was a game she and her grandmother played together.

As she grew older and more serious, she also became close to Tonio, *"Zio Tonio,"* as she called him, "Uncle." Tonio, then in his mid-twenties, became the girl's trusted confidant, someone she often saw in Milan during the winter and played with in Torre. She never forgot his affection for her; once when she was recovering from a throat operation, he put a mattress on the floor next to her bed and slept there for a month so she would not feel lonely and frightened. She always slept with the doll Puccini had brought her from America, although she was jealous because he had brought a more beautiful doll from Paris for Wally Toscanini, her best friend. "Wally is like your older sister," Puccini explained. "Every so often, we have to make her happy, because she deserves that."

Little Elvira had fond recollections of her grandparents' comfortable home, its colorful carpets, paintings, good food, and pleasant garden. Although her bedroom was far from Puccini's studio, the night was so quiet that she could hear the guests' conversations and the sound of the piano when Puccini played. "[He] loved to compose, even at night; sometimes he played the piano until three in the morning, while his friends played cards in the salon" (Blignaut, p. 14).

This is not to say that Puccini always felt like the proud *capofamiglia,* the traditional Italian patriarch. During Little Elvira's visit in July 1912, he complained to Sybil about his discomfort. "I'm playing at being a sailor, but it's not very amusing. On the contrary, I'm bored at not having any work to do, and I don't get much fun out of life. The family weighs on me! My wife is—well, never mind! And I have to bow my head! A pig of a life! Long live Anarchy! And forward to the day of the long, last sleep" (GP to SS, July 19, 1912, in Seligman, p. 220). He was in deep mourning at this time, which of course colored his views.

The spring of 1914 brought Little Elvira back to Torre. Staying all summer and into the autumn, she met many of Puccini's colleagues and remembered their discussions about the war, in which Italy was originally mentioned. Dante Del Fiorentino described how violent arguments about the war erupted in the community around Massaciuccoli. Everyone in Puccini's household followed the international news. "The *Corriere della Sera* was publishing a lot about the news of the day: the war. [Should Italy] intervene, or not intervene? [Puccini] shot back: 'You all know I hate politics, with its rackets and swindles; and the nationalist factions make me angry. I'll stay neutral as long as I can.'" In the loudest "nationalist faction" was Toscanini, whom Gatti-Casazza described as a "rabid nationalist" in a letter to Otto Kahn (Sachs, *Toscanini,* p. 136). One evening the guests at Villa Puccini included the librettist Giovacchino Forzano, the painter Gianni Morandi, the composer Ildebrando Pizzetti, who had been Puccini's severe critic and had begun to change his mind about his music, the journalist Carlo Paladini, and the writers Renato Fucini and Ugo Ojetti. Gabriele D'Annunzio was to have been there as well, but he had remained in Paris to await the outbreak of the war, which, he said, he wanted to see with his own eyes. Puccini had urged D'Annunzio to come home.

Little Elvira remembered sitting in the salon one day, watching the adults play *briscola*. When the conversation turned to D'Annunzio and his refusal to leave France, Grandmother Elvira, sharply critical of him, said, "Maybe he's hoping his private problems will be wiped out by a greater drama." Everyone agreed with her, for they all knew about his huge debts and his flight to escape his creditors. The child would later remember Puccini and his guests talking about film, for cinema and the legal issues it raised worried Puccini, who wrote to Casa Ricordi about film producers' projects and sought protection for his rights. One evening, an embarrassing moment came when Grandmother Elvira left the room to make coffee. In her absence, someone had the courage to ask Puccini about his attachment to Sybil Seligman. "No! No!" Puccini protested. "She's only a trusted friend." Little Elvira also remembered people talking about their fear of an Austrian invasion of Italy (Blignaut, p. 15).

Puccini invented a nickname for Little Elvira. One day, baby-sitting for her on the veranda in Torre, resting in his rocking chair, he had laid his big hat and a handful of matches on a low table beside him. Still in hunting clothes and leather boots, he rocked and watched her. On the lawn below she had arranged a lot of ripe fruit on the lawn tables and was running from one table to another, singing and talking to herself. Puccini laughed as he watched, but at first he said nothing. Then she spoke to him, asking what he had shot that day. "Nothing. So you see, you were right to stay home. And now come over here, you little rascal, and tell me about all this merchandise." Gesturing toward the fruit, he added, "Wouldn't it be better to put a little German order into that?" Little Elvira begged him not to be cross with her. Then, in a small voice, she said, "And besides, I like to do what I want." Puccini gave a loud laugh. "She's just begun to go to school, and now this little scamp wants to have her own way! I'll have to take you to America the next time I go! People over there like independent women."

At that, she twirled around, dancing pirouettes for him. Then he told her to go inside. Stubbornly, the child refused to leave. "Grandfather, don't call me Elvira. If you like, you could call me 'Viri' or 'Biri.'" Puccini responded in an instant: "Well, you little actress! From now on, you'll be 'Biri,' and that's the end of it. And you must call me 'Tato,' because 'Grandfather' makes me seem old, and I'm not old." But that was not the end of it, for Puccini loved to play with words. As if in a game, he rang changes on "Biri," getting to "Biribichi," "Birba," "Birbante," and "Biribichina." Finally he settled on "Bicchi," the nickname that stayed with her until her death in 1999, although she used the spelling Biki in her profession (Blignaut, p. 12).

He also took her fishing on Lake Massaciuccoli, and sometimes even went to sea with her. These excursions were especially exciting after he bought his yacht, the *Cio-Cio-San,* for he dashed through the Burlamacca Canal on the way to Viareggio. Playing at the roles of captain and sailor, they saluted each other, cap to cap, both dressed in yachting outfits. Summer ended with Puccini looking forward to hunting, and Bicchi wanting to go with him. Nicche, Puccini's former hunting partner and employee, was home on furlough from the army; and one morning Puccini asked him to bring in the dogs. Then a maid dressed the child in the little hunting costume Puccini had given her and pulled on her new leather boots, which she could not manage alone. Decked out in high fashion, Bicchi went hunting with her grandfather. Sometimes she and Franca went out on the lake alone, and once they rowed out and hid in the duck blind, scaring everyone. In addition to these visits to Torre, Bicchi later stayed with her grandparents in Viareggio, where Puccini often rented. He later built his last villa there. (These and her other personal accounts from this period are from my interviews with her and from Blignaut.)

One of Puccini's jobs every year was to check up on his properties. Although he had sold the house at Abetone, he still had his land in Viareggio and had kept Chiatri and other houses, including the family home in Lucca. His little house across the lake in the village of Massaciuccoli was not very well maintained, and at the beginning of January 1915 he asked Antonio Bettolacci for help. He wrote from Milan: "Dear Tonino, I had your dear, dear letter with news of Maciuccoli [*sic*]. Poor building! Please perform an act of charity. I know you go there often; you went there, and I even sent you there a long time ago. Last year, it also made Gianni unhappy to see this house in that condition. So take care of it, [and] I will get this burden off your back." He also mailed "the three operas," probably scores or librettos, to Bettolacci and sent a bulletin on his health. He was in Milan, he said, "a little under the weather with influenza. I want to come down there, but you tell me there is [no reason for coming], so I will wait" (GP to AB, January 27, 1915, Tollett and Harman Collection).

The following year he was trying to buy yet another house, an ancient pile at Torre della Tagliata in the Maremma. Dante placed his own curse on this area in his trip through Purgatory when he had Pia lament, "Siena made me, the Maremma destroyed me." And a Tuscan folk song of the nineteenth century takes up the mourning cry:

> Everyone says "Maremma, Maremma"
> But to me it is a bitter Maremma.
> Birds lose their feathers when they fly there,
> And I have lost someone I love.
> Damn the Maremma.
> Damn the Maremma and everyone who loves it.
> My heart trembles whenever you go there,
> And I am afraid you will never return.

Puccini finally got the lonely house in Torre della Tagliata, and soon he came to hate it.

World War I and the Break with Toscanini

By the end of 1914 several European countries were at war. Archduke Franz Ferdinand of Austria had been assassinated in Sarajevo on June 28; in July Austria invaded Serbia; and on August 4 Germany invaded Belgium. Italy declared its neutrality that same month, and Puccini also claimed to be neutral. Under other circumstances, his stance might have remained a private matter; but other artists—Italian, French, and English—were rushing to support patriotic causes. He was first approached in November by Hall Caine, an English writer, who was collecting statements to protest Germany's aggression in Belgium. Many important composers rushed to help, but Puccini did not. Instead, he described his neutrality in a personal letter to Caine, saying he had refused all requests to sign such protests or take part in benefits. Those who knew the music business saw this as his private campaign to prevent boycotts of his works and keep his royalties flowing.

Another public statement by the European arts community came after the Germans bombed the French city of Rheims, but again Puccini's name was not there. That provoked Léon Daudet into attacking him in *L'Action Française* in February 1915. Defending himself, Puccini claimed not to have known about the letter; then he said he had not been asked to sign it in time. After that, many suspected him of pronounced pro-German sympathies. In spite of his efforts, Germany boycotted his operas, believing incorrectly that he had signed the Rheims letter. At the height of the controversy, he had assured the German society of composers and dramatists that he had never denounced Germany. From that moment, the French attacks on him continued, even after the spring of 1915, when Italy entered the war.

On the day Italy joined the Allies, Dante Del Fiorentino, who was then a young seminarian, was in Torre del Lago. He had been spending all his free time there for years, seizing every chance to talk to Puccini, his idol. The two men he courted most assiduously were Nicche, whom he called "Gnicche," using the local dialect pronunciation, and Arnaldo Gragnani, one of two brothers who were Puccini's neighbors in Torre. Del Fiorentino said he was with Gragnani when someone told them that Italy had gone to war. They ran to Puccini's house and found him alone in his studio. He, too, had heard the news. His piano was closed. "War, war," he said. "It's the end of civilization." He railed against the loss of human life, and against profiteers. A further blow came when a telegram brought the news that Tonio was volunteering for the motor corps.

Del Fiorentino was not called into service at once. After his ordination, he was sent to assist the priest at Mutigliano, where Puccini had once played the organ. To his delight, Canon Roderigo Biagini, Puccini's cousin, was living in the rectory. Don Roderigo encouraged him in what he called his "Puccini studies" and let him play arias from Puccini's operas on his grand piano. The two became fast friends, and the older man provided him with material he later used in his biography of Puccini. Finally Del Fiorentino received his draft notice. Before leaving, he went to Torre to say good-bye; there he found Gragnani making light conversation with Puccini and trying to cheer him up. Puccini, who had come to love the young priest and always called him *"Gonnellone,"* "Big Skirt," and *"Pretino,"* "Little Priest," was truly sorry to see him go. "Giacomo was overwhelmed with sadness. He came out to bid me farewell, an old man, gray, taciturn, plunged in thought, the prey to sorrows. I stood there, holding my round beaver hat, overcome with the yearning to say many things to him, but he looked so overburdened that no words came to my lips. He nodded sadly, waved his hand gracefully, and began to pace up and down the garden, engrossed in his own thoughts. He looked as lonely as a grave" (Del Fiorentino, p. 159–165).

Later, the young priest was stationed in Cormons, a town the Italian army had occupied. It was in Austrian territory and just outside "accursed" and fatal Gorizia, the city whose very name struck fear into Italian hearts. As a popular song had it, when troop trains left for Gorizia, mothers wept, their sons wept, and "many of them would never return." In Cormons, Del Fiorentino and another Tuscan won over the formerly hostile local physician by playing and singing Puccini's music under his window.

When he was furloughed back to Quiesa for two weeks, he went to look for Puccini in Torre. Learning that he was in Pisa for a performance of *Butterfly,* he sought him out there and told him how

> his music had brought peace to an obscure Austrian village and how it kept up our courage in the fighting. He was the same, simple-minded, generous, understanding person I had known before. The tenor who was playing Pinkerton suffered from stage fright. Hoping to steady his nerves, the conductor told him beforehand that the Maestro would be there, but this had the effect of making the tenor even more nervous. During the love duet, his voice gave out completely. Giacomo went to see him during the intermission. To the tenor's astonishment, he was greeted warmly, told not to be afraid, and above all, he must not punish himself with regrets. *"Una stecca non è la fine del mondo,"* Giacomo said, throwing his arm around the unfortunate tenor. "One cracked note doesn't bring about the end of the world. You'll do better next time. You'll see. This kind of thing happens to everyone who is serious about his art, and nothing gives me so much pleasure as to see one of the 'Gods' taking an occasional tumble."
>
> Then the reporters pressed forward with their absurd questions. "What is the right kind of music for people? What is going to happen after the war? What kind of mood will the people have?"
>
> Giacomo shrugged his shoulders. He was accustomed to these questions, and knew no answers. He beckoned to me, and said, "You tell them, *Gonnellone.*"

"All I know," I said, "is that they like your music. It's the same with the soldiers. Sometimes they like their music gay, and then at other times they like music with deep religious feelings."

It was not much of an answer, but Giacomo seized on it.

"You see, it's all there, gentlemen," he exclaimed. "The important thing is that human emotions are not changed by the wars. Life is fundamentally simple, and so is my music. The wars pay attention to frontiers, but people don't." [Del Fiorentino, pp. 167–168]

Never physically threatened by the conflict, Puccini fell into a profound depression during the war, as Del Fiorentino saw. To Adami he wrote,

Loneliness is as wide as the sea; it is as smooth as a lake; it is as black as night; and it is also as green as bile! My present indecision exhausts me, wears me out, irritates, and depresses me. . . . I am turning into an imbecile, like a rock that stands silent and turns gray as it is weathered by time. . . . The Austrians have my crown [*Gli austriaci hanno la corona mia*], and I no longer have it: I'm like the king in the Tarot cards. What about music? I don't answer.—[It's] gone with the wind, with the wind, like the ashes of suicides that drift away. [Tito] Ricordi's proposals humiliate me. All said, this state of affairs can't continue. I am alone. You can imagine what fun! Nicche has been called back into service and has left. Tonio is in Milan. Let me hear from you. I won't tell you to come because I know you can't. But if you were free, what joy you would give me! [GP to GA, March 11, 1915, in Adami, p. 196]

On October 10, 1915, with Italy already in the war, Puccini made a private statement about Italian art, one he never tried to publish. "Although I recognize great merit in these French musicians, the direct followers of the Russians, yet I say that our art is, must be, and has been the ruler of the world, and I insist that we Italians are [not so cruel] as foreigners. Italian geniality, even if it is less rich in technique, imposes itself on the world. And [should] we seek to depreciate it by accepting, desiring, and encouraging conglomerations and intrigues of notes? No, no, no! Clear Italian light must restore our [strength]" (GP to Carlo Vanbianchi, October 10, 1915, in Charles Hamilton catalogue for Auction No. 146, May 20, 1982).

Puccini's neutrality and his failure to help with benefits and fund-raisers would eventually have cost him Toscanini's friendship in any case; but

in fact they had a bitter argument over politics just as the war was beginning. According to Harvey Sachs's account, the conductor was vacationing in Viareggio in 1914, the very summer Puccini was renting Villa Motta
for himself and Josi. Having been friends for nearly twenty years, they
spent a great deal of time together, and it is entirely possible that Toscanini knew about Josi. One evening they talked politics. Everyone knew
that to Toscanini, Italy was sacred. Nevertheless, Puccini said he felt Italy
needed the Germans to come down and put things in order—"German
order," the same words Bicchi remembered him using. Evidently this was
what he really believed, but there can be little doubt that he was
influenced, at least in part, by his love for Josi. Toscanini, livid with rage,
ran to his house, slammed the door, and stayed inside for a week. From
that moment, he considered Puccini disloyal or worse, and even when
Puccini came to try to make peace, the conductor refused to see him, although they were reconciled (if briefly) soon afterward. Then they became enemies again (Sachs, *Toscanini,* p. 125).

After this, Toscanini had little to do with Puccini for the next seven
years. After all, Toscanini's father had fought with Garibaldi to drive Austria out and create the Italian nation. The conductor, fiercely patriotic,
never feared taking a stand, and never feared taking a stand for Italy. He
made such an extraordinary effort for his country that, according to
Harvey Sachs, his income fell to almost nothing. He began organizing and
conducting benefit concerts in Milan, Rome, Turin, and other cities, to
audiences of as many as forty thousand people. At one of them, 150
wounded Italian soldiers were brought in. Even when many singers were
not available, he directed a special opera season at the Teatro Dal Verme,
asking all the participants to contribute their services to help jobless musicians.

Defying death, Toscanini even conducted on the battlefield, heading a
military band that moved with the Italian troops in war-wracked Friuli
and Venezia Giulia. Those areas, north and east of Venice, became the
most dangerous war zones, served by the one main road that led from
Austria through Tarvisio and Carnia to Udine and Venice. The road and
the rail line that runs beside it became the pipelines of the war. Italy's
largest military hospital was in Udine, where Toscanini's son, Walter, and
Guido Vandini's son lay among the wounded. Toscanini, undaunted by
the carnage, led his little corps of musicians so far into the field that they

were caught at Monte Santo, the battlefield that became "the graveyard of young men" *(il cimitero della gioventù),* and is now a national monument. At the height of the fighting, shells or fragments of shrapnel rained down on them, ripping open the bass drum; but, as one musician remembered, Toscanini refused to give up and shouted *"Viva l'Italia!"* after every piece. Toward the end of the war, he and his men were in Cormons. Even there, Toscanini kept his men playing during a retreat, then helped them escape in wagons and railroad cars (Sachs, *Toscanini,* pp. 135–136). The Italian newspapers, carried splashy stories about his exploits. Bicchi remembered Grandmother Elvira reading one story to Puccini and saying, "The Lord sent that shell through the drum and saved our friend." Puccini shook his head and said nothing.

The Italian government took notice of Toscanini's heroic acts and decorated him for bravery under fire. Puccini did little for the war effort, but he did help individuals and families affected by the conflict. At first, he moved around freely: Torre, Viareggio, and Milan, with occasional trips to Rome, Lucca, and Florence. He even went twice to Monte Carlo and, as we have seen, to Lugano. But apart from these trips, most of which were for business, he lay low during most of the war. Unfortunately, he and his controversial "neutral" stance made him the target of countless attacks, even after he dropped it. People said he was pro-German because he was writing under a contract with an Austrian theater. Musicians thought he was after money, and they may have been right, for he was rumored to be notoriously tightfisted. At a time when Toscanini was donating time and energy to the cause, sacrificing his earnings to do so and making donations of a thousand lire to charitable organizations, Puccini never appeared at an Italian benefit, so far as we know. If he donated money to some cause, we do not know it, but he could surely have afforded to do so. Nor did the war cause his financial woes in 1915; those he brought on himself when he decided to buy property in Viareggio and to keep the several other places he already owned. In November 1916 he did contribute something to the war effort, writing a short piano piece, *"Calmo e molto lento,"* for an album to be sold for the benefit of the wounded. This was noble, yet he continued seeing Josi, a German citizen, during three of the four war years, from 1914 until the end of 1917, and for some time after the war.

Puccini and his family remained physically comfortable throughout the war. In Viareggio, people complained of bad bread and a shortage of meat and other foods, all of which he mentioned in his letters, but they were never at risk of being bombed or encountering hand-to-hand combat in the streets. Bicchi remembered the resort town being full of film stars, singers, ballerinas, princesses whose children had governesses and tutors, and upper middle-class women with their children's nurses, all mingling with men from the Italian army, air force, and navy. In the morning the boardwalk along the sea looked like an artist's palette: bodices of red, green, and blue velvet, buttoned over the nannies' bosoms, and pink and blue lace and shiny buttons on the children's clothes. The nurses, dressed more conservatively, chatted in Italian, but with different accents: Swiss, French, and English. They all stayed in villas or the great hotels, the most famous of which was the Grand Hotel Royal. The ladies came out in the late afternoon and stopped at the Caffè Giacosa or Caffè Margherita or some other fashionable retreat before dressing for a society ball.

Bicchi remembered the elegant fashions, her mother's pale blue chiffon gown, and the long ermine coat that one of Fosca's friends wore. At these events, aristocrats and nobles mingled with officers from the Italian and Allied forces, and Fosca attended all of them. Puccini and Elvira saw Fosca and the children regularly in Viareggio, for the Leonardis' villa and his rented one were close together, both in the center of town. Bicchi remembered running to tell her dear Tato about seeing the king of Italy pass by in his limousine. Fosca's wartime effort centered on the Red Cross balls, where money and packages for the troops were being collected. In Milan, Carla Toscanini, an early Red Cross volunteer, was untiring in her efforts, and she made Wally, her daughter, sew clothes for the soldiers. As Wally once said, other girls' mothers took them to church, while her mother took her to hospitals. On the Puccini "front," Elvira had taught Bicchi to knit, showing her how to make men's sweaters; Elvira sent one sweater to Tonio, who had volunteered for service and was driving an ambulance (Blignaut, pp. 17–26).

Once, when Bicchi asked Puccini why he never went to those elegant balls, he responded, "I have to work, and anyway I like simpler things." At the very least, his answer suggests something about why he acted as he did during the war. He worked on *La Rondine* and, later, the *Trittico*, hunted, and avoided public events, especially formal ones, although he could not get out of attending banquets in his honor. Dreading publicity, he simply could not make a spectacle of himself, and in the opera business, the fact that he could not make speeches became a matter of public knowledge. Furthermore, his diabetes plagued him, more on some days than others, but it needed constant monitoring and a diet that he had trouble following at public luncheons and dinners. His disease often left him tired. Still, he adjusted to circumstances. After the Italian government sequestered his automobiles, he walked; then he bought a motorcycle with sidecar and drove it all over the Torre-Viareggio neighborhood and as far as Lucca. Selling his yacht, the *Cio-Cio-San,* which was expensive to operate and maintain, he fell back on rowboats, some powered with outboard motors.

Through this entire period, Puccini's interest in politics was close to zero, as it had been all his life, so far as one can judge. He seemed almost indifferent to everything from mayoral elections in Viareggio to cabinet appointments in Rome. William Ashbrook, discussing his politics, wrote, "Puccini as both man and artist was Italian to the marrow and proud of his *italianità*. . . . [But] there is an even more fundamental root to Puccini's orientation. For him home was not Italy, but quite specifically Torre del Lago" (Ashbrook, *The Operas of Puccini,* p. 158). As Puccini told Tito Ricordi, Florence was his capital. Tuscany was his state; and above all he was a Lucchese, loving his home and privacy, his soil, the lake, and good bread. While Toscanini was making his noble contribution to the war effort, Puccini was turning out a surprising amount of work: the full-length opera that *Rondine* had become and the three one-act operas of *Il Trittico.*

Getting *La Rondine* Onstage in Wartime

Puccini struggled with *La Rondine* throughout the conflict, although largely without the support of Casa Ricordi. Adami remembered his saying that Tito Ricordi, afraid to back something that was likely to fail, had no faith in the opera. Puccini told Sybil that Tito had written it off as "bad Lehár." In another letter, he rued the "dog days" and said his nerves were strung out like snakes. "I am vomiting over the orchestral score." Finally things began to go more smoothly. Puccini completed and then rethought the third act; by Easter of 1915, *La Rondine* was finished, although, as always, he had things to add. The opera was completely finished in October 1915. Of course, for Puccini the words "absolutely finished" almost always meant that more changes were in store, something that proved as true with *La Rondine* as it had with the other operas. Finally, though, he was satisfied. In trying to arrange the world premiere, he faced several problems, because he was contractually obligated to present it in Austria, where he now could not travel. Because his operas were boycotted in Germany, he might even be denied permission to give it in Vienna at all. For a while, it seemed *La Rondine* might never reach the stage. Worse, he needed the income at a time when opera companies had shortened their seasons or canceled them altogether.

With a finished work lying on his table, Puccini had to get it published. In December 1912 he and Tito had argued over his refusal to sign a contract with Casa Ricordi for his future work. Now, after offering *Rondine* to him many times—a hundred times, Puccini claimed—Tito, because he could not own the exclusive rights, was not interested. As Ashbrook observes, the problem started with Puccini's complicated arrangements about the rights. He had been able to meet the Austrian impresarios in Switzerland before all travel had been stopped, and he renegotiated his contract during that meeting. No longer required to give the world premiere in Vienna, where the war prevented its production, he had to cede his rights for Austria, Germany, and the United States, three major markets. Tito could not accept that. Also, as Puccini told Adami in August 1915, Tito did not believe in the opera, finding it was just "pleasant," and nothing more.

In the end, however, this long dispute was resolved. Ashbrook quotes Puccini's letter of December 1916, which said that so long as Tito was the head of Casa Ricordi, he would be offered the first option on any future work (Ashbrook, *The Operas of Puccini,* p. 160). As Puccini told Schnabl, he and Tito were in complete agreement, and everything was fine. Loyal to Ricordi, he sold only *La Rondine* to Casa Sonzogno, which awarded the premiere to Monte Carlo. News of the premiere and the planned cast of *La Rondine* appeared in a dispatch from Paris, dated January 1917. It also appeared in the February 10 number of *Musical America,* which announced that the Polish soprano Rosa Raisa would sing Magda. According to Raisa's biographer, Charles Mintzer, the threat of submarines was so great that she could not cross the Atlantic, and another singer had to be engaged. It was Gilda Dalla Rizza.

Puccini went to Monte Carlo to prepare the opera, staying at the Hotel de Paris with Elvira and Fosca, and getting there early enough to hear Gino Marinuzzi conduct the first orchestra reading, which went splendidly. His early doubts about Dalla Rizza's costumes and appearance were soon set aside, and she became the star of the production. The opening, on March 27, 1917, had her as Magda, Tito Schipa as Ruggero, Ines Maria Ferraris as Lisette, Francesco Dominici as Prunier, and Gustave Huberdeau as Rambaldo. With more than twenty curtain calls, as he wrote to Guido Vandini, it was "a true success" that left him very happy (GP to G. Vandini, March 30, 1917, in Pintorno, letter 202). On April 3 Prince Albert I of Monaco awarded Puccini the Order of Saint Charles.

After *La Rondine,* Puccini seized on Dalla Rizza as an ideal singing actress for some of his operas; and she repaid his loyalty with marvelously conceived interpretations of his roles. Her idiosyncratic technique and odd voice, with its marked vibrato, enhanced her performance; and on every stage she overcame the handicap of her tiny body, for she was very thin and barely five feet tall. By the end of her career, this intelligent singer could count seventy operas in her repertory, having honed her dramatic skills until she was seen as "the Eleonora Duse of opera." Born in 1892 in Verona, she studied in Bologna, where she made her debut in *Werther,* but she soon moved into Puccini's orbit with an exciting Minnie in *Fanciulla* in Florence, performed under Puccini's stage direction. Two years later, she sang *Manon Lescaut, Bohème,* and Massenet's *Manon* during her first South American tour, often performing with Caruso. She then returned to La Scala, the Costanzi, and other major theaters. After the world premiere of *Rondine,* Puccini assigned her two roles in the first Italian production of the *Trittico,* composed Liù in *Turandot* with her in mind, and corresponded with her until his death.

With her brilliance and beauty, she arguably did more to promote Puccini's operas than any other Italian woman of her generation, partly because of her versatility. Toscanini, who saw her *Suor Angelica* in Rome, coached her to become the unforgettable Violetta of his landmark *Traviata* of 1923 at La Scala. Dalla Rizza's last performance was a *Suor Angelica,* sung in 1939 as a benefit for the Italian Red Cross in Vicenza.

Teaching voice at the Benedetto Marcello Conservatory in Venice, she became *"la nostra Gildina,"* "our little Gilda," as the Venetians called her, a woman loved as much for her wit and spirit as for her dark Venetian dialect. For years, she was the darling of the Gritti Palace Hotel, where she held forth as a cult diva, surrounded by students and faithful fans.

When I interviewed Dalla Rizza in 1969 in her home in Bassano del Grappa, she was in her late seventies. I saw a powerhouse, packed into this porcelain figurine; and the size and richness of her speaking voice was simply astonishing. She remembered Puccini calling *Rondine* his "dear, forgotten child." She said: "It seems to be an easy work, but it isn't. *La Rondine* is not an operetta, but a full-scale opera. Vocally, it is enormously difficult. The first act is every bit as challenging as the first act of *Traviata;* and the tenor role demands an artist of the caliber of Schipa. It must be staged with sensitivity and taste. *La Rondine* ought to have a theater that is not too large, although it can hold up in big theaters, as we proved at the Colón in Buenos Aires." In his letters to Dalla Rizza, Puccini often mentioned the opera, "my poor *Rondine,"* even in the last months of his life. The soprano remarked about Puccini's love for it, "He died with the wound of *Rondine* in his heart" (Phillips-Matz, "First Ladies of the Puccini Premieres: Gilda Dalla Rizza," *Opera News,* January 24, 1970).

The publicity generated by the premiere of *La Rondine* set off another furor in the French press. Again it was Daudet who blasted it as an "enemy opera." That virtually sealed its fate in France, for this time Daudet attacked both Puccini and the impresario of the opera in Monte Carlo, making it difficult for other French theaters to book the opera. Always reluctant to engage in a public controversy, Puccini answered directly this time, with a letter to the *Corriere della Sera* and the French papers. First he explained the details of his contracts and subsequent negotiations with the Austrians, then he defended Adami as the Italian author of the Italian libretto, and the publisher, Sonzogno, who was also Italian, not Austrian. He had committed no crime, he said. Quite naturally, this uproar tarnished the auspicious launching of *Rondine.* Worse, its early promise faded. Tito's hostility again flared. On June 29, 1918, Puccini told Sybil about his new struggle with Casa Ricordi and said he would be willing to open negotiations with an English publisher. By his definition, his existing agreement with Ricordi meant nothing, for Tito had only the right of first refusal, so anyone who offered him a big fee for a new opera—around

250,000 lire—would put Ricordi out of the running. "How happy I should be to come to an arrangement with an English publisher and to be able to get out of the clutches of these publishers of ours!" (GP to SS, June 29, 1918, in Seligman, pp. 278–279). A few weeks later, however, he and Tito made peace again.

In May *Rondine* was featured in the Buenos Aires season, again with Dalla Rizza, who sent Puccini good news about its success. The first production in Italy, given in June at the Teatro Comunale in Bologna, got indifferent reviews, as did the inadequate *Rondine* at the Dal Verme in Milan in October. It left Puccini furious over Mugnone's tempos and the singers, whom he denounced as "dogs, dogs, dogs." A planned production in Lucca never materialized, and his and Sybil's attempts to sell it to Covent Garden came to naught. In 1920, when he finally got to Vienna for *Rondine* at the Volkstheater, he contradicted himself by saying, "It went well," but the whole evening left him dissatisfied and unhappy (GP to ?, October 17, 1920, J. & J. Lubrano, Music Antiquarians, catalogue of PADA Exhibition, St. Moritz Hotel, New York City, April 18, 1999). The opera reached the Met and La Scala only after Puccini's death.

And Again the War

Not until 1917 did Puccini seem completely overwhelmed by the horrors of the war. Fosca remembered his reaction when the troops began to fall ill with malaria, jaundice, and flu. Hospitals were full, and soldiers were dying of their wounds. Frightened people had begun to take to the streets in bread riots and peace demonstrations. Then, when news came of the revolution in Russia, Italians began fearing anarchy. October 24 brought the shocking Italian defeat at Caporetto. This triggered the retreat that sent Toscanini and his musicians running for their lives. At the moment that Italy seemed lost, D'Annunzio stepped forward as a patriotic writer and orator and even took part in a naval mission. On his return, the city of Milan greeted him as a national hero. Then he returned to Viareggio and to his villa, to begin living his new, grand role.

Puccini did nothing heroic, but he did use his connections to help people. When Guido Vandini's son was wounded and hospitalized in Udine, he arranged to have him moved to the hospital in Lucca. As in the past, he wrote many letters of appeal and recommendation, some to officers, asking them to help soldiers with promotions, transfers, or furloughs. After Tonio enlisted, he was stationed at Monza in summer 1917, as he told his parents in a telephone call. They left Milan the next day and rushed to see him. He then asked to go to the front, so in September he was stationed in Verona as an ambulance driver operating out of a depot for motorized vehicles.

Two of the battlefields, Pasubio and the *Altopiano* or High Plain of Asiago, saw Italian victories. At Mount Pasubio, the Italian infantry held off the Austrians for months and finally defeated them in July. Fighting raged on the *Altopiano* in 1917 until Italy drove the Austrian forces back across the border. Only a few weeks after the Battle of Pasubio, Puccini was at the front himself, visiting both battlefields. He may also have visited Tonio or paid his respects to the troops. In any case, this was a dangerous excursion, through heavily mined territory, with the Austrian army just to the north. Fighting would also erupt on the *Altopiano* in 1918. Puccini sent a card to the mayor of Viareggio. "Greetings from the Front. Today Pasubio, tomorrow the *Altopiano*" (GP to Cesare Riccioni, card, August 20, 1917, in Pintorno, letter 206).

As his letters show, the war took a toll on him. In the artistic community, a new sadness came in January 1918, when Arrigo Boito fell ill. Puccini, writing from Viareggio, told Tito how worried he was over the old man's condition. Because Boito was Italy's most revered intellectual and artistic icon, composers, poets, and theater people flocked to his bedside, to his hospital room, and, after his death on June 10, to the wake. Toscanini was among those who helped in Boito's last days, and he spent an entire night at his bier. With Boito's death, a generation of Italian creativity ended, Verdi's era ended, and with it the highest aspirations of Italian art. Puccini regretted not going to Milan for the funeral, but he explained to Tito that he had been too ill to travel. "My doctor [and] my wife would not let me leave; and I am now suffering here, alone! Thanks for sending me a telegram right away. With Boito's death, the last of our Sig[nor] Giulio's companions has gone!" (GP to TR, June 11, 1918, in Gara, pp. 461–462). Boito had left his opera *Nerone* unfinished. He had, however, told Toscanini he wanted it produced at La Scala and wanted him to conduct it. After his death, Boito's executor asked Toscanini to oversee the work of finishing *Nerone*, using the composer's musical sketches. He did so with the help of Antonio Smareglia, Vincenzo Tommasini, and Casa Ricordi's staff, seeing the project to its end. It was produced at La Scala on May 1, 1924. Harvey Sachs describes the effort for *Nerone* as the most difficult undertaking of Toscanini's reign at La Scala and perhaps of his entire career. Its premiere was staged as a great operatic gala and a national event for Italy.

Il Trittico

Puccini, evidently troubled about his own future in a chaotic time, focused on Rome and the Teatro Costanzi, where he could see *La Rondine*, talk to Emma Carelli, who was then managing the company, and plan productions of his new work, the *Trittico*, which he had written during the war. It was made up of three one-act operas, *Il Tabarro*, *Suor Angelica*, and *Gianni Schicchi*.

When Puccini had first faced Giulio Ricordi's strong opposition to the idea of three one-act operas, he set the project aside for several years, but he never gave it up. Finally, he found three suitable subjects. Adami was his librettist for the first, *Il Tabarro*, mentioned earlier, which Puccini composed while he was working on *Rondine*. He orchestrated it in 1916, while he was considering two other works, which would have librettos by Forzano. *Gianni Schicchi* was a story about a Florentine schemer. *Suor Angelica* was set in a convent. Many elements of it closely resemble Soldani's sprawling story about Saint Margaret of Cortona, which Puccini had rejected; but the plot of *Suor Angelica*, unlike that of Saint Margaret of Cortona, is taut. This is clearly one of "Puccini's Pascoli operas," a hymn to Tuscan nature: he finished composing it in autumn 1917.

Among many letters about casting the *Trittico*, Puccini sent one to Carlo Clausetti, mentioning the upcoming Rome production and another in Buenos Aires.

> I sent you a telegram just now, but are you really suggesting [the soprano Virginia] Guer[r]ini? And why not Marianna, who is walking the streets in Milan? As you say, [Walter] Mocchi has had misfortunes, defections, but should I have to bear the burden of that? It is absolutely obvious that I'm not going to throw my opera away in B[uenos] Aires, unless I have heard it here [in Rome]; and the conductor there must be the same as the one here, otherwise, with three operas that require so much care to be taken about

the sets and costumes, you are headed for an American production: [it will get] few rehearsals and then [you run it out] before the public. Not that, really no! I care too much for these three works of mine, and I cannot nor will not show them where things are uncertain or worse. And you, as [my friend] Claudio and as the representative of the House [of Ricordi], will tell me I am right.

For *Tabarro,* we need someone in addition to [Carlo] Galeffi, a woman who can do the opera itself [and] can do *Schicchi* as well; but for *Schicchi* we need an ingenue, small, and with a fresh voice that is not dramatic, etc. etc. Dalla Rizza (who would not be ideal for *S[uor] A[ngelica]*) can do Lauretta in *G[ianni] S[chicchi]* very well. I say that she would not be ideal for *S[uor] Ang[elica]* because I had dreamed of a woman with another kind of *allure,* but so be it, go for Dalla Rizza, who certainly would do a good job in the end. But, as you say, we are in deep water, even with Galeffi. But a heavier sea is coming, where that pig Conrad [von Hötzendorf, the Austrian general] is planning new attacks on our Italy, may God protect us; but also (and let us hope for this) things may go better. With this new blow, it would not be correct to give the operas. I fixed [the date], I gave my word to give them before our infamous and enormous [defeat at] Caporetto. So I will wait until you tell me yes or no, and [then] get out of it. [GP to CC, April 8, 1918, Tollett and Harman Collection]

After visits from Emma Carelli and Tito, he decided against giving *Trittico*'s world premiere in Rome and awarded it to the Metropolitan Opera instead. The Costanzi would present the first Italian *Trittico.* Although its baptism meant another important world premiere for him, Puccini referred disparagingly to his new operas as *"le 3 operettacchiole,"* "the three miserable little operettas" (GP to LP, June 27, 1918, in Gara, p. 462). In the event, they were anything but miserable. Puccini was still retouching *Schicchi* and the revised *Rondine* that summer. He and Elvira stayed in a rented house on Via Giotto in Viareggio, where they could entertain Bicchi, Franca, and Fosca.

At the height of the vacationers' invasion, however, he abandoned Viareggio for Chiatri (where he had his piano tuned for the first time in ten years), then summoned Adami and turned back to *Rondine.* As Puccini told Sonzogno, he intended to make small changes in the first act; but some were major, as were those in other acts. Prunier was to move down from his original tenor register to baritone; Lisette's tessitura would be raised; Rambaldo would become stronger, Ruggero less naïve, and Magda's character would be more carefully developed. In the course of the reworking, he also decided to change the setting of the opera, discarding the crinolines for contemporary costumes, in the style of the Tuscan painter and scenic designer Umberto Brunelleschi or of Caramba, the costume designer responsible for the *Trittico* in Rome. He wanted to set the last act in Ruggero's family home, but later gave that up. By mid-September, when little had been accomplished on *Rondine,* Puccini blamed Adami, who had cost him an entire summer.

Other correspondence from that time includes letters about the scenic designer Galileo Chini, who had been working with Puccini on the *Trittico.* Far from satisfied with Chini's proposals, he stood by his ideas and particularly defended the characters in *Il Tabarro.* In September he also had a visit from the conductor Roberto Moranzoni, who would conduct the world premiere of the *Trittico* for the Met. After going over the operas with the composer, he picked up the scores and the costume and set designs in Milan.

All this theatrical business was conducted as if the war were on some other continent. But the fact was this: Italy seemed certain to fall in the summer and early autumn of 1918. Austria had mounted a new offensive near the *Altopiano,* while the Italian army had lost all of Carnia to the east and the Cadore, in the mountains north of Venice. The Austrians, who had bombed Venice, Padua, and Treviso from the air, were advancing all along the front. In June they mounted a general attack, with the Piave River as the main line of Italian defense. Having occupied Belluno and crossed the Piave, they could march straight to Venice. Italy, however, made an astonishing recovery, for the Piave saw the nation's last and greatest battle of World War I. On October 24 the Italians mounted their counteroffensive, and within a few days they were fighting decisive engagements along the river and in Vittorio Veneto, forcing the enemy back to the north and east, in full retreat. With that, the Austrian generals asked for an armistice, which was signed on November 3 and took effect the next day, ending the war on the Italian front. Puccini, who had followed the news, wrote to Luigi Pieri on November 3, looking forward to the end and praising the courageous Italian troops who had fought so bravely in Vittorio Veneto. Finally the Italian army drove Austria out, but at a dreadful cost in human life and destruction. Recovery came, but slowly.

The Metropolitan Opera gave the world premiere of *Il Trittico* on December 14, 1918, but Puccini could not attend because travel was still limited. The war having ended a month earlier, this was a more subdued event than the first night of *Fanciulla*. The large cast for *Il Tabarro* featured Luigi Montesanto as Michele, Giulio Crimi as Luigi, and the enigmatic Claudia Muzio as Giorgetta, a role that suited her perfectly. In the 1940s several singers and stagehands at the Met remembered Muzio as very tall and beautiful, but she said very little to anyone, lived like a recluse with her fanatically religious and demanding mother, and "acted as if we were all devils." Muzio was nevertheless a consummate professional, the daughter of a stage manager who had worked for years at Covent Garden before he moved to New York. She, however, was raised in Italy, where she launched her career and sang roles in new operas by many of Puccini's contemporaries. Puccini did not particularly like her in *Tosca,* but it was the role of her Met debut in 1916. One critic called her singing "one long, tragic cry," something that made her a perfect Giorgetta. Crimi, whom Puccini knew very well, had a respectable success. According to one review, he sang with real fire. Surprisingly, the coarse and self-absorbed Montesanto failed to bring Michele to life.

With Geraldine Farrar in the title role of *Suor Angelica,* this exquisite opera was perhaps doomed from the start, for the soprano had lost her voice and had a throat operation that had put all critics on the alert. When she described the opera in her autobiography, she said, *"Suor Angelica* put no further strain on a throat now fairly strong"—but not strong enough to save the opera, although one critic praised her subdued acting. Other worldly New York critics greeted it with scorn, compared it to a Christmas card, and wrote of monotony, sentimentality, and cheap theatrical effects. Puccini reported to Sybil that Farrar had "no voice left." Then, he said, Rosa Raisa took over the role and sent the Chicago Opera audience into a delirium of enthusiasm over it. Because he called this opera his favorite of the three works, any hint of success was welcome.

Gianni Schicchi became popular when people fell in love with its bright comedy. After the Met premiere critics greeted the "froth, spray," and "sparkle" of Puccini's score. One wrote, "Action and speech, voices and orchestra are inseparable in an ebullient flood." It was Puccini's "most Italian opera." Henry Krehbiel, writing in the *New York Tribune,* said that it blew through the theater like "an invigorating breeze, a modern version of old-fashioned Italian *opera buffa.*" Giuseppe De Luca brought the comic title role to vivid life; the veteran English soprano Florence Easton was a delicious Lauretta, a real feat, given the many heavier roles she was sing-ing at the time. She had to repeat *"O mio babbino caro,"* which became an instant hit and was hailed as "the pearl of the evening." Crimi's Rinuccio was "easily his best part so far" at the Met. Moranzoni, who had studied the scores with Puccini, was the ideal conductor for them (Krehbiel re-view in Seltsam, p. 336; other reviews are quoted in Tuggle, pp. 151–153).

On December 13, the day before the Met premiere, Puccini was already installed at the Hotel Quirinale in Rome, preparing the first Italian *Trittico* at the Teatro Costanzi. He ordered things he needed from Milan: the gold powder for the miracle of *Suor Angelica* and bells that rang with an au-thentic "convent" sound. Rehearsals were going slowly, he reported to Tito, but the orchestra sounded fine, at least in *Schicchi.* He was particu-larly pleased with the expert editing and beautiful parts Ricordi had sent. Never before had he seen a score so finely done, he said; and he thanked Raffaele Tenaglia, who had taken care of the many revisions he had made after the premiere.

I learned something about the singers' view of his production when I interviewed Dalla Rizza in 1969. The rehearsals of *Schicchi* went smoothly enough, she said, but she was overcome by the difficulty of *Suor Angelica.* She said she threw herself so completely into the role that she went home exhausted, night after night. "My God!" her mother cried, "It's killing you." Finally Puccini felt he had whipped his forces into shape; and the Costanzi production went off brilliantly on January 11, 1919, with the king, the queen, and the royal family present. Gino Marinuzzi conducted. In *Il Tabarro,* Galeffi, as planned, sang Michele; Maria Labia, Adami's sister-in-law, was Giorgetta; and the Canadian tenor Edward Johnson, singing un-der the name of Edoardo Di Giovanni was Luigi. The cast of *Suor Angelica* included Dalla Rizza in the title role and Matilde Blanco Sadun as the Princess. Galeffi returned in the title role of *Gianni Schicchi* with Dalla Rizza as Lauretta and Di Giovanni as Rinuccio.

Although the reviews were somewhat mixed, Dalla Rizza rang up a big personal success. The critics loved everything about her—her makeup, movements, and sense of poetry. She gave the audience the "soul of the role," had a magnificent voice, and expressed all the emotions Puccini had put into the opera (Gara, p. 479). The public liked the operas so well that Puccini could send good news to Luigi Pieri. "Here everything is moving full steam ahead, sold-out houses, last Sunday the box office for the matinee was 28,000 lire. Yesterday, Sunday, at standard prices, a tremendously good house, 21,000 lire" (GP to LP, January 27, 1919, in Gara, pp. 478–479). The reviews, however, were not unanimous, although all praised Puccini's technical skill and artistry. This was an all-important event for Puccini, showing the music world the new directions he had chosen and the risks he was willing to take. It was so successful that it was given seven times, and Puccini stayed in Rome until the run ended. Before he left, the mayor hosted a banquet for him at the Grand Hotel, another of the events he so detested. With it, he closed out a satisfying six-week adventure and returned in peace to "boring" Torre del Lago.

Safe at home, he started making changes to the scores of the three operas and continued in his old habit of helping others. Would [Giorgio?] Alberti, a highly placed official in one of the ministries in Rome, see that two of his relatives got decorations?

I am sending a portrait of myself as a souvenir. I left without saying good-bye to you. Please forgive me, but all the bother of leaving kept me [from taking care of it]. Is Adami still there? I read about his Ibsen-style success, but I think that it would be better for him to go back to something refined, spiritual, and sweetly sentimental [something like his old plays]. I thank you again for everything you did for me. Now I must ask a favor of you. There are two of my relatives who would like to be crucified [receive the Cavalier's Cross, a decoration]. One is my nephew Carlo Marsili, director of the B[anca] di Sconto in Livorno. I am enclosing the papers for his application, which has already been sent. The other is my brother-in-law, a little old man of 65 years, who has been for 30 or 35 years a model [of public service] as the inspector of the Commune of Pescia (Tuscany). His name is Renato Franceschini; from Lucca. I believe he has not yet filled out any papers. He wants this very much, enormously; it would bring immense joy to this dear man and royal functionary who is so alert and so respected in his whole town. Please forgive me for my boldness. And if what I am asking should be even a small bother to you, just let it go. Thanks and many cordial wishes from your very devoted and affectionate G. Puccini. [GP to Alberti, February 21, 1919, Tollett and Harman Collection]

As a successful composer, Puccini would normally have gone directly to other productions of the *Trittico,* but in such a difficult time he found it hard to sell. In short, it fell victim to the circumstances of the day. At the same time, major changes were taking place at Casa Ricordi, where Tito either resigned or was forced out of the firm. Renzo Valcarenghi and Clausetti, the new heads of Casa Riccordi, both sympathetic to Puccini (Clausetti more, Valcarenghi less), stepped into the administration; but disruptions were many, after more than a century of the Ricordis' rule. The new directors were sometimes torn between conflicting loyalties as they managed the affairs of Puccini and other, new composers. Neither had Giulio Ricordi's practical experience in theater, and neither understood staging as Tito did. As Puccini remarked in 1921, Clausetti had only a limited knowledge of his operas, although he could defend his rights and reputation. Business practices also changed, as they had after Giulio Ricordi's death; but this time Casa Ricordi became what Puccini angrily called "a bureaucracy worse than the one in Rome." Now neither his handwritten receipt for money nor his brief thank-you letter was enough, for the firm required him to sign a printed form and return it to Milan. This, too, was a moment when many were asking whether he would ever compose another truly popular opera. As several writers have observed, he had not had a big hit since the *Butterfly* of 1904. In 1919 and for years to come, many theaters were closed, while others could barely manage to give standard operas, which the singers knew very well and for which they had costumes and scenery. Just as Giulio Ricordi had predicted, Puccini's three one-act operas were expensive to produce and hard to cast. Singers had to learn new roles in works that would be infrequently performed; and this meant a net loss for them. Also, there was the matter of public taste, for critics and audiences obviously liked *Gianni Schicchi* better than *Il Tabarro* and especially disliked *Suor Angelica.*

Toscanini, famous as he was, did damage of his own by criticizing the *Trittico;* his criticism deepened the chasm between him and the composer. When Puccini heard that Toscanini had walked out during a production of the *Trittico* and had expressed unfavorable opinions about the operas, he responded by trying to prevent Covent Garden from hiring him for the

Trittico in London. To Sybil he wrote, "I protested to Ricordi because I don't want that *pig* of a Toscanini; he has said all sorts of nasty things about my operas and has tried to inspire certain journalists to run them down too. . . . One of his friends (of the *Secolo*) wrote a beastly article under his inspiration—and I won't have this *God*. He's no use to me, and, as I say, as I have already said, when an orchestral conductor thinks poorly of the operas he has to conduct, he can't interpret them properly. . . . There remains the personal question [about the controversy during the war], and I shall do all I can not to have him. I have no need of *Gods* because my operas go all over the world. . . . If you see Higgins or any of the others, tell them too that I don't want this *pig*; if he comes to London, *I shan't come*" (GP to SS, March 16, 1919, in Seligman, pp. 292–293). The *Trittico* did rack up some successes, in January and February 1920, at the Teatro Regio in Turin and the San Carlo in Naples. In April the revised *Rondine* was given in Palermo.

With the war over, his sequestered automobiles returned to him, and highways and rail lines being repaired, Puccini could at least travel, so in January he took two friends to Torre della Tagliata, the old tower in the Maremma that he had finally managed to restore. With the sea almost at the door, he loved the place at first for its sun and primitive landscape, but later found it was the loneliest place imaginable. He spent about a month there, fishing and hunting with his guests and with Nicche, who was home from the army, keeping him company and doing the cooking. In October he, Elvira, and Tonio went to Vienna, where again he was a world-class celebrity. Two long letters to Sybil told about the first Austrian *Rondine*, which he criticized, and mentioned his encounters with Lotte Lehmann and the Moravian soprano Maria Jeritza, whom he called "perhaps the most original artiste that I have ever known." Having heard her in *Tosca*, he praised her, saying that she did certain things marvelously and that she was very good as Giorgetta in *Tabarro*. He had discussed Jeritza's future plans with the idea of luring her to London for *Il Tabarro* and *Suor Angelica*, even as the Austrian impresario was trying to keep her in Austria. He also praised Lehmann's performance in *Suor Angelica*, saying she could expect a warm welcome in London. Further revisions of *Rondine* claimed some of Puccini's time, but he did the most important work of the year on his new opera, *Turandot*.

CHAPTER TWELVE

~❧❧~

The Unfinished Turandot: *Spring 1919–November 1924*

Italy's painful postwar era ran through the 1920s and 1930s, during which time people everywhere suffered from poverty and a lack of services. In the once prosperous Veneto, shattered buildings, craters, military fortifications, and cemeteries reminded every Italian of what the country had lost. Men returned from military service to find their jobs gone, and farms no longer turned a profit. Families mourned those who had been killed or injured. With the country demoralized and uncertain about recovery, strikes and riots broke out, sequels to earlier disorders reaching back into the 1890s. Like the earlier uprisings, these were put down by the police and the army. Milan's once-solid economy virtually collapsed, and the government in Rome appeared ineffectual.

The Composer in the "New" Italy

In this chaos the opera houses were also at risk, because they were easy targets for anarchists. Impresarios got bomb threats; in 1921 a bomb was actually set off in the Teatro Diana in Milan. Money for new productions was difficult to find. Worse, many singers and conductors had moved to the United States, South America, and, after the armistice, even to Russia.

Puccini, very bitter about his country's condition, believed that England, rich and beautiful, had won the war, while Italy had lost it. Although he was not among the poor, he suffered as all composers did, with reduced royalties from an opera industry that was struggling back to life. Throughout this period, he dreaded going to Milan, a city he had never

· 257 ·

liked. He wrote to Schnabl: "I am very troubled about going to Milan. I am not used to the new Italy; and Milan is the university of new ways" (GP to RSR, December 25, 1920, in Gara, pp. 499–500). La Scala could not reopen until December 26, 1921, when Toscanini conducted *Falstaff.* Bicchi remembered Puccini reading about the opening night in the *Corriere della Sera* and seizing the occasion to make sarcastic comments about Toscanini. However concerned the composer may have been about Italy, he was even more worried about the European theaters, especially those where his works had been banned during the war. Naturally, some of his most popular operas recovered quickly, but others fought to stay alive. *Rondine* did not sell; and when the *Trittico* was given for the first time in Cologne, the critics wrote it off as such a failure that the impresario took it off the program after only three or four performances.

Puccini as Father Dante's Parishioner

Puccini saw unwelcome change come even to his paradise, his "Eden" at Torre del Lago. First, he came close to losing his hunting rights, after thirty years on Lake Massaciuccoli. Then he began protesting the peat factory that the government had built in the peat bog, the *torbiera,* near his house. Its work siren shattered the pristine silence several times a day, while its dredges fouled the place with odors and noise. He discussed his problems with the village's new, young priest, Dante Del Fiorentino, who had been assigned to the parish just after the armistice, arriving in Torre in spring 1919. His job: to work in a church where the senior cleric was too old and ill to manage his pastoral duties alone. Del Fiorentino was, as we have seen, the composer's avid fan. Having known Puccini slightly for years, he gradually became a trusted friend. At first hand, he observed Puccini trying to adjust to a world he could hardly recognize. After Del Fiorentino arrived, the Gragnanis and other neighbors did what they could to keep him close to his idol. His first postwar personal encounter with Puccini came during the parish's annual spring blessing of the houses, *la benedizione.*

Because none of the village's priests had ever managed to get Puccini to come to Mass, they and the local conservatives saw him as an unbeliever. One rite, however, the composer did accept from Del Fiorentino, and that was the blessing of his villa. In Italy, the priest and two altar boys make the rounds of the parish every April, sprinkling holy water and reciting prayers in homes, shops, cafés, bars, and even the local train station. Most people let them in, but nonbelievers and others of anticlerical persuasion close their doors and hide. In divided families, the believers welcome the priest and his attendants into the kitchen or hall, while nonbelievers stay in a bedroom or go outside to rage against the Church. In public places such as the train station, practicing Catholics let the priest sprinkle them, while the ones the priests call atheists turn their backs and mumble curses and threats. In 1919 the job of doing the spring blessings in Torre fell to Del Fiorentino. He began his rounds, and having blessed the Gragnanis, he turned toward Villa Puccini, only to be stopped by one of his altar boys.

"We never go there," he said. "He's an unbeliever."

Del Fiorentino, undaunted, asked Nicche, Puccini's fellow hunter and jack-of-all-trades, whether Puccini would like to have his house blessed. The Maestro was still in bed, Nicche said, but he would be happy to have the priest come in. Room by room they went through the ground floor, with Nicche beside them and two of Puccini's hunting dogs in tow. Del Fiorentino sprinkled holy water in every room, and he prayed. Then they started upstairs.

"Hey, *Cappellano* [Chaplain, which Del Fiorentino had been in the army], come along in," Puccini shouted. He was propped up against pillows in a huge bed, with his windows facing the lake and the mountains on its far side. In his own gruff way, the composer asked Del Fiorentino how his music and studies were going. Both men speaking the local dialect, they reminisced about the night Puccini had consoled the tenor in Pisa. Then Puccini said, "You were a young soldier then, and now who would ever dream I would be calling you *mio cappellano!*" He also joked for a while about how he had first dubbed Del Fiorentino "Big Skirt," or *Gonnellone*. With that, he shouted to let Elvira know the priest was coming to her room.

"Elvira! Elvira! Wake up! The *Capellano* is here. *Gonnellone* has come to bless you. Get a good dose of holy water. You need it!" Del Fiorentino said he was so afraid to enter her room that he simply reached around the door and sprinkled, without looking to see what he had done. Then Puccini called them back and began to chat about life in Lucca. He also warned them not to sprinkle his music, but he said, "Do a good job with your holy water sprinkler and intercede for me with your prayers." Before they left, he handed Del Fiorentino a cash donation and invited him to come back (Del Fiorentino, pp. 175–178).

Del Fiorentino remained in Torre from 1919 until 1923, when he went briefly to the United States, only to return to Torre, Viareggio, and Puccini in the summer of 1924. His warm friendship with the composer went somewhat beyond the close association some priests have with their parishioners, and Puccini had enormous respect for the young cleric. In Italy, the parish priest serves as a counselor and personal advisor, with everyone in the community aware of his power. What he says can change people's perception of one, particularly in a small town or village. When the priest writes a *raccomandazione,* a letter of recommendation, he signs it, embosses it with the parish's metal seal, then drops hot wax near his signature, pressing yet another seal into it. All authorities, practicing Catholics and nonbelievers alike, take such a letter very seriously.

When he was first assigned to Torre, Del Fiorentino was young and inexperienced, but he was an ordained priest, and he was a native of Lucca, as Puccini was. According to the codes of Italian society, this set him above others, even above a parishioner as famous as Puccini, who respected the dignity of his post. As we have seen, Puccini asked Del Fiorentino's advice about sending money to Josi von Stängel. And more, he evidently enjoyed his affection and admiration. In Torre the two men chatted in the composer's studio, sat together in the café, watched water carnivals, and listened to band concerts on saints' days and national holidays. Sometimes Puccini drove the priest to the villages across the lake, particularly to Quiesa, the Del Fiorentinos' home parish, where they attended the local saint's day festivals in the summer. In Del Fiorentino's memoir, Puccini appears at his best, generous and decent, contributing five hundred lire toward the price of a new bell for the church, or taking pity on Fedele, the mentally retarded beggar who pestered him almost daily for small change. Del Fiorentino described something "essentially childlike" about him, saying that he loved to laugh and play silly jokes on people (Del Fiorentino, pp. 172–184).

This idyll of rural Tuscany ended all too soon, as the postwar political and social upheaval forced itself on this ancient, stable world. Once, when Puccini took Del Fiorentino out on the lake in his motorboat, an angry fisherman shouted at him, "It's your turn now, soon it will be our turn!"

Del Fiorentino, who took the man for a communist, said the composer seemed to ignore the threat, but soon Puccini spoke sadly: "Let's go home." During the rest of their outing, he complained that the world and Italy were morally sick. Disease had come even to Tuscany. "Why should that man hate me?" the composer asked. "There was hatred in his voice and in his face" (Del Fiorentino, p. 194).

The new hostility, the peat factory, and other aggravations eventually drove Puccini out of Torre. Having often rented villas on a temporary basis in Viareggio, Puccini began building his own house there, although he and Elvira stayed on in Torre while it was under construction, sometimes alone and sometimes with Tonio, who helped oversee the work. In 1920 Fosca sent Bicchi, now a teenager, from Milan to Torre for her summer visit with Puccini and Elvira. Even after his new house was ready, Puccini never completely abandoned Torre, for he returned there often, sometimes to hunt, but usually to visit with his old cronies.

Del Fiorentino went with Puccini to the Viareggio job site, where the composer argued with Tonio about whether to have a radio in the house; but when he saw the ugly aerial crowning his roof, he ordered it taken down. The villa was not ready until December 1921, nearly three years after Del Fiorentino had come to live in Torre. Then, and for the rest of the composer's life, he followed Puccini around and kept a record of their meetings. Over the decades that followed, he also amassed a large collection of Puccini's letters, mostly written to local figures. Because his own sister lived in Viareggio, the priest had had an excuse for going there and seeing the Maestro regularly.

Choosing *Turandot*

Even before the world premiere of the *Trittico* and its successful first European production in Rome, Puccini had begun to hunt obsessively for a new subject. For a time, his choice was *Cristoforo Sly*, the libretto for which he hoped to get from Forzano, the recent collaborator who had written well-made librettos for two operas of the *Trittico*. *Sly* went slowly, even with Forzano, Puccini's neighbor in Tuscany, close at hand. A tall, thin, somewhat eccentric man of middle age, he had built a small wooden house on the beach at Lido di Camaiore, where he worked on the *Sly* scenario and tried in vain to satisfy the demanding composer. Puccini also had another project in mind—*Oliver Twist,* a production of which he had seen in London. At the composer's request, Adami began to prepare a scenario, working alone at first and then with an established critic and editor, Renato Simoni.

Like Adami, the genial Simoni was a native of Verona and was a prominent dramatist and journalist; but unlike the sweet, modest Adami, he was full of himself, proud and somewhat arrogant. Only in D'Annunzio had Puccini faced such a temperamental artist, for Giacosa, in spite of all his fame, had been essentially a simple, unpretentious man. The composer had actually met Simoni years before, when Giacosa brought them together. Simoni had begun writing in 1914 for the *Corriere della Sera* in Milan. At least at the beginning, a solid professional relationship developed between him and Puccini, helped along in part because of Simoni's close friendship with Adami and with Fosca, who often invited both to dinner in her home. After Puccini's death in 1924, both men turned to Fosca in their grief and were prominent among the mourners chosen for the final ceremonies for Puccini in Milan. Simoni eulogized his demanding Maestro in essays and articles, but when Puccini most needed him, he was not nearly as helpful as he might have been.

In October 1919 Puccini was complaining to Adami that he had not worked in two years. Then, in early March 1920, he met Adami and Simoni for lunch in Milan, just as he was about to leave for Rome. Adami later published his recollection of the day's events. He, Simoni, and Puccini were sitting in a restaurant discussing several dramas when the subject of the Venetian playwright Carlo Gozzi came up. In fact, it was Simoni, the author of a play called *Carlo Gozzi,* who suggested that Puccini should look over his works. Puccini already knew something about Gozzi and his "theatrical fables," as later correspondence shows. According to Adami, Puccini suddenly inquired, "What about *Turandotte?*" Simoni, who had a copy of the play in his apartment, gave it to Puccini, who left Milan that afternoon and read it on the train. What he read was not authentic Gozzi, but a second-generation adaptation by Andrea Maffei of the original play, which had had its premiere in Venice in January 1762.

Carlo Gozzi, the heir of a noble family in sharp decline, wrote his *Fiabe teatrali,* his theatrical fairy tales, as gorgeous, sardonic, and even brittle responses to the popular comedies of Carlo Goldoni. During this local war of style against style, Goldoni, in his total reform of the theater, tried to drive out the traditional Venetian *commedia dell'arte,* with its air of magic and fantasy. Instead, he populated the stage with such down-to-earth characters as tavern layabouts, shopkeepers, housemaids, valets, and scheming relatives. This is not to say that Goldoni completely ignored tragic and tragicomic themes, for among his early works were a *Belisario* and a *Don Giovanni Tenorio;* but he found his true element in the comedy of the everyday lives of real people.

Gozzi, Goldoni's hated rival, shot back with his *Fiabe,* which brought legend, myth, and wild creativity to the Teatro San Samuele. Temporarily turning back the Goldoni tide, he presented *L'amore delle tre melarance, Il corvo, Il re cervo,* and *Turandotte.* He had enhanced his plots, some taken from *A Thousand and One Nights* and collections of fables, with his own clever use of *commedia dell'arte* figures. It was a question of the right moment and the right theater. The San Samuele, known for its extravagant scenery, was the perfect house for Gozzi's flights of fancy. In that theater in 1753, the Venetian architect and scenic designer Antonio Codognato had built a brilliantly lighted set with huge Venetian mirrors, a daring idea for its time. Not to be outdone, another designer decorated a production with crystal; then Codognato retaliated with a setting so beautiful that the impresario had to open the theater during the day, charging admission for people to look at it. It was entirely fitting that Gozzi's exotic play should follow Codognato, "The Mirror Man," onto the San Samuele stage.

At the beginning of the nineteenth century, Gozzi's original five-act *Turandotte* was adapted and translated into German by Schiller; that adaptation was later translated back into Italian by Maffei, Verdi's friend and librettist. Puccini and his librettists were also familiar with other versions of Turandot's story, many of which had made their way out of Venice and even into the opera repertory. Puccini might have heard about Antonio Bazzini's *Turanda* (1854), for Bazzini had taught him at the Milan Conservatory, and he knew of a *Turandotte* north of the Alps, where Ferruccio Busoni had expanded one of his scores into a two-act opera called *Turandot.* Even as Puccini was beginning to consider this subject, the Russian director Yevgeny Vakhtangov was planning a major production of

Gozzi's play at the Moscow Art Theater, where it was produced as *Princess Turandot*. Puccini, who had never been intimidated by others working on a subject he liked, went on with his own project.

Within days of the Milan luncheon, Puccini was giving Simoni specific instructions about the structure of the opera and his emphasis on "the amorous passion of Turandot, who has suffocated for such a long time under the ashes of her great pride." It is entirely possible, however, that he and the playwright had discussed Gozzi as early as 1919, when both were vacationing in Bagni di Lucca. At the end of summer, Puccini invited him to come to Torre to talk and "enjoy the air of swamp and sea." He also mentioned the Max Reinhardt production of *Turandot,* photographs of which he expected to get from an acquaintance (GP to RS, March 18, 1920, in Gara, pp. 490–491).

At that moment, however, his first concern was keeping the *Trittico* intact, as he battled with impresarios and even with Casa Ricordi to prevent it from being broken up. First, impresarios wanted to omit *Suor Angelica,* then *Il Tabarro,* from the single-evening program. As always, Puccini wrote to Sybil about his problems. He was feted in Covent Garden in June 1920 when the *Trittico* was first produced. At that time, all three operas were given as he had written them. Vincent Seligman, describing the evening as a wonderful personal triumph, said Puccini was nervous when the first opera began, but became calmer as he realized the evening was a success. The king and queen invited him to the royal box and offered their congratulations. As the critic of the *Times* put it, "What would Covent Garden be without Puccini?"

He left England confident that the *Trittico* would enter the Covent Garden repertory. His main problem was finding a replacement for Dalla Rizza, who had to go to Buenos Aires. He already feared *Suor Angelica* might be set aside. "I don't like the idea of this opera becoming a *Cinderella,*" he told Sybil (GP to SS, June 27, 1920, in Seligman, pp. 307–308). To his dismay, he soon learned that Henry V. Higgins, the director of Covent Garden, had indeed taken *Suor Angelica* off the program; when Sybil pleaded its case with Higgins, he refused to listen. Feeling that the audience disliked it, he said he would never stage it again. Puccini, dumbfounded, railed at this turn of events, but he had to give in, authorizing Covent Garden to give *Schicchi* and *Tabarro* without it. But worse was to come. Higgins then decided to drop both *Suor Angelica* and *Il Tabarro* and pair the successful *Gianni Schicchi* with the Russian ballet. "This is a real betrayal," Puccini protested to Sybil (GP to SS, July 15, 1920, in Seligman, pp. 309–310).

Puccini sent that depressing news to Dalla Rizza, writing from Torre della Tagliata, where he was overseeing the stonemasons' work on his house. "It is all right, but it's terribly lonely, and melancholy sets in. . . . Here everything is rotten, one lives badly, without order, without any protection from the national government. . . . How I long to live abroad!" (GP to GDR, July 5, 1920, in Gara, pp. 491–492). He then referred briefly to the strikes and riots that had erupted all over Italy. By the end of the month, he had taken refuge in Bagni di Lucca to avoid the summer crowds in Viareggio, which was rapidly being developed. It had grown from a fishing village to a town, and then to a small city, swollen with tourists and long-term visitors in winter and summer. While not yet a major resort, Viareggio had become the capital of the Versilia, an important gathering place for European royalty and the wealthy foreigners and Italians whom Bicchi loved to spy on. Not even this fast growth had given Viareggio a decent theater, so Puccini refused to let his operas be given there, although later he developed an ambitious plan to build an opera house and even a national theater in the town.

As he firmed up his ideas about *Turandot,* Puccini told friends about his new project. To Sybil he wrote, "Perhaps I shall do an old Chinese play, *Turandot.* The poets Simoni and Adami are coming here [to Bagni di Lucca]" (GP to SS, July 18, 1920, in Seligman, p. 312). Things were going well for him. Royalties had again begun to pour in. Writing to Schnabl about his search for a new opera, he mentioned his interest in *Cristoforo Sly* but said he would not decide about it until autumn, when he could see the play onstage. Adami and Simoni had provided a very original scenario of *Turandot;* at that moment, he preferred it to everything else.

Work Begins

A few days later, he was discussing the opera with Adami and Simoni, for both were with him in Bagni di Lucca. During their stay, they listened to Chinese tunes played on a music box that belonged to one of the composer's acquaintances, Baron Fassini-Camossi. Baron Fassini, a collector of Oriental art, had brought it back from the Far East. William Weaver, who tracked down the music box decades later, spoke of his discovery when I asked him about it in January 2001.

> Baron Fassini was a diplomat from Lucca. When Puccini was alive, the baron, then retired, was staying at his villa in Bagni di Lucca. That is where he played this music for them. Then, after World War II, Michael Rose of the BBC found that Baroness Fassini was in Rome, so he called her. We went to her home with a tape recorder, and I interviewed her. It was a pretty little music box made of rosewood, but when she tried to start it, it didn't work. We were horrified when she jabbed at it with a screwdriver, but finally she got it to play. The music was absolutely what Puccini used; there were five tunes, and three of those were quite obviously in *Turandot*. It was an eerie experience with this tinkly music and the idea that Puccini had had this very box. He kept it forever. After we listened to it, we made the tape.

Weaver played his tape on a Metropolitan Opera Saturday broadcast intermission feature. As he said, Puccini used pieces from the music box to create Chinese elements in the score. According to Mary Ellis Peltz, the former editor of *Opera News* and archivist of the Metropolitan Opera, Puccini wrote in 1920 or 1921 to Gatti-Casazza, asking him to go to China-town, find some "Chinese music," and send it to him. (Although that letter can no longer be found, we have no reason to doubt that it existed.)

After the meeting in Bagni, the librettists began building a text on their scenario, while Puccini took care of other business. He was, however, desperate to begin work. Just before leaving to hunt in Torre della Tagliata, he described his mood to Simoni:

> "My anxiety—I would almost say suffering—over idleness and my frenzy to be working—that is, for the tyrannical Princess—are growing day by day. I think that it was August, when you described the scenario to me! Twenty days from now, it will be Christmas! I am not criticizing you, but if my words had spear-points, you, you pure-blood thoroughbred, would think someone was driving spurs into your flanks. Don't be angry at me. People tell me that when you talk about our work and my impatience, sparks fly from your eyes. If you only knew that every day I jot down themes and conceive processions, I whisper hidden choruses, I invent un-earthly harmonies. But for heaven's sake, hurry, both of you hurry. And I

would like all the work to be finished, tight, balanced, fine, and polished. I can already savor the goodness and beauty of the verses, the images, and above all the clear and moving humanity that is in this story, full of poetry and of special perfume." [GP to RS, December 4, 1920, in Gara, p. 497]

A much more tentative spirit emanates from a letter to Clausetti, written while Puccini was expecting Adami in Torre della Tagliata. "As you know, it is not certain that I will write *Turandot;* that depends on how the whole [libretto] develops. Especially the third act, the very heart of it, if I can manage to do it right" (GP to CC, [December 1920], in Gara, p. 498). Adami came, with a first act that was far too long, long enough for a whole opera, in fact. So Puccini ordered Adami to cut it. He needed quicker action and words flooded with "luminosity."

Still afflicted with the sadness that, he said, was always with him, he spent the rest of December in Torre della Tagliata, waiting for sunny days and resisting a move to Milan. On New Year's Eve he wrote a devastating poem called *"Scirocco,"* its title referring to the heavy, warm wind that blows across the Mediterranean from Africa. He sent it to Simoni.

At Tagliata: The Melancholy of the Maremma at the End of the Year 1920
Oh the false spring of the Maremma!
Falcons sail through the air, their wings spread wide.
Herds of sheep and cows, barely moving,
are strewn around as far as Maccarese.
Ravenous crows strip flesh from carcasses.
From nearby swamps comes the smell of sewers.
The sea leaves tree trunks and seaweed on the beach,
along with trash from shipwrecks.
Woods of oaks, lentisk [mastic] trees, and myrtle,
Thorns that rip off your skin!
Today, a rotten scirocco, lifeless, nauseating!
Far away, the swan grunts, the lapwing shrieks.
 And what of those weary horses on the edge of the ditch?
 How heavy the air is!
 How it smashes your bones!
O friends, watch out for malaria! [Gara, p. 500]

Puccini was alone, and the year was over.

In January 1921 he described *Turandot* to Alfredo Vandini as very original, an ancient Chinese legend, and a fantasy. He was hoping to get a good libretto. Still, with two librettists hard at work, and the project under way, he had further doubts and fears, and he confessed that he was thinking about writing something else, something based on a smaller subject. Tired and afraid of old age, he soon realized he had chosen something far grander and more difficult than he had first imagined, a project that required a huge commitment from him and was, as he said, far from easy. In many letters he expressed concern about his ability to finish it, and he once told Sybil outright that he doubted he ever would. There is no doubt that its scale weighed on him. As we have seen, Giulio Ricordi had often begged him to compose something big and important; but the 1910 *Fanciulla* had remained his only large-scale effort. With *Rondine* and the *Trittico,* he had reverted to the small, although they were challenging. In *Turandot,* at least as he and his librettists developed it, he had to manage a sprawling drama. As he complained to Sybil, it was too big, and he regretted not having a more manageable project in hand.

The grandiose scale of *Turandot,* the sumptuous, exotic settings, crowd scenes, rituals, rites, and characters suggest nothing more than *Aida.* The manly hero, Calaf, resembles Radamès. Both face life-threatening challenges, and both aspire to a woman's hand, believing that if they overcome the obstacles put before them, they will win and the woman will be theirs. Liù, the hapless slave girl, is the true child of Gozzi's slave Adelma; Liù is willing to die for Calaf, the alpha male, just as Aida rushes to die for Radamès. The cruel, haughty Princess Turandot resembles Amneris, the Egyptian princess. Turandot's father, the Emperor of China, matches the King in *Aida,* even in wanting to give his daughter's hand to the conquering hero. Timur resembles Amonasro, insofar as both are caught in the enemy's court; both conceal their identities; and both risk dying in a hostile place. The riddle scene of *Turandot* and the trial scene of *Aida* turn on thrice-repeated formulas. In *Aida* these are the accusations of treachery that the priests hurl at Radamès, while in *Turandot* they are the riddles that Turandot pitches to Calaf. In both cases, Calaf/Radamès will live or die depending on his answers to the three challenges put to him.

The parallels between *Turandot* and *Aida* also extend to the huge choral masses gathered in royal courts. In both operas the chorus pleads with the ruler to spare a life. All of this follows the formulas for *Aida,* which *Turandot* resembles even in its grand march—royal and Egyptian in *Aida,* imperial and Chinese in *Turandot.* This opera is also characterized by Puccini's return to closed pieces, to separate and identifiable arias, duets, and choral ensembles. It is an old-fashioned opera.

Given its size, no one should be surprised at the difficulties Puccini faced in composing it, but after 1923 his failing health added to his other serious problems. Dealing with diabetes every day, he was also plagued with the throat ailments that were eventually diagnosed as cancer. In spite of his illness, he continued pressing Adami and Simoni for an acceptable text. He sent them requests, then demands and orders; finally, when he became convinced they were ignoring him, he made many desperate pleas for cooperation. Often he waited in vain for the text, without which he could not compose; but sometimes he had composed the music and asked to have poetic lines written to fit it, just as he had done years before with Illica. Part of the equation, unspoken but very real, was his well-deserved reputation for tormenting his librettists with countless demands for revisions. Another element: both Adami and Simoni were busy with their own lives and projects, for both were active professional writers. The struggle to get the *Turandot* libretto in shape reached from spring 1920 until shortly before the composer's death in 1924. Over that span of time, he fretted about his own works, old and new, and, sometimes, those of rival composers.

Mascagni and *Il Piccolo Marat*

Early in 1921, while his librettists worked on the new opera, Puccini began stewing about Mascagni, whom he still saw as a threat, and never so much as after the war. This was the case even though Puccini had long been recognized as one of the richest and most famous composers in the world. That spring would see the premiere of *Il Piccolo Marat,* which the critics were awaiting with great interest. Mascagni's earlier collaboration with Illica had produced *Iris* and *Isabeau.* His prewar *Parisina,* which reached La Scala in 1913, was composed to the D'Annunzio libretto that the poet had tried unsuccessfully to peddle to Puccini and Franchetti. Overly long and written for an orchestra of more than a hundred instruments, it nevertheless won Mascagni high praise for his skillful orchestration, artistic growth, and psychological insights; and it stayed in the repertory in the composer's reduced version. Mascagni's next opera, *Lodoletta,* was taken from Ouida's *Two Little Wooden Shoes.* This was *I Due Zoccoletti,* which Puccini had fought so hard to win for himself and had then rejected. With a libretto by Forzano, it was launched at the Teatro Costanzi in Rome in 1917 and soon reached many Italian cities, Buenos Aires, and Rio. At the Metropolitan, Geraldine Farrar took the leading role for its first performance. Mascagni's next success came in 1919 with a sophisticated operetta, *Si,* which had a cast of dukes and showgirls, along with witty modern touches and sly references to high life in New York City. Popular in Italy and Austria, where Mascagni presented it with a revised score, it succeeded where Puccini's *Rondine* had failed.

Il Piccolo Marat was to have its premiere in May 1921 at the Costanzi, Puccini's preferred venue in Rome. Also composed to a libretto by Forzano, it told a tight story of the French Revolution and boasted a substantial musical, political, and dramatic heft that quickly set it apart from Giordano's ever-popular *Andrea Chénier.* Dalla Rizza, who sang Mariella, the leading soprano role, kept Puccini abreast of the progress of the rehearsals, and he went to Rome for the premiere. His reaction: "*Nicht!* Lots of noisy music without any heart." Although he did not like *Il Piccolo Marat,* the critics did; and its success set Mascagni on the road to receive new honors from the king. Soon after the premiere, the critic of the *Giornale d'Italia* described Mascagni as "*il creatore più nobile della musica italiana,*" "the noblest creative artist in Italian music." Writing to Simoni and Adami, Puccini said the article turned his stomach. And what about Verdi? "At least Verdi will be the leading trumpet player!" he wrote (GP to GA and RS, June 20, 1921, in Gara, p. 508). All the new publicity instilled in him the fear that Mascagni might be named Senator for Life of the Kingdom of Italy before Puccini won that title for himself. Puccini's own patriotic effort, the "*Inno a Roma,*" had been a hymn to Rome composed in 1920 for Princess Jolanda of the reigning House of Savoy and performed as a celebration of the country's capital. But he had few illusions about it. In a letter to Elvira, he dismissed it as "a real piece of crap," but he may have thought it would boost his chances to become Senator Puccini. In the event, he had a long wait before he received the nomination, which would come only in 1924, shortly before his death.

Rose Ader, *"La mia adorazione"*

Still very much alert and aggressive in the early 1920s, Puccini kept watch over his operas then, just as he had done earlier. He was horrified and sickened, he said, by a sloppy production of *Fanciulla,* which he had seen while he was incognito, hidden in a box at the Dal Verme in Milan. It had, however, sold out; encouraged by its success, he tried to get an open-air production of it mounted.

Still promoting it, he oversaw a production of *Fanciulla* in Ravenna, where he worked for the first time with Fausto Cleva, who was then an assistant conductor. Cleva went on to conduct in almost every major theater in the United States. Of Puccini, whom he later also saw in Milan, he said, "He was always a very nostalgic man, a very sentimental man. And the perfect gentleman. I never heard his voice loud; and he always talked very gently and seemed to be measuring his words before he would say anything. You know why? He was afraid of offending somebody. He would not hurt anybody for anything in the world. Above all, Puccini never thought of his own importance. He was very humble" (Cleva with Freeman). Just before Easter 1921, Puccini went to Monte Carlo for the *Trittico* (some good performances and some only fair, he said) and *Fanciulla* (very, very good, with Dalla Rizza as Minnie). Had he not lost twelve thousand lire gambling at the casino, he would have had a perfect trip, but even that loss seemed not to bother him much. In high spirits and fully rejuvenated, he told Simoni that the air in Monte Carlo was "saturated" with *Puccinismo.* Even better, he bragged that four beautiful young women had driven him to the customs station at the Italian border. Not bad for a "little old man like me," he joked. He was past sixty.

Soon that *vecchietto,* that little old man, fell smashingly in love again, this time with the soprano Rose Ader. He simply adored her, called her *his* Rosa—and began corresponding with her. He asked her to send letters to a secret box in Viareggio—just as Josi had. No one who knew Puccini well would have been surprised to learn that his *vita galante* was not yet over, but so far as we know, he did not tell Del Fiorentino about his latest affair, which began in 1921. It started when Ader wrote, asking him for a photograph of himself. He responded, signing it and sending kind wishes. In March, when she sent thanks and two photographs of herself, Puccini was captivated by her image. "How darling she is!" he exclaimed. He was able to spend time with her when they met in cities where he oversaw his operas. If Elvira was again jealous, no trace of it appears in his letters; but she may never have known about Ader.

Simonetta Puccini gave a brief sketch of Ader's life in her edition of Puccini's letters to Schnabl. Born in Oderberg in 1890, Ader made her opera debut in 1915 at the Hamburg Opera, where she continued singing until 1918. In 1918–1919 she was at the Vienna Staatsoper, but in 1920 or early in 1921 she returned to Hamburg, where the *Trittico* finally reached the stage on February 2, 1921. Coached by Schnabl, she sang the title role in *Suor Angelica* (S. Puccini, *Giacomo Puccini lettere*, pp. 120–121). Soon letters were flowing between her and the composer. Puccini wrote more than a hundred, several of which, all very passionate, have come on the New York market in the last decade. In one, he sent Ader the news about Mascagni and *Piccolo Marat*. Then came a declaration of love, as he called her "the woman I adore, *la mia adorazione*. You know you are *my life*. I live only for you." In the same letter, he complained about a photograph that Ader sent him from Berlin, saying, "It doesn't look at all like you" (GP to RA, May 10, 1921, Tollett and Harman Collection, Catalogue 21). While in Berlin, Ader also got to know Margit Vészi, whom she met through Puccini, who encouraged them to correspond with each other.

Although Ader may not have been a superior artist, she was at least good enough for Emma Carelli to give her the role of Mimì in the Teatro Costanzi production of *Bohème* in a short February–March season in 1922. This visit brought him and Ader together for weeks as he managed the rehearsals. After her first appearance, he told Schnabl she had sung "deliciously." She had a small, even voice and was very likable (GP to RSR, March 12, 1922, in S. Puccini, *Giacomo Puccini lettere*, pp. 169–170). After eight performances, she left for Palermo, where she sang the title role in *Suor Angelica*. Later in 1922 Puccini wrote to Gatti-Casazza, asking him to engage her; but nothing came of his request. Gatti answered on June 19: "I've been in Vienna. I saw Signorina Ader, and I have to say that there is nothing possible for her here at the Metropolitan. She belongs to a category of artist that we have plenty of in America, and we are obliged to favor them because of local politics" (Gatti Casazza to GP, June 19, 1922, in Ashbrook, *The Operas of Puccini*, p. 205). So far as we know, Puccini continued to love her for the rest of his life. After he died, according to Simonetta Puccini's notes, Ader sang in 1928 and 1930 in Amsterdam; and in 1933 she sang *Bohème* at La Scala. Because she was Jewish, she left Germany and, after her last performances in Austria, moved to South America; she died in Buenos Aires in 1955.

Again, *Turandot*

On August 5, 1921, Puccini wrote a lively bit of doggerel for Buzzi-Peccia, who had asked his old friend what he was doing.

> I am writing a Chinese opera;
> In it are all kinds of adventures
> Of the beautiful Turandotte.
> The first act is beautiful and fast,
> And alluring. I hope it goes well.
> When I have covered the words [with my music]
> My troubles will end.
> There are three acts, very entertaining,
> And a setting no one has ever seen;
> Fast and slow tempos;
> And let's hope it won't fail!
> Turandot, the princess,
> Is a soprano with high notes.
> There is a tenor who never stops singing;
> And there are scenes without singing.
> There's a really darling slave
> Named Liù. There are choruses.
> There are dances that won't bore you,
> And scenes worthy of [Adelaide] Ristori.
> Xylophone, bells, and tam-tam,
> Gong and saxophone and carillon,
> There are men who look like orangutans;
> There are smart guys and fools.
> If you want exact information
> For the American papers
> Just send your questions to me here
> And I will satisfy your every wish.
> Your G. Puccini. [GP to AB-P, in "The Composer of *Turandot* Writes to an Old Friend"]

A month later, Puccini became infected with his old, chronic self-doubt. Losing faith in the project, he had begun to think about turning *Turandot* into a two-act opera, in spite of the fact that the two-act structure had been partly responsible for the failure of *Butterfly.* Worse, a colleague had told him that the opera, as it stood, was headed for "shipwreck." By November, he had had so little communication with his librettists that he wrote "with a troubled heart" to ask whether he had perhaps committed some serious crime. Was he to be punished for it? But he still was "infected" with the desire to work. January 1922 began with his lament over lost time, as he complained that he would be decrepit or dead when *Turandot* was finished. To Simoni he wrote:

> Tell me the truth. You no longer have faith in me! Why haven't you yet sent me the third act that you promised? Have you done it? Perhaps not— and here I am torturing myself because it seems I have lost the faith you had [in me]—perhaps you believe that I am working to no purpose—That may even be true. The public that listens to music no longer has good taste [*il palato apposto*]. It loves or endures illogical music that makes no sense. Melody is something no one writes anymore—or if they write it, it is vulgar. People believe symphonic music must rule, and I, on the other hand, believe that this means the end of opera. In Italy, people sang; no more. Crashes, discordant chords, faked expression, diaphanous stuff, opalescent, and lymphatic. All Celtic diseases—true syphilis from across the Alps.
>
> But, returning to us, may I know where you are? Why leave me alone like this, with repeated promises that you don't keep? I've heard nothing more from [the attorney] Giordani. Ricordi says nothing. Is he under the spell of the fox-trot? I have heard nothing more from Milan. I beg you [and] Adami to tell me something, so I at least may know whether Turandot is still our Princess, or whether she has gotten lost in chaos, like the children of heaven. Ciao, affectionately, your Puccini. [GP to RS, May 1, 1922, in L. Marchetti, illus. 273, 274]

In June, he was still pleading: *"The third! The third! The third!"* He would go on singing variations on the same refrain for more than two years.

That spring, he wrote again to Margit Vészi. By then she was a published author, with two books that had come out in Budapest. Puccini had just returned to Viareggio from Rome, where he had sat as a judge on the competition for new composers.

> Dear Margit, Finally! And how many times did I say to myself "Why doesn't that dear signora let me hear from her? Where can she be? How is she?" . . . Rosa [Ader] was [in Rome]. She sang deliciously as Mimì at the Costanzi. Now she is in Palermo for *Suor Angelica*. Teatro Massimo. Write to her, she would be overjoyed, because we often spoke of you.
>
> My work has been stopped for 7 months! Horrible to say, at my age! But the libretto was no good, and it had to be redone. It's not yet finished, and I am afraid that my faith in it is a little shaken. Or, to put it better, I am feeling a bit *cold* about this work. There is hope that I will get back into it, and I hope this myself. But I am not at all happy. I am suffering from a lot of things. And I would like to have Rosa near me, and instead I'm in pain. . . . I won't come to Berlin. I hoped that Harmann would do the *Trittico,* and instead he has set it aside. Instead I went to Paris, where they treat me like a charity case by producing only *Schicchi* at the Opéra Comique. . . . Monte Carlo would only give it as a benefit evening, because my new operas make too much money, and this gets on the nerves of my colleagues in France. O Fraternity! Don't tell anyone I wrote this. A thousand affectionate greetings, G. Puccini. [GP to MV, March 14, 1922, The Pierpont Morgan Library, New York]

He also confided his worries to Buzzi-Peccia: "I'm working on *Turandot,* which is a difficult, serious work [*un lavoraccio serio*]. I'm in a bit of trouble because of the libretto, which is not yet the way it should be. But it will be all right, but when? When my poets are here with me, they make promises and make a lot of noise, but when I go away, they say they are working hard, but they get lazy, and don't care, and don't work. Here, too, we have new music. Not new music but old carcasses, no ideas. Color, color, music that does not attract you, but wears you out. Goodbye, old cow. Your Pig" (GP to AB-P, March 22, 1922, in "The Composer of *Turandot* Writes to an Old Friend"). A much more troubling letter went off to Buzzi-Peccia in July, when Puccini said he had been ill and was in a very bad humor. "Music disgusts me. The sea air irritates me. . . . Maybe I'll go to the mountains. *Turandot* is here, sleeping, just as a snake sleeps in winter. I finally have the whole libretto. I will do it, but I'll take my time. I won't go to Milan right now. Maybe in winter, but only for a short while, because winter in Milan is really bad for me. We're old, but what can we do?" He mentioned a visit from Gatti-Casazza, whom he had not seen in six years. Then, almost as an afterthought, "Do you know *La Rondine?* It is my most beautiful opera. In Milan! In Milan they wreck it for me; but you will see that it will live again; that will have to happen, if there is any justice in the world." He then quoted a line from *La Traviata, "Amami, Alfredo!"* ("Love me, Alfredo!"), and he signed it: "Your Violetta, with Parmesan cheese" (GP to AB-P, July 25, 1922, ibid.).

Toscanini: Rifts and Reconciliations

At this point, Puccini had worked for years without the support of the one man who could perhaps have helped him most: Toscanini. The chasm that opened between them during the war years had widened after the conductor expressed an unfavorable opinion of *Il Trittico.* Puccini was told that he had even walked out of *Il Tabarro.* Thus, their stormy relationship followed its unpredictable course, with Puccini railing to Carlo Paladini about Toscanini's edict forbidding encores at La Scala and criticizing him for making recordings with his orchestra. "As far as I'm concerned, he has a great, prodigious memory; but music has to make the soul vibrate. In his hands, its physiognomy changes. . . . Toscanini is fine for concerts, especially if he is conducting Debussy's embroideries and cold and colorful things. For the rest, where the soul vibrates humanly— *nihil*—or little more" (GP to CP, 15 February 1921, in Sachs, *Toscanini,* pp. 155–156). Later that year, when Puccini urgently needed Toscanini to conduct the *Trittico* at La Scala, he appealed to Clausetti, asking him to mend the breach between himself and the conductor, but the strategy failed. Puccini told Schnabl that Toscanini, who was evil, untrustworthy, and heartless, would conduct only *Falstaff* and operas that he already knew. Although Puccini said he didn't care about Toscanini's opposition to the *Trittico,* he clearly worried about having another conductor in charge (GP to RSR, [July 1921], in S. Puccini, *Giacomo Puccini lettere,* letter 81). Writing to Simoni later that summer, Puccini called Toscanini "a thorn in my side," a relentless enemy. In the end, Ettore Panizza conducted La Scala's *Trittico,* which had a fair success, with most praise going to *Schicchi.*

By August 1922 peace had been made; Clausetti may have brought the two men together. In any case, Puccini and Toscanini were collaborating on the planned thirtieth anniversary production of *Manon Lescaut,* which Toscanini would direct at La Scala. He came to Viareggio in mid-August to discuss the cast, staging, and the changes he had made in the score. Puccini then left on the twentieth for a long trip to northern Europe, traveling by car with Tonio and Angelo Magrini, a friend from Viareggio. Three days later, he sent Toscanini a card of good wishes, with remarks about his future plans and the beauty of the Dolomites (GP to AT, card, August 23, 1922, NYPLPA, Music Division, Wanda Toscanini Horowitz Donation).

While the three men were in a restaurant in Ingolstadt, a small Bavarian city, Puccini almost choked to death on a bone from a platter of roast duck. He had so much difficulty breathing that Magrini and Tonio rushed to the car and went for a doctor, who probed for the bone and removed it. As Magrini recalled, it was a dangerous and frightening incident. Next came a visit to Holland and a September jaunt up the Rhine. By the middle of the month, he was home, fending off a new *Casanova* libretto from Motta, whose works he had once sworn he would never use. Later that autumn, Puccini's sister Iginia, Sister Giulia Enrichetta, died in the convent at Vicopelago, where she had become the Mother Superior. Referring to her in letters as "my poor little Nun," the composer expressed profound grief and resignation over the inevitability of death, saying that all the Puccinis were dying.

At the same time, he worried about the casting for "this sow of an opera, *Rondine,*" which was on the schedule in Vienna; and he arranged to have copies of the scores of his operas sent to Erich Wolfgang Korngold, another composer he liked and often helped. A planned trip to Paris with Elvira and Tonio was postponed indefinitely after Vanni Marcoux, the protagonist in *Gianni Schicchi* at the Comique, fell ill. At that point *Turandot* was asleep, Puccini said, and much work on it lay ahead. Although some of his sketches had been lying untouched for months, he planned to compose again in late autumn. He had also asked Simoni for a small revision in *Tabarro* and was working on yet another revision in *Fanciulla,* expanding the Minnie-Johnson duet that ends the second act; but in the event, the singers engaged for subsequent productions could not manage the high C in his new passage. If the singers refused to sing that C, he said, it meant they were not the right artists for *Fanciulla.*

(Later, as we shall see, he found singers who could manage it.) First, however, came *Manon Lescaut.*

On December 26, 1922, *Manon Lescaut* opened at La Scala, Toscanini conducting. It was beyond doubt one of the greatest evenings of Puccini's entire career. Having attended some rehearsals and overseen others, he spent weeks eagerly awaiting the moment, saying he loved the music as he never had before. Then came the first night, such a triumph that Puccini, overcome with emotion, threw himself into Toscanini's arms during their third-act curtain call. It was a gesture of such spontaneity and such fierce ardor that the audience fell silent for a few moments. Especially affected by the performance of Aureliano Pertile, Puccini sent his congratulations to the great tenor, the best Des Grieux "I could ever wish for." Like Martinelli, Pertile was a native of Montagnana, near Padua, and both had sung in the same church choir. Where Martinelli was tall and handsome, Pertile was not; instead, he owed his success to a total intellectual and emotional commitment to his roles. (Mario Del Monaco once told me about how Pertile affected him. Then young and unknown, he was in the top balcony at La Scala for Pertile's performance in *Otello.* He said the experience of the last act was so shattering that he began to cry; he broke down sobbing so violently he had to get up and move to the back of the section for the rest of the opera.) Otello and Des Grieux were certainly Pertile's best roles, and the recordings of him in *Manon Lescaut* let us hear something of what Puccini heard.

Quite naturally, Puccini shared his satisfaction with Sybil, writing to her in early January 1923 that the first five performances of *Manon Lescaut* had gone splendidly. Five days later, the house was still sold out. As Eugenio Gara noted, this superb revival kept the opera on the program at La Scala for many years to come. Puccini also told Sybil about the planned gala on February 1, the thirtieth anniversary of *Manon,* when a banquet would honor that opera and celebrate his whole career. After the event, he reported with some pride that nearly five hundred guests had dined in the elegant Ristorante Cova, across the street from La Scala and a step from his own apartment. "The fête for the thirtieth anniversary of *Manon* was fantastic, and the performance was a miracle of execution and of enthusiasm. The returns [were] 110,000 lire. At last Milan has honored me" (GP to SS, January 6, 11, 26, and February 5, 1923, in Seligman, pp. 343–

345). For the moment, Puccini's self-confidence was fully restored. The sold-out houses reflected sheer enthusiasm for his work, while the respect tendered to him on the street and in shops showed him that *Manon*, at least, was not an "old carcass," as he sometimes called his earliest operas.

And to Toscanini he wrote:

Dear Arturo, You have given me the greatest satisfaction of my life. In your interpretation, *Manon* surpasses what I thought [it was] in those far-off times. You have performed this music of mine with poetry, suppleness, and a passion that no one will ever match. Last evening, I truly felt all of your great soul and the love you have for your old friend and companion from our first struggles. I am happy because you, above everyone else, have understood all my youthful and passionate spirit of thirty years ago! Thank you from the bottom of my heart! To the good Signora Carla, I send all my grateful friendship for her effort for last night's celebration. I embrace you as a brother, *fraternamente,* your G. Puccini" [GP to AT, February 2, 1923, photocopy from Walfredo Toscanini's collection]

He addressed Toscanini with the intimate form, *"tu,"* and signed himself *"tuo G. Puccini."* When *Manon Lescaut* returned to La Scala in December 1923, Puccini was delighted to have Dalla Rizza in the title role.

With his *Manon* celebrations behind him, he and two of the Magrinis planned to drive down to Torre della Tagliata in his expensive new car, which he had fitted out expressly for the trip. For this eight-cylinder Lancia limousine he had paid ninety thousand lire. "Marvelous," he described it, "splendid," even though the price represented about one fourth of his six-month royalties. "I came to the conclusion that one has one's life only once," he wrote to Sybil, to whom he also confided his terror of old age and illness (GP to SS, January 26, 1923, in Seligman, pp. 344–345). But before the end of the year, he was trying to trade it for a new Hispano Suiza. Restless and bored with Milan and family life there, he was "not well . . . and nervous" (GP to SS, February 12, 1923, in Seligman, p. 345). His mind was on Viareggio and hunting, and he was even thinking of going to Monte Carlo. Simoni was ill, so *Turandot* was delayed again.

Puccini and Tonio went to Vienna in May, returning to his old suite at the Hotel Bristol. While there he heard Maria Jeritza in *Tosca*. "Sublime," he wrote, describing a delirious audience and more than fifty curtain calls.

The Czech soprano, a stunning blonde with a radiant voice, was then past thirty. Richard Strauss had chosen her for the title role in the premiere of *Ariadne auf Naxos* in Stuttgart in 1912, and she had been singing at the Volksoper in Vienna since then. She also created Marietta in Korngold's *Die Tote Stadt* in 1920 in Hamburg. In her Puccini found an ideal inter-preter of his most difficult works. The Vienna opera management also presented *Bohème*. During his visit, Puccini wrote to Toscanini about the theater's scheduled production of *Manon Lescaut*. It had been delayed, Puccini said, and would be given later, not with Lotte Lehmann but with Jeritza. "And when is *Bohème* at La Scala? I think it will be soon; I'm sorry not to be there for the first night. But I can't leave here; but I hope to ar-rive [in Milan] before the last performance" (GP to AT, May 14, 1923, NYPLPA, Music Division, Wanda Toscanini Horowitz Donation).

From Vienna, Puccini also wrote to Margit Vészi to say that he was there with Tonio and a friend. His affairs were a mess, because the season was too far along for the theater to risk a fiasco. This meant *Manon Lescaut* would be given in September. "Lehmann got sick, sick from love and sick from contracts; she no longer wanted to sing [the title role], and Jeritza has taken it. . . . I am going back to my work a bit tired, not that I am tired, but that the opera is tired; but I hope to get back my enthusiasm because finally the libretto [of *Turandot*] is finished—after two and a half years! I had the third act redone four times! It is beautiful. Now it is here. . . . I am fairly well, getting old little by little. . . . Many affectionate greetings from your old and faithful friend, G. Puccini" (GP to MV, May 21, 1923, The Pierpont Morgan Library, New York). Of course, in Puccini's vocabulary, the word "finished" meant anything but.

He also sent Elvira three affectionate letters about his visit, describing a reception and concert the Italian ambassador gave in his honor and an-other offered by an important cultural organization. Korngold invited him to tea, and old friends had dinner with him. Fully energized by all this attention, he considered taking an airplane to Budapest, where the *Trittico* was on the schedule, but Tonio vetoed that idea. Mentioning his health, he said he took naps in the afternoon, ate no sweets, drank no wine, and was hoping that insulin, which he had just begun using, would help his diabetes. When *Manon Lescaut* was postponed until autumn, he passed the days rehearsing the singers for *Butterfly*, but in general he felt he had wasted his time. He complained about the high price of a restaurant meal in Austria and about the big tips he would have to hand out to hotel and garage employees. In a word, he longed to be home.

Two weeks later, from Viareggio, he sent Toscanini a telegram about La Scala. "Tonio telegraphed me about your wish to have me come to Milan for the *Bohème* rehearsals. Stop. If you do not conduct, I have no interest in being there. Stop. If you can, I will be very, very happy to hear my opera again, as it was when it was given for the very first time in Turin, and I will leave at once" (GP to AT, telegram, May 28, 1923, NYPLPA, Music Division, Wanda Toscanini Horowitz Donation). As Harvey Sachs says, Puccini's refusal irritated Toscanini, who was ill and not able to take on this heavy assignment. In the event, the conductor kept his temper and did not criticize Puccini for his failure to help with the final rehearsals and his absence on the first night at La Scala, when Franco Ghione conducted. Puccini said he had been notified by telegram about its success, but he complained about "The God," that is, Toscanini, not conducting. The cast members, apparently, were unaware of the conflict between conductor and composer. The sprightly Edith Mason, whom I interviewed in her summer home in Cortina d'Ampezzo, sang Mimì in this production. Like Dalla Rizza and many other singers, she called Puccini a gentle and thoughtful man, "the most serious musician imaginable," even though he gave her no guidance on that important occasion in Milan.

Again at home, Puccini turned to other professional and personal matters. Generous as always in writing letters of recommendation, he addressed an army colonel whom he knew and sought help for a young corporal, Giuseppe Palumbo. Ordered into service as a machine gunner, Palumbo, who had been one of Ricordi's accountants in Milan, hoped for a better assignment. "He is asking whether he could possibly be used . . . in some regimental office," Puccini wrote (GP to ?, Alexander Autographs, Inc., catalogue, p. 306; sale of October 2000). In July 1923 Puccini also gave Del Fiorentino a letter of introduction to the Italian ambassador to the United States, to be used in Washington when he took his first trip to the States.

At this time, Puccini was not composing, and Bicchi, who had come for her regular summer vacation, wanted to know what was wrong with Grandfather. She had always heard him playing, well into the night. "Tato, it was so beautiful to listen to you when you fought with your characters. But for some time, I've heard nothing but silence when you're in your studio," she said. "I've lost my voice, Birichina, and I want silence," he replied. "And anyway, Turandot is asleep." Looking at him, she thought he seemed unusually tired (Blignaut, p. 31).

During the summer of 1923, Puccini helped to plan *Fanciulla* in the Teatro Politeama in Viareggio, where he had finally agreed to a production of one of his works. With Giulia Tess as Minnie and Carmelo Alabiso as Johnson, it was sung with the difficult, high-lying lines he had added to the tenor-soprano duet. While he did not say so, his effort for Viareggio was surely part of his hopes for the establishment of a national theater in the city. Puccini and Cesare Riccioni, the mayor, felt that the theater was, at the very least, worthy of the attention of Mussolini and the government. As it turned out, their hopes were dashed, for Florence organized the Maggio Musicale Fiorentino, to which Mussolini decided to lend his weight, endorsing it as the national festival event.

That autumn Puccini took Elvira to Vienna with him for the long-postponed *Manon Lescaut.* As he had the previous spring, he complained about how expensive everything was; but he could only be happy at the reception the city gave him. From Vienna, he sent a card to Carla Toscanini, with news of the opera. "I hope you are all well. Arturo will already be busy with the rehearsals [for the new season at La Scala]. Give him my best regards" (GP to CT, card, October 14, 1923, NYPLPA, Music Division, Wanda Toscanini Horowitz Donation). *Manon* was given the next day. The opera went well, and Puccini was particularly impressed with it.

As the Puccinis prepared to leave Vienna for Viareggio, Elvira took to her bed with a backache, delaying their departure. This was the first of many bouts of illness that would afflict each of them over the next year. When they did return, he had to get back to *Turandot,* which sometimes went well and at other times not so well. On November 9 he wrote to Margit Vészi, who had written while he was in Vienna. After describing his trip, he mentioned a suit involving him and Casa Ricordi. "My dear friend, . . . The suit with Ricordi did not mean that my relationship with the Casa has been broken off. *Turandot* already belonged to [Ricordi] by contract. . . . *Turandot* is dragging herself to the end, but when? I don't know. I would like to stay at work, and instead I take trips, I go hunting, and *fritter away the time.* Very affectionate wishes, your G. Puccini" (GP to MV, November 9, 1923, The Pierpont Morgan Library, New York).

But the following day, writing to Pietrino Malfatti, an old friend from

Torre, he struck a different note, saying he was rested and ready to return to *Turandot,* and he regretted that its composition had been "neglected and interrupted." Added to the letter was his order for twenty-five jars of preserves—anything but currant, which he disliked. And, finally, he said he regretted growing old, but was hoping that friends would make the process very gradual and even tolerable (GP to PM, November 10, 1923, Sotheby's catalogue, December 11, 1989). All that autumn, poor health— his and Elvira's—left him depressed. She stayed in bed and recovered in time for Christmas; but she was often ill, sometimes with back problems, sometimes with bronchitis. His mind turned to work whenever he could summon the energy for it. As he said, he urgently needed to finish *Turandot.*

December brought another annual trip to Rome, where Puccini sat again as a judge in the national opera competition. This he did unwillingly, for he had often complained about the lack of talent uncovered there; he had threatened to resign from the panel, although in the end he remained on it. Now he found the young composers' operas mediocre, and felt that the prizes had been awarded more as a token of encouragement than as an award for true accomplishment. Some satisfaction, though, came from his *Gianni Schicchi,* which was very successful in Rome. During this visit to the capital, he also pressed on with another of his many campaigns to help friends and relatives who were looking for jobs or trying to get favors or decorations from the government. As he had before, he turned to Commendatore Alberti, the secretary general of the Chamber of Deputies, to avoid the bureaucratic red tape he so hated. He also continued supporting Korngold, whose career he assiduously promoted. At the end of November and the beginning of December, Korngold was in Rome to present a concert of his own works; and Puccini, as always, spoke out for him. All this is described in another letter to "Carissimo Pietrino" Malfatti (GP to PM, December 1, 1923, in Smythe Auction catalogue, autumn 2000).

In that letter Puccini also mentioned an appointment he had on that day with Benito Mussolini, whom he referred to as *"Il Duce."* In the Italian edition of his *Giacomo Puccini,* Michele Girardi describes the composer's earlier meeting with Mussolini, in November, when he had made his bid for the projected national theater. Mussolini had risen to power through the Fascist movement, which he had founded in 1919. In 1922 the Fascists' march on Rome had led the king to ask Mussolini to lead the country as its prime minister. Using his power, Mussolini created the Fascist state in 1923. Girardi also describes the moment in spring 1923 when the local heads of National Fascist Party in Viareggio sent Puccini a membership card, *ad honorem*. Although he did not send it back, he remained resolutely apolitical, and he hoped that Mussolini might restore order. Also, he may have felt this would help in his long campaign to be nominated Senator. He was still hoping to get the nomination before Mascagni did. At that time, though, nothing happened (Girardi, p. 435).

Puccini's Christmas letter to the Toscaninis, addressed to Carla, again thanked the conductor. *Manon Lescaut* had just returned to La Scala, with Toscanini conducting and Dalla Rizza in the title role. He wrote, "Dearest Signora Carla, Cordial and friendly wishes and greetings. I want to tell Arturo everything in my soul, which is always full of affection and great esteem. He follows his path, which is full of that holy belief in art [*piena di quella santa fede per l'arte*] that has put him above all the greatest interpreters; and I am grateful to him for my *Manon,* which, under his direction, has taken on forms I never dreamed of; and the audience has repaid us richly for it. Good wishes to you all, and be well and happy. I am laboring on *Turandot,* underneath my pine trees. Affectionately, Giacomo Puccini." In a postscript in the margin he added, "All good wishes from Elvira, who is now much better." A second postscript, written above the first, and at right angles to the rest of the text, says, "Remember me to Wally, Walter, and Wanda" (GP to CT, December 23, 1923, NYPLPA, Music Division, Wanda Toscanini Horowitz Donation.)

He was indeed working on the orchestration that December, when, as he said, almost all of the score of *Turandot* was safe in the vaults of Casa Ricordi in Milan. He still had the third act duet to finish, but he had sent the words for it and the last scene back to Simoni for changes. And, as he told Schnabl on December 22, it was the fourth time he had asked the librettist to revise this part of the opera (GP to RSR, December 22, 1923, in Gara, p. 545). Weeks had passed, and he had received nothing, so he wrote to Simoni the same day: "You have forgotten me. Remember that I urgently need the duet, which is the key to the opera. I have begun orchestrating to gain time, but my soul will never be at peace until this duet is finished. Please do me the favor of getting busy on this last bit of work.

Be kind, as you have always been; steal an hour from your busy life, and dedicate it to this poor, old maestro, who urgently needs to finish this great work" (GP to RS, December 22, 1923, in Gara, pp. 545–546). By then, the librettist was obviously discouraged, although he excused himself with Puccini by saying he was simply trying to do a good job.

The Beginning of the Final Year

In January 1924 the composer was planning to take a ten-day cure in the spa at Salsomaggiore, where he sought treatment for his sore throat and persistent cough. Through it all, he went forward with *Turandot,* though sometimes haltingly. He remained confident through the middle of the month, even though he still had not received Simoni's revision of the duet. At that point Puccini asked Adami to keep after the poet and also begged Clausetti to hound him by telephone. On his own, he sent Adami a storm of letters about specific verses. In one he described himself as "sad, sad" and "unhappy about everything—even *Turandot.* I can't wait for the moment when I will be free of it" (GP to GA, January 19, 1924, in Adami, p. 291). Quite predictably, when the revised verses came, he asked Adami for changes, although he felt that he and Adami could extract a satisfactory version from the first three drafts that then existed. They were enthusiastic, and Adami was working swiftly, something Simoni could not do. As for himself, he said he rarely moved from his desk, where he went ahead orchestrating the second act. When he finally got the text in his hands, he felt Simoni had still not got it right. Reluctant to send it back or even to criticize, he handed it to Adami, who would undertake the fifth version. In the spring he finished orchestrating the entire second act of *Turandot* and half of the third.

In February he described himself to Dalla Rizza as "more of a savage than ever. I work from morning to night; I am doing very well, almost finished. And I am also very convinced that my labor is worthy. We'll see how the cruel princess will be welcomed, when she steps before the great window [of the opera house proscenium arch]. But I worry very little about this evil [idea]. I am doing well, and I am enjoying that" (GP to GDR, February 25, 1924, in Gara, p. 549).

A revealing letter to Clausetti also showed him hard at work on the new opera, but still critical of what other composers were doing. "Today people move toward atonal music, and have fun doing handsprings in it; and the ones who are farthest off the true path think they are on the right road. And in the field of opera, we don't have even the tiniest victory. Three hours or more of music like that will kill you. It's fine in a concert, because it's followed by Beethoven and others (according to them, those men are relics of the past), who set your spirit straight and make you forget all the tired smears left behind by composers looking for something new, no matter what the cost" (GP to CC, March 25, 1924, in Gara, pp. 549–550).

Toscanini and Boito's *Nerone*

It was at this moment, in the spring of 1924, that anger over a professional matter again erupted between Puccini and Toscanini, with the dispute arising over Boito's *Nerone,* the world premiere of which was to be given at La Scala on May 1, 1924. Harvey Sachs gave a detailed account of these events in his *Toscanini;* and Charles Mintzer, author of *Rosa Raisa,* has recently uncovered new information about it.

At his death in 1918, Boito had left the unfinished *Nerone,* a long, difficult work to which he had devoted many years. Hiring someone to complete it had been a moral obligation for Casa Ricordi, and for Italy it was a matter of national pride. Boito had, after all, been the country's most respected intellectual. The solution to the problem lay with Toscanini, who had known Boito very well and had discussed with Boito his desire to have Toscanini conduct the opera at La Scala. It thus fell to Toscanini to complete the orchestration of the opera, for which Boito had left only a piano-vocal score. Toscanini began the job in 1923 with Antonio Smareglia and finished it with another composer, Vincenzo Tommasini. Much of the work was done during a long work retreat in the Italian Alps, north of Milan.

After creating a usable score, they returned to the city, where *Nerone* was put on the Scala program for the 1924 spring season. At some point someone told Toscanini that Puccini had mocked his and Tommasini's efforts. What Puccini said in conversations with colleagues is not known, but in a letter to Schnabl he criticized Toscanini and Tommasini, saying that they were working in "some villa on Lake Como" to "manipulate" the opera. Toscanini, hearing the criticism, became furious, because he was very much satisfied with their work. Whatever his feelings, Puccini asked Clausetti, in his March 25 letter, to get him a seat for the world premiere. "Tell me, can you get me some place in a little corner for *Nerone?* If I don't find a place, it will be useless for me to come; and I care very much about attending the world premiere" (GP to CC, March 25, 1924, in Gara, pp. 549–550).

From the beginning Toscanini had tried to keep anyone from hearing the music of *Nerone* before the day of the dress rehearsal. To that end, Mintzer says, he had even sent a warning to Chicago, to Raisa, the leading soprano, and Ettore Panizza, the conductor who was coaching her in her role. On shipboard from New York to Europe, he said, they were to conduct their sessions in a completely private room, where no one could hear them. He had also closed all rehearsals at La Scala.

Raisa arrived in Milan about three weeks before the premiere, and started rehearsing. Puccini, defying Toscanini's edict, slipped into the theater during one of the last rehearsals. He was probably hidden backstage. When Toscanini found him there, he ordered him out. Raisa left an account of how she escorted Puccini to the stage door, apologizing all the way. To that Puccini replied, "That's the way he is."

Toscanini then ordered the staff at La Scala to keep Puccini out of the much-anticipated dress rehearsal of *Nerone,* which took place on April 29. Puccini, for his part, had apparently decided to attend it and the premiere. Nothing suggests that he tried to crash the rehearsal; and, indeed, Clausetti must have assured him that he could get in. He wrote to Sybil about his plan to hear "the famous *Nerone,* in which I believe very little — but we'll see." To his mortification, he was kept out of the dress rehearsal, on Toscanini's orders. Shocked and shamed before his colleagues, he retreated into himself. Quite naturally, *Nerone* meant one thing to Puccini: profound injury. Toscanini's insult, delivered publicly in Italy's grandest opera house, gave people something to gossip about for months and tormented the composer at a time when poor health had begun to figure in his daily calculations.

To Toscanini's satisfaction, the first night of *Nerone* was a success, its premiere celebrating Italy, its culture, and its history. Even on the first night, however, many in the music business wondered whether it could enter the repertory; and it did not, in spite of Casa Ricordi's promotional campaign. Puccini did not attend.

Progress on *Turandot*

Work on *Turandot* went forward that spring. In March Puccini wrote to Clausetti to say that he was about to send Casa Ricordi "all of the second [act] and half of the third, orchestrated. I beg you to put them into the works right away. As soon as they have been copied, I want to look at them again. I think I have done something good [*Mi pare di aver fatto cosa buona*] (GP to CC, March 25, 1924, in Gara, pp. 549–550). On that same day, he told Simoni that he had worked "like a dog" for four months on *Turandot*. "I am almost at the end: I lack only the final duet. All the rest is orchestrated. I will send Tonio to Casa Ricordi with it in a few days. I believe I have done good work; perhaps, though, I have made a mistake, with all the new things people are trying today, following rough-sounding paths and discord, where sentiment—that sentiment that gives us joy and tears—has been abandoned. I have put my whole soul into this opera; we shall see whether my vibrations match those of the public" (GP to RS, March 25, 1924, p. 550).

He then turned once more to the troublesome problems in Simoni's text for the duet. "Your duet had good things, but it was not varied and lively enough; Adami and I have worked together, and I feel we have succeeded, especially in the different sections of it. When I come to Milan, we could look at it together, if you can and will do this, if only to give it some additional imagery and some 'little Chinese' touches. But I wanted something human, and when the heart speaks, whether in China or Holland, it says only one thing, and the outcome is the same for everyone. . . . Ciao, my dear Renato. With such hard work, and so many ups and downs, we are finally almost at the end of our work. Praise God!" (ibid.)

But at the end of March, his throat hurt more, and he had begun his long search for relief, going to several nearby doctors and specialists and receiving a series of incorrect diagnoses. As he confided to Sybil, his throat had been tormenting him since January, and he was about to see a specialist in Milan. However, he reassured her that he was working on the *Turandot* duet, saying that although it was difficult, he would do it, and then "the opera (if God wills) will be finished" (GP to SS, [end of March 1924], in Seligman, p. 355). By May everything had changed. Soon after he was turned away from La Scala, he told Angelo Magrini he was not well. "I can't work. I wanted to finish my work quickly, but I cannot find the way to put myself into it [*la via di mettermici*]" (GP to A. Magrini, May 18, 1924, in Gara, p. 551). He did, however, summon enough energy to meet Galileo Chini to discuss the scenery; Chini was to take his sketches to Casa Ricordi. He also tried to force himself to face the problems of the last duet. Having sent Adami's text back to Simoni, Puccini received what must have been the fifth or perhaps the sixth version of it. As he told Adami in May, Simoni had finally sent him the prose text, which would now be turned into poetry. However, he asked for help on both the structure and the poetry, as he stipulated matters of meter and warned them to keep the rhythm that had been established. He begged to have the work as quickly as possible.

Still worried about his throat, he went to Salsomaggiore in May, five months after he had first planned to take the cure there, and spent ten days at the Grand Hôtel des Thèrmes. Writing to Sybil about his treatments, he complained that his throat had not gotten better. *Turandot,* "this P[rostitute] of an opera," was lying unfinished on his desk. "But I *will* finish it—only just at present I've got no desire to work" (GP to SS, May 27, 1924, in Seligman, p. 355–356). Within days, again from Salso, he sent her discouraging news, saying once more that his throat had not improved, although the doctors told him it would eventually get better. At that point, he admitted that he had "so much work" still to do on the opera. It was hot, he was lazy and not feeling very well (GP to SS, June 1, 1924, in Seligman, p. 356). This is Puccini's last letter to Sybil although they would meet later that year.

In July he wrote to tell Adami how bored he was. "I have to finish this *Turandot.*" And again he begged for the poetry, saying that getting back to work would be good for him. Puccini often drove over to Torre del Lago, although he never found his old sense of tranquillity in the village. One of his visitors in Viareggio and Torre in 1924 was Dante Del Fiorentino, who had gone to the United States at Puccini's urging the year before, armed with the composer's letter of introduction. Devastated by homesickness, the young priest returned to Italy twice to visit his sister, his former parish, and, of course, Puccini, whom he found old and ill. As in the past, he spent all the time he could with the composer and his friends. Once in these late years, Puccini confided to Del Fiorentino that he was "no good at all," and that his eyes were failing. The priest also recalled that Nicche, who was Puccini's longtime hunting companion, arranged to have others go out with him, so that when Puccini aimed at a bird, another man would shoot at the same time and give Puccini the credit for the kill. Believing that he had actually brought something down, the composer would say, "There's life in the old veins yet!"

He once actually spoke to the priest specifically about his illness, when they met outside the post office in Torre. He had such a coughing fit that he could not speak at first. Recovering, he took a scrap of paper and a pencil and drew a picture of his throat to show Del Fiorentino "the tiny little pimple trying to strangle me."

In his last years, Puccini also enjoyed visits with other personal friends. Sybil came to Viareggio for a visit in August 1924 and was struck by how ill he looked. His throat was still sore, and he was still coughing, but a specialist had told him nothing was wrong; he was told at first that he had tonsillitis or laryngitis. To while away the time, Puccini spent hours with the poet and novelist Renato Fucini, who had written poems the composer loved, among them the text for his own song *"Avanti Urania!"* Del Fiorentino remembered their off-color jokes, but he said that when their language became too racy, Puccini always raised his hand and said, "No, Renato, we simply must not talk like that. *Gonnellone* is here."

Then there were the days when the great baritone Titta Ruffo, another Tuscan, came to visit Puccini and played practical jokes on him. Instead of going to the door of the villa, Ruffo would hide in the shrubbery outside and sing in full voice until Puccini, recognizing his voice, would shout, "Shut up, you baker!" After making fun of Ruffo's working-class background, he brought Ruffo inside for dinner and hands of *scopa* or *briscola*. Some visitors came from abroad, and among them, in the summer of 1924, was the coach and voice teacher Romano Romani, a native of Livorno, who returned to Tuscany accompanied by Rosa Ponselle. Romani, another of the dozens of people Puccini had helped with letters of recommendation, had befriended and coached the soprano some six years earlier, as she was leaving the vaudeville stage and preparing for her Metropolitan Opera debut. At the Met, though, she sang no Puccini operas, although she had recorded Puccini arias. When Gatti was choosing

the artists for the world premiere of *Il Trittico*, he asked Ponselle to prepare the role of Giorgetta in *Il Tabarro. Tosca* was another opera Gatti kept
on her active repertory list, so Ponselle continued to study it, though she
never sang it, perhaps because Gatti found others more suitable for the
role. For their stay, Romani rented a villa in Livorno and arranged for
them to visit Puccini. Del Fiorentino was there, sitting in a Viareggio café
with the composer and sipping a cool drink. Suddenly, he said, a young
woman came and sat down unannounced at their table. It was Ponselle,
in high spirits and ready to tease Puccini a bit. Sure that he would be interested in any attractive woman, she pretended to speak little Italian. This is
Del Fiorentino's account.

"I am *Pellerossa* from New York," she said simply. *Pellerossa* means 'Red-
skin.' It was evident that the young lady, though she was tanned, had no
Red Indian blood. "My father is a Red Indian chief," she went on, with
mock seriousness.

"That's fine," Giacomo murmured, without enthusiasm.

"I am *Pellerossa,*" she repeated. "I am making my debut in one of your
operas. I can't remember the title!"

"Let's hope you remember the music," Giacomo said dryly.

"Thank you, Maestro, for your deep interest. I am *Pellerossa* . . ."

And it went on indefinitely. Giacomo was unimpressed, bored, incredu-
lous. Who was this person who kept talking about Redskins? She was certainly beautiful. Also, he had the curious feeling that he had seen her before. Suddenly, he realized that she was playing with him, just as a
fisherman plays with a fish.

"Who the devil are you?" he demanded at last. She said she was Rosa
Ponselle; and he was immediately captivated. The idiotic game was over.
His son Tonio arrived at that moment. "Tonio can smell the presence of a
woman the way a hunter smells game," Giacomo said. "He's a good boy,
though. I don't know what he is going to do to earn a living." Puccini then
went on teasing his son about his extravagance and lack of a formal education. [Del Fiorentino, pp. 201–202]

When Romani finally put in an appearance, he, Puccini, Ponselle, and
Tonio went to the villa for a longer visit and the obligatory photographs.
Ponselle also sang for Puccini, who had nothing but praise for her voice.

Del Fiorentino also described Leoncavallo's visits with Puccini after the two had forgotten their old bitterness and had made peace. He was

> an ancient relic of the past, an old man with a large head, a squat body, and short legs. He wore a moustache like the Kaiser's. His glory had faded. He was poor, and lived in lodgings in Viareggio. Everyone was aware of his great humility. Once when he was asked to play an "Ave Maria" of his own composition in a small church in Viareggio, he accepted as though a great honor had been bestowed upon him. "I'm as excited as a boy!" he told me, and then, looking down at his legs, "You know, Dante, I have only once in my life played a harmonium with foot pedals. I wonder whether these old sticks will stand it!" Puccini said of him, "He had the head of a lion, the body of a horse, and the honest heart of a boy." [Del Fiorentino, p. 203]

The last time Del Fiorentino went to see Puccini in Viareggio, the composer spoke again about his health. "Well, I'm not so stupid as to underestimate the seriousness of the affair. If I can only finish *Turandot!* Yes, God's will be done!" He told him what the priest had already learned from Tonio: that he intended to go to Brussels for treatment. Then Del Fiorentino went back to his parish in Elizabeth, New Jersey, from where he corresponded with the composer. On September 26 Puccini wrote a note to answer one of Del Fiorentino's telegrams (it is in Pintorno's collection): "Thanks, dear Little Priest [*caro Pretino*], for your telegram. Affectionate greetings, G. Puccini." He also wrote to Del Fiorentino from Brussels during the last weeks of his life. After Puccini died, the priest repaid him royally, and in music. For the next forty years he presented Saturday night concerts, heavily larded with Puccini's music, in parish halls, using singers and conductors from the New York City Opera, the San Carlo, and other companies. First he gave these concerts in New Jersey, then in the 1940s in Glen Cove, Long Island, and finally in the parish of St. Lucy's in Brooklyn. By then, Del Fiorentino was a monsignor; but early and late, he dismissed the title and proudly described himself as "a *Lucchese* and Puccini's most loyal fan."

Reconciliation with Toscanini

On August 4, three months after the incident at the *Nerone* rehearsal at La Scala, Puccini decided to write a long letter of reconciliation to Toscanini, perhaps because he had received an encouraging letter from Carla, the conductor's wife.

Dear Toscanini, Even before I got Signora Carla's kind letter, the newspapers had given me information about your trip to Paris [where he had discussed guest performances by the La Scala company]. I thought of you at that time in a friendly, loving way [*con amore d'amico*] and about your terrible grief [over the death of Toscanini's mother, Paolina]. And because of an association of one idea with another, with my mind wandering through unforgettable memories of long ago, in a flutter of emotions that came to life as I remembered those times, there came to me the idea of opening my heart to you in a letter. The episode of my being excluded from the dress rehearsal of *Nerone* was, I must confess to you, a violent shock to my sensibilities and to my feeling of friendship and comradeship. I had come to Milan precisely to take part in the event that was to mark the apotheosis of Arrigo Boito; so I had come to Milan with the heart of a friend and the legitimate curiosity of an artist. And to see myself shut out of the dress rehearsal, and really by you, was so painful for me that I, an unwelcome guest, left just a few days later, full of bitterness. Back again in the quiet of Viareggio, I thought for the first time of writing to you, also because of the most fantastic gossip and lies that were soon circulated about me, and particularly about supposed judgments I had made about *Nerone*, as unfavorable as they were ill-timed. [These] threatened to cast a cloud over our old friendship; and that is exactly what happened, as far as I can see. However, I did not, because I did not yet have enough serenity of spirit to do so.

It seemed evident to me that a mysterious and malign force had thrust itself between us. A hidden force, which I would gladly destroy, just as you smash a snake's head, were I able to find out exactly what individual was behind it. Someone near you at La Scala, a sailor who hoists his sail according to the way the wind is blowing, has set himself to the evil job of making trouble between us. Who will ever know why? and to what purpose? And, by a strange coincidence, even the *Corriere della Sera,* as I have been told by a reliable source, has given orders to take a decisive attitude boycotting me. Perhaps also this effect comes from my nonexistent judgments about *Nerone,* very probably attributed to me by the usual hidden snake. I wanted to unburden myself to you, because of our old friendship, about which I care, and because you, now, may help me discover the evil person or persons who are conspiring to harm us. I don't know how to accept the fact that wretched people can cause trouble in the friendship of two gentlemen bound to each other by so many years of friendship, esteem, and memories.

Dear Arturo, you can understand me, it's truly painful for a man who, like me, has worked all his life, and not without glory, a man whose name keeps itself alive and unconquered in the world, and who, because of his age, should have the right to some respect, to see himself treated in this way in his native land, and by the best [people]! Yes, it is truly troubling and unjust, and I cannot tell you how sad my heart is over it. You will make me very happy if you will write to me, [and if you will] appreciate, as it deserves to be appreciated, the feeling of loyal friendship that has moved me to write to you. If you cannot do it yourself, make Signora Carla write to me. If we could see each other, it would be even better. I think I will stay here until winter, except for a few days in the second half of August.

Turandot is about to be finished, but I am taking it very easy [*ma io me la prendo assai comoda*], all the more because I don't intend to give the opera this year. It surprised and saddened me that *Manon* is not included in the repertory of La Scala [at the] Paris Opéra. I feel that I don't deserve this war on all fronts! [GP to AT, August 4, 1924, NYPLPA, Music Division, Wanda Toscanini Horowitz Donation]

He was at first dismayed when he got no answer. By then his sore throat had been bothering him for seven months without respite. As he told Angelo Magrini and Schnabl, it hurt, and he was thinking of going to Switzerland or Germany to find a specialist, because the four doctors he had consulted recommended four different courses of action. He was in a foul humor, he said, and had not worked in months. On August 4 he told Dalla Rizza how sad, nervous, and discouraged he was. He did recover his spirits occasionally, he said. One day at the beginning of September he helped his brother-in-law plan a day of hunting on Lake Massaciuccoli. Sick as he was, he even offered to meet Franceschini on his side of the lake or go to La Piaggetta to arrange things. At the end of October, Puccini hunted for the last time on the lake. Fortunately, he then got back to work, and he wrote to Adami, who had not had a word from him in nearly two months. He had suffered through tremendous emotional and physical crises, he said; but now that he had been told he would recover, he felt better. He could return to *Turandot,* which he had laid aside for six months, and he hoped to "see the end of this blessed princess" soon.

On September 7 Toscanini, who had never replied to Puccini's letter, was persuaded to go to Viareggio to meet Puccini and discuss the opera. With him was Wanda, his daughter, who described their visit to Simonetta Puccini. And to Adami the composer wrote, "All the clouds have vanished, and I am very, very happy. We are in perfect and cordial agreement, and finally I can breathe. So the nightmare that has hung over me since April has now ended. We spoke of the duet, which we did not like very much [*che non piace molto*]. What to do? I don't know. Maybe Toscanini will ask you and Simoni to come to Salso. I'll come too, and we'll see if we can find a way to improve this. I see only darkness [*Io vedo buio*]. By now this duet has made our heads swell until they are as big as an elephant's. You, too, must talk to Renato. And we have to get out of this, because I'm standing in water up to my throat" (GP to GA, September 7, 1924, in Adami, p. 297). On the same day he reassured Schnabl that the opera was safe in Toscanini's hands and was to be given in April (GP to RSR, September 7, 1924, in S. Puccini, *Giacomo Puccini lettere,* p. 11).

The conductor visited Puccini three or (as Guido Marotti told Simonetta Puccini) four times in all, once when he and Forzano drove over from Bologna, where they were staging *Nerone;* once when Toscanini came down from Milan; and then during the first week of November. According to Forzano, Puccini showed the conductor the score of *Turandot.* Walter Toscanini, who accompanied his father on one of these occasions, noticed how Puccini's voice had changed. "I remember how his voice seemed strange toward the end, how he joked with Forzano (the *Gianni Schicchi* librettist) and my father about singing the tenor part himself" (Walter Toscanini with John Freeman). Wally Toscanini said her father discussed *Turandot* with Puccini, although she was not sure whether he actually played much of the score for him. Puccini, however, told Adami in his September 7 letter that Toscanini liked "that little bit" of the music that he played. (But in a private conversation in the 1970s, Wally said her father was not particularly enthusiastic about what he heard.) It is certain, that the two men came to an understanding about Toscanini's role in preparing the opera and conducting it. At that moment, Puccini thought he had six or seven months to finish the last act, and he believed he had all the time he needed "to finish the little that I still have to do," as he wrote to Schnabl in his September 7 letter, cited above. He was also thinking about casting, writing to Dalla Rizza about Liù and to Beniamino Gigli, whom he wanted in the leading tenor role.

Had Puccini been well, work might have gone on that fall, because on October 8 the composer could finally tell Adami that he had received the revised duet from Simoni. Even then, however, he asked Adami for minor changes, but now he could pay attention to the stage action and concentrate more on the sets. With one casual, modest, tossed-off line, Puccini told Adami that he had been named Senator at last. Punning, he signed himself *"Sonatore del Regno,"* a "Musician of the Kingdom." By the tenth, however, he was not working, because the "two or three verses" he had asked Adami to do had not come. "Am I really not to finish *Turandot?"* Also worried about his other operas, he asked Clausetti why the *Trittico* was so rarely produced; at that moment it looked as if it might join *Rondine* on the list of commercial failures.

He went to Florence on October 10 to consult Dr. Torrigiani, a specialist he had perhaps seen before. He had also been examined by a Dr. Toti from that city. On the eve of his visit to Torrigiani, he wrote to Clausetti, saying he was considering treatment in Berne or Lausanne, and he hoped he was not seriously ill. Sometime before the twenty-ninth, he was told that his problem was a benign growth, a papilloma. It was not serious, one of his doctors said, but it must be removed, at once. To Clausetti he wrote, "I telegraphed to Professor Gradenigo [a Neapolitan specialist]; I have to get an operation, with radium or X rays. We shall see what Gradenigo says. As for getting the radium treatments, Florence or Paris. What a fine bother! But at least I know what the illness is that has been worrying and tormenting me for months. . . . Let's hope I can get well, and take up *Turandot* again. For the moment, the only music in my house is sadness and silence" (GP to CC, October 29, 1924, in Gara, p. 557). Finally, Dr. Gradenigo came to Torre to examine him; in the end, Puccini decided to go to Brussels.

Charles-André Gouras, a writer for the Brussels newspaper *Comoedia,* reported later that both Gradenigo and Torrigiani had advised Puccini to go to the Institut Chirurgical, a hospital for surgery and radiology at 1 Avenue de la Couronne in the suburb of Ixelles. There he could get a "new method of treatment for supposedly intractable throat problems." Radium treatments had been used there for about two years and had sometimes been successful. However, as Gouras learned from Dr. Jean Matthieu Ledoux, the head of the Institut, the Italian doctors had serious reservations about Puccini's condition. Whether Puccini knew it or not, Ledoux had been corresponding that autumn with Gradenigo and Torrigiani, who had sent long, detailed reports about their patient. He was old, they said; he had a low resistance to infection, and he had a heart condition, which they described as *"la faiblesse du coeur."* He had also grown very thin. Reading these reports, the Belgian doctors went so far as to advise their Italian colleagues not to send Puccini to Brussels. In spite of these warnings, however, Gradenigo and Torrigiani recommended that he go (Gouras).

On October 22 Puccini, writing to Adami, sounded thoroughly discouraged. He would leave soon for Brussels, he said, to consult a Belgian specialist. Would he have surgery? Could he be cured? Or was he doomed? Sad because he had not finished the opera, he told Adami and others how worried he was about the premiere, which La Scala had already announced, complete with a cast, for the spring season. In one of his last letters to Adami, he described the final duet: "Two beings almost out of this world become human [*entrano fra gli umani*] because of love, and at the end, an orchestral peroration must make this love possess everyone onstage [*deve invadere tutti sulla scena*]" (GP to GA, October 22, 1924, in Adami, pp. 300–301).

With the trip now planned, Puccini fulfilled one last obligation, making his long-promised and long-awaited visit to Celle. On October 26 he was photographed on the rough steps in front of his ancestors' home, surrounded by friends and local dignitaries. A band member, trumpet in hand, stood in full uniform at the edge of the group, and two women were at the door of the house. As William Weaver remarked in "Puccini Pilgrimage," the composer made this "symbolic journey" because he was "always profoundly family-conscious" and was "returning to his roots."

On November 1 he wrote to tell Ferruccio Pagni that he was going to Brussels for radium treatment and asked him to have the caretaker pick up a dog that some priest was sending from Florence. As Simonetta Puccini noted, this was his last letter to a friend he had known for more than thirty years (S. Puccini, "Puccini and the Painters," p. 12).

The Trip to Brussels

Puccini left Viareggio for the last time on November 4, driving to Pisa, where he and Tonio boarded the late afternoon express train, which took them to Milan and Ostend, then to Brussels. Elvira, who had been ill for months with bronchitis and a chronic backache, stayed home, with Fosca to care for her. Both intended to join Puccini later. He took his musical sketches for the *Turandot* finale with him, evidently believing he could work in the hospital. In Belgium he entered the Institut Chirurgical, where Dr. Ledoux was his primary physician, and remained there incognito for almost two weeks, with the staff protecting his privacy; but on November 18, a story about his stay in Brussels appeared on the front page of *Le Soir.* "The Italian composer Giacomo Puccini, creator of *Tosca* and *La Bohème,* is being treated in a clinic in our city. Soon he will undergo an operation: the removal of his larynx."

Dr. Orsini Barone, the Italian ambassador, immediately issued a denial, although Puccini had often been recognized in the city. He frequently left the hospital with Tonio, having luncheon downtown every day and taking long walks in the historic center of Brussels. Once they strolled through the marketplace, where the composer noticed a lot of woodcocks, and regretted he had not brought them down himself. He even slipped unnoticed into the Théâtre de la Monnaie to see *Butterfly;* but according to a newspaper article about his visit, he became ill during the performance and had to return to the hospital. To outward appearances, though, he was in fair health. For the first ten days, radium was applied externally for part of each day, kept in place by a wax collar, which he hated. During these early stages of treatment he had several visitors, among them the Italian ambassador, who paid his respects every day, and the papal nuncio, Monsignor Clemente Micara.

Some of Puccini's first letters from the hospital reflect limited optimism, but in confidence he told Adami how frightened he was, although he had had little pain from the early treatment, and the doctors assured him he would not suffer much from the later procedures. Nevertheless, in his last letter to Adami he said he had lost any hope of getting well. In letters to others, however, he expressed hope. He was trying his best, he said.

Puccini's Last Interview

One day, probably on November 21 or 22, Puccini agreed to let Nino Salvaneschi, a journalist, visit him in the Institut. The interview was published in *Le Soir* on November 23, with a bold headline:

GIACOMO PUCCINI IN BRUSSELS
A VISIT TO THE ILLUSTRIOUS PATIENT

Their meeting took place in what Salvaneschi described as "a warm, comfortable room" in the hospital. Because Puccini had met Salvaneschi earlier in Italy, he seemed very much at ease. Salvaneschi first described the circumstances of their previous meeting:

> The last time I met him was in Viareggio, in a room in an art gallery, flooded with beautiful light; he was looking at the works of a Florentine painter, one who had inherited the technique and style of the *"Macchiaioli."* The Maestro seemed to be enjoying himself as he looked at these much-loved pictures of his Tuscany. Perhaps he got just as much pleasure from strolling in the beautiful *pineta* in Viareggio, smoking one of his cigars.
>
> I found him in a room in this clinic on Avenue de la Couronne, cordial, smiling, but very unhappy about having to give up his cigars. However, he welcomed me with good humor and with that open simplicity that his glory has never stolen from him. The extraordinary success of *La Bohème, Tosca,* and *Mme. Butterfly* and his triumphant popularity have changed nothing about the Maestro, who has given up none of his old habits, and has gone on writing music and smoking his *toscani* [Tuscan cigars].
>
> "I have come here to get care, on the advice of my doctors," Giacomo Puccini told me. The Maestro has been in Brussels for several weeks; he followed his course of treatment without being recognized. And M. Orsini Barone, the Italian ambassador, was careful to deny all the indiscreet stories, when a hint appeared in the "Petite Gazette" of *Le Soir.*
>
> "I was suffering with my throat for some time, when Dr. Gradenigo, who is from Naples, and Drs. Toti and Torrigiani advised me to get radium treatments. I had to choose between Brussels and Berlin. You see the choice I made. And anyway, I was already familiar with Brussels, and I loved it; but just think of how much I will love it when I get my health back."

Puccini speaks very slowly; his voice, which had once been coarse and heavy, has become strangely sweet. He also speaks with some difficulty, and Professor Ledoux does not want his patient to get tired.

In any case, the Maestro is an ideal patient. [Puccini said], "The doctors will tell you that I am the most obedient of all their patients; and I do not want to know what the doctors are going to do to my throat. It seems that in a few days they will apply the radium internally, and that ought to destroy the disease. What dismays me, though, is that I have abandoned my work. I had some pages to finish, but here I can't get into the right spirit, which I need."

The musician's slow, calm words fit in with the warmth in the room. Sister Herman-Joseph takes care of the man who made Musetta sing, along with Floria Tosca, and the little geisha. [The nurse] moves from the bed to the door, her chaplet and cross making a tinkling sound, as if they were made of crystal.

"And that's the whole story," Puccini said. "In Brussels, I am surrounded by friends; and I am waiting patiently for the moment when I can take up my work again."

Each day, the Italian ambassador comes to see this patient, who also has his son Antonio at his side. Contrary to what has been bruited about, Puccini is not in Brussels to have an operation; but he is here to follow this treatment. He does not have to stay in bed, and sometimes he even takes walks outside. But Puccini has to avoid getting tired, and Sister Herman-Joseph watches over him. [She said], "He will certainly get well, because Monsieur Puccini is such a docile patient." He will recover: that is the news that everyone in the world is waiting for. [Salvaneschi]

(This and other clippings from *Le Soir* were found by Anne Vandenbulcke, archivist-conservator, City of Brussels, Department of Culture, Archives. Jan Van Goethem, the archivist of La Monnaie, provided them for this book.)

The Last Week

Tonio reported the news to Riccardo Redaelli, who had sent Puccini an encouraging note. "His general condition is fairly good, up to now; he has had the radium applied externally; beginning Monday, he will have it applied internally, and Monday they will operate on him to insert the nee-

dles. He has 'ups' and 'downs' all the time, but—poor man—the 'downs'
are more frequent. He is braver than I would ever have imagined. He is
not in bed. In fact, we go out every day for lunch; but beginning on Monday, he will not be able to go out for the next eight or ten days, which is
the length of the internal application treatment, which ought to cure him
[*che dovrà guarirlo*]. Poor Papa! When you can do so, go keep Mother company for a while. Who knows how she is, poor woman. With many affectionate greetings from Papà and from me, I send you an affectionate
embrace. Tonio" (AP to Redaelli, November 22, 1924, in Pintorno, letter
249).

Puccini's spirits sank as he thought of the second phase of treatment,
scheduled for Monday, November 24, because he would have a tracheot-
omy, with a breathing tube placed in his throat. Then the needles would
be inserted, in the hope of reaching the growth. Just the idea of the tube
horrified him, he said, as he remembered his reaction to a man from
Lucca, who had used one all his life. For all his fear, however, he was
rarely alone. Fosca had arrived from Milan, while Elvira stayed in the Puccini apartment on Via Verdi. With Fosca was Carla Toscanini, her closest
friend. Clausetti soon followed, as did Angelo Magrini. Magrini reached
the hospital just a few hours after the needles were inserted, and he realized that although Puccini was fully conscious, he could say very little, because of the breathing tube. In spite of that, he managed to communicate
by sign language, handwritten notes, and barely mouthed words. Puccini
asked Magrini whether the Maremma was beautiful that autumn and
whether the hunting was good. On a pad, he wrote a note saying he had
been massacred, and felt as if he had bayonets in his throat.

Le Soir of November 26 ran another story about the treatment: "Yesterday Giacomo Puccini underwent a surgical operation. . . . They applied
radium needles in his throat to destroy two little tumors inside that organ. However, the creator of *Tosca* was on the table only a little less than
three hours, between nine and noon. His son Antonio and his daughter
Fosca are with him. The composer, who was strolling around the streets
of our city just day before yesterday, will soon be able to take up his wan-
derings again. He is in excellent condition."

So even in those dire moments, the news was reassuring. Clausetti
wrote to Adami that things had gone better than anyone could have imagined. Tonio also told some of Puccini's nieces that there was reason to

hope. And when the head of La Monnaie asked Dr. Ledoux about the condition of its famous patient, Dr. Ledoux's response was optimistic: "He will live through this." This, too, was reported in the newspapers. Puccini also thought the operation a success. On November 27 he beckoned for Fosca to lean over him, smiled weakly, and mouthed an optimistic message: "Fosca, I'm making it! [*Fosca, me la cavo!*]"

His hopes proved unwarranted, however, for a major crisis followed when his heart began to fail. Clausetti sent Adami a telegram, saying that a "catastrophe" lay ahead. In the emergency, the surgeons removed the needles. Then Puccini, writing a desperate note on his pad, said he was worse and wanted a sip of cold water. Although his breathing became regular around four the next morning, the doctors told Fosca and Tonio there was no hope. The Italian ambassador and Monsignor Micara arrived between seven and eight, with the nuncio remaining alone briefly with Puccini to give him the last rites of the Church. Puccini died at 11:30 in the morning on November 29.

The news reached Milan almost at once. As soon as Adami heard it, he rushed to find Toscanini, who was in a rehearsal at La Scala. Seeing Adami's face, the conductor knew what had happened. Adami said that Toscanini, completely overcome, rushed to his dressing room, began sobbing, and threw himself in a chair; soon he left to break the news to Elvira. The *Corriere della Sera* ran a special bulletin that said: "Giacomo Puccini, the gentle maker of melodies of sorrow and grace, died at 11:30 on November 29 in Brussels. The Maestro died without being able to speak, but he was fully conscious."

The Rites in Belgium

As soon as the death was announced, the Brussels papers ran headlines, "THE DEATH OF GIACOMO PUCCINI," and gave the details, describing the letters, telegrams, and flowers that had arrived. Among others, the Queen sent her personal condolences to Fosca, Tonio, and the rest of the Puccini family. Said *Le Soir*, "The people of Belgium and Brussels in particular have been enormously moved to learn of the death of the great musician, who had won over the greatest possible understanding and sympathy from everyone." Bulletins described telegrams that had come from Italy, with condolences and public expressions of grief from the king, the pope, and Mussolini. The Italian papers prepared full-page and double-page stories.

The rites that followed were formal, and attendance at some was limited to Puccini's family and friends. The customary viewing of the dead, which in Italy is held in the family home, took place in a hospital room in the Institut Chirurgical. Although it was open only to an invited few, Charles-André Gouras, mentioned earlier, managed to get in and interview Dr. Ledoux, whom he knew. Gouras then wrote a long article about the composer, describing his "thin, frail body," which lay on a simple metal bed. His description of the dead man matches what one can see today in a newspaper photograph that was published in *Le Soir.*

In the hospital Monsignor Micara held a brief funeral service, with only Fosca, Tonio, and their closest friends present. That night, the management of La Monnaie honored the "immortal musician" by presenting a large wreath onstage and having the orchestra play the Funeral March from Beethoven's Third Symphony. The audience was asked to observe a two-minute silence before the opera, which was *La Bohème.* In addition to Puccini's other popular works, the company there had given *La Fanciulla del West,* and it was planning to produce *Gianni Schicchi.*

A large, official funeral followed, in one of the city's biggest center-city churches, the cathedral-like Church of Sainte Marie, which stands on a hill on Place de la Reine. A monument to Romanesque-Byzantine architecture, this imposing mass of stone has flying buttresses and arches worthy of Ravenna. According to *Le Soir,* Mussolini had sent the Italian ambassador a telegram, asking him to represent the Italian nation at the funeral and announcing that the Italian government would pay for it. For the occasion the church was fully draped in black, inside and out, and the bells tolled slowly. In the surrounding streets, a large crowd watched the hearse arrive, followed by three open funeral cars, all heaped high with grand wreaths and bouquets of chrysanthemums, roses, dahlias, and lilacs. At the altar the bier was covered with a cloth bearing the insignia of Italy's royal family. Again, Monsignor Micara officiated. The music included *Kyrie Eleison* and *Pie Jesu,* sung by a soprano from La Monnaie, Madame Laure Bergé; the organist played hymns by Gounod and Franck, among others. A long procession then wound its way through the city, with the hearse followed by hundreds of mourners. Just after six in the evening, a ceremony with military honors took place at the train station, where the Italian ambassador and the Brussels city officials saw Puccini's coffin placed in a private car that was added to the train for Ostend and Milan.

Italy Honors a Hero

When the train arrived at the Stazione Centrale, the mayor of Milan, Toscanini, Giordano, Pizzetti, Zandonai, Panizza, and a delegation of singers from La Scala were all present on the platform. In Rome that same day, Mussolini made a formal announcement about Puccini's death to the Chamber of Deputies, summoning them and the Italian people to national mourning. In the Senate, to which Puccini had so recently been named, a formal session was held. The president gave an address in which he said that everyone should remember Puccini for his achievements, first as a celebrated musician, then as a popular one. His gifts were recognized throughout the world, he said; and with his music, Puccini had brought honor to his country.

On December 3, the day of the funeral in Milan, the streets were draped with black mourning silks and ribbons. La Scala remained closed. Archbishop Tosi and the national and local authorities planned a state ceremony and requiem Mass in the great gothic cathedral, the Duomo. Over the bronze doors was hung a drapery with an inscription reading, "Tears and prayers for Giacomo Puccini, who from earthly glory has ascended to glory in Heaven." Inside the church, which held thousands of people, the family group was seated near the altar. It included Elvira, Tonio, Fosca and her husband, their children, Puccini's nieces, other relatives and in-laws, and the Toscaninis. Clausetti and Valcarenghi represented Casa Ricordi. Official committees came from Viareggio and Lucca, and near them were the Milanese dignitaries and a cabinet member who had come from Rome for the day. During the service Puccini was hailed not just as a musician, but as a "protagonist of history." Some of his music was also heard, for Toscanini and the La Scala orchestra and chorus performed music from *Edgar,* including the Funeral March and "Addio, addio, mio dolce amor," which Hina Spani sang.

Afterward, crowds jammed the streets as the funeral procession moved through a pounding rain. The hearse stopped for a few minutes in front of La Scala, where members of the administrative staff, the stage crew, and singers from the company stood in silence on the sidewalk. Puccini was also saluted at the Monumental Cemetery with full military honors, and he was given a temporary burial in the Toscanini family tomb. Two years later, his body was moved to the parish church in Torre del Lago, where a simple rite was read. Finally, he was buried in the little mortuary chapel that Tonio had created at his father's lakeside villa.

Puccini's death prematurely ended the career of a distinguished artist. It also marked the end of the Puccini dynasty in music, the fifth and last generation of its composers.

AFTERWORD

Turandot *Reaches the Stage*

With PUCCINI DEAD, Casa Ricordi was again left with a famous composer's unfinished opera, as it had been when Boito died and left *Nerone* behind. Clausetti and Valcarenghi, who believed in *Turandot,* knew they held an important asset; but they also had to act quickly, because La Scala had already announced the premiere for the 1924–1925 season. Of course it could not be produced then, but if they could hire a composer to finish it, the work could be saved. It might even crown Puccini's career.

Toscanini, who had worked so hard on *Nerone,* now oversaw *Turandot.* According to Harvey Sachs, the Casa Ricordi team first approached Zandonai, who had been on their roster for years. Born near Verona in 1883, he had become a Ricordi composer in 1908 and, as we have seen, Tito Ricordi's protégé. Zandonai, after composing *Conchita* from the text Puccini had rejected, wrote *Francesca da Rimini* (1914) to a D'Annunzio libretto. Successful after its premiere, it has survived into our own time. His idiosyncratic *Giulietta e Romeo* followed in 1922, with a premiere at the Costanzi in Rome. When Puccini died, Zandonai was writing *I Cavalieri di Ekebù,* the premiere of which Toscanini conducted at La Scala in 1925. Zandonai's brilliant orchestrations would likely have made him a good candidate for the *Turandot* job; but Tonio Puccini apparently rejected him on the grounds that he was too famous. If that was true of Zandonai, it was far more the case with Mascagni, whose name appeared in one New York newspaper as the right composer for the job. A lesser light, Vincenzo Tommasini, who had worked with Toscanini on *Nerone,* was also briefly considered.

Then Casa Ricordi turned to the Neapolitan Franco Alfano, a dedicated, serious composer whom Toscanini and Tonio Puccini readily en-

dorsed. In 1924 he was a distinguished teacher and versatile composer
with a wide musical culture. He launched his opera career with *Risur-
rezione,* premiered in 1904 in Turin under Ricordi's umbrella. *La Leggenda
di Sakùntala,* based on an Indian play, resembled *Turandot* in its oriental
setting and heavy orchestration. *Sakùntala* had its premiere in 1921. Although Alfano never became as popular as Puccini or Mascagni, his works
nevertheless had respectable runs.

According to Alfano's own account, which appeared in the *Corriere
della Sera* and is summarized in Sachs's *Toscanini,* he showed Toscanini his
work in progress several times as he worked from Puccini's *Turandot*
sketches. At first, Alfano said, the conductor asked him to expand the last
scene of the opera beyond the version he had originally created. He followed those instructions, but when it was done, Toscanini found it too
long and ordered him to shorten it. The first version is called "Alfano I,"
and the second, "Alfano II." As John Freeman noted in a recent conversation, the Alfano II version is often performed with further cuts, notably
Turandot's aria *"Del primo pianto."* Toscanini sometimes gets blamed for
this, but the published Alfano II shows that his cuts were not as drastic as
the ones we often hear now. Toscanini understood that *"Del primo pianto"*
is dramatically necessary; William Ashbrook makes an even stronger case:
that Puccini's sketches run up to the first phrases of the aria. For this and
other reasons, he believes the aria should be performed, because it makes
Turandot's change of heart convincing. "Puccini's sketches show that he
did want the aria, and he left indications of how he wanted it to begin"
(Ashbrook, *The Operas of Puccini,* pp. 224–225). Ricordi published both
Alfano I and Alfano II, the first in time for the world premiere, and the
second in the standard score issued later.

In an interview that Raymond Roussel conducted with Alfano and
published in *Musical Leader and Concert-goer* on October 22, 1925, Alfano
cleared up much confusion about his assignment. Here is Linda B.
Fairtile's description of that interview: "[Alfano] outlines his strategy for
completing the final scene of *Turandot,* using Puccini's sketches and
drafts. Roussel reveals that Casa Ricordi had decided not to use Alfano's
conclusion for the opera's premiere, but will end that performance at the
point where Puccini ceased composing." As Fairtile says, most accounts
of the premiere represent "this action as a spontaneous decision by the
grief-stricken conductor" (Fairtile, p. 188). Clearly, however, Toscanini and

Casa Ricordi planned all along to end the first night's performance with the last notes Puccini wrote.

In recent years many scholars have examined Alfano's finale. Among them is the American conductor Steven Mercurio, who served five years as music director of the Spoleto Festival and conducts regularly in the States and abroad. His version has been used in three productions, in Philadelphia, Washington, and Detroit, and has been received with hearty critical and audience response. Robert Baxter, a critic who heard Mercurio's finale in Philadelphia, says he finds it very effective. Interviewed in 2001 for this book, Mercurio described his work on the Alfano score as "a performing version based on Alfano I, using the improvements of Alfano II and a previously unused Puccini sketch, with a slight reworking of both climactic moments, the revelation of the name (Calaf), and the moment of 'the kiss,' as well as some adjustments in the Alfano orchestration to bring it in line with the rest of the opera." More recently, Luciano Berio has also composed a new ending for it.

The world premiere of *Turandot* took place at La Scala on April 25, 1926, with the great Polish dramatic soprano Rosa Raisa as Turandot. Maria Zamboni was Liù, because Edith Mason, whom Puccini had originally wanted, was pregnant at the time. Miguel Fleta sang Calaf. The evening ended just as Alfano knew it would, with Toscanini stopping the orchestra after Puccini's last notes. He played Liù's death and the chorus that follows it, then he stopped the orchestra, put down his baton, and turned to the audience. "Here the opera ends, because at this point the Maestro died."

After the first night, Alfano's revised ending was played for the remaining performances of that run, as it also was when *Turandot* returned in the 1926–1927 season. In spite of all the advance publicity about the opera, the premiere failed to get universal praise from the Italian press, although the reviews, many of which are quoted in Eugenio Gara's *Carteggi pucciniani,* were generally favorable. Some critics thought it Puccini's best work, while others, including the reviewer from the influential Turin paper *La Stampa,* expressed reservations. Some saw Liù as the protagonist, a true Puccini creation and the only believable, human figure in the opera. The others were marionettes. Other writers exalted Turandot, but few seemed to understand her. One writer swore that Puccini's reputation would survive because of Mimì and Manon, not because of *Turandot;* and another praised the composer for his symphonic music. Carlo Gatti called it "a noble opera: Italian in its manner and in its forms," while others spoke of foreign influences in Puccini's music. Among later critics, Joseph Kerman dismissed *Turandot* as void of any true emotion, with a score of "café-music banality." Worse was the "bogus Orientalism" that is "lacquered over every page of the score" (Kerman, pp. 205–206).

The next important production was mounted in Puccini's old fortress, the Teatro Costanzi in Rome, where *Turandot* opened four days after the premiere at La Scala. Outside Italy, the opera was first given at the Teatro Colón in Buenos Aires on June 25, 1926, with Claudia Muzio as Turandot, Giacomo Lauri-Volpi as Calaf, and the delicious Rosetta Pampanini, a beloved Butterfly, as Liù. This cast then took it to Rio de Janeiro. In September it was given in Venice; in Dresden in July it was heard in a German translation; in October it appeared at the Vienna Staatsoper, the theater that had so often refused to give Puccini's early operas; and in November it reached Berlin. In December 1926 the Théâtre de la Monnaie in Brussels gave it in French. *Turandot* got a very mixed reception at London's Covent Garden in June 1927, with Bianca Scacciati in the title role. A British soprano, Eva Turner, later emerged as one of the great Turandots of her generation.

The first Metropolitan Opera production opened on November 16, 1926, with Jeritza as Turandot and Lauri-Volpi as Calaf. Martha Attwood sang Liù. Robert Tuggle described that *Turandot* as "the grandest production in the history of the Metropolitan." According to a newspaper account, "Puccini's portrait, a more than life-size photograph framed in laurel branches and violet satin bows, was hung over the parterre box promenade rail in the Broadway entrance. During the performance a census of those singing onstage and mostly visible to the house showed these large totals: 120 opera chorus, 120 chorus school, 60 boy choir singers, 60 ballet girls, 30 male dancers and procession leaders, 30 stage musicians, 230 extra supers—650 persons in all, beside the eleven-star cast and a hundred orchestra players in the pit." On her entrance, Jeritza was "unforgettable," for she seemed to be "a sudden, gleaming apparition" as she sent yet one more suitor to his death (Tuggle, pp. 210–211).

Not every critic in the States appreciated *Turandot*. In the *New York Times* Olin Downes said the stage production deserved more praise than the music, which he found only occasionally interesting. Puccini had made but limited progress with this opera, Downes said; his advances were technical and theatrical and lacking inspiration or power. All in all, he denounced the opera's effects as exterior, spectacular, studied, and craftily concocted (this last because Puccini had learned long before where and how to plant his devices on the thread of the story). In short, Downes defined it as a "full-night success and an ultimate failure" and "much ado about nothing" (review in Seltsam, pp. 466–467).

In spite of this and other unfavorable views, *Turandot* opened the next season, again with Jeritza and Lauri-Volpi, and remained in the Met repertory for several years. It then fell out of favor in New York, until the lavish Met revival of 1961, which had Birgit Nilsson, Franco Corelli, and Anna Moffo. The Puccini Festival in Torre del Lago opened in 1930 with *La Bohème* under Mascagni's direction and with Forzano as the director, but *Turandot* did not appear on its program until 1954.

In spite of all the effort spent on it, *Turandot* falls short of what Puccini hoped to create, partly because Alfano's ending seems so thin. What might it have been? For Puccini, as for us, the confounding enigma remains.

List of Puccini's Works

This list was compiled from those prepared earlier by Linda B. Fairtile for *Giacomo Puccini: A Guide to Research* and by Dr. Dieter Schickling for the Giacomo Puccini Centro Studi in Lucca. My thanks to both for helping with this section of the book.

1875: Short pieces for organ

1875 (in any case, before 1880): *"A te"* for voice and piano

1876: *Preludio sinfonico* in E minor-major for orchestra (lost)

1877: *I Figli d'Italia Bella* for solo voices and orchestra (lost)

1877: *Motetto per San Paolino "Plaudite populi"* for baritone, mixed chorus and orchestra

1878: Credo for tenor, chorus and orchestra

1878?: *Vexilla regis prodeunt* for male chorus and organ. Written for the parish church in Bagni di Lucca to a text by Venantius Honorius Fortunatus

1878–1880: *Messa a quattro voci con orchestra* for tenor, baritone, mixed chorus, and orchestra

1879: *Prime fantasie,* waltz (lost)

1880–1881: Suite *"Allemande, Corrente, Gavotta"* for piano

1881 or 1883: *Melanconia* for baritone and piano. Text by Antonio Ghislanzoni (lost)

1881?: *Adagio* in A major for piano

1881: *Scherzo* in A minor for string quartet

1881–1883: *Largo adagietto* in F major for orchestra

1881–1883: *Fughe a quattro voci. Moderato* in D minor; *Largo* in C minor; *Allegro moderato* in G major; *Moderato sostenuto* in C major; *Largo* in E minor and other keys; *Andante mosso* in G major; *Piuttosto lento* in G minor

1881–1883: *Fughe reali. Andante poco mosso* in C minor; *Andante sostenuto* in A major

1882: *Preludio sinfonico* in A major for orchestra

1882: Trio for two violins and piano

1882: *Ah! se potesse* (fragment) for tenor and piano (lost)

1882 or 1883: *Ad una morta!* for baritone and piano. Text by Antonio Ghislanzoni

1882 or 1883: Quartetto d'archi in D major

1882 or 1883: *Salve Regina* for soprano and harmonium. Text by Antonio Ghislanzoni

1883: *Mentia l'avviso* for tenor and piano. Text by Felice Romani.

1883: *Storiella d'amore* for soprano or tenor and piano. Text by Antonio Ghislanzoni.

1883: *Capriccio sinfonico* in F major for orchestra

1883: *La Sconsolata* for violin and piano

1883–1884: *Le Villi.* Opera. Text by Ferdinando Fontana

1884: *Tre minuetti* for string quartet

1886–1889: *Edgar.* Opera. Text by Ferdinando Fontana

1888: *Sole e amore* for soprano or tenor and piano

1888: *Solfeggi* for three voices

1890: *Crisantemi* for string quartet

1890–1893: *Manon Lescaut.* Opera. Text by Ruggero Leoncavallo, Marco Praga, Domenico Oliva, Giuseppe Giacosa, Luigi Illica, Giulio Ricordi, and Giacomo Puccini

1894: *Piccolo valzer* for piano

1894–1896: *La Bohème.* Opera. Text by Luigi Illica and Giuseppe Giacosa

1896: *Avanti Urania!* for voice and piano. Text by Renato Fucini

1896: *Scossa elettrica* for piano, arranged for band in 1899

1897: *Inno a Diana* for voice and piano. Text by Carlo Abenicar

1899: *E l'uccellino,* lullaby for voice and piano. Text by Renato Fucini

1896–1900: *Tosca.* Opera. Text by Luigi Illica and Giuseppe Giacosa

1901–1904: *Madama Butterfly.* Opera. Text by Luigi Illica and Giuseppe Giacosa

1902: *Terra e mare* for voice and piano. Text by Enrico Panzacchi

1904: *Canto d'anime* for voice and piano. Text by Luigi Illica

1905: Requiem for three voices, viola, and harmonium or organ. Composed in memory of Giuseppe Verdi and performed at the Casa di Risposo per Musicisti

1905: *Ecce sacerdos magnus* for four-part chorus. Liturgical text

1907 or 1910: *Piccolo tango* for piano (perhaps not by Puccini)

1907 or 1910: *Foglio d'album* for piano (perhaps not by Puccini)

1908: *Casa mia, casa mia* for voice and piano. Text by Giacomo Puccini

1908–1910: *La Fanciulla del West.* Opera. Text by Carlo Zangarini and Guelfo Civinini

1912 or 1913: *Sogno d'or* for voice and piano. Text by Carlo Marsili

1914–1916: *La Rondine.* Opera. Text by Giuseppe Adami

1915–1916: *Il Tabarro.* First opera of *Il Trittico.* Text by Giuseppe Adami

1916: *Pezzo per pianoforte: Calmo e molto lento* for piano

1917: *Suor Angelica.* Second opera of *Il Trittico.* Text by Giovacchino Forzano

1917?: *Morire?* for voice and piano. Text by Giuseppe Adami

1917–1918: *Gianni Schicchi.* Third opera of *Il Trittico.* Text by Giovacchino Forzano

1919: *Inno a Roma* for voice and piano. Later orchestrated. Text by Fausto Salvatore.

1920–1924: *Turandot.* Opera. Left unfinished at Puccini's death and completed by Franco Alfano. Text by Giuseppe Adami and Renato Simoni

Puccini and His Contemporaries: Opera Composers and Their Works

Alfredo Catalani: born 1854, Lucca
Giacomo Puccini: born 1858, Lucca
Ruggero Leoncavallo: born 1857, Naples
Alberto Franchetti: born 1860, Turin
Pietro Mascagni: born 1863, Livorno
Umberto Giordano: born 1867, Foggia

WORKS

1880: Catalani's *Elda*

1883: Catalani's *Dejanice;* Puccini's one-act *Le Willis*

1885: Puccini's two-act *Le Villi*

1886: Catalani's *Edmea*

1888: Franchetti's *Asrael*

1889: Puccini's *Edgar*

1890: Catalani's *Loreley* (revision of *Elda*); Mascagni's *Cavalleria Rusticana*

1891: Mascagni's *L'Amico Fritz*

1892: Catalani's *La Wally;* Giordano's *Mala Vita;* Franchetti's *Cristoforo Colombo;* Mascagni's *I Rantzau;* Leoncavallo's *Pagliacci*

1893: Leoncavallo's *I Medici;* Puccini's *Manon Lescaut*

1894: Franchetti's *Fior d'Alpe;* Giordano's *Regina Diaz*

1895: Mascagni's *Silvano* and *Guglielmo Ratcliff*

1896: Mascagni's *Zanetto;* Leoncavallo's *Chatterton;* Puccini's *La Bohème;* Giordano's *Andrea Chénier*

1897: Franchetti's *Signor Pourceaugnac;* Leoncavallo's *La Bohème*

1898: Mascagni's *Iris;* Giordano's *Fedora*

1900: Puccini's *Tosca;* Leoncavallo's *Zazà*

1901: Mascagni's *Le Maschere*

1902: Franchetti's *Germania*

1904: Puccini's *Madama Butterfly;* Leoncavallo's *Der Roland von Berlin*

1905: Mascagni's *Amica*

1906: Franchetti's *La Figlia d'Iorio;* Leoncavallo's *La Jeunesse di Figaro*

1910: Puccini's *La Fanciulla del West;* Leoncavallo's *Maia* and *Malbrouck*

1911: Mascagni's *Isabeau*

1912: Leoncavallo's *Gli Zingari* and *La Reginetta delle Rose*

1913: Mascagni's *Parisina*

1915: Franchetti's *Notte di Leggenda;* Leoncavallo's *La Candidata*

1916: Leoncavallo's *Prestami Tua Moglie* and *Goffredo Mameli*

1917: Mascagni's *Lodoletta;* Puccini's *La Rondine*

1918: Puccini's *Il Trittico*

1919: Mascagni's *Sì;* Leoncavallo's *A Chi la Giarrettiera?*

1921: Franchetti's *Giove a Pompei;* Mascagni's *Il Piccolo Marat*

1923: Leoncavallo's *Il Primo Bacio*

1924: Puccini's *Turandot*

From my article "Friends and Rivals," *Opera News* (January 2000). Reproduced with permission of The Metropolitan Opera Guild, Inc.

Selected Bibliography

BOOKS

Abbiati, Franco. *Verdi,* vol. IV. Milan, 1963.

Adami, Giuseppe, ed. *Epistolario Giacomo Puccini.* Milan, 1928 (an early collection of Puccini's letters, edited by one of his librettists). Published in English as *Letters of Giacomo Puccini,* translated by Ena Makin. New York, 1973.

Ashbrook, William. *The Operas of Puccini.* New York, 1968. Second ed., 1985.

Ashbrook, William, and Harold Powers. *Puccini's "Turandot": The End of the Great Tradition.* Princeton, 1991.

Belli, Aldo. *Tramontate Stelle: Puccini e Torre del Lago.* N.p., 1989? (photographs and essays on Viareggio and Torre del Lago).

Bernardoni, Virgilio, ed. *Puccini.* Bologna, 1996.

Blignaut, Hélène. *La Scala di Vetro.* Milan, 1995.

Carner, Mosco. *Giacomo Puccini.* New York, 1958. Third ed., 1992.

Catelani, Bice Paoli. *Il Teatro Comunale del "Giglio" di Lucca.* Pescia, 1941.

Del Fiorentino, Dante. *Immortal Bohemian.* New York, 1952.

Eaton, Quaintance. *The Miracle of the Met.* New York, 1968.

Fairtile, Linda B. *Giacomo Puccini: A Guide to Research.* New York and London, 1999.

Gara, Eugenio, ed. *Carteggi Pucciniani.* Milan, 1958 (mainly, but not exclusively, Puccini's correspondence with Casa Ricordi, his librettists, and other professionals).

Girardi, Michele. *Giacomo Puccini.* Venice, 1995.

———. *Puccini: La vita e l'opera.* Rome, 1989.

Gozzi, Carlo. *Fiabe.* Venice, 1805.

———. *Memorie inutili della vita di Carlo Gozzi scritte da lui medesimo e pubblicate per umiltà.* Bari, 1910 (modern edition; this was first published in Venice in 1797).

Hoelterhoff, Manuela. *Cinderella & Company.* New York, 1998.

John, Nicholas, ed. *Madam Butterfly, Madama Butterfly.* An English National Opera Guide. New York, 1984 (includes essays, John Luther Long's story, and the complete libretto of the 1904 production, with notes about revisions).

Kaye, Michael. *The Unknown Puccini.* New York, 1987.

Keolker, James. *Last Acts.* Napa, Calif., 2000.

Kerman, Joseph. *Opera as Drama.* Revised edition. Berkeley, 1988.

Levarie, Siegmund. *Musical Italy Revisited.* New York, 1963.

Lopez, Guido, ed. *La Casa di riposo per musicisti Giuseppe Verdi in Milano.* Milan, 1988.

Mangini, Nicola. *I teatri di Venezia.* Milan, 1974.

Marchetti, Arnaldo, ed. *Puccini com'era.* Milan, 1973 (a collection of Puccini's letters, other correspondence, and extensive notes).

Marchetti, Leopoldo. *Puccini nelle immagini.* Torre del Lago, 1968 (photographs).

Mintzer, Charles. *Rosa Raisa.* Boston, 2001.

Noble, Helen. *Life with the Met.* New York, 1954.

Osborne, Charles. *The Complete Operas of Puccini.* New York, 1982.

Pagni, Ferruccio, and Guido Marotti. *Giacomo Puccini intimo.* Florence, 1926 (an early personal memoir).

Pasi, Mario. *Mascagni.* New York, 1989.

Pintorno, Giuseppe. *Puccini: 276 lettere inedite.* Milan, 1974 (Monsignor Dante Del Fiorentino's collection of Puccini's letters, with other documents).

Porter, Andrew. *Music of Three Seasons: 1974–1977.* New York, 1978.

Puccini, Simonetta. *Giacomo Puccini Lettere a Riccardo Schnabl.* Milan, 1981.

Rescigno, Eduardo, ed. *Giacomo Puccini, "Il Trittico."* Milan, 1997.

Reynaud, L. *Rome, a Pocket Guide. Holy Year Edition: 1899–1900.* Rome, 1899.

Sachs, Harvey. *Toscanini.* New York, 1978.

Seligman, Vincent. *Puccini among Friends.* London, 1938 (personal account of Sybil Seligman's friendship with Puccini, together with English translations of the composer's letters to Sybil).

Seltsam, William H. *Metropolitan Opera Annual.* New York, 1947.

Smith, Patrick J. *The Tenth Muse.* New York, 1970.

Taviani, Ferdinando, and Mirella Schino. *Il segreto della Commedia dell'Arte.* Florence, 1992.

Torrefranca, Fausto. *Giacomo Puccini e l'opera internazionale.* Turin, 1912.

Tuggle, Robert. *The Golden Age of Opera.* New York, 1983.

Vetro, Gaspare Nello, ed. *L'allievo di Verdi, Emanuele Muzio,* with chronology by Thomas G. Kaufman. Parma, 1993.

———. *Antonio Carlos Gomez, carteggi italiani raccolti e commentati.* Milan, 1977 (also contains essays by Giampiero Tintori and Marcello Conati).

Weaver, William. *The Golden Century of Italian Opera: From Rossini to Puccini.* London and New York, 1980.

———. *Seven Puccini Librettos.* New York, 1981.

Weaver, William, and Simonetta Puccini, eds. *The Puccini Companion.* New York, 1994.

Wilson, Conrad. *Giacomo Puccini.* London, 1997.

Zorzi, Alvise. *Canal Grande.* Milan, 1991.

ARTICLES, ESSAYS, BROCHURES

Ashbrook, William. "The Chrysalis of *Butterfly.*" *Opera News,* December 10, 1956.

———. "*Turandot* and Its Posthumous *prima.*" *Opera Quarterly* 2, no. 3 (Autumn 1984).

Atlas, Allan W. "Belasco e Puccini: 'Old Dog Tray' e gli indiani Zuni." In *Puccini,* edited by Virgilio Bernardoni, Bologna, 1996.

Bajoni, Maria Grazia. "A Chronology of Puccini's Life and Works." In *The Puccini Companion,* edited by William Weaver and Simonetta Puccini, New York, 1994.

Brown, Angela K. "University to Perform Lost March by Puccini." Associated Press, July 24, 2001 (newspaper unidentified).

Burton, Deborah. "The Creation of *Tosca,* Toward a Clearer View." *Musical Quarterly* 12, no. 3 (Spring 1996): 27–34.

———. "The Real Scarpia, the Historical Sources for *Tosca.*" *Musical Quarterly* 10, no. 2 (Winter 1993–1994): 67–86.

Buzzi-Peccia, A. "The Young Puccini as I Knew Him." *Musical Courier,* November 25, 1926.

Cleva, Fausto, with John Freeman. "Poem of the West." *Opera News,* January 8, 1966.

"The Composer of *Turandot* Writes to an Old Friend [Buzzi-Peccia]." *Musical Courier,* November 18, 1926.

De Schauensee, Max. "Toscas of Yesterday." *Opera News,* December 8, 1952.

De Stefano, Paolo. "'[Pascoli] Borghesuccio,' 'pedagogico' e 'arretrato.'" *Corriere della Sera,* September 23, 2000, p. 33.

Dell'Orso, Attilio. "Giacomo Puccini nel Cinquantenario della Morte." *La Follia di New York,* May 1974.

Domingo Plácido. "The Magic That Is Opera." AARP (May–June 2002): 28–30.

Ebani, Nadia. "Pascoli, parole scritte nelle lingua degli uccelli." *Corriere della Sera,*

April 29, 2001 (this is excerpted from the critical edition of Pascoli's *Canti di Castelvecchio,* published by La Nuova Italia in May 2001).

Elphinstone, Michael. "Le Villi, Edgar, and the 'Symphonic Element.'" In *The Puccini Companion,* edited by William Weaver and Simonetta Puccini, New York, 1994, pp. 61–110.

"Epistolari: I lamenti di Pascoli." *Il Gazzettino* (Venice), April 25, 2001.

Freeman, John. "Mascagni nel nuovo mondo." In Mario Pasi, *Mascagni,* New York, 1989.

"Giacomo Puccini e la Guardia di Finanzia [di Torre della Tagliata]." *La Follia di New York,* May 1974.

Giacosa, Giuseppe. "Parole commemorative di Giuseppe Giacosa." Milan, 1901 (speech delivered by Giacosa during the Verdi Commemorative Concert at La Scala).

Gouras, Charles-André. "La mort et les obsèques di Puccini." *Comoedia* (Brussels), December 4, 1924 (dated December 2).

Groos, Arthur. "The Lady Vanishes." *Opera News,* January 7, 1995.

Guinther, Louise T. "Another View." *Opera News,* January 7, 1995.

Handt, Herbert. "Bohemian Quartet." *Opera News,* January 11, 1997.

Henderson, W. J. "Puccini, the Foremost Operatic Composer of Today." *Munsey's Magazine,* [1907?], pp. 549–551 (in Metropolitan Opera Archives).

Kestner, Joseph. "Bridge of Dreams." *Opera News,* January 7, 1995.

Miyasawa, Duiti. "Madama Butterfly's Original Melodies." *Opera News,* January 28, 1952.

———. "Tamaki Miura and Puccini." *Opera News,* December 10, 1956 (excerpts from a biography of Miura.)

Morini, Mario. "Un omaggio di Puccini a Volta." *Rassegna musicale Curci* 32, no. 2 (August 1979): 9–14 (cited in Linda B. Fairtile, *Giacomo Puccini: A Guide to Research,* New York and London, 1999).

"La mort di Giacomo Puccini" and "À la Chambre Italienne." Both articles dated November 30, 1924, in Brussels City Archives.

Museo Casa Natale Giacomo Puccini. [1990s] (brochure: guide to the house where Puccini was born).

"Museo Pucciniano a Celle di Pescaglia." *La Follia di New York,* May 1974.

Nicolosi, Luciano. *Omaggio a Giacomo Puccini, con note biografiche e storiche.* Fondazione G. Puccini, Lucca, n.d. (booklet).

Patison, Dolly. "Puccini as Seen by His Intimate Friends." Undated article from unidentified publication, in the Metropolitan Opera Archives.

Phillips-Matz, Mary Jane. "First Ladies of the Puccini Premieres," a series in *Opera News*. March 1956 (Cavalieri); December 1956 (Storchio); February 1958 (Ferrani); April 1959 (Darclée), April 1960 (Muzio); April 1961 (Raisa); January 1962 (Destinn); February 1962 (Farrar); March 1967 (Mason); January 1968 (Easton); January 1970 (Dalla Rizza).

———. "Friends and Rivals." *Opera News,* January 2000.

———. "The Last Desperate Chance: Puccini and *Manon Lescaut.*" Spoleto USA Program Book, 2001.

———. "Puccini's America." In *The Puccini Companion,* edited by William Weaver and Simonetta Puccini, New York, 1994.

———. "*La Rondine:* This Swallow Flies Away." Royal Opera Program, London, May 2001.

———. "Turandot and Her Sisters." Royal Opera Program, London, February–March 2001, pp. 21–26.

Pinzauti, Leonardo. "Giacomo Puccini's *Trittico* and the Twentieth Century." In *The Puccini Companion,* edited by William Weaver and Simonetta Puccini, New York, 1994.

Pizzetti, Ildebrando. "Giacomo Puccini," in *La Voce* (1910), reprint in *Musicisti contemporanei,* Milan, 1914, pp. 49–106.

Puccini, Simonetta. "Puccini and the Painters." *Opera Quarterly* 2, no. 3 (Autumn 1984): 5–26.

———. "The Puccini Family." In *The Puccini Companion,* edited by William Weaver and Simonetta Puccini, New York, 1994.

Puccini, Simonetta, and William Weaver, with Michael Elphinstone and William McKnight. "*Dramatis Personae.*" In *The Puccini Companion,* edited by William Weaver and Simonetta Puccini, New York, 1994.

Puccini Reisewege. 1994 (brochure published by the *Azienda di Promozione Turistica* and the *Centro Studi Giacomo Puccini,* Lucca).

Raboni, Giovanni. "Pascoli, il Giovannino [Pascoli] che visse cento volte." *Corriere della Sera,* September 23, 2000, p. 33.

Ricci, Luigi. "Fleta e le note filate presente Puccini." *Rassegna Musicale* (Milan), April 1977.

Romersa, L. "Una giornata di malinconia sul Lago di Puccini." *La Follia di New York,* May 1974.

Rossi, Nick. "At Home with Puccini." *Opera Quarterly* 2, no. 3 (Autumn 1984).

Sachs, Harvey. "Manon, Mimì, Artù." In *The Puccini Companion,* edited by William Weaver and Simonetta Puccini, New York, 1994.

Salvaneschi, Nino. "Giacomo Puccini à Bruxelles, une Visite à l'Illustre Malade." *Le Soir* (Brussels), November 23, 1924 (discovered by Anne Vandenbulcke, Department of Culture, City of Brussels; provided by Jan Van Goethem, archivist of La Monnaie).

Toscanini, Walter, in collaboration with John Freeman. "New Masks for Old Faces." *Opera News,* March 4, 1961.

Waters, Willy Anthony. "Composer Largesse?" Letter to the editor of *Opera News,* April 2000.

Weaver, William. "In *Tosca,* a Touch of Family History." *New York Times,* Arts and Leisure section, July 16, 2000.

———. "Puccini Pilgrimage." *Opera News,* July 1974.

———. "*Turandot* through a Modern Mind." Royal Opera Program, London, February–March 2001, pp. 10–15.

Zirato, Bruno. "The Last Days of Puccini." *Opera News,* March 4, 1961.

———. "*Uno scherzo poetico di Puccini.*" *La Follia di New York,* May 1974.

PRIVATE AND PUBLIC COLLECTIONS
(IN ADDITION TO THE AUTHOR'S)

Accademia Filarmonica, Bologna, Italy

Archivio di Stato, Pistoia, Italy

Biblioteca della Cassa di Risparmio di Parma e Monte di Credito su Pegno, Busseto, Italy

Enrico Caruso Museum of America, New York, N.Y.

Frank Celenza Collection, New York, N.Y.

Metropolitan Opera Archive, New York, N.Y.

Metropolitan Opera Guild Archive, New York, N.Y.

Monsignor Dante Del Fiorentino Collection, New York, N.Y.

Museo Teatrale alla Scala, Milan, Italy

New York Public Library, New York, N.Y.

Nino Pantano Collection, New York, N.Y.

Pierpont Morgan Library, New York, N.Y.

Tollett and Harman Collection, New York, N.Y.

Walfredo Toscanini, New Rochelle, N.Y.

Wally Toscanini, Countess Castelbarco, Collection, Milan, Italy

Wanda Toscanini Horowitz Donation, the Toscanini Legacy, and other collections in the Music Division of the New York Public Library for the Performing Arts, New York, N.Y.

William Weaver Collection, New York, N.Y.

OTHER REFERENCES

Celenza, Frank. Lecture on *Turandot* at the Columbus Club, New York City, March 2000.

Celenza, Frank, and others. Seminar on *La Fanciulla del West,* Long Island, New York, August 2000.

Opera Quarterly 2, no. 3 (Autumn 1984). This special commemorative issue, prepared under editors Sherwin Sloan and Irene Sloan, is an invaluable tool for Puccini research.

Index